eBusiness:
A Beginner's Guide

eBusiness:
A Beginner's Guide

ROBERT C. **ELSENPETER**
TOBY J. **VELTE**

Osborne/**McGraw-Hill**

Berkeley   New York   St. Louis   San Francisco
Auckland   Bogotá   Hamburg   London   Madrid
Mexico City   Milan   Montreal   New Delhi   Panama City
Paris   São Paulo   Singapore   Sydney
Tokyo   Toronto

Osborne/**McGraw-Hill**
2600 Tenth Street
Berkeley, California 94710
U.S.A.

For information on translations or book distributors outside the U.S.A., or to arrange bulk purchase discounts for sales promotions, premiums, or fund-raisers, please contact Osborne/**McGraw-Hill** at the above address.

eBusiness: A Beginner's Guide

1234567890 CUS CUS 01987654321
ISBN 0-07-212744-9

Publisher	**Proofreader**
Brandon A. Nordin	Pat Mannion
Vice President & Associate Publisher	**Indexer**
Scott Rogers	Jack Lewis
Acquisitions Editor	**Computer Designers**
Ann Sellers	Mickey Galicia
Project Editor	Gary Corrigan
Jennifer Malnick	**Illustrators**
Acquisitions Coordinator	Michael Mueller
Timothy Madrid	Robert Hansen
Contributing Writers	**Series Design**
Jenna Noller, Rob Rammer	Peter F. Hancik
Technical Editor	**Cover Design**
Nick Payton	Amparo Del Rio
Copy Editor	
Robert Campbell	

This book was composed with Corel VENTURA™ Publisher.

For Henry and Janet—RCE

For Mr. V., the best dad anyone could ask for—TJV

AT A GLANCE

CONTENTS

Part II

E-Business Servers and Clients

Part III

Building an E-Business Infrastructure

Part IV

Securing E-Commerce Environments

ACKNOWLEDGMENTS

When you look back over the reasonably short period of time it takes to write a book like this, you realize how many people helped, in one way or another. My old friend Darren Boeck deserves big thanks for his input. It's necessary to thank him here in lieu of any sort of cash payment. It's important to thank my patient wife, Janet, and baby boy, Henry, who had to tolerate long evenings of Dad upstairs working on "the book." From the resulting couple pounds of paper and glue you're holding in your hands now, I hope that they can be assured that I wasn't playing video games all night under the guise of working. (That isn't to say I didn't slap the Galactic Empire around now and again.)—RCE

The folks at FireSummit (especially Jim Flom and Marty Rice) deserve recognition, because in addition to their own work, they had to answer my questions. Krista Schmidt at our front desk should be recognized as the fastest FedEx in the west. From Osborne/McGraw-Hill, Wendy Rinaldi and Ann Sellers made this book happen and are always a delight to work with. The artists and editors have my thanks—their fast, professional turn-around on every facet of this project was magnificent. Tim Madrid and Jenny Malnick delightfully provided essential information and gently prodded to keep the book on schedule. Thank you also to Bob Campbell and Pat Mannion for whipping the book into shape. Most importantly, I want to thank our contributing editors, Rob Rammer and Jenna Noller, for without their contributions the book would not be. Dr. Velte may be reached at tjv@velte.com —TJV

INTRODUCTION

▼

I t's no secret that e-business is the latest, greatest wave in commerce. Not since loaves of bread came presliced has commerce taken such a fantastic turn—for both the buyer and the seller. It is a convergence of the world's oldest profession (selling stuff) with the technology of the millennium (computers). The growth of e-businesses has been exponential and the success stories have been the stuff of legend.

But the biggest problem with e-business is that everyone knows about it (or at least they think they do); however, when it comes time to actually implement an e-business solution, finding the solid answers and solutions are not easy. Sure, there are consultants out there you can throw fistfuls of money at, but how do you know that they're doing the right thing? And who is giving them direction? It's easy to find information about the business end of e-business, but when it comes time to design a network and start pulling cable, the resources begin to dry up. Although you may not be the one to design, implement, and troubleshoot every aspect of your company's e-business solution, you need to cut through the hype and understand the essential components and potential pitfalls.

That's why we wrote *eBusiness: A Beginner's Guide*. This is a one-stop resource for information about both the business side as well as the technological side. In this book you will find the information you need to understand the issues that surround e-business—from developing your organization's business model to selecting the right server software and making sure traffic flows smooth and unfettered through the ether.

E-BUSINESS AND YOUR BUSINESS

With all the hype surrounding e-business, you may feel like a caveman if you don't already have some sort of online presence or e-business solution in place. There's a load of information, opinion, and buzz out there about e-business, but no one really tells you how to get your business online from both a business and technological standpoint.

Developing an e-business solution is more involved than installing a couple pieces of software, developing a clever marketing campaign, and waiting for the IPO to turn you into a gazillionnaire. Turning your business into an e-business is anything but a simple task that can be worked out on a piece of scratch paper. In order to do it properly, you'll have to follow a number of steps:

1. You'll have to perform some research to understand how your business currently functions.
2. Then you have to decide how you want technology to help change it and improve it.
3. Finally, you'll have to develop the technological infrastructure, tools, and applications that will deliver those results.

But even within each of these steps are complex choices and issues that you must understand to develop the best e-business solution.

Just mentioning the term "e-business" brings to mind images of Amazon.com, Priceline.com, and all the other dandies of the new economy. But e-business is a much wider, more encompassing term and philosophy than selling to consumers. A much larger, more prolific type of e-business is business-to-business (B2B) sales. It is the online conjunction of two businesses that are able to improve their operations and profitability through technology. For many businesses, the B2B benefits of e-business are taking them from conventional business practices to a new, paperless office.

Whatever organization you currently have, it's more likely than not that computers are a major component of its day-to-day operations. Once deciding to take the next step on to the Internet, the technological requirements of your organization increase dramatically. To do this effectively, it's necessary to understand computer networking, hardware, and application needs.

Further, we have endeavored to present information about a variety of companies and products so that you can get a better handle on your choices, lest you think there is any one company out there that should do it all.

Within these pages, you'll be able to understand the issues that are involved for the business side, the networking side, the application side, and the functional side of e-business.

WHO SHOULD READ THIS BOOK

This book is aimed at a range of people in your organization or anyone with an interest in e-business. First and foremost it is meant for the chief decision maker who will be implementing an e-business solution. But the content is also appropriate for IT staffers, CEOs, and anyone else with an interest or stake in your organization's e-business goals. Anyone reading this book can understand the principles, theories, and applications behind the different e-business issues.

But that isn't to suggest that individuals with a higher level of technological or business expertise can't get valuable information from this book. The world of business and technology is changing rapidly, and—because of the nature of e-business—there are different concepts and ways to conduct business and utilize technology that are unique to the merger of business and technology. We discuss those issues here.

WHAT THIS BOOK COVERS

eBusiness: A Beginner's Guide is structured around five parts, each one explaining a facet of e-business development and implementation. The first part conveys the message of what e-business is all about from a perspective that business managers and technical staff new to e-business will enjoy. This introductory section is divided into two chapters:

▼ **Chapter 1:** *E-business Comes of Age* This chapter deals with the history and evolution of e-business and introduces many terms and concepts that are essential to understanding e-business.

▲ **Chapter 2:** *Business Cases for E-business* This chapter explores the business case for implementing e-business and punctuates this with examples of organizations that have deployed e-business solutions.

The second part of this book is where *eBusiness: A Beginner's Guide* separates itself from other e-business books. This section discusses e-business development and deploying custom e-business solutions by examining the servers and clients involved.

▼   **Chapter 3:** *Network Operating Systems*   This chapter talks about the importance of operating systems to e-businesses, then compares and contrasts the most popular, prevalent operating systems on the market. By the end of the chapter, you should be able to decide which operating system is best suited for your e-business solution.

■   **Chapter 4:** *Configuring an E-Business Server*   Servers provide the functionality of your e-business. It is on these machines that customers can connect, browse, and purchase. Behind the scenes, servers are used for many back-office functions that keep your online presence humming away.

▲   **Chapter 5:** *Preparing Clients for E-Business*   Where servers are the computers you use to deliver content, clients are the computers that your customers will use to access that content. This chapter talks about issues surrounding client computers and tells you about several technologies you can take advantage of to make your customers' visits more memorable and useful.

The third section contains five chapters and brings you from the computers used in e-business to the network infrastructure. In this section, we talk about basic networking concepts and how they apply to an e-business environment.

▼   **Chapter 6:** *LANs*   The first chapter in this section looks at the basic network that serves local users—a local area network (LAN). In this chapter we discuss LAN technologies and their impact on e-business. We also talk about the hardware components you'll need to build an effective, useful LAN.

■   **Chapter 7:** *Introduction to WANs*   The second chapter in this section focuses on wide area network (WAN) technologies that are used in e-business. WANs are the networks that span great distances and can connect remote branches and customers to a central computer network. In this chapter, we illustrate how to plan for and set up a reliable connection to the Internet and other remote organizations. In addition to concepts and construction, we also talk about the hardware that is instrumental in WAN construction.

■   **Chapter 8:** *Quality of Service*   This chapter takes a fresh look at a very hot area—Quality of Service (QoS). As more and more applications become bandwidth hogs, mission-critical data can find itself mired down in the ether. Providing fast, reliable service is essential for a successful e-business.

■ **Chapter 9:** *The Thinking Network*   Following on the concepts and the ideas presented in Chapter 8, this chapter takes you to the next level of networking—the future of networking and e-business. We will show you what it's going to take to make a world-class network in the years to come. This vision is called The Thinking Network and builds upon the network infrastructure in place today.

▲ **Chapter 10:** *Maintaining and Optimizing E-Business Sites*   Just building an e-business network is not enough. Like a high performance racecar, constant monitoring and tuning will deliver optimal results. The last chapter in this section shows you how to manage and optimize the new infrastructure you just built.

The fourth section deals with another key component to building effective e-business solutions—security. The three chapters in this section show how to secure your e-business solution from your network to your servers.

▼ **Chapter 11:** *Creating Secure Networks*   A common-sense way to make a secure network is by building it to be secure from the ground up. This chapter talks about basic network security by building a safe network infrastructure, including using firewalls, passwords, and other physical means.

■ **Chapter 12:** *Public Key Infrastructure*   The second chapter in this section uncovers a relatively new technology called Public Key Infrastructure (PKI). PKI will play an important role in user authentication and non-repudiation, which is important for both your and your customers' security.

▲ **Chapter 13:** *Securing E-Business Servers*   The third chapter in this section tells you how to lock down your e-business servers from outside intruders. This chapter covers such concepts as IPSec, permission management, and how to Hacker-proof a server.

The last section addresses integration, an important issue facing anyone creating e-business solutions. Since few, if any, e-business solutions will be built from the ground up, this is section will help mix the old network with the new.

▼ **Chapter 14:** *Connecting E-Business Solutions*   The first chapter of this section examines integration issues *within* an organization and explores Electronic Data Interchange (EDI). We'll talk about integrating e-business solutions with other corporate applications as well with existing EDI solutions.

▲ **Chapter 15:** *E-Commerce Application Service Providers*   Building an e-business solution doesn't have to be an all or nothing proposition. You can chose to build as much or as little of your network as you like. The last chapter in this book shows you how to outsource many of the e-business solutions to an Application Service Provide (ASP), which can relieve some of your e-business burdens.

HOW TO READ THIS BOOK

This book has been written with beginners in mind. It is designed so that you can pick it up, flip to any chapter, and find the information you need. We do assume, however, that you have some very basic understanding of networking, computers, and the Internet. If you already know as much as you want about the business side of e-business, you can skip over the first section and proceed directly to the chapters related to the technological side. If you want specific information on security, for instance, you can easily turn to that section for the appropriate chapters.

PART I

E-Business Through Technology

CHAPTER 1

E-Business Comes of Age

In the Peanuts comic strip, young entrepreneur Lucy Van Pelt doled out psychiatric advice—a nickel at a time—from a roadside stand. In the twenty-first century, however, it would be hard not to imagine that Lucy would run her operation from her own Web site—probably www.psychiatricadvice5cents.com or something like that—rather than from the side of the road. And it's anybody's guess how she would make out after the initial public offering.

Dot coms seem to pop up like lawyers at a traffic accident. At first, e-businesses were invincible, money-making juggernauts. Put up a Web site and watch the cash roll in. But after more than a few cyberfailures, it's becoming obvious that e-businesses aren't just some cool thing that makes money. Now that e-business is maturing, organizations are realizing that there's more to e-business than slapping ".com" after your organization's name.

Like any other endeavor, e-business is still rooted in complex business processes and procedures. However, e-business adds a new twist—the element of technology. To be successful, businesses must balance the knowledge and expertise of business along with the exponential development of technology and its impact on society.

THE FUTURE OF BUSINESS IS E-BUSINESS

Every decade brings its own colloquial phrases. In the early part of this decade, the phrase that you'll hear a lot of is, "soon, all business will be e-business." Sure, it's not as catchy as "Where's the beef?" but it is dead on the money.

Each year, more and more people get connected to the Internet. As the chart in Figure 1-1 shows, in 2000, 336 million people were online. By 2003, that number is expected to hit 926 million.

Eventually, those people will make their way around to buying something or just visiting a company's Web site. Once they get to the site, it's important that something be there the people want to see and buy.

But the extent of the business that can be gleaned from the Internet isn't limited to people sitting in their living rooms surfing the Web. Businesses that sell to other businesses are discovering just how useful the Internet is to reinforce existing business partnerships and nurture new, profitable relationships.

In this section, we'll talk about why e-business is big business and how it can be used to rake in more money for your own organization. We'll also take a closer look at the Internet's biggest winner, Amazon.com, and it's first big loser, Toysmart.com. From this information, you'll get a better understanding about the soft, furry exterior of the Internet, but we'll also warn you about the sharp teeth that you may not be expecting.

The Explosion of E-Business

If you thought companies like Amazon.com and eBay.com were shaking things up, you haven't seen anything yet. E-business is still young and formative, and the future looks nothing but bright for companies that decide to conduct business online.

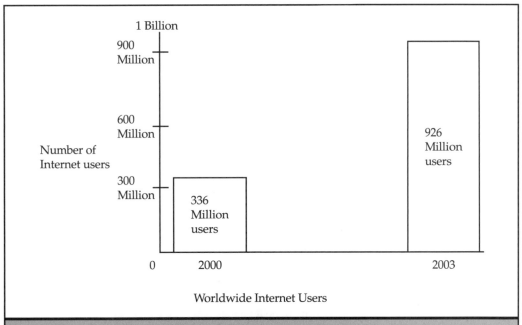

Figure 1-1. The number of consumers on the Internet worldwide will triple in the next three years

According to Dataquest (a unit of Gartner Group, Inc.), there will be a rapid overall growth of e-business in the years leading up to 2003. In 1999, worldwide e-business reached $31.2 billion, up from $11.2 billion in 1998. As Figure 1-2 illustrates, similar U.S. figures reveal a 1999 tally of $20.5 billion, rising sharply to $147 billion in 2003.

As a business professional, you must be asking the question, "How can I get a piece?" The answer comes from your level of involvement and willingness to make some cold, hard business decisions. Some companies will naturally bring their own name recognition to the game, thus gaining instant customers. For example, consider what happened at Victoriassecret.com.

In late 1998, just three months before officially launching its Web site, Victoria's Secret posted a splash page at the site's address. The page requested that visitors leave their e-mail addresses. Even without advertising the address, the company collected e-mail addresses from more than 300,000 customers.

That's great for a company with such strong name recognition as Victoria's Secret, but they aren't the only ones doing well. Think about all the e-business sites you routinely visit—were they all well-known companies before the Internet? If you frequent sites like Priceline.com, Amazon.com, eBay.com, or Buy.com, then you see the power of the Internet.

Other forward-thinking business professionals and customers see the power of the Internet too, and that's why it's becoming more and more powerful. As Figure 1-3 shows, it's a cyclical phenomenon.

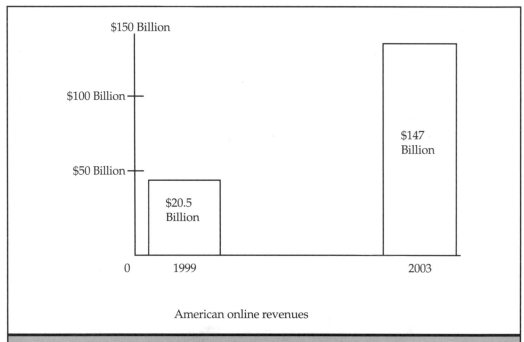

Figure 1-2.   E-business revenues are expected to grow at fantastic rates

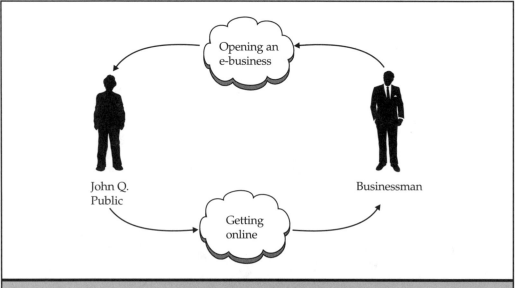

Figure 1-3.   Customers look for online businesses, which draw more businesses because of the abundance of customers

Customers are drawn to the World Wide Web because of everything there is to offer (including online stores). This, in turn, brings more businesses to the Web in search of the customers, which brings more customers to the Web, and so forth.

The Benefits of E-Business

To be sure, you've heard more about businesses on the Internet than Monica Lewinsky and Elián Gonzales combined. Leaving aside all the meaningless buzz out there, what can the Internet *really* do for your company? Quite a lot, actually.

By taking your business into the Internet's realm, you open your operation up to vistas you would never encounter if you were limited to a shop on Main Street. The benefits to your company are great. If you design and implement your e-business correctly, you will see great advantages in your company's finances and greater speed in getting your products and services to market; you'll also reach new customers; even the tiniest company can seem like a big wheel.

Financial

There's one reason to be in a for-profit business: to make money. Whether it's a lemonade stand on the side of the road or a multinational corporation with thousands of employees, the whole reason you want to take your organization to the Internet is to make money—and lots of it if possible.

If the lessons of the past continue, there is money to be made on the Internet. Take the example of Amazon.com founder Jeff Bezos. Starting with just three Sun workstations and a dream he turned his garage in suburban Seattle into the biggest success story of the Internet. Its success propelled his personal stock to $10.5 billion and made Amazon.com a household name.

Will any other company have that kind of success? Probably not, but it's best to never say never. After you put your company online, your personal wealth may not top $10 billion, but you will most certainly tap into a broad, diverse range of customers.

Businesses know that "there's gold in that thar Web." According to the *Wall Street Journal,* dot coms spent more than $3.1 billion in advertising in 1999. Additionally, Network Solutions tells us that 86 percent of the Internet domain names are registered to companies. This fantastic growth and business presence will continue and mean more money for e-businesses that know what they're doing.

Speed

In the past, if you wanted to sell something, you had to rent a storefront, hire employees, stock the shelves, spend a few bucks on advertising, maybe mail out some catalogs, and wait for customers to come in or mail in their order forms. This may sound just fine—after all, that's how business has, conventionally, been done. But with the Internet on your side, the time between developing your product or service and having it ready for the consumer is whittled down considerably.

Now, you needn't wait for catalogs to be printed and shipped to customers, followed by the wait for their mail-order requests to arrive. Naturally, there is a drop in immediacy on the customer's side. After all, once a product is ordered, it has to work through the shipping and handling channels. But that's a problem for future Internet innovators to overcome. In fact, some e-tailers have collocated their warehouses with the post office and Federal Express to cut down on shipping times.

In addition to speed, there's more availability of product than in a conventional store. Let's say you want to buy a boxed set of James Bond DVDs. You could put on your coat, get in your car, drive to the store, and hope to find a set of the DVDs on the shelf. If it isn't your day, they will have sold the last set or—maybe even worse—just have the Roger Moore boxed set in stock. Either way, you're not a happy customer.

Conversely, you could simply log onto a site like Buy.com, find exactly which DVDs you want, type in your credit card, and wait for the package to arrive. Even if Buy.com doesn't have the DVDs in stock, there are more sites out there where you can find what you're looking for—that means you don't have to trudge back to the car and drive to another store in a vain quest.

Expanding Your Reach

Years ago when the hippies started going on and on about "one world" this and "one world" that, it was easy to dismiss them as unbathed weirdoes who liked Grateful Dead music. But now the Internet is doing more to pull the world closer together than all the Hacky Sack tournaments and Earth Days combined ever could.

When customers go to an e-business site, they don't have to physically go to any store. Once they get online, their computer will link to the e-business, where the customer can browse, shop, and make a purchase. This means that physical limitations need not keep anyone away from your company.

For example, let's say you sell Christening gowns for babies and have a shop in San Antonio, Texas. Without the Internet, you depend on customers who walk into your shop and a few call-in orders from word-of-mouth. But the bulk of your sales are reliant on people who actually come in the shop, look at the gowns, and buy one. However, if you decide to put your business online, people from all around the world can look at your stock and decide if you have what they want. Now, a grandmother from Lino Lakes, Minnesota, who needs a Christening gown for her grandson can easily buy from your shop—half a continent away.

Actually, the physical store (if there is one) could be thousands of miles away from the server housing the e-business content, which in turn could be thousands of miles away from the consumer, as is illustrated in Figure 1-4.

As you see, one of the major benefits of the Internet for e-business is bringing your company with its products and services to people anywhere in the world.

Be a Big Shot Even If You're a Pipsqueak

The other benefit of conducting e-business is that the Internet is the great equalizer. Everything comes across to the customer the same way—it comes across on the customer's computer however the company presents it. It doesn't matter if Dale's Elk Meat Emporium is in a tiny little shop in an obscure strip mall and his competition, "Super Mega

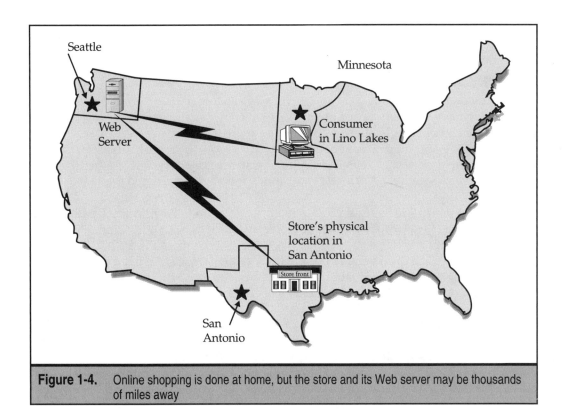

Seattle

Minnesota

Web
Server

Consumer
in Lino Lakes

Store's physical
location in
San Antonio

Store front

San
Antonio

Figure 1-4.   Online shopping is done at home, but the store and its Web server may be thousands
of miles away

Meat Mall," is in a giant store right off the interstate. On the Internet, the only thing limiting Dale's presence is himself.

When you are developing a Web site, the only thing that limits your presence is your ability to develop the Web page. To be sure, the big boys will hire big shot consultants, but with a little knowledge, a little effort, and the right software, even Dale can develop a top-notch Web site.

What Works and What Doesn't—Case Studies

Conventional logic tells us that there's a right way to do something and a wrong way. Up until early 2000, it seemed that in the realm of e-business, there was no wrong way. Every company that went online was successful. Then the bottom dropped out.

For some e-businesspeople and analysts, the change in e-fortune was an omen, a specter that all should fear. For others, the fallout was a natural part of business—a Darwinian effect where the weakest sites were weeded out and only the fittest survived. But now that we have a clearer picture that not every business's online presence will be successful, we can take a look at two examples of e-business in action. The Cinderella story of the e-business world—Amazon.com—will serve as an example of what works on the Internet.

Conversely, ill-fated Toysmart.com is a study in what didn't work. Each contains its own share of the owners' decision-making processes and the fickle hand of fate.

Amazon.com

Unless you've lived in a lunar cave with your eyes squeezed shut and your fingers in your ears, you've probably heard about Amazon.com. (In all likelihood, you probably bought your copy of this book from the online superstore.)

On July 16, 1995, Amazon.com opened its virtual doors to the world. No multimillion dollar ad campaign or slick television commercials marketed the site. Rather the site's founder, Jeff Bezos, told the 300 friends and family members who tested the site to spread the word.

Within a month, Amazon sold books in all 50 states and 45 countries. By Christmas 1995, the company was ready to top $1 million per year. This is the e-business site that entrepreneurs dream about.

But Bezos's vision didn't end at book sales. Gradually, the store has expanded to include DVDs, CDs, videos, gardening tools, auctions, and space for individuals who want to open their own shops. That might seem like all the goods that one store can sell, but Bezos wants more expansion and more goods for sale.

If all goes according to his vision, within a few years Amazon will handle everything: washing machines, Prozac, nails, exercise machines, marmalade, model airplanes—everything but guns and live animals. By the end of 1999—at peak holiday sales time—Amazon's stock price had soared to $94 and the stock had split three times. In 2000, sales are expected to top $1 billion.

A New Way to Sell   From a business point of view, Amazon provides a new way to sell things. It creates a "flow experience." This experience, in theory—and seemingly in practice—keeps customers coming back to Amazon.com to read product reviews or one another's "wish lists." It also smoothes out the online shopping process from when you finalize your order (via Amazon's patented "1-Click" button) to when your stuff shows up on your doorstep.

Amazon's half-dozen warehouses are part of a nationwide distribution network uniquely designed to handle e-commerce. The warehouses are located in low- or no-sales-tax states around the United States. They are also designed to handle goods differently than conventional warehouses: they ship materials from the warehouse to the customer rather than pallet goods and ship to a retail store.

The marriage between a bookstore and the Internet was perfect. When Amazon was started, there were no giant mail-order book companies, because the catalog would be as big as a phone book and far too expensive to mail. On the Internet, this wasn't an obstacle.

Fortune   Luck also played a helpful part in the success of Amazon. When Bezos approached book wholesalers, he discovered that books were one of the most highly databased items in the world—the wholesalers even had their databases on CD-ROM. This, again, helped get his fledgling e-business up and cashing in.

To get the site up and running, Bezos borrowed $300,000 of his parents' retirement money. Call it the investment of the millennium, because today—as six percent owners of Amazon—his parents are billionaires.

Initially, Amazon was headquartered in a small, two-bedroom home in Bellevue, Washington. The garage was converted into a work area, and three Sun workstations were connected. From its modest initial public offering (it started at $18 per share in 1997), the stock began to climb. By the end of 1999, Bezos's stock was worth $10.5 billion.

Toysmart.com

Were Bezos and Amazon just in the right place at the right time with the right service, or could the bright light of fortune shine on any business that could buy a couple servers and register a domain name? As you probably know, so many companies tried their own hand at online success. Some won, some lost. Toysmart.com lost.

The first major e-business casualty was three-year-old Toysmart.com. It became an e-statistic after its partner, the Walt Disney Co., decided not to go through with additional funding. To compound matters, venture capitalists decided not to throw the toy company a life preserver, and its highly anticipated stock offering was hampered by a lagging tech stock market.

The result was unrecoverable. Creditors soon forced Toysmart into bankruptcy. Some may say that Toysmart "took one for the e-business team." Its downfall illustrates just how quickly a capable business venture can shudder, break apart, and burn in the ether.

How It Grew   Toysmart was a promising e-business when it started in 1997. Its founder, David Lord, joined Holt Education Outlet. The small, family-owned, suburban Boston toy company specialized in educational toys, and Lord moved the company into e-commerce by putting the store's wares online. At the end of 1998, Lord and a partner bought the company from the Holts.

After Lord took over the company, renaming it Toysmart, the company started to grow. It grew so fast that by August 1999 it needed more money. Twenty-five million dollars in funding was offered by a capital investment firm, but Lord rejected the offer, opting for a partnership with Disney. Disney's investment included $20 million in cash and $25 million worth of free advertising across Disney's vast media belongings.

That deal didn't just buy his company money and time—it bought him a partner with a controlling interest in the company. It was that shift of power that would pave the road to disaster.

How It Fell   Toysmart's every move required Disney's stamp of approval. Because Disney was used to operating at the pace of a conventional company, Toysmart was about to get itself into trouble.

Trouble poked up its head at Christmas time, when the company sold $6 million worth of merchandise, far less than the anticipated $25 million sales. A few months later, when the stock market started to think twice about e-business investments, Toysmart's public offering went out with a whimper. And, in another stroke of bad luck, Disney decided to shift its Web focus from commerce to entertainment.

The company shut its virtual and physical doors in May 2000, and in June creditors pushed Toysmart into bankruptcy proceedings. In the end, Toysmart owed $21 million to scores of creditors, including Zero Stage Capital and Citibank for $4 million each; Arnold Communications for $2.5 million; and Children's Television Workshop for $1.3 million.

The ripples of Toysmart's failure radiated outward, affecting hundreds of people—both employees and those who had business dealings with Toysmart. First, almost 200 employees lost their jobs and saw their version of the new American Dream—turning stock options into millions—dashed on the rocks. Then, one must consider the scores of toy makers, software companies, advertising partners, plumbers, carpenters, distribution companies, vendors, and any other service providers that can be linked to a company that was left with $21 million in unpaid invoices.

Toysmart left associated e-businesses scuffling for cash and struggling to survive the e-business earthquake. The companies, including Shopnow.com, Lifeminders.com, eGreetings.com, Christmas.com, Garden.com, Go2Net.com, and Yesmail.com, are still waiting to collect $15,000–$200,000 in bills.

So what does Toysmart's rise and fall mean to the rest of the fledgling dot coms out there? Analysts predict that the shakeout for Internet retailers has just begun. Forrester Research estimates that the 50 largest Web sites need an average of $43 million each to continue building their businesses through 2000. But with more than 300 online retailers competing for money, Forrester predicted that most Web stores would go out of business by the end of 2001.

SUCCESS IN E-BUSINESS

To be successful with your e-business, you can no longer think in terms of your bricks-and-mortar operation. Too often—and to their detriment—managers, CEOs, and presidents think they can simply move their businesses online and expect to conduct business as usual. But that isn't the case anymore.

Since e-business is a marriage of business and technology, it is vastly important to understand the technological side of the union along with how technology affects the existing business. In this section, we'll be talking about how your business needs to change to be successful online. We'll talk about how you should structure your business, the need to change the way your think about business, and the practice of integrating technology into your business.

Restructuring Your Business

Because technology is a major component of e-business, business changes are harder to manage because of the sheer magnitude of the changes. And, as Figure 1-5 illustrates, because of this change, a company's value isn't found in tangible assets, like products and materials. Rather, value is found in intangibles: branding, customer relationships, and supplier integration.

Unfortunately, many businesses have not developed an information-based business design to deal with the necessary business change. Changing the flow of information

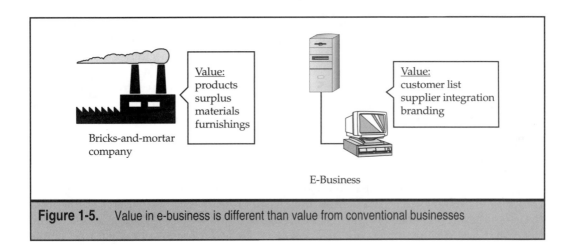

Figure 1-5.   Value in e-business is different than value from conventional businesses

requires companies to change not only how they deliver their products, but the environment in which they compete. An enterprise must develop a precise plan to accommodate the increased flow of information; otherwise, it will find itself expending its resources trying to stay solvent.

Businesses that don't adapt to the changing marketplace will find themselves looking for a great bankruptcy attorney. The most common problem for companies is failing to change at all or not changing fast enough or effectively enough to stave off disaster. The problem sits squarely on the shoulders of management—too often they are not able to foresee change in the marketplace; they become overconfident and cocky; they simply lack the ability to implement changes; or they fail to manage properly once the changes have been made.

E-business is fast-paced and extremely volatile. The constant change in the marketplace means that businesses must engender a discomfort with the status quo. When things seem to be sailing along nicely, it's time to take a step back and figure out what's wrong. They have to see the changes before their competition does, make rapid changes, and be able to make drastic changes to their business model.

Outsourcing

A way to smooth out the constant change in business models is to start with a business model that accommodates rapid, continuous change. To deal with this rapid change, many businesses have seen outsourcing as a solution. Since companies cannot do everything on their own, they can get the help they need from third parties.

Outsourcing comes in many sizes and shapes. At first, outsourcing was focused on technology management. Recently, contract manufacturing has become popular in the technological world. But even as the work is subbed out to another company, the two parties must work closely together. It isn't enough merely to get the job done—now, it has to get done quickly, effectively, and efficiently. That means that the outsourcing company must act almost as a division of the contracting company.

In the current business climate, you'll hear these outsourcing relationships called e-business communities, clusters, and coalitions. As technology develops and expands, outsourcing alliances become easier and easier to implement, especially if both sides are using compatible business application software.

These types of complex outsourcing alliances aren't just an easy, trendy way to do business—they're crucial. Managers simply don't have the tools they need to stay on top of all the changes in business, so they must ally themselves with someone who can help them stay competitive.

Tearing Down

Businesses will find their value is in the needs being served, not the products being sold. *Disaggregation* is an exercise that lets businesses separate the means (in this case, the product) from the ends (the customers' needs). Disaggregation requires your business to identify, value, and nurture what your business is all about. Ultimately, this will lead you to reevaluate what service you are providing to your customers and what role your products play in that service.

Disaggregating, as shown in Figure 1-6, allows your managers to take apart the business, rethink its core purpose, and identify where new value can be developed and created.

Building Up

But once your company has been disaggregated and studied, it must be *reaggregated.* Reaggregation allows you to streamline your company's value chain, and it also serves your client's needs in important, valuable new ways. Reaggregation allows new and burgeoning companies to serve a new niche. Consider, for instance, Priceline.com.

Before Priceline set up cybershop, there was no lack of travel companies operating on the Internet. The travel industry hadn't handed over all its business to the Internet, but there was a reasonably strong presence of online travel agents. Rather than look for another way to sell the same product, the founders analyzed an important need—lower price—and figured out how they could deliver less expensive airline tickets.

By disaggregating the business and looking at it from the customer's point of view, Priceline's founders determined that customers would not only like less expensive tickets but would actually enjoy bidding for them.

Here are the steps that you must follow to effectively disaggregate and reaggregate your business:

1. Challenge the traditional ideals of value.

2. Define value in terms of your customers' needs.

3. Engineer the end-to-end value stream.

4. Create a new technology-based enterprise that is based on customer needs.

5. Make sure your company's leaders understand how to continue the self-examination process.

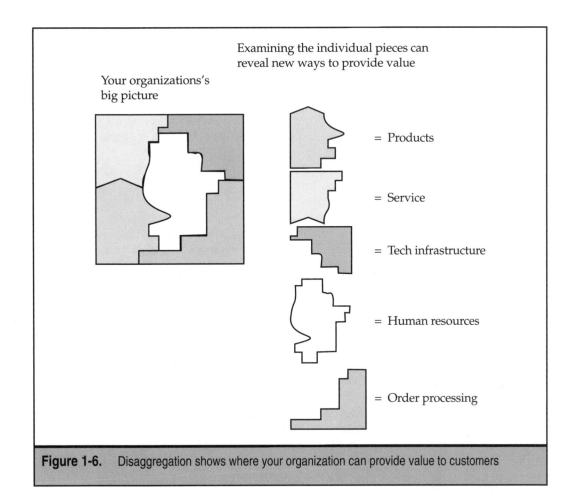

Examining the individual pieces can
reveal new ways to provide value

Your organizations's
big picture

= Products

= Service

= Tech infrastructure

= Human resources

= Order processing

Figure 1-6. Disaggregation shows where your organization can provide value to customers

When you develop your e-business, using technology to reaggregate the value chain
is your trump card.

Change Your Paradigm

The word *paradigm* is a cliché in the business world. Unfortunately, nowhere do the concept and the term fit better than when we talk about adapting your company to an
e-business environment. In every business, if you want to make customers happy (thus
shedding some light on the presidents holed up in their wallets) you must address at least
one (if not all) of these four points:

▼ **Price** No one likes to think they got cheated, and no one will ever think they
    spent too *little* for something. Businesses that offer unique services and
    products for a reasonable price will do well.

- ■ **Convenience** In the fast-paced dot-com world we live in, efficiency is critical. One-stop shopping is nice, but customers also want the process to move smoothly and with few steps. Once again, consider the case of Amazon.com. Using its patented "1-click" shopping, customers need only select their purchases, then wait for the mail to show up.

- ■ **Speed** No one likes to wait. For customers, there can never be such a thing as "too fast." To stay competitive, you must deliver your products and services as fast and efficiently as possible.

- ▲ **Personalization** Customers want to be treated as individuals. The more choices customers get for their products, and the fewer decisions made by the company, the happier they'll be.

As you develop your company to compete in an e-business arena, you should be thinking about how you can use technology to address these needs. If you can figure it out, you'll be a step ahead of the pack.

Remember, improving your business means looking at it from the customer's point of view. Innovative businesses look at what *new* things customers want, rather than the differences among the customers. Don't focus too much on market segmentation—that only works in a stable business climate. In the budding world of e-business, "stable" isn't a word that's used very often.

Technological Changes

We've pumped up the necessity of identifying what's valuable for the customer. Now it's time for the curve ball—technology is changing your customers' notion of value. All of the services we just talked about—speed, personalization, convenience, and price—have grown critical in the high-tech world in which we live.

Because of these innovations, customers are now faced with many companies offering the same goods and services. Because of this information overload, customers find themselves making decisions based on:

- ▼ What's cheapest
- ■ What's most familiar
- ▲ What's the best quality

Any business performing at less than 100 percent in any of these categories sets itself up for failure.

"What's cheapest" doesn't mean that the product or service is inferior; it means that all the extra costs between the manufacturer and the customer have been minimized. Remember what we talked about—no one likes to pay any more than they have to. If there's a Web site out there that offers your products for less, kiss the sales good-bye.

"What's most familiar" lets customers know what they're getting. Especially in an e-business environment where you can't touch, taste, or feel what you're buying, brand recognition is extremely important. If your online retailing site is selling "JoeTech VCRs," customers might have more concerns than if you offer a line of Panasonics. Of course, if yours is a company that strikes the right note with consumers, you'll earn that brand recognition faster than you can say "Yahoo!" or "Amazon.com."

"What's the best quality" means a lot of different, complex things. It encompasses all the things that make a business successful. It means giving the customers what they want, when they want it, and at a value they appreciate. It's a moving target, and it's one of the most critical issues for any business.

All of these factors are important considerations, especially in the high-tech, innovation-rich world of e-business. If you want to stand out from the crowd and ensure you're appealing to your customers, make sure you've got at least one of these bases covered.

Changes for the Customer

Customers are no dummies. They know that better technology should result in a better shopping experience. In e-business, it isn't enough just to identify new ways to make your customers happy and find the services that they want. In order to attract customers and present something new and valuable, organizations must innovate the entire customer experience.

Especially in the case of e-business, customers are swarming to sites that give them something more for their shopping experience. Now, customers have come to expect a little something extra for their cyberbuck. That extra value, that extra perk is something that creative businesses that understand their customers and what their customers want will develop.

Let's consider Amazon.com, once again. The site's initial value for customers is when they log onto the site, find the book they want, and check out with ease. But the value to the customer doesn't end there. Customers can write online reviews about favorite books (or not-so-favorite books); they can create a wish list that family and friends can check at gift-giving times.

One of Amazon's competitors, Buy.com, got a lot of my business for a while, because every time I ordered a DVD, they sent a package of microwave popcorn with it. Their prices were comparable to Amazon's, and the little added bonus of the microwave popcorn was a nice touch.

Companies that realize the value of using technological innovation to serve customers—not just to push products—will be successful. One of the problems that many e-businesses experience is that they simply build a Web presence to have a Web presence. There has to be something that brings customers to the business that they can't get anywhere else—there has to be something that sets the e-business apart from other e-businesses and even the company's physical store.

Integrating Technology into Your Business

When you're ready to make the big move to e-business and integrate technology into your business, the first thing you should do is prepare to be overwhelmed. Integrating technology into e-business is not as simple as it may seem—sure, the Internet is pervasive and new dot coms pop up seemingly overnight, but to make an effective, useful solution, you must make some complex technological changes.

Integration means that your organization must have a solid, seamless set of applications that must work fluidly not only at the point where customers and supply-chain partners would encounter them but for everyone from the CEO to Larry in accounting.

The process requires a major application overhaul so that you can develop a back-end infrastructure that allows your e-business functions to work seamlessly. The necessity for integrated applications isn't a new concept—it's only gotten more important where e-business is concerned. It's important because it harks back to a common theme we've been developing—customers expect and want something more out of online businesses. In the past, customers had little choice in the e-business arena. Now, however, with so many choices, customers can decide to spend their money at a site with efficient service. With the knowledge that shopping efficiency is a factor in business design, the need for an integrated infrastructure should become very clear.

Are You Ready to Integrate?

As you decide to put your business online, an important question to ask is "do I even have any business going online?" If you've thought it out and know how you will serve your customers and will serve an unmet need, then you can press forward. However, if you aren't sure what you will do, there is little point in building a Web site and putting it online.

Often, managers put the responsibility for the e-business squarely on the shoulders of their IT managers. With all due respect to IT managers, this is not the best way to conduct business. The responsibility for the technological side of an e-business solution is the IT manager's department; however, the business planning and modeling behind the solution should not be delegated to the technical department.

Your task in developing an e-business solution is to identify how you can deliver what the customer wants via technology. In many cases, you'll find that integration is not simply a technological obstacle that must be negotiated. For example, consider Manna Freight Systems of Mendota Heights, Minnesota.

To remain competitive in the freight hauling industry, Manna developed a computerized system that links them with airlines and trucking companies. Unlike other freight companies, Manna is able to discover if there is enough room in an airplane before it lifts off and before the customer's goods are left behind, causing a late delivery (this is illustrated in Figure 1-7). Once Manna discovers there is a problem with a particular flight or hauler, they are able to consult their online system and locate another mode of transportation. This system has afforded the company a 95 percent on-time rate. Interestingly enough, the rest of the industry doesn't bother keeping track of how often deliveries are on time.

This example shows how application integration (Manna is linked via computer with their subcontractors) enables Manna to serve its customers in a more effective way than the competition can.

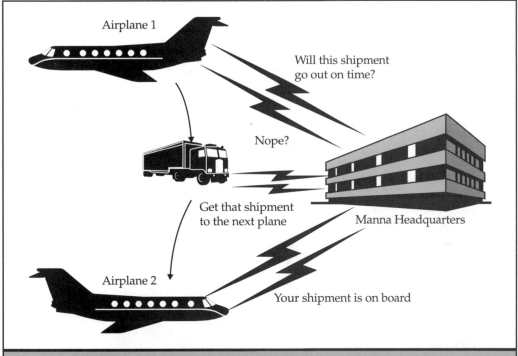

Figure 1-7.   Manna Freight Systems uses integrated applications to make sure its cargo is shipped in a timely manner

Getting It Together

But how do you know how to make an e-business strategy work? To be profitable, organizations must pay attention to new architectures that support organizational agility in terms of business applications. *Agility* means that the company must be able to meet the needs of the market without excessive costs, needless delays, organizational disruption, or loss of performance.

Especially with e-business, agility is an important feature. Your organization must keep pace with your customers' wants: variety, price, quality, and fast delivery. If you have a static model with no room for change, none of these needs can be met. The models becoming increasingly popular are customer-centric and support a number of complex business designs.

Designing an integrated, agile e-business infrastructure requires decisive choices in many different disciplines. When designing an e-business infrastructure, it is necessary to make sure those decisions are well researched and well tended. Too often, e-business infrastructures fail, but not because the technology was faulty; rather, somewhere between the problem and the execution, the solution slipped off the track. The main reasons e-businesses run into trouble are because their solutions were poorly linked to an organizational plan, the strategies and tactics were flawed, the plans weren't properly executed, or an organization failed to understand all the facets of its problem.

WHO IS YOUR CUSTOMER?

In *The Art of War* by Sun Tzu, great warriors are required to "know the enemy and know yourself." But that bit of wisdom doesn't only apply when taking on an army of vicious Mongols; e-business requires the same level of knowledge. At first blush, one might think that there is only one type of customer out there—someone at home surfing around for goods or services. Though this is an important customer, the Internet is ideally suited for business-to-business (B2B) sales. In fact, if you have a supply-chain partner with whom you need to be in constant contact, the Internet can provide an inexpensive link between your companies.

In this section, we'll help you define who, exactly, you are selling to and why you should target those customers.

John Q. Public

The most visible example of e-business actually claims the smallest share of the e-business pie, although it's the one we hear about most often. Consumers account for about 10 percent of all online sales; if your business caters to the public, then it's important to realize how to get at that 10 percent.

Even though they are the smallest group represented in e-business, consumers are probably the most fickle and the hardest to market to. Consumers want good deals, efficient transactions, and decent customer service. If you want to attract consumers to your e-business, you must ensure that you have something that they want—or at least you have it cheaper than the next guy.

When you are selling to the consumer, the same rules apply online as in a store—sort of. Consumers expect a little more out of the Internet. They want it cheaper, they want it faster, or they want something cool with it. Naturally, if you are one of the innovators who will take e-business to the next level, there's sure to be something new and exciting that the general public wants.

B2B

According to analysts at Goldman Sachs, business-to-business e-commerce will be a $1.5 trillion market by the year 2004, and many analysts predict that it will rapidly outpace consumer commerce on the Web. According to researchers at Dataquest, consumer e-commerce will be "only" a $380 billion market by the year 2003—well below Goldman Sachs's prediction for business-to-business e-commerce.

The boom of the Internet has meant great things for companies that deal with other companies. Now, companies can fuse their internal systems with its suppliers, partners, and customers. This fusion makes companies integrate systems they share with other organizations and improves efficiency and effectiveness. Simply put, supply chain management is the coordination of material, information, and financial flows between and among supply chain partners.

An example of this is PartMiner.com, which eases the buying and selling of electronic components on the Internet.

As shown in Figure 1-8, one of PartMiner's partners, Atlas Services, is a $300-million-a-year distributor of electronic and computer components. When Atlas gets a bill of materials from a computer manufacturer, it goes to PartMiner and finds out which suppliers have the parts on hand. In the past, this was a telephone-based effort that was extremely

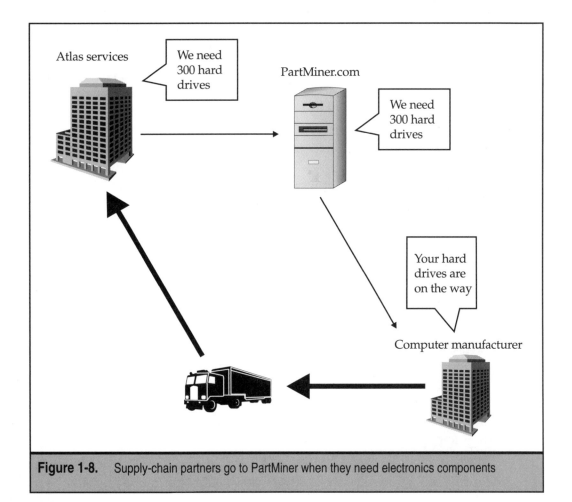

Figure 1-8. Supply-chain partners go to PartMiner when they need electronics components

time-consuming. After switching to the Internet to fill orders, Atlas has saved 15 percent on product-procurement costs, not to mention all the time spent on the telephone.

With the Internet handy to help marshal information between your company and your partner, you will cut costs and overhead.

BECOMING A DOT COM

When you finally decide to make the plunge and open your e-business, you will have to plan for both the inevitable business and the technological changes that come with opening your virtual doors.

The first step in developing an e-business plan is to take a look at where your organization is. What is the status quo? Who are your customers? What do they need? Are you serving them adequately? How can you serve them better? Next, you have to turn the microscope back on yourself. Is your organization ready to make the move online? What do you have, now, that will accommodate the move? What will you need to become a viable e-business? Finally, you have to develop your e-business design. What kind of model will you follow, and how can you make it your own?

This section shows you how to look at your own business and decide who your customers are, evaluate your preparedness, and design the most appropriate business model.

Do Some Digging

In an earlier section, we talked about the different kinds of customers. But that isn't the extent of what you need to know about your customers. Now, we need to know more specific things about them. By asking (and answering) these questions, you can understand your customers' priorities. The sad reality is that most managers don't truly understand what their customers want. Further, the relationship between the customer and profit is also hazy to many who should know better. If you take the time and make the effort to ask the hard questions about your customers' wants and needs, you'll be able to design a profitable e-business solution.

Identify Your Customers

This may seem like a silly question to ask, because the answer is so obvious—my customers are the people I'm selling to. To an extent that is correct, but it's not adequate enough. You also need to know the different customers within that broad group. It's necessary to break that large group into smaller groups whose behavior can be analyzed systematically.

Let's say you own a video rental store. Here's how your customers might break down:

▼ **Occasional renters**   These are the customers who come in once in a while. They don't come in with any regularity. They rent movies sporadically and usually just one at a time.

- ■ **Regulars**   These are the customers who come in at least once a week (normally on the weekends) and rent a couple movies. You can depend on them to be there Friday evenings, and maybe on Saturdays, too.

- ▲ **Hardcore renters**   This has nothing to do with that little room in the back of the store. These are the renters who come in daily and pick up a new set of movies after they've dropped off the ones from the night before. On the weekends, these are the folks who will walk out of the shop with six or seven movies in their hands.

Now that you understand how customer segmenting works, you must ask the following question of each group: *What is important to each customer segment?* The customers who buy from you also buy a number of other goods and services. By figuring out what's important to that segment, you can apply this information to your e-business.

Next, answering the following questions will help you figure out what your customers want:

- ▼ What are five new products and services that have become popular in the last five years?

- ■ What customer segments are buying these products and services?

- ▲ Why do these customer segments like these products and services?

By answering these questions, you'll get a better insight into your customers' needs. There are two types of customer needs: spoken (explicit) and unspoken (implicit). It should be easy enough to determine your customers' explicit needs—they'll tell you. It's the implicit needs that are trickier (yet more rewarding) to determine.

Now, you answer the question, "Who are my customers?" The answer to this will determine how you should measure performance. If you are providing the services and goods that your customers want, then you should be able to determine if you're meeting that need.

What Are Their Needs?

Your customers' needs are truly a moving target. If you become complacent and just focus on the here and now, you won't be around long. The finesse in staying on top in business is realizing what your customer wants, then reacting before they've moved on to something new. The main problem companies have is that they are resistant to change because their business models are so static. This is bad news for that organization, because before you can say "click for more information," an upstart has seen the market, swooped in, and taken that business away.

To understand what your customers want, there's an easy, underused method—listen to them. The best place to start is to fix what your customers tell you needs fixing. What do they tell you when they write in? Is there a common complaint managers hear? Have you asked them?

While moving into the digital realm, you'll have to anticipate what a new batch of customers who interact with you online will want. Ask yourself, who will my customers be in three to five years? What will they need? How can I supply it? The best way to look into the future is to look at the past. What were your customers like five years ago? Based on how they've changed, what will they be like five years from now?

How Can You Serve Them?

Once you've figured out who your customers are and what they want, you have to address the question of what you can do with your company to serve them. Do you have a new, exciting product that they'll be scampering for? Do you have a company that will streamline operations for other companies? Your customers want value, innovation, and savings. Do you offer your customers some sort of savings? Do you make things more convenient for them? How do you add new forms of value?

The question "how do you add new forms of value" is important when migrating from a bricks-and-mortar company to a dot com. Ideally, in addition to ordering new computer equipment and phone lines, you're prepared to answer this question.

If you're still unsure of how to add more value, at least avoid putting too much stock in industry assumptions. For instance, for years DVDs didn't catch on because the industry was wary of the format. In each of the last three years of the 1990s, however, DVD machine sales doubled from the year before.

But ultimately, when we talk about e-commerce, the most important thing to determine is how you can use technology to serve your customers. If you're having trouble with this question, you may run into some e-trouble.

Other Considerations

Of course, we're just making a brief overview of the types of questions you should be prepared to answer. Most likely, your marketing department should prepare a battery of information about your customers and what their needs are. Some of the other important issues you should be prepared to address in relation to your customer preparedness include these:

▼ **How can I become my customers' favorite?**   The best way is to knock them off their feet with your service. An easy way to think about this is to look at a casino. For their high-rollers (and even some of the low-rollers), gamblers are treated to free hotel rooms, meals, drinks, and flights. These incentives are proven ways for casinos to instill an element of brand loyalty in their customers.

■ **Do I understand the environment?**   We're not talking about getting to know squirrels, here. Rather, are you aware of how your industry and the marketplace are operating, and are you prepared to roll with the punches as the environment changes?

■ **Am I knowledgeable about technology trends?**   This is really a billion-dollar question. If you were precognizant enough to predict technology's roller-coaster of changes, you'd be the next Gates or Bezos. But unless the fickle hand of fortune is ready to tap you on the head, your best bet is to know your core technology as best you can. Think about the technology you're using and ask yourself, "Is the technology going through changes?" "Am I diversified, or if this technology fails will I go under?"

- ■ **Do I know my supply chain?**   Here's a cliché we haven't used yet: a chain is only as strong as its weakest link. That applies to supply chains, too. You have to know what's going on with your supply chain and what its dynamics are. What do the upstream suppliers want? How can you make the chain more efficient? Without a good knowledge of how that chain works, you could be the weak link.

- ▲ **Who are my competitors?**   Not so quick, this isn't as easy a question to answer as it may sound. Sure, you can probably think of a handful of competitors right off the bat. But not all villains are wearing black top hats and twirling their mustaches. Are there other companies that might not seem like a threat but offer the same product or service? Booksellers probably didn't think that an online store would be that successful. (After all, don't people want to page through books before they buy them?) It was that blind spot that left a lot of them smarting when Amazon.com went online. Take a look at all angles of this question and then make sure someone can't offer your customers something you should be offering.

Being aware of your customers, their needs, and the market's dynamics are invaluable tools, not just in the realm of business in general, but e-business in particular. When you've prepared this information, you're ready to take a look at your organization's capabilities.

Are You Ready?

You wouldn't run a marathon if you were 50 pounds overweight, smoked a carton of cigarettes a day, and ate three helpings of fried cheese every day. This self-awareness may seem a silly example, but too many companies decide to take a shot at e-commerce without knowing if they're organizationally ready.

To find out if your organization is capable of making a leap into e-business, you must consider two important questions: "What are my abilities?" and "How can I improve?"

What Are Your Abilities?

An important element of self-examination is to review your organization's strengths and weaknesses. Take a look at the traits listed in Table 1-1. This is a good (albeit brief) set of assets to revisit from time to time, because—given the ever-changing business world— what is a strength today may be a weakness tomorrow. For instance, five years ago the prevailing wisdom for training employees was to let them attend night courses somewhere. Now, there's a trainer willing to come to the office and give them the training they need, thus saving time and money.

Employees	Infrastructure	Technology	Customer Interactions	Production
Skills	Financial systems	Legacy applications	Sales	Manufacturing
Training	Human resources	Networking	Marketing	Supply chain management
Knowledge	Research and development	Web site and intranets	Customer service	Distribution
Commitment by executives	LAN/WAN	Security	Call centers	Production scheduling
Happiness		IT skills	Distribution channels	Inventory management

Table 1-1. Areas of Evaluation

Since we're talking specifically about e-business, let's take a closer look at technology. When you are considering moves to e-business models, consider how a technology implementation can either assist or impede an organization's ability to acclimatize to changing business environments. You must also take a closer look at your IT department and determine if they have a different business philosophy from management. This is one of the biggest points of failure in companies where the application infrastructure is not in alignment with the business's objectives.

How Can You Improve?

Now that you've taken a close look at your organization, it's necessary to develop a plan to help bridge the gaps you've uncovered.

NOTE: If you didn't uncover any gaps, look again.

Next, you must align your capabilities with your organization's vision. If you don't (or can't) do this, you'll likely have problems achieving success. With a clear destination for your company in mind, you will need to specify the requisite capabilities needed for each function, those that will lead to your goal. For the traits you identified earlier that are not up to snuff, you should develop a transition plan describing how each function must change or be improved so that your plan will mesh with the final functional strategies.

You must also develop a solid enterprise architecture, one that will provide a logical, consistent plan of activities and coordinated projects that will lead your business applications and infrastructure from their current state to the final goal.

This is a comprehensive plan that must include the specifics of each department, plus a plan that will allow them to develop in conjunction with one another. Further, the plan must include the overall strategy and the migration steps. Since application integration is an important part of your e-business, your plan should also include guidelines to show how integration can occur.

Design Your E-Business

Finally, you can start thinking about how your e-business will be designed. With all the earlier data at hand, you can make a specific decision about how your e-business will be built. Designing your e-business is a two-step process. First, you should consider what design you want to model your e-business after. Then, you should personalize it and make it your own.

Choose a Design

Look at the basic e-business designs in Table 1-2. Which of them comes closest to what you're trying to accomplish? Naturally, if yours is large or especially ambitious, you may be trying to accomplish a few of these in one fell swoop.

Once you've found the pigeonhole in which your e-business fits, it's time to make it gel with your company.

Make It Your Own

After you've selected the model your e-business is suited to, you should look back to the questions posed in the section "Do Some Digging" earlier in this chapter. By applying those answers, you'll be able to develop an accurate picture that will help tweak out the e-business model so that it best suits your organization and its goals.

By applying the information you've discovered about your organization and your customers, you'll be able to customize and add your own sources of value to these stock e-business models.

Further, you should continually analyze your e-business to ensure that it is unique. Some of the traits you should analyze to guarantee you are not duplicating another's e-business offering include:

▼ Products that are superior

■ Marketing channels that provide quality responsiveness, convenience, and information

■ Service and support geared toward your customers' needs and urgency

▲ Price, which includes both the net purchase price and the cost savings to the customer who will use the product

Design	Description
Category killer	You want to use the Internet to define a new market by identifying a unique customer need. If you're aiming for this model, be aware that you'll have to be one of the first to market and stay ahead of the pack. *Example: Amazon.com*
Channel reconfiguration	You want to use the Internet as a new channel to deal directly with customers, which will include sales and order fulfillment. This model first aids and then replaces physical distribution. *Example: Compaq.com*
Transaction intermediary	You want to use the Internet to process purchases. This model performs all the end-to-end functions that a customer would need from searching to comparing with other products to sales. *Example: eBay.com*
Channel mastery	You want to use the Internet for sales and service. This model is used to support existing sales rather than supplant them. *Example: Eddiebauer.com*
Infomediary	You want to use the Internet to make searching easier and less expensive. This model allows your customers to gather information about a product they want to purchase. *Example: HomeAdvisor.com*
Self-service innovator	You want to use the Internet to provide human resources services that your customer's employees can use directly. This model allows them to develop a personalized relationship. *Example: Ceridian.com*
Supply-chain innovator	You want to use the Internet to make the transactions between all members of a supply chain more efficient and streamlined. *Example: McKeeson.com*

Table 1-2.　E-Business Models

Given all the variables, research, and study involved in developing your e-business, it's obvious that this isn't something that can be written on the back of an envelope or in the few minutes before a meeting. To develop your e-business requires a fair amount of study and critical self-reflection. In the end, however, when you consider the many benefits that come from a quality e-business solution, the work should seem well worth it.

CHAPTER 2

The Business Case
for E-Business

Most businesses are designed, built, and open their doors in the bricks-and- mortar world. But realizing the benefits and rewards of e-business takes more than hiring a consultant to develop a Web page and making a deal with the post office for shipping. In order to develop a successful, efficient e-business, it's necessary to understand how your organization needs to be shaped, how to keep customers happy, and how the traditional model of business is changed on the Internet.

For the past 15 years, the business term that you've come to know and loathe is the ever-present cliché, *paradigm*. It's time to introduce the latest business concept, which is sure to become the first truism of the new millennium—*integration*. We're going to talk a lot about integration in this chapter. We're going to tell you why it's important for your company's right hand to know what its left hand is doing at all times and across all your vital systems.

In this chapter, we'll talk about those issues. We'll talk about making sure your company and its infrastructure are organized in a way that facilitates e-business. Next, we'll take a look at the age-old issue of making sure your customers are happy. As you can imagine, e-business presents a new way to attract and keep your customers. We'll also look at how technology helps your supply- and selling-chain management in the changing world of twenty-first century business.

ENTERPRISE RESOURCE PLANNING

It should be obvious by now that turning your organization into an effective e-business goes further than taking a trip to the local electronics shop and registering your domain name with Internic. In addition to the technological changes that come with an e-business, so must core business practices.

When you put your company on the Internet, you must also shelve 25-year-old back-office systems and embrace a new way of conducting business. With proper planning and streamlining, you can greatly enhance the performance of your organization. This process is called enterprise resource planning (ERP); in this section, we'll talk about ERP, why it's so useful, how you can implement it in your own organization, and some of the issues around it.

What Is ERP?

ERP is a way to streamline the information flow in your business. It improves the exchange of data between your divisions by bringing important processes together, as shown in Figure 2-1.

More than 70 percent of Fortune 500 companies are implementing an ERP system or intend to do so in the coming years. But that big businesses are embracing ERP doesn't mean small businesses are incapable or unwilling to do the same. As prices fall, more and more small businesses are willing to jump on the ERP bandwagon.

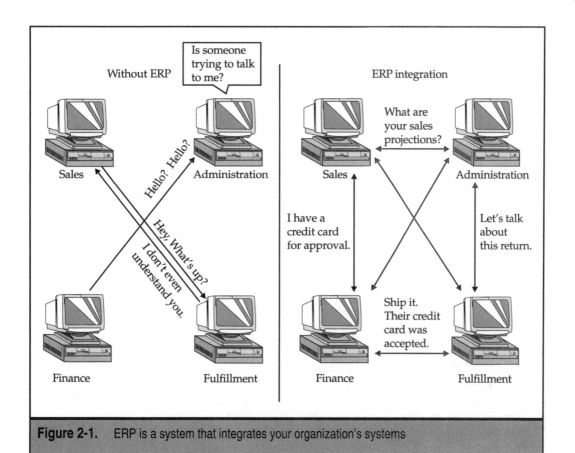

Figure 2-1.   ERP is a system that integrates your organization's systems

For large companies, ERP is the answer to their prayers. For many companies, corporate computing is a 20-year-old ledger system on a mainframe that has long since been rendered obsolete. The mainframe worked great—when orders had to be filled in a few weeks. Now, the Internet has spoiled customers. They have the gall to expect their purchases to be shipped in a prompt, timely manner.

To speed up the process and streamline in-house systems, the first step is to send those old, clunky computers to a museum. (Better yet, take them out behind the building and let employees take baseball bats to them, working out years of pent-up rage. Make a company picnic out of it.) Next, you should bring in the new, ERP-integrated suites.

ERP isn't a single system; rather, it is a network of systems, which includes all the divisions of your organization, including administrative applications (finance and accounting) and human resources applications (payroll and benefits). ERP brings your organization's business units together under a single software complex. ERP is extremely important; it's akin to the e-business operating system. What Microsoft Windows 2000 is to your computers, ERP is to your e-business as a whole.

The greatest benefit of ERP is integration. If you add a new sales order to the system, everything related to the order is instantly updated, including commissions, inventory levels, manufacturing schedules, and the balance sheet. With ERP-enabled integration, all employees can use the same information and business processes and get the same results when the system is queried.

The High Demand of ERP

The importance of ERP is realized when you consider the remarkable increase in efficiency, which, in turn, translates into increases in profits. Consider the case of Petsmart, a pet store chain. Since it integrated all its systems in preparation for the Year 2000 problem:

▼ The integrated system allows programmers to work in a single development environment.

■ With Petsmart's legacy system, it took the IT staff 12 hours to process daily store transactions and updates. With the new ERP system, it takes 2 hours to handle 600,000 daily updates and 5 million sales transactions.

▲ Between reduced system maintenance costs and the lower cost of processing transactions, Petsmart officials forecast their five-year savings will total $3.5 million.

Figure 2-2 shows how ERP integrates all your organization's major functions into one seamless commerce machine.

ERP has been picking up steam since the early 1990s, but as e-business started to skyrocket, ERP slowed down because many of the ERP packages were unable to handle e-business. The basic functionality of ERP and the Internet are different. ERP is an integrated transaction-processing system that handles businesses' internal information. The Internet is a delivery method and doesn't involve a lot of processing. Of course, the information flowing through the Internet is becoming more open to processing all the time, with advances like Java and XML. But it's still processed by applications, and the best business applications are still enterprise packages from major vendors. Though e-business and ERP seem at odds, ERP is as necessary as it ever was and simply needs to evolve to thrive in the Internet age. But why is ERP so popular? For these reasons:

▼ The need for a system that improves customer order processing

■ The need to consolidate key business functions for an internal good, like interconnecting, manufacturing, accounting, administration, and fulfillment

■ The need to integrate separate technologies, along with the functions they provide, into a common, organization-wide organism

▲ The need to provide a solid foundation on which next-generation technologies and applications can be built

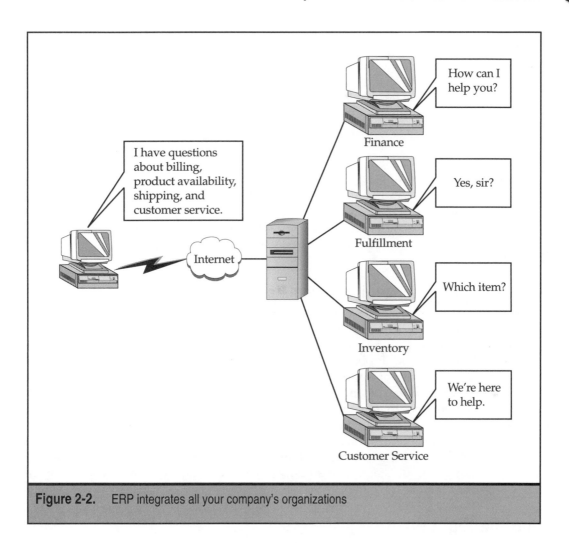

Figure 2-2.   ERP integrates all your company's organizations

But the most important reason for ERP comes down to money: e-business demands a smooth, efficient, effective ERP. Why does ERP give your organization an e-business edge?

Get Control

Even though we're in the middle of the Information Age, business managers can't get access to the information they want—especially on legacy systems. They want to know immediate details about how much they've sold, how much money they've made, how much they've shipped, and a fleet of other matters. Most legacy applications can't provide this information, but ERP can.

Work Globally

This is the age of multinational, worldwide operations. For you to manage your local activities while still being able to keep your finger on the pulse of your operations in Europe, applications must be able to accommodate distant facilities. To manage and work effectively, your applications must be able to talk to each other and do it quickly. This is beyond the capabilities of legacy applications.

The Feds' Demands

Governmental edicts can have an impact on your systems, and if those systems are not properly equipped to handle them, you may find yourself shelling out bucks for a new system to accommodate the government. For instance, consider the Year 2000 problem. The U.S. government mandated that computers be Year 2000–compliant. If yours is a system that can make the appropriate changes when the government says so, you'll save a lot of headaches and money.

Improve Information and Decision-Making

Even in the "we're all a team" atmosphere of business, the truth of the matter is that every business is still a group of disparate tribes working together for a common goal. But, really, do your tribes (accounting, HR, production, fulfillment, and so on) know what's going on with the others? Probably not. Because so many departments use different applications, the sharing of information is difficult. This leads to confusion, misunderstanding, mistakes, and an incomplete use of corporate assets. By implementing an ERP, you can bring the tribes together with common applications. This will not only improve the flow of information in both directions, but it can also reduce the tribe mentality.

Integration is an organization's dream come true. It eases the IT department's burden and it brings the company's information together by including everyone in the same system. Now that you understand the necessity of ERP, let's talk about how you can introduce ERP into your organization.

Getting the Right Fit

Many companies, when looking for an ERP solution, fall into an unfortunate trap. To find a good fit between a company and an ERP application product family, too many companies don't look far enough down the road. Often, they look at the individual applications and base their decisions on what features come with each application. What they should be doing is making a more introspective decision based on what kind of company they want to have.

Getting a good fit with your ERP can be challenging, but it is crucial. Take, for example, FoxMeyer Drugs—an organization that came to a disastrous end when it implemented a bad ERP. The $5 billion pharmaceutical wholesaler wound up filing bankruptcy because the consultant hired to perform the upgrade, they alleged, made false promises about its effectiveness. Not every company has this rough a ride, but enough organizations are feeling the sting of bad ERP implementation.

One of the biggest problems for evolving businesses is finding the happy balance between business and technology. Many managers forget that ERP—though it has tech undertones—is really a business foundation. If the business side and the tech side don't come together, it's certain disaster for any e-business solution. Too often, the task of finding an ERP solution is delegated to the IT manager—bad idea. With all due respect to the IT managers out there, they don't know the ins and outs of business management any more than the HR manager knows how to configure a 100 Mbps Ethernet switch.

Change in business isn't just a technological issue, though lately it has been driven by technology. ERP adoption will have direct effects on your organizational structure, processes, people, and procedures. To make sound, solid business decisions, management needs to understand the technical foundation for business and e-business functionality, as well as the return on technology investment.

To that end, management needs to ask itself some important, pointed questions:

▼ What *is* our business?

■ What are our issues *today*?

▲ What will be important *tomorrow*?

The answers to these questions will help your organization make the best ERP decision.

The Right Software

Although, as we've said, ERP is as much a business initiative as it is a technological one, there is one undeniable fact of ERP—the core of any implementation is technology. But when you decide to develop an ERP solution, what kind of software will you use to enhance your e-business? Will you try to find something off the shelf or build it yourself?

In the past, there were only two ERP architectures: a complex, custom-designed application that would meet the organization's specific needs and use the existing legacy equipment; or an off-the-shelf application that was designed to adapt to a changing marketplace and to be implemented more rapidly at a lower cost.

Though custom-designed applications give organizations functionality unique to them, they tend to be large and overly complex and take a long time to design, develop, and implement. By the time they are ready, your organization could be on to a new way of doing business. Additionally, maintaining and updating this kind of infrastructure is expensive and requires more manpower than you'd like.

Off-the-shelf applications, on the other hand, provide broad functionality; improved integration with existing systems; and greater flexibility to upgrade, expand, and change. Table 2-1 shows a list of vendors who offer off-the-shelf ERP software.

Company	Product	Contact
SAP	IMPRESS/OIS	www.sap.com
BAAN	BaanERP	www.baan.com
Oracle	Oracle eBusiness Suite	www.oracle.com
Lawson	Insight II	www.lawson.com

Table 2-1.   Off-the-Shelf ERP Software

Besides the aforementioned reasons in praise of off-the-shelf software, a number of other, important factors show how off-the-shelf software is a good solution:

▼ Custom software is expensive. Only organizations with a stack of extra money can maintain the high cost of ownership that custom ERP solutions demand.

■ Installed applications are becoming outdated, and the continual redesign of how business is done (especially in a dot-com world) makes existing software useless.

■ Off-the-shelf software uses only the best practices from a diverse collection of industries. Your ability to use these practices will only help your organization.

▲ Oftentimes, software development simply fails. About 70 percent of internal software projects fail. To ameliorate this problem, more and more organizations are using outside consultants to develop their solutions.

But off-the-shelf software isn't a panacea. Off-the-shelf software requires organizations to rethink and change established business practices to fit in with the new applications. Alternatively, the applications can be purchased but then modified and customized to fit in with the organization. Altogether, the off-the-shelf applications have a higher initial cost if they are customized. Also, if you want to maintain your company's "bleeding edge," be aware that any software you buy from a third party, your competitors can also buy.

Capabilities of ERP Solutions

In spite of some of the initial sticker-shock associated with an off-the-shelf solution, your organization can only benefit from the functionality they impart.

▼ **Integrate the back office**   By integrating your back office, you'll be able to leverage your capabilities and present a more functional face to your supply-chain partners, customers, and suppliers.

■ **Ease business changes**   Business isn't a static model. Especially in the dot-com age, your organization and the way you operate must remain flexible. You can use the best practices found in off-the-shelf software to help ease the change.

▲   **Ease technology changes**   ERP architecture is designed to work in a variety of complicated systems, and to do so in such a way that users never have to know how complex the underlying system is. Further, the software can be modified to accommodate specific business practices and processes without users' having to worry about the technical infrastructure that lies beneath.

Though finding and customizing an ERP solution is complex, the work isn't finished. Implementing the changes and upgrades requires a bit of work.

Implementation

Implementing your ERP software solution requires work on two fronts: your organization's leadership and your technological infrastructure. Remember, because ERP is, at its heart, a business issue, it can't all be managed with a CD-ROM and two technicians from the IT department.

Successful implementation requires attention to both technology issues and business issues. Because these issues are complementary, both your tech and leadership sides must work in tandem so that the final product is not lopsided or misguided.

Technical Implementation

On the technical side, the work is fairly straightforward—it's the job of the IT staff and consultants to conduct the actual installation, testing, and migration. But this can't be done in a vacuum. It's important to stay in contact with management so that important issues can be passed along for each side's benefit.

Phase	Description
Project preparation	The project is organized, and the project team is recruited. At this stage, project resources, costs, and activities are estimated.
Blueprint	Your consultants will document your organization's requirements and its business processes.
Pilot	Software is configured to match your organization's structure. The technical team plans the interfaces and data integration application infrastructure of the new system.
Final	The work from earlier stages is consolidated. This phase includes the final system test, user training, and the final data migration.
Assessment	The system is reviewed to verify that all your organization's requirements were met. This includes checking business processes, the technological components, and the users.

Table 2-2.   ERP Implementation Phases

Fortunately, off-the-shelf vendors have identified many of the issues related to upgrading an ERP solution, and they have tried to reduce deployment times and headaches with implementation plans. There are five key steps, shown in Table 2-2, to a smooth, reasonably glitch-free implementation.

But the technological implementation is just the beginning. After the new applications are installed, some leadership follow-up is important.

Leadership Issues

As technology changes the face of business, leadership must also change. The traditional role of issuing orders and watching the result is morphing into an environment where coordination and lateral leadership are necessary. (I sense a lot of traditionalists shivering out there. Don't worry, it'll be fine.) Successful coordination management can be achieved with the following capabilities:

▼ **Strategic thinking** With so many delicate issues swirling around ERP, it's crucial to make the best decisions. ERPs, unfortunately, require you to choose between speed of installation, cost, and functionality. One of the biggest mistakes managers make is getting caught up in the hype of a new process and not taking the time to really understand it.

■ **Process reengineering** You may have managed your billing for 20 years and want to hang on to those methods. However, it's impossible to implement a comprehensive ERP solution without having to reengineer the way you do your business. The fact of the matter is, the software simply won't allow it. If the same processes are attempted on the new system, you'll wind up with a "square peg, round hole" scenario.

■ **Managing the implementation** Because of the sheer complexity of ERP solutions, they often come in after deadline and over budget. Because of the seemingly inevitable headaches, it's important to be able to roll with the punches and manage effectively. This isn't to suggest that you should sit idly by when things go wrong. One way to alleviate these problems is to develop a good relationship with your consultants. For instance, Bay Networks put in place a "gain-share" with its consultants. If the consultants deliver the project on time and with a high degree of accuracy, they're paid more. If they're late, they get paid less—a lot less.

▲ **Transition management** Once the solution is installed, work with the employees begins. Resistance to change is a big problem in any new computer system and can lead to disastrous results. To lessen this problem, you can find way of helping the users understand the vision behind the changes. Have them participate in the implementation and get them working on it as soon as possible.

Once you've overcome the leadership and technological hurdles that come with an ERP solution, you'll reap the benefits that come to an organization that has streamlined its processes. Especially in the world of e-business, speed and efficiency are vitally important.

CUSTOMER RELATIONSHIP MANAGEMENT

It's no secret that successful businesses will have happy customers who can't wait to come back and buy more things. In the world of e-business, finding and keeping customers and making them happy is a different affair than in a traditional bricks-and-mortar shop.

To attract and keep customers in an e-business setting, you must successfully engage in *customer relationship management (CRM).* In this section, we'll give you a more complete description of CRM and what you can do to make your customers happy, spending customers.

What Is CRM

It's easy enough to develop a product or service that people will want to buy—once. The real trick is to develop a system and an organization that bring customers back over and over. CRM requires that your whole organization work in tandem to bring customers back through your cyberdoors. That means that everyone has to do a good job, from the customer's point of view. For instance:

- ▼ The marketing department has to create an image of the company that the customer can't do without.
- ■ The online catalog has to be easy to use and complete enough to give all information customers want.
- ■ The fulfillment department has to get orders out the door as fast as possible.
- ▲ If there is a problem with an order, the customer service department has to respond to the customer's concerns as quickly and accurately as possible.

To ensure that you have the business framework in place to accommodate solid, effective CRM, you must focus on the following goals:

- ▼ **Expand sales with existing customers**   Take a good, hard look at your existing clients. What do they want and how can you provide it?
- ■ **Use integrated information**   Use the information you already know to enhance your customers' stay at your site. You shouldn't ask repetitive questions of your customers at different stages of their visit.
- ■ **Use more repeatable sales processes**   With more and more ways for customers to come in contact with your organization, they're bound to come into contact with many different employees. Customers like to know how things are done, so ensuring that all the avenues for sales are identical will make them comfortable and happy shoppers.
- ■ **Create value and make customers loyal**   No matter how you accomplish it, you have to do something that will make your customers value your organization and make them "brand loyal." It may be your consistently low

prices, your great customer service, or your speedy delivery. Whatever it is, make sure you have some way to keep customers coming back.

▲ **React before it's too late**   Consistently look at your organization through your customers' eyes. Ferret out and find issues *before* they become problems.

CRM is a comprehensive, multifaceted issue. To be successful, you have to ensure that you're delivering the best value for your customers, whether yours is a B2B or business-to-consumer (B2C) endeavor. Two of the biggest issues in CRM are bringing in new customers and then ensuring you have enough of what they want so that they'll stay.

Get Them and Keep Them

Effective CRM revolves around three separate concepts: getting customers, enhancing your relationship, and keeping them. Each of these stages is important, because your relationship will steadily evolve with your customers through these different phases.

Figure 2-3 shows the three phases of CRM and how they affect your customers.

Let's take a closer look at each phase in the CRM cycle and then talk about why they're important and what you can do to deliver a solid, successful e-business solution that enhances these phases. All of these phases are interrelated, but doing all three components well is a tricky job—so tricky that many organizations have chosen to focus on

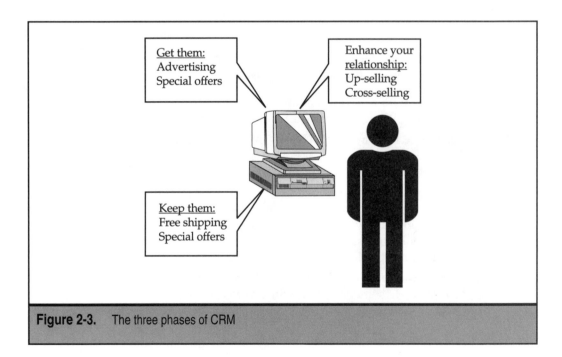

Figure 2-3.   The three phases of CRM

just one. However, be aware that providing emphasis on one phase does not mean forsaking the others.

By picking one of the three, you should be looking at your organization and where your strengths are. Further, you must also be aware of the technical requirements and underlying infrastructure of each.

Get Them

As with any business, attracting customers to your business is crucial. But with the Internet, you're playing with a different set of toys. It's not the same as slapping up a banner on your wall proclaiming a "Grand Opening Sale." Naturally, there is an element of advertising involved, but don't forget the core functionality of the Internet. Technology and streamlined service are great ways to get your customers to stick around.

For instance, I recently bought a computer from Compaq. Online, I was able to configure exactly the computer I wanted. A few minutes after ordering the computer, I got a call from Compaq verifying my credit card and shipping information. Because of their integration, the order-processing department was able to send an instant message to the order validation department, which then contacted me to make sure no one was trying to steal a computer.

First, I was impressed that they were making the effort to make sure that someone wasn't using a stolen credit card (mine!), and second, that instant—human—contact with Compaq was very reassuring. How could it have been better? The lady verifying the credit card information wasn't able to tell me when my computer would arrive or anything else about the order, except to check my credit card. Though that first contact was nice, there was still room for improvement.

Another way e-businesses attract new customers is with special offers for first-time customers. A couple years ago, customers of Amazon.com got a special offer from Drugstore.com—customers of Amazon.com could get their first $20 in merchandise free from Amazon's new sister site, Drugstore.com. There's nothing like free stuff to bring in customers.

Ultimately, when you're looking at bringing in new customers, make sure you take advantage of the technology at hand to give them something of value.

Enhance Your Relationship

Now that you've attracted new customers to your business, if you enhance that relationship, you can encourage up- and cross-selling. This deepens your relationship with the customers and encourages their loyalty.

NOTE: We talk about up- and cross-selling in the next section.

For example, at some customer service centers customers call with any number of questions, not just to complain about a broken item. Often, customers call with specific questions about a product they're thinking about buying. Recognizing this as an opportunity to enhance the company's relationship with a customer, the representatives may suggest an item complementary to the one the customer is calling about—for example, a Caller ID box for a new telephone (this is cross-selling) or a higher-quality item like a cordless telephone (this is up-selling).

Customers are thus getting an extra bonus because not only are they getting their questions answered, they're gaining additional information, which can provide them with a better alternative.

Keep Them

Once you've got them, you don't want to lose them. A returning customer is the most valuable asset to a company. Take this statistic, for instance: The odds of selling a product to a new customer are about 15 percent. The odds of selling a product to an existing customer are about 50 percent. Clearly, your business will benefit from happy, returning customers.

As e-business continues to grow, you've probably seen your own examples where customer service and incentives have bloomed. For instance, periodically at Buy.com the store offers customers free shipping. This is a great time for customers who want to buy a number of items to place an order, because the shipping charges will be eliminated, making for a less expensive sale.

Because there are so many e-businesses out there, retaining customers won't simply be a good idea, it will be a requirement to stay in business. At this time, there are any number of online sellers customers can choose between. One of the things that will make or break a company is how well it tends to its customers' needs.

Customer-Centric Architecture

As important as an integrated design is for your back office (as we discussed in the last section), it's just as important for your customers. It's a pain in the neck for employees to have to monkey around with conflicting applications and software packages. It's another thing entirely when customers—who can take their business elsewhere—have to wade through the quagmire of a poorly designed, implemented, and integrated Web site.

Now's the Time

But if yours is not a company that provides a customer-centric architecture, there's good news. There's a high demand for integrated applications that are designed to make your customers happy.

E-business applications are becoming increasingly customer-focused, which means focusing CRM activities around the customer, not marketing, sales, or other internal tasks. As a result, it's the input from your customers that drives changes and enhancements in the CRM process. What the customer wants becomes the driving force, which allows the e-business to change with the customer's wants and needs.

This isn't meant to suggest that you can simply drop everything and immediately implement an organization based solely on what your customers want—you may not be ready to supply such a service. You may have to restructure your business, especially the points at which you interact with the customer. A company's internal organizations are designed to compartmentalize the different units that deal with customers. Because of this, customized service is difficult to give.

Process Competencies

To counter this, companies that know how to give good customer service manage their customers in a way that cuts across the company's organizations. By addressing these issues as individual, customer-oriented processes, the company can ensure that it delivers the service

CRM Process Competency	Description	Applications Needed
Cross- and up-selling	Offering a product or service to enhance an existing product or service (cross-selling) or offering something that is better than the product or service that the customer is seeking (up-selling).	Software for sales calls, records about sales activities, and the ability to check the status of customer orders.
Direct marketing and fulfillment	Providing information about your products and services that your customers might be interested in. Also, making sure that when they ask for information, you provide it as fast as possible.	Software to provide direct mail responses, pricing or billing issues, and requests for literature.

Table 2-3.   CRM Process Competencies

CRM Process Competency	Description	Applications Needed
Customer service	Providing support for customers who are having problems with a product or service and to help resolve those problems.	Software to verify customer status, open trouble tickets, track specific tasks needed to resolve problems, maintain incident records, and capture support costs for charge-backs.
Field service operations	The extension of customer service when the problem can't be solved over the telephone or via e-mail. Field service and repair personnel can help solve large, complicated issues.	Software for scheduling, dispatching, managing inventory and logistics, and handling contracts and accounting.
Retention management	Providing your resources to your most important customers. By gathering detailed information about customers, you can locate those who are likely to spend more money with you and weed out those who bring in less money and cause more headaches.	Software that will allow study of customer account histories and transactions.

Table 2-3.   CRM Process Competencies *(continued)*

that its customers want. These processes are called *process competencies*. To build a solid CRM architecture, you need to design it with a series of process competencies.

Table 2-3 details process competencies that will provide for a customer-centric e-business solution. While looking at the table, you should try to identify any that would apply specifically to your organization.

To find out more information about some vendors offering CRM applications, consult Table 2-4.

Strong customer relationships are no secret to any company. However, with the added technological features of the Internet and developing applications, value can be

Vendor	Product	Contact
Oracle	Oracle eBusiness Suite	www.oracle.com
Lawson	Insight II	www.lawson.com
PeopleSoft	PeopleSoft 8 Enterprise Performance Management	www.peoplesoft.com

Table 2-4.   CRM Application Vendors

delivered to the customer in a number of new, creative ways. By understanding your customers and responding to their needs (even before they know what their needs are), you are assuring a successful e-business solution.

SELLING-CHAIN MANAGEMENT

Selling something is easy, right? You put up a Web page, throw a few items on there, wait for the orders to roll in, slap them in boxes with some foam peanuts, and call the UPS guy. If only the process of selling was that easy.

Not only do you have to worry about customers knowing about your product, but also you have to make sure it's exactly what they want. You have to worry about your current systems—are they fast enough, are they giving your customers what they're looking for? Then, you have to worry that the products are getting out in a timely manner. The first time a customer thinks, "Hey, I might like to buy that" until the money makes it into your account, there is the chance for a problem.

Since the days when Grog first negotiated with Kunk to buy an antelope leg in exchange for five coconuts to a current multimillion dollar sale between Sun and a Fortune 500 company for supercomputers, the face of sales has changed. Realizing how sales is changing is especially important, least of all so you aren't trying to sell supercomputers and expecting antelope haunches in return.

What It Is

Selling-chain management is, simply put, streamlining the sales process so that customers get what they want, how they want it. E-business is changing the way sales are made. Like other aspects of e-business (ERP and CRM, for instance) selling-chain management is an integrated approach. And, like ERP and CRM, selling-chain management at its heart involves a change in business thought, with technology coming in to mop up the details.

When we talk about integrating selling-chain management, we mean that every step in the life cycle of an order is integrated with the other steps. We mean that the order isn't merely passed on to the fulfillment center and then forgotten about. We mean that the selling process is viewed through the customer's eyes, which will only help when it comes to winning their loyalty.

Goals

Think back to the example used earlier in this chapter about ordering a computer from Compaq. The process was entirely integrated, giving the customer a sense of control and the ability to understand where the machine was in the construction process. Here's how it worked:

1. Advertising alerted me to the fact that companies would let you configure your own computer, rather than take what comes preconfigured from the factory. After checking out different companies, I decided to place an order with Compaq.

2. After selecting the base model at the Compaq Web site, I was able to add or remove features like hard drives, DVD players, and processors. A running total in the corner of the screen told me how much my customizations would cost.

3. I paid for my order, and then the Web site showed me a link I could follow to check on the status of my computer.

4. Anytime I wished, I could check that URL and find out where, in the process, my computer was. As it was being built, I knew it was under construction.

5. When the computer shipped, I was given the tracking number so that I could see where my computer was. One day it was in Texas, then it was in a UPS depot in Ohio, and finally it arrived in Minnesota.

In addition to upping customer satisfaction, this process integrated the sales process and took a lot of the headache and worry out of custom-ordering a computer. Incidentally, the steps I outlined and the resulting sale fall almost perfectly in line with the goals of selling-chain management.

▼ **Make it easier for the customer**   Streamline the process. I didn't have to go to a shop, wonder if they had the components I wanted, then worry that they'd take their sweet time building my computer. Rather, I knew that Compaq—which obviously sells a lot of computers this way—knew how to build me a custom computer and do it fast with all the benefits that come from a job in the factory.

■ **Add value**   This doesn't mean making sure the product is valuable; rather, it means making sure the *process* is one the customer values. I found the process at Compaq very easy to follow and beneficial. The process gave me more control over what I wanted to buy.

■ **Make it easy to order custom products**   This means making it easy to match what the customer wants with what you're selling. I wasn't prepared to buy one of the machines that Compaq had ready-made. It was the ability to add more processing speed and a beefier hard drive that sealed the deal.

■ **Increase sales force effectiveness**   In spite of the immediate productivity enhancements technology has added to the sales process, there is still more that can be done. There is still work to be done in terms of increasing sales volume, cutting back on the sales cycle time, and lowering the cost per sale. For example, as smooth as the process was, could the process have been sped up? It took about 10 days for the computer to arrive. As the customer, I don't care how long it takes them at the factory; I would have preferred to get the computer the same day.

▲ **Coordinate team selling**   As companies spread across the world like the British Empire did in the eighteenth century, it's more and more important to coordinate between the office in Budapest and the one in Nome. The need to coordinate activities and share information is extremely critical for businesses. When the order for my computer was placed, it originated in Arizona. Then, the information was transmitted to the factory in Houston, where it was built and shipped out.

We're a long way from Grog and Kunk negotiating for the leg of an antelope. But as the process of sales changes, so must the organizations that want to make money and flourish in the new economy.

The Value of Integration

Although many companies like Compaq and Amazon have customer-friendly, integrated systems, the fact of the matter is, most companies do not. Even though Web pages are popping up for every company under the sun, the order acquisition process has undergone little or no change at all.

Happily, technology is providing the tools you need to streamline and integrate your sales process. In the networked economy, the sales organization has a great deal of impact on decisions made across the company, as well as the decisions that affect outside suppliers. Sadly, management is widely confused about what to do and how to do it using the available software applications. Making the issue even more complex is the ever-changing, dynamic world of both business and technology.

How Business Is Shaping the Need for Selling-Chain Management

Within the last decade, there have been a number of issues that have driven the need for selling-chain management applications: the increase in self-service shopping, presales issues, cost of orders, more channels, and product complexity.

Companies are able to deal with and overcome these issues by implementing selling-chain management systems. The first step is to integrate the sales systems with the rest of the organization's systems to bring all the organization's information to the point of sale, be it a salesperson's laptop, a Web site, or the call center's terminal.

Next, companies must integrate sales and acquisition applications with the rest of the business's systems. This allows them to increase sales throughput, reduce mistakes, lower costs, and increase customer satisfaction. Let's take a look at the different obstacles blocking effective sales and how selling-chain management can help you negotiate and eliminate those obstacles.

Increase in Self-Service Shopping

If anything is indicative of commerce on the Internet, self-service shopping is it. Shoppers can find virtually anything they want online, and they don't need some guy in a polyester suit with a big, white belt and matching shoes standing over them dripping pomade. This goes beyond buying a book or a CD at Amazon.com. Now, customers can track down used cars using Carsoup.com or Auto-By-Tel. Customers need (and sometimes want) less and less help from a salesperson.

Presales Issues

As technology makes even toasters more complicated to operate, you can imagine how tough it is to effectively describe a product and its functionality to a customer if you don't have knowledgeable staff. This isn't just a problem of going into an electronics store and asking detailed questions about a new television and hearing, "Umm…I…Uh…" from the 16-year-old clerk. This is an issue that reaches into any business where the service or product is complex.

This sort of problem can lead to expensive presales issues, especially when it comes time to prepare a bid for a client. It's especially difficult if you're trying to offer a product or service online and trying to include the relevant information in a format that is accessible for everyone.

Cost of Orders

There's an ugly, dark side to all the automation and order sophistication we enjoy from our computers. If we dumb humans don't tell them the right things, mistakes happen— big mistakes. For instance, if we're selling new cars online and we forget to tell the Web page that the teal/pearl gloss coat is not available on the GTX body, when a customer orders that exact configuration, he's not going to pay for the mistake—we are.

This happens all too often and is an increasingly expensive problem for organizations that don't have a good selling-chain management system in place. Organizations that do not integrate their systems will continue to get slapped when these expensive errors pop up.

More Channels

At first blush, you might wonder why having too many points of sale would be a problem. More chances to sell the product must be a good thing, right? To an extent, that's correct, but the more open channels, the more you need to be able to serve the clients and customers who make use of those channels. And to complicate the matter further, different channels require different levels of support and involvement. For instance:

▼ Telesales requires someone in a cubicle with a terminal.

■ Web sales require a Web server and the associated infrastructure.

■ In-store sales require someone in the store to talk to customers.

▲ Third-party sales may require some degree of warranty or support work on your part.

Obviously, without some solid, effective integration, there is the possibility for a lot of loose ends out there—and you don't want your customers hanging Indiana Jones–style from any loose ends.

Product Complexity

As our great economy chugs forward, the marketplace is flooded with new products. From the consumer's standpoint, this is great—better stuff delivered faster, who wouldn't love it? Well, if you're the salesperson who has yet to fully understand how the SUX 6000 works, you're not looking forward for the SUX 7000's release.

As more products come out at a faster rate, this reduces the earlier products' shelf life and increases the burden on the salesperson to understand the new products. In addition, the plethora of new products steepens the learning curve for consumers trying to keep themselves educated. This just accentuates the need for up-to-date, comprehensive information about a product or service.

The Selling-Chain Infrastructure

So, how do you solve all the problems plaguing the sales process in the new millennium? You'll kick yourself for asking—we integrate.

First, unique applications are developed for each aspect of the automation process. These applications include catalogs, pricing engines, proposal systems, and sales compensation systems. Next, these applications are interconnected and then integrated together.

Coordinating sales across your enterprise is extremely important when you're selling products with long, complicated sales cycles; when there are multiple organizations selling jointly; or when there are many decision makers to keep in the loop.

Integration can keep every person in the chain informed about what each other person is doing. The sales team can share information about pricing updates and the customer's purchase history. They can also share a number of details—including who the key decision makers are, important issues in follow-up discussions, and a multitude of other issues that would be left out to dry without an integrated system.

Within the selling-chain management infrastructure are five key features that are critical to the process.

Catalogs

If you can't show or adequately describe what you're selling, how is the customer going to know? Luckily, in this day of the Internet, providing your customers information about your product is as easy as clicking the Web site—the tricky part is making sure the Web site is ready.

Another useful tool is marketing catalogs. These are intelligent documents that connect sales reps and customers to the company's most current and complete product information. As soon as official changes are made to the products, they are posted to the marketing catalog, and it is immediately broadcast across the network where sales staff can use it to provide the most up-to-date information to clients.

Sales Configuration

We've become spoiled. Nowadays, we *expect* to be able to pick what color we want our car, how fast we want our computers, and how loud our stereo can be. Don't we realize how much of a burden the ability to get what we want is for organizations?

It's especially difficult, because without an integrated system, salespeople—for instance—have to call the office to make sure that particular configuration will work. As a product line evolves and changes, the ability to check the custom configurations for a particular product grows complicated.

Modern configuration applications go beyond simply making sure that the customer's selections are doable. Rather, they are comprehensive tools that give customers what they want and enable the sales force to create accurate configurations and quotes at the point of sale.

Pricing and Distribution

Pricing is a complicated issue. For instance, have you ever checked the price of a car online? The first question—even before "do you want leather seats or cloth"—is "what's your zip code?" All too often, the differences in pricing can have a brain-chilling effect when you try to balance such issues as:

▼ Special discounts for certain customers

■ Pricing based on changing market conditions

■ Different prices based on geographical location

▲ Complex promotional offers

It doesn't take a genius to see that you need a computer to keep up with the dynamic changes within your pricing structure. This problem is exacerbated when you extend selling channels with resellers and partners. Because of all the issues related to these complicated sales scenarios, a new sales configuration type has been born: pricing configuration. Pricing configuration helps growing companies as they manage and position pricing and discount plans for selling channels.

Incentives

An important aspect of any sales system must include some sort of incentive component. The applications that track this kind of information are used for designing, processing, and analyzing complicated incentive programs. There are three core systems in commission software:

▼ Incentive design

■ Incentive processing

▲ Incentive analysis

Incentive design software allows the development of complex commission and bonus rules for a range of performance goals. Incentive processing requires systems to use nonrevenue performance issues (like customer satisfaction and service quality) to determine commissions and bonuses. Incentive analysis capabilities allow managers to get a real view of the entire sales process from account to product to customer-level analysis.

SUPPLY-CHAIN MANAGEMENT

You should probably be noticing a trend by now. The topics we're discussing—though they involve technology to achieve these goals—are first and foremost firmly rooted in business practices. And, like the other acronyms we've thrown at you in this chapter, supply-chain management (SCM) is no different.

And, as with the other topics we've discussed, the key to SCM comes from integration. But in this case, the customer isn't a consumer, it's another business. Further, for SCM to work, each business in the supply chain needs to have its applications and organization integrated.

In this section, we'll talk about SCM: what it is, how technology is streamlining the process, and just how supply chains work.

What Is Supply-Chain Management

A supply chain is a series of companies, linked together and supplying parts, materials, and services to others in the chain. The first link in the chain is the raw materials; the last link is a business selling a finished product. Take a look at Figure 2-4, which will illustrate a supply chain.

1. The first link in the chain is a mine in Minnesota's Iron Range. Once the iron is mined, requisitions come from a smelter that turns iron into salable pieces.

2. The iron is sent to Smeltworld, where it is turned into beams, bars, and rods.

3. Next, Smeltworld sends the iron to Ron's Wrought Iron Furniture, where it is turned into furniture.

4. Finally, a lawn and garden store orders its furniture from Ron.

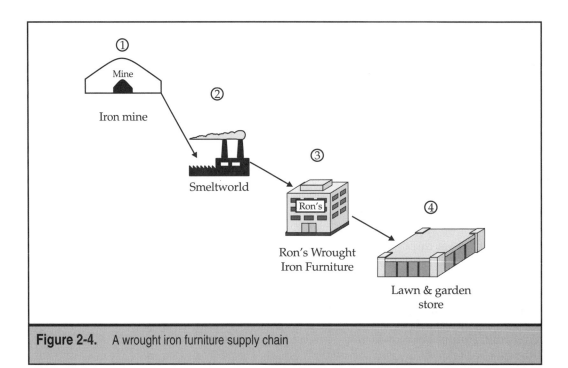

Figure 2-4.   A wrought iron furniture supply chain

This is the natural, logical flow of a supply chain—from raw material to the consumer. If, however, at any point in the chain, people decide they need more materials from one of their partners, they can requisition them.

In practice, this model works in the reverse order. Customers come into the lawn and garden store and buy the chairs. This causes the store to reorder chairs from Ron's Wrought Iron Furniture. But because he needs the iron to make the chairs, Ron calls Smeltworld for more. Smeltworld, in turn, calls the mine to ask for a few more tons of freshly mined ore.

And it isn't just the flow of materials that is important in the chain. Ultimately, everyone along the chain expects to get paid, so the chain works both ways—product flows one way, money the other.

In our furniture model, we have four steps, but that number of steps isn't cast in iron (sorry about that). If you're selling vegetables from a roadside stand, you may have two links in the chain—the farmer and the stand. Or if you're building cars, you have a very complex supply chain; in fact you're likely to have several chains—one for tires, one for seats, one for hub caps, and so on.

As you can imagine, as supply chains get more complex and as customers want products faster and faster, you need to be able to manage your supply chain. Here's where a new business paradigm and technology come into play. SCM is the coordination of material, information, and financial flows between and among all the partners.

How Technology Streamlines SCM

Our earlier example of wrought iron furniture was very straightforward and simple. However, complex products involve even more chains that can have very many links. As you can imagine, if you're building computers, you'll have suppliers for a broad range of components: plastic cases, keyboards, processors, hard drives, monitors, mice, software, motherboards, modems, preprinted manuals, FireWire ports, and so forth.

Each one of those suppliers must get its materials from other sources. For instance, the company making the hard drives has to get the platters from one supplier, the cases from another, the connection ports from another, and so forth.

Every time a customer buys a computer, you have to make sure you have enough of the components in stock. If not, you have to rattle the respective links in your supply chain to make sure you have enough materials.

As you can see, if your organization (and your partners' organizations) are integrated and interconnected, the supply-chain process is much, much smoother. Rather than having to fill out forms in triplicate and submit them to your partners, if you're integrated and connected (like the furniture manufacturer shown in Figure 2-5), when your supplies run low, your system will instantly contact your supply-chain partner and requisition new materials.

If your supplier's system realizes that it is getting low on an item, it can immediately requisition additional materials from its supplier, and so on. Ideally, the only time a manager would ever know that supplies were low would be when examining a report that mentions the statistic.

SCM Trends

In addition to the obvious speed and efficiency factors we talked about earlier, there are a number of forces motivating companies to jump on the e-bandwagon and integrate their supply chains.

▼ **Worldwide need**   The demand for goods that are tailored specifically for a local market has increased.

■ **Channel unpredictability**   Because so many channels are open to the customer, organizations must handle those channels much better. This requires more sophisticated coordination of several distribution channels.

■ **Responsiveness**   The traditional inventory management process has been supplanted by faster, customized orders from clients.

▲ **Companies will accept lower margins to maintain market share**   Many organizations are redesigning their supply chains to "trim the fat" and get rid of any slow, nonproductive processes.

As the market becomes even more streamlined, this forces individual companies to find ways to streamline. Customers and retailers expect more, and this also drives manu-

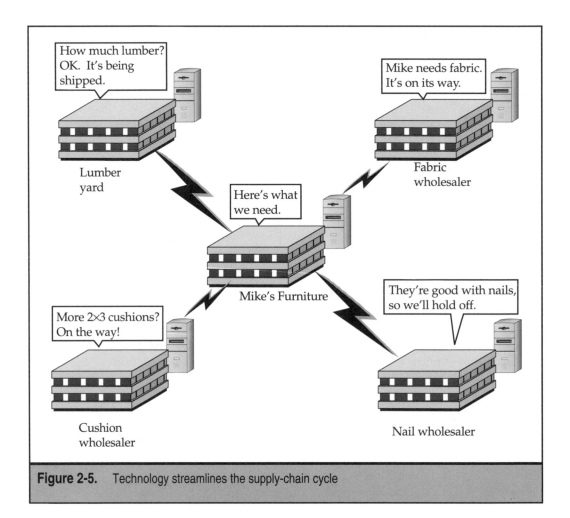

Figure 2-5. Technology streamlines the supply-chain cycle

facturers to improve their planning capabilities and better manage their link on the supply chain.

By implementing new technology, companies can ameliorate these pressures. New SCM applications are streamlining the supply-chain process. For instance, enabled directories (like Microsoft's Active Directory) can be used to keep your supply-chain partners informed about your company's needs. Other important technology improvements are:

▼ The Internet, which provides the technological infrastructure for businesses to communicate

■ Data acquisition applications

■ Data manipulation tools

▲ Data dissemination tools

The paradigm shift for businesses is that they are managing less inventory and managing more information. By understanding the information, a manager will have a better handle on SCM. This will be important as the world of business moves from a world of businesses competing against each other to one where the supply chains are duking it out for business supremacy.

How an Internet-Based Supply Chain Works

SCM seems to be the heir apparent to the B2B and business-to-enterprise (B2E) in the coming decade. But, as with any developing technology and business process, there is no prepared roadmap to lead managers through the twists and turns of SCM implementation and through the dense forest of SCM applications. But that doesn't mean that SCM is a total mystery. By understanding how an Internet-based SCM works, you can arm yourself with the right tools to navigate that maze or hack through the forest.

Integration[2]

The most important part of SCM is integrating integrated organizations—maybe you want to call it Integration[2]. This means that not only do you and your supply-chain partners need to have integrated applications, but your organizations must then be integrated together.

NOTE: Don't worry about integrating away the security and stability of your organization. The extent of your integration with another company includes what is essential for business, not your financial records.

Businesses hate excess inventory—it's stuff that they couldn't sell. The dream behind SCM is that integration will reduce excess inventory because, ideally, Larry in purchasing won't order too much inventory. Nowadays, customers are able to shop around, so the demands they place on suppliers can change drastically from order to order. Because of this, organizations are looking to SCM to further reduce excess inventory. Ideally, they'd like to cut inventory to zero and erase just-in-time ordering.

Types of Integrations

But when it comes time to actually integrate two organizations, there's no one model that works for all organizations in all situations. There are basically three types of supply chains that will form the foundation of your solution.

Responsive   *Responsive* supply chains respond quickly to a customer's needs. An important attribute of this is the available-to-promise factor. Businesses need to know what resources are available before they can promise a delivery date to their customers. Available-to-promise systems provide a system-wide, real-time look across the entire supply chain to show what is available and if it can be delivered on time.

Enterprising   The world of business is dynamic and your supply chain must be *enterprising* to keep up with the twists and turns of commerce. Supply chains must be able to be quickly reconfigured to respond to customer demands. Businesses on the chain must be able to look forward and be able to make the appropriate changes.

Intelligent   *Intelligent* supply chains are like hot rods. You're always tweaking or tuning different components. But it's the tweaking and tuning that gives you the extra edge. The components being tweaked and tuned are the weakest links in the chain.

Supply-Chain Planning

SCM is a business framework that is made up of several applications, split into two camps: planning and execution.

▼   The planning process emphasizes demand forecasting, inventory simulation, and transportation and manufacturing planning. These applications are designed to improve forecast accuracy, sharpen planning, and reduce costs.

▲   The execution process is where the rubber meets the road. It concerns itself with procuring, manufacturing, and distributing goods throughout the supply chain.

Let's take a closer look at each of these processes.

Planning

Supply-chain planning (SCP) can be broken down into five components, as shown in Figure 2-6.

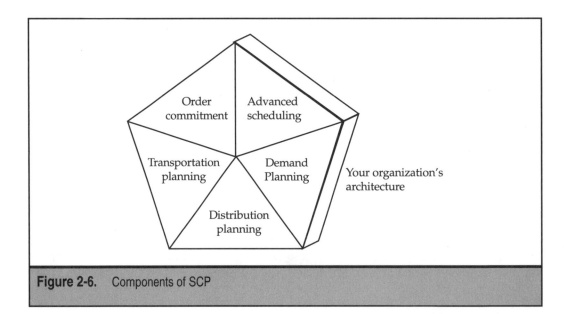

Figure 2-6.   Components of SCP

1. **Order commitment**   This module allows vendors to know, exactly, when a product or service can be delivered. It looks across the entire supply chain and is able to determine what the chain's resources are.

2. **Advanced scheduling**   This module provides in-depth coordination of all manufacturing and supply activities on the basis of customer orders. This module is execution-oriented and generates job schedules for managing the process as well as simple logistics.

3. **Demand planning**   This module takes all the demand forecasts from all units in the chain and combines them into one comprehensive forecast. Using statistical tools, this module is used for a big-picture view of demand.

4. **Distribution planning**   This module works in conjunction with the demand planning module to develop a complete model of the supply chain and its ability to fulfill orders.

5. **Transportation planning**   This module ensures that materials and finished goods are delivered at the right time to the right place in accordance with the planning schedule and at a minimal cost.

With so many variables at play with one organization, coordinating them across two or more enterprises can be quite a juggling act. That's why it's so important to utilize these sorts of SCP applications so that an accurate view of your supply chain can be generated and its actual abilities are measured. From there, you can decide if you are ready to move foreword. If you are, then supply chain execution is your next stop.

Execution

The second half of planning your supply chain is much more customer-centric. After all, it's the execution that the customer sees—not if you've got a good transportation plan in place. Planning is good at reducing your costs, but the customers won't see that. All they care about is that the goods get to them as ordered and when promised.

Like the planning phase, execution is divided into five components, as shown in Figure 2-7.

Let's take a closer look at the five kinds of supply chain applications:

1. **Order planning**   Because customers expect more when they make a purchase and because of short fulfillment deadlines, it's necessary to have an effective execution plan that reduces the time from when an order is placed to when it ships from your organization. One way to accomplish this is through backward planning. It considers all the steps in the supply chain and identifies any place there may be issues, including such seemingly minor details as truck sizes and when the drivers work.

2. **Production**   Because so many products are modular in nature, it's important that the completed components come together at the right time. Most often, subassemblies are conducted in conjunction with the timeline for the final

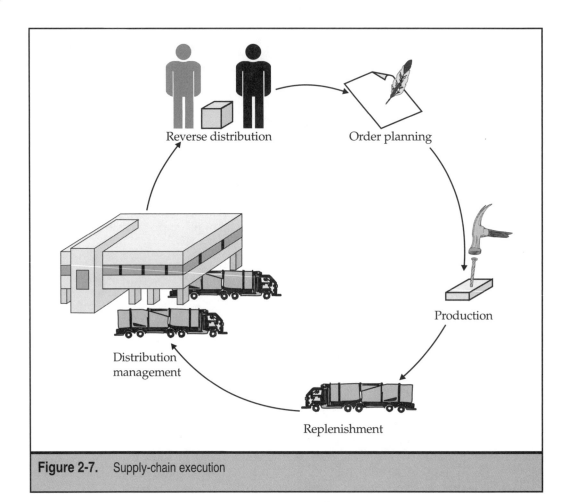

Figure 2-7. Supply-chain execution

assembly. Another piece of this puzzle is ensuring that the right quantities of raw materials are ordered and ready to go.

3. **Replenishment**   Production leads to the issue of replenishment. This is necessary so that there are enough resources available without overloading on excess inventory.

4. **Distribution management**   Once a product has been constructed, it must be distributed. Distribution management encompasses the whole process of getting the product from the assembly line to the distribution center to the customer. Distribution management has been streamlined and improved by merging it with transportation planning. This gives users the ability to check on the status of a shipped item.

5. **Reverse distribution**   But the process doesn't end when the customer opens the box. What if something's wrong? It's the wrong size; it's the wrong color; it's leaking phosphorescent goo; whatever. In these cases, the item will have to be returned to the manufacturer. But it isn't simply a matter of picking up the box and taking it away—it must also be accounted for, and the money or a new product must be returned to the customer.

Vendors

Table 2-5 lists some vendors that offer SCM applications. For more information, visit their Web sites.

Building a viable e-business is not as easy as it seems at first blush. To develop a good, profitable, successful e-business, you have to keep a great many balls in the air.

Vendor	Product	Contact
Oracle	Supply-Chain Planning	www.oracle.com
	Advanced Supply-Chain Planning	
	Demand Planning	
	Global ATP Server	
	Supply-Chain Execution	
	Advanced Pricing	
	Configurator	
	E-Commerce Gateway	
	Inventory	
	Manufacturing Planning	
	Manufacturing Scheduling	
	Order Management	
	Receivables	
	Release Management	
Baan	BaanSCS	www.baan.com
PeopleSoft	PeopleSoft Supply-Chain Management	www.peoplesoft.com

Table 2-5.   Off-the-Shelf SCM Applications

PART II

E-Business Servers and Clients

CHAPTER 3

Operating Systems

W ithout operating system (OS) software, computers would be little more than heavy boxes costing a couple thousand dollars that sit on your desk and hum. (Oh sure, you could still watch the little Caps Lock light go on and off by repeatedly pressing the button, but that won't get you any closer to developing an e-business solution for your enterprise.) Even though you bought a computer that purports to be the fastest, with the most memory and a gazillion other bells and whistles, without OS software you can't do anything with it, as you can see from the following illustration.

Computers need operating systems
to function

No operating system

Operating systems provide the functionality for your computer and, by extension, your e-business. Certainly you will augment your OS with e-business-specific client and server applications, but some bare-bones tools built into your OS can help you develop, run, and maintain your enterprise.

Contrary to what the Justice Department and the attorneys general of 20 states argue, there are more operating systems out there than Microsoft Windows. Sun has done very well with its Solaris OS, Novell is well into the fifth version of its popular NetWare OS, and Linux isn't just the dandy of the newsgroups anymore.

But talking about operating systems is a lot like talking about cars: you have a Ford, but your buddy swears by Chevys. The only thing you can agree on is that the guy down the street who owns a Toyota is out of his mind. It's just about the same when talk turns to OSes. Talk to one network administrator and you'll hear that Sun is the only way to go. Another swears by Microsoft, and yet another says open-sourced Linux is where it's at. The truth of the matter is, they may all be right. Each OS has its own pros and cons.

In this chapter, we'll look at your best OS bets for e-business. Many books have been written about each of these OSes, their functions, and their features. We only have a chapter to talk about them, so we'll only be able to touch on the highlights. For more information—and a fair dose of marketing—you should visit their respective Web sites.

First, we'll talk about what functions and features you are likely to need from an OS for your e-business enterprise. Then, we'll talk about the OS offerings from Microsoft, Novell, Sun, and Linux and what each one brings to the e-business table. Finally, we'll look at what they can do for you, what hardware you'll need, and—very important—how much they cost.

THE FEATURES YOU WANT

In essence, all OSes do the same thing: they make your computers work. But beyond that simple requirement, they each do their thing with differing features and differing results. When considering an OS for your e-business, there are four main features that you want to ensure your OS has. These features are reliability, scalability, interoperability, and security.

Reliability

It's happened to us all. At a crucial point in our work on a computer, the keys stop responding, the screen freezes up, and the mouse seems to have run into a hole in the wall. No matter how many times we try to recover the system, the writing is on the wall—the computer has crashed and you must reboot. As much of a hassle as it is for someone using a single computer, crashes can mean big trouble for an e-business, as you can see in the following illustration.

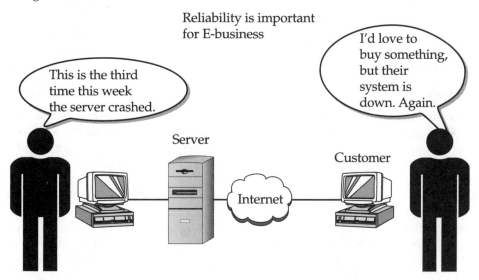

Reliability can be achieved in a number of ways. First, strong programming and good testing can stave off problems. But reliability extends beyond the OS itself. Much of your system's reliability will depend on how you construct your network. If you've figured a number of redundant systems into your network, you're less likely to suffer when things go awry. We talk more about the best way to configure and build your networks in Chapters 6 and 7.

Scalability

Building an e-business system will cost a couple bucks. But when the time comes that customers are maxing out your hardware, if yours is a system that can be expanded, it's much cheaper and much easier on your network to simply add more processors to beef up the system. Adding more processors is called *scaling;* it is an important consideration in picking a good OS for your e-business.

An important detail when considering an OS for its scaling features is how many processors you can include on each node (Windows 2000 and Linux allow up to 8 processors per node, Solaris allows 64 per node, and NetWare only supports 1 per node).

Apart from the question of future upgrades, scalability is an important feature if you want to hit the ground running with a fast network.

Interoperability

You could sink stacks of money in the best system in the world. It could be the fastest, it could be the most reliable and the most stable, but unless you can link up with other systems and run applications created on other machines, that sweet system will do you little good. To that end, an important feature of your e-business system is the capability to talk with other computers and share information.

Two of the most important aspects of interoperability in an e-business enviroment are, first, the adherence to and acceptance of standards and, second, the capability to use an enabled directory.

Standards

Since a different company develops each operating system, it's unlikely that each company will independently develop software that can readily communicate with the software of the other companies. This is where the notion of *standards* comes into play. Standards are sets of parameters for applications that ensure they will be operable across a multitude of systems.

Unless you're a relative newcomer to the world of computing, you'll probably remember a time when a word processing document created on one computer could not be read on another. If you tried to read the file on a nonconforming system, you only got pages and pages of gibberish. To cure that problem, one example of a standard is a basic text file. A word processing document saved as a text file can be read on any computer, because ASCII is a standard.

Another way to understand standards is to look at the Internet. Web sites are programmed and developed using Hypertext Markup Language (HTML). HTML is a standard that allows the same content to be accessed by every computer with a Web browser. For instance, consider two people accessing your network. Let's say a customer is running Windows and receives an HTML page. Because HTML is a standard, the Windows machine understands it. In another case, consider a supply chain partner accessing your network. In this case it receives a file but cannot understand it because it is not a standard. In this case, your partner, who is using a Linux computer, was expecting the file to be in a standard J2EE format. As you can see, your partner was unable to read the file. The following illustration is an example of these situations.

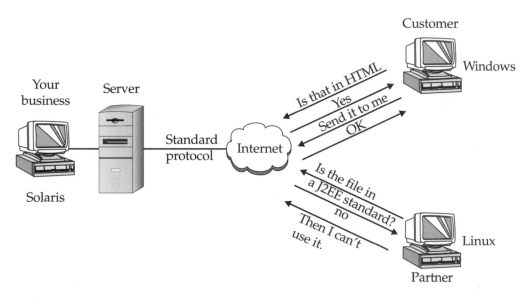

Standards let computers share information

If you select a system that adheres to standards, you will have vastly more flexibility when it comes to upgrading software and hardware. If, on the other hand, you lock yourself into a proprietary vendor, you will be at their whim if and when they decide to upgrade.

Enabled Directories

Another way to ensure interoperability is to use an X.500-based directory. Enabled directories allow you to manage not only files and applications, but also users and clients, what they can access, what they can't access, and how you want them to be able to utilize your resources.

Enabled directories are giant databases containing information about your system and the components in it. Like any databases, enabled directories contain fields of information. We can compare enabled directories to your personal address book. The fields of information in the address book (names, addresses, and phone numbers in your address book) are similar to fields these enabled directories hold.

But if you use an X.500-based enabled directory, it isn't maintaining phone numbers and addresses for your friends, family, and business associates. Rather, it is holding bits of information (like names and descriptive information) about objects in your network.

The enabled directories' logical, hierarchical structure allows the database to be sorted from the largest element down to the smallest. To continue the address book example, it would start with the broadest category (like what country someone lives in) down through smaller fields (like states and area codes). This relationship is shown in Figure 3-1.

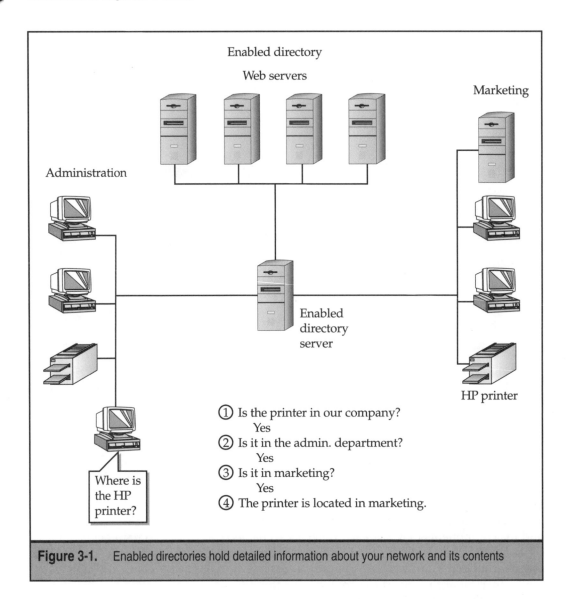

Enabled directory

Web servers

Marketing

Administration

Enabled
directory
server

HP printer

① Is the printer in our company?
   Yes
② Is it in the admin. department?
   Yes
③ Is it in marketing?
   Yes
④ The printer is located in marketing.

Where is
the HP
printer?

Figure 3-1.   Enabled directories hold detailed information about your network and its contents

So how do enabled directories help your business? These intricate directories help you create secure, customized relationships between your network and those of your customers and partners. Directory-enabled products can provide automated provisioning, improved security, customer profiling, electronic wallets, automated notification systems, customized Web interfaces, and virtual private networks (VPNs).

You can share e-business solutions with your partners by establishing mutually beneficial relationships between varying company networks. On the customer side, they can securely maintain customer-accessible directories. E-business partners can communicate directly with and update each other's directories. Suppliers can immediately know when and how much inventory to ship.

Let's take a look at a couple things you can do with directory-enabled applications.

Customer Profiling   Customer profiling allows you to gather information about customers as they browse your Web site. You can extract a profile of your customers and their shopping habits by tracking certain bits of information:

1. **Observed information**   This is what customers reveal about themselves through their patterns of movement through the site.

2. **Stated information**   This is the information customers tell you about themselves through online surveys and questionnaires.

3. **Transactional information**   This is information about your customers derived from what they buy.

With this information stored in your directory, you can tailor your offerings and services to each customer or supply-chain partner.

Figure 3-2 shows how certain information can be extracted from a customer's visit with directory-enabled applications. Next, it is stored in the directory, where it waits for another application to retrieve it and create personalized Web content.

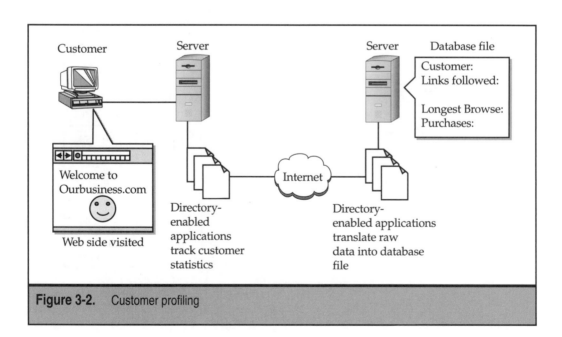

Figure 3-2.   Customer profiling

Supply Chain Management   Enabled directories will undoubtedly help you optimize service to partners in your supply chain. Rather than your having to track stock information and reorder supplies manually, your network can be configured so that shortages of material can be automatically reordered.

Let's use the Tastee-Crisp Snack Cracker Company as an example (see Figure 3-3). Four components go into a box of their crackers: cheese, flour, plastic bags, and preprinted boxes. When the company ships a crate of crackers, they must order more materials to make more crackers.

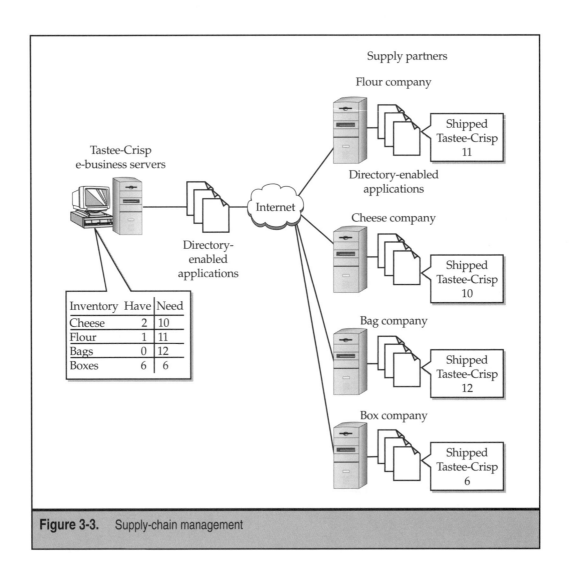

Figure 3-3.   Supply-chain management

By using directory-enabled services, Tastee-Crisp can give its cheese, flour, bag, and box suppliers access to its materials inventory database so that they will instantly know when to send out fresh supplies.

Security

Probably the biggest issue on your mind as you think about bringing your business onto the Internet is security. A crucially important part of any e-business solution is to ensure that a solid security system is in place to keep troublemakers at bay.

Each operating system we're looking at uses many common security features, such as the Secure Sockets Layer, Single Sign-on, and authentication systems. But the systems also offer differing layers of protection in the form of different features. In addition to what the specific OSes offer, we talk about security issues for networks as well as the OSes in more depth in Chapters 11, 12, and 13.

MICROSOFT WINDOWS 2000

Let's get right into the OSes with a talk about the 900-pound gorilla—Microsoft. In many regards, Windows 2000 and NT can be discussed together. Though Windows 2000 is improved over NT, the two OSes still contain a number of the same tools that function more or less the same. Since Microsoft is putting its muscle behind Windows 2000 and more or less phasing out NT, and also for the sake of simplicity, we're going to talk specifically about Windows 2000.

Windows 2000 Versions

Microsoft has introduced three different versions of Windows 2000. Windows 2000 Professional is the version that is used on corporate desktops and clients, while Windows 2000 Server and Advanced Server are meant, naturally, for network servers. The functionality is the same; the only difference between them is the addition of certain tools on the server versions.

Windows 2000 Professional and Server

Both the desktop and server versions of Microsoft's new flagship feature a multitude of improvements that will keep your e-business up and running. The following are a few of the features that will enhance your servers and clients.

Reliability   To curtail corruption of key files, Windows File Protection guards the platforms' core files. If a key file is overwritten, Windows 2000 automatically rewrites it with the proper version. Improved device driver certification ensures that drivers haven't been tampered with and will function properly.

Windows 2000 Server improves network reliability and increases uptime over earlier versions of Windows. Kernel-Mode Write Protection prevents errant code from corrupting system operations. Internet Information Services Application Protection keeps Web applications running separately from the Web server, preventing server crashes.

Management The Microsoft Management Console is featured in all versions of Windows 2000 and gives users a consistent environment for managing Windows resources. Windows 2000 Professional users can manage their resources locally; Windows 2000 Server users can administer the resources of a network.

Security Windows 2000 ensures security by encrypting its files on local and network drives. The process is invisible to users, and the information remains encrypted when files are backed up or archived. Both versions also support Kerberos user authentication and smart cards.

Windows 2000 Server employs several security methods to safeguard employees, partners, and customers. The latest security standards are supported, and a variety of encryption tools are used for data protection.

Dynamic System Configuration Windows 2000 Server has a complete set of tools for configuring systems without taking them offline. Volumes can be added, disks can be defragmented, and processes gone haywire can be halted without affecting end users. This is an improvement over Windows NT, which required the system to be rebooted for almost every change made to it.

Windows 2000 Advanced Server

Windows 2000 Advanced Server provides all the features and functions of Windows 2000 Server, but it adds additional tools and capabilities for enhanced e-commerce and network needs. Table 3-1 illustrates those enhancements.

	Scalability	Memory Support	Advanced Clustering Abilities
Windows 2000 Server	4-way scaling	Up to 4GB RAM	
Windows 2000 Advanced Server	8-way scaling	Up to 8GB RAM	Allows network load balancing, cluster service, and enhanced cluster wizards

Table 3-1. Functional Enhancements of Windows 2000 Advanced Server over Windows 2000 Server

NOTE: Microsoft's most robust release of Windows 2000 is its Datacenter, which is expected to be available late in 2000. Datacenter promises 32-way scalability and will provide even more power for e-businesses.

Internet Information Server 5.0

Microsoft's Internet Information Server 5.0 (IIS) is an extremely handy tool that comes bundled with Windows 2000. IIS is the core tool that will help you build, develop, and maintain your Web presence.

NOTE: Windows NT users cannot use IIS 5.0; it's designed and closely woven in with the Windows 2000 architecture. If you are using NT, however, you can still use IIS 4.0 and get many of the same functions as in version 5.0.

Shipped with Windows 2000 Server releases, IIS 5.0 has many features that are interconnected with the operating system, providing a solid base in functionality and reliability. Such benefits as improved security and administration tie in directly with Windows 2000 improvements and are immediately accessible to the user.

Reliability

Reliability and stability are key features of IIS 5.0. It is easier and faster to restart IIS in the event of a failure than with previous versions. In earlier versions of the software, an administrator had to restart four separate services after every stoppage. Now, using IIS Reliable Restart, administrators can restart IIS without having to reboot the computer.

HTTP support has also been enhanced in IIS 5.0. Site administrators can use customizable error messages, which can be a benefit if a customer has stumbled across a dead link.

Application protection allows Web applications to be run in a pooled process that is separate from core IIS processes. That means that if something goes afoul in one of the applications, the rest of the IIS services are not affected.

WebDAV

The World Wide Web provides a great way to publish content, but document collaboration has been difficult. Traditionally, it has been easier to view pages than to make changes.

Microsoft's Web Distributed Authoring and Versioning (WebDAV) is an extension to HTTP 1.1, enabling remote authors to manage files and directories on a server over an HTTP connection. Because of IIS's intertwining with Windows 2000, WebDAV takes advantage of the security and file access features of Windows 2000 Server.

With WebDAV, you can allow remote users to move, search, edit, or delete files and directories from the server. In fact, other OSes have begun to support WebDAV, making it a standard for Web file management. Figure 3-4 shows how documents are shared using WebDAV.

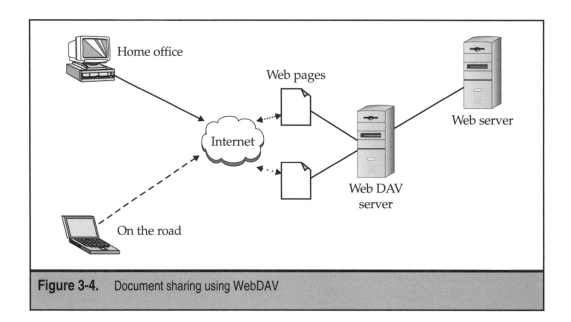

Figure 3-4. Document sharing using WebDAV

Application Environment

IIS 5.0 extends the Web server's application development environment by building on new technologies included with Windows 2000 Server. Active Directory and Component Object Model (COM+) along with Active Server Page (ASP) enhancements are particularly useful for developers.

ASP—the chief way to launch dynamic content under IIS—has seen great enhancements in the latest version of IIS.

▼ The ASPerror object enhances error handling by letting developers catch errors in script files. Flow-control capabilities allow the server to execute other pages without the traditional round trips that are required by server-side redirects.

▲ Scriptless ASP pages are enhanced by a new check in the parsing stage. In the past, many sites would use .asp file extensions for all their pages, so they wouldn't have to change links if script was later added to an HTML-only page. Unfortunately, this practice would launch the default scripting engine, even when there was no code. The new check detects when executing requests are waiting for internal components and automatically supplies the resources to allow other requests to continue processing.

ASP is bundled with several prebuilt components for such tasks as logging, accessing data, accessing files, and using counters. The components are fast and scalable, and the Browser Capabilities tool can support capabilities described in cookies sent by the browser. This allows flexibility in running server code that reflects the features supported by the client.

Active Directory

The core feature of Windows 2000's manageability is its directory-enabled service called Active Directory (AD). Active Directory, simply put, is a database of your network. It maintains lists of data about the different attributes of objects in your system.

Benefits of AD

AD is an exceptional way to manage your network resources. The system takes traditional directory services and allows you to manage them with much more control and flexibility. Other benefits of AD include the following:

▼ Management is easier because of the centralized nature of the Active Directory database.

■ Active Directory uses a series of equal domain controllers rather than a hierarchical structure. What this means is that if one of the servers containing a domain controller crashes, the other domain controllers will pick up the slack and minimize impact to your enterprise. This feature adds an extra layer of reliability through redundancy.

■ Scalability is enhanced, allowing Active Directory to hold millions of pieces of information without having to modify the administrative model.

▲ Searchable catalogs let you quickly and easily search through network resources and services.

Structure

How Active Directory is structured is important. When you read about and deal with X.500-based directory services, you'll encounter a structured, hierarchical way to manage your resources. The language of X.500-based directory services includes organizational units (OUs), domains, forests, and trees. These are the building blocks not only of Active Directory, but of other enabled directories, as well.

Figure 3-5 shows the structure of Active Directory and other enabled directories. OUs are groups of people, computers, files, printers, or other resources that need to be combined into one unit. Domains are collections of OUs. Trees are collections of domains. Forests are collections of trees. This network hierarchy allows you much more precise control over your network and its attributes.

Another key part of Active Directory is the *schema*, which is the database's internal structure. The schema defines relationships between classes of objects. For instance, using the address book example, you may have a class called "Name," which has the attribute "first and last name," which specifies that objects in the Name class must contain first and last name information. Classes can inherit from other classes, forming a hierarchy of classes.

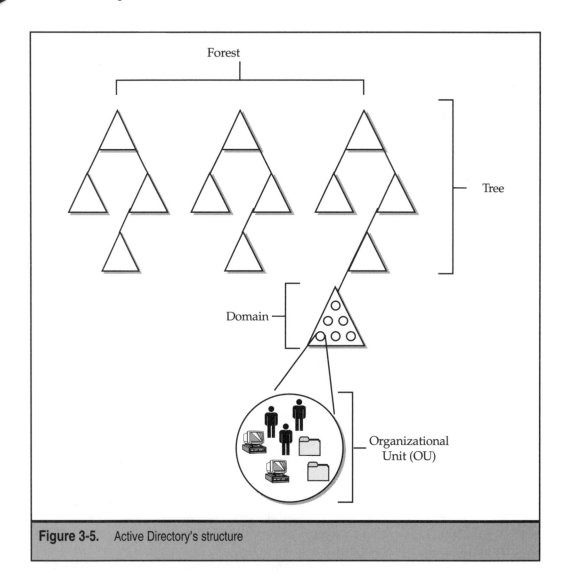

Figure 3-5.   Active Directory's structure

Managing AD

With such a powerful tool as Active Directory, there are a number of ways to manage the resources within. Two of the chief ways to manage AD are by establishing a solid security foundation and by administering who can access its various levels.

Security   One of the main security improvements in Windows 2000 is the addition of Kerberos. We'll talk more about network security specifics in Chapter 13, but in a nutshell

Kerberos is a shared secret authentication protocol, which means that both the client and the Key Distribution Center computer know passwords. This prevents other computers from pretending to be clients or servers.

Delegation of Control   One of Windows 2000's most eagerly awaited features is its capability to delegate control of specific functions to users in the network. Under the NT system, to assign one function (such as creating or deleting user accounts), you had to give full administrative rights. By delegating control of specific functions, administrators can keep a safe and secure system but still allow work to get done, as you can see in the following illustration.

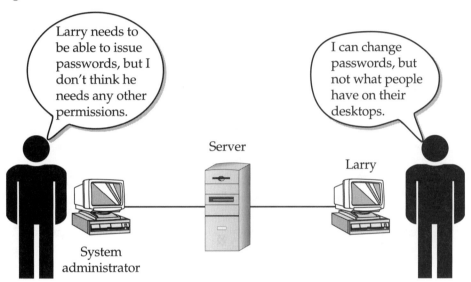

SUN

Sun Microsystems is no stranger to the e-business world. About half of the systems administering e-business applications run on Sun systems, so it's only natural to consider their operating system and software for your enterprise.

Solaris Version 8

The latest version of Sun's Solaris OS is version 8. The newest system's most notable improvements are greater availability, management, and security.

Availability

Availability—the ability to keep your servers and, subsequently, your business running—is enhanced with several new features in Solaris 8. One of the greatest improvements on Solaris 8 is its increased availability. Here are some of the improvements that allow for greater availability in Solaris 8:

▼ **Dynamic Reconfiguration**   This allows you to add or subtract system resources such as memory, hard drives, or processor cards without ever having to shut down your server. You simply add the hardware while the server is running and tell the OS you have made some physical changes; it will progressively make use of the new hardware.

■ **Policy Transfer**   Another, similar, feature allows you to create policies that transfer resources from one domain to another without having to shut down and restart either. This is a useful tool if your e-business solution gets a spike in traffic at certain times of the day or if you need to increase capacity.

■ **Live Upgrade**   With Live Upgrade, you can create a new installation on a clear partition while earlier versions of Solaris are still running. Then, you simply reboot and activate the new OS. Though there will still be a brief amount of downtime, it will be limited to the amount of time it takes to reboot the system. If you've ever had to migrate to a new OS, you'll appreciate the simplicity of the upgrade, plus the diminished downtime. Another benefit is the presence of the old OS. In the event something does go awry with the new OS, you can fall back to your original setup.

■ **Hot Patches**   If you have to fix bad or faulty code, Sun has made it possible to do so without shutting down your servers. These hot patches allow dubious kernel code to be redirected to the hot patch without interrupting any applications that are running. This fix allows you extra time to figure out a plan to correct the problem, while keeping your services available to employees, customers, and partners.

▲ **Solaris Resource Manager**   This offers management of resources through a common graphical user interface and enables administrators to balance loads across both system and network resources for better availability and Quality of Service.

Security

Another improved part of Solaris 8 is in the realm of security. The following points highlight some of Sun's new security features:

▼ **IPsec for IPv4**   IPsec is a popular security protocol, which prevents spoofing (where the true IP address is hidden) and increases security in VPNs. The protection includes confidentiality, strong integrity of the data, partial sequence integrity, and data authentication.

■ **Smart Cards**   These are credit card–sized cards that contain security information about users and are used for authentication.

- **Role-based access control (RBAC)** This allows permissions to be granted across the network using roles, execution profiles, and authorizations. This allows selected permissions to be granted to select users or groups of users who perform similar tasks.

▲ **Single Sign-on (SSO) Authentication** This provides the client-side Kerberos infrastructure. Kerberos provides strong user- and server-level authentication, integrity, and privacy support.

Management

Sun has included a variety of management tools that are meant to improve the overall management of Solaris system resources. Some of the noteworthy additions that will aid your e-business are:

▼ **Web Start** This tool installs the operating system using a Web-browser interface. It includes upgrade capability and the "kiosk," which allows users to review documentation (as Web pages) while the OS is being installed.

- **DHCP Manager** Written in Java, this manager provides a graphical user interface for configuring and managing Solaris's DHCP server. This lets the administrator use a single tool to manage DHCP resources such as servers, client options, and IP addresses.

- **WBEM Services** Web-Based Enterprise Management (WBEM) is an initiative on Solaris 8 to make management application development much easier. The applications can manage software systems and the Solaris OS.

- **Product Registry** This streamlines software installation and uninstallation.

▲ **LDAP** Support has been added in the Solaris naming system to support searches in the LDAP directory.

Networking

Sun has improved the networking functionality of Solaris 8 with the addition of several new features and tools. Tools range from naming services to Internet protocols. The majority of these tools will certainly enhance and improve performance for e-businesses. Some of the most noteworthy are these:

▼ **DNS Support** The Domain Name System (DNS) is a powerful and popular name service that increases the ease of network and system object management.

- **IPv6** A new version of the Internet Protocol (IP), this uses 128-bit address fields and extends the number of available IP addresses to meet future demands of Internet devices. IPv6 is implemented alongside its predecessor, IPv4, and increases future Solaris functionality.

- **Mobile IPv4**   Mobile IP enables the portable systems to have their IP traffic proxied to their current connection point without data loss.

- **WebNFS Software Development Kit**   The WebNFS Software Development Kit provides remote file access for Java applications using WebNFS technology.

- **Sendmail 8.9.3**   This version of Sendmail improves storage and security functionality. It includes features that prevent denial-of-service attacks; hooks that enable spam restrictions; and virtual hostings that allow e-mail to be received using different domain names.

- ▲ **Service Location Protocol (SLP)**   This standards-based protocol is used for discovering shared resources (such as printers and file servers) in an enterprise network. Also included are the APIs to enable developers to write SLP-enabled applications.

Java

Java is a programming language that, when introduced in the mid-1990s, was supposed to change the way content is developed and delivered on the Internet. Since then, it has grown from a simple programming language to a tool that is used for developing stand-alone applications, and for server-side programming. The face of Java has changed, but the core language remains the same.

Java software comes in several flavors, the most common being the stand-alone application, and the applet. An *applet* is a piece of code that runs under the control of a Web browser, as distinguished from the application, which requires an interpreter.

Included with Solaris 8 is Java 2 SDK, Standard Edition. The new version is redesigned to address the needs of both Java server and client environments. It includes the new Java Virtual Machine, tuned libraries, fine-grained security, and enterprise services for accessing corporate resources. It delivers improved performance and Web deployment for Java applets and applications, and it offers optional packages such as Java Media Framework, Java3D, and XML.

With this release, enterprise Java developers can quickly create client and server applications that interface with existing corporate resources. It also enables these applications to be deployed over the Web to distributed, heterogeneous environments.

New Features

There are many new features in Java that make Java client- and server-side applications run faster and more efficiently. Among the highlights:

- ▼ **HotSpot Performance Engine**   With dedicated client and server virtual machines and compilers, this release is able to optimize Java applications according to their intended environments. The result is faster performance for client applications and greater scalability for server applications.

■ **Java Naming and Directory Interface (JNDI)**   JNDI is now a standard part of Java, and it provides an easy gateway to enterprise directory services, such as LDAP-supported directory software. Java applets and applications can now communicate with enterprise information repositories such as those containing user names, address and telephone information, access privileges, and more.

■ **Remote Method Invocation over Internet Inter-ORB Protocol (RMI/IIOP)**   This feature enables cross-platform communication between Java and traditional back-end enterprise applications, in distributed environments. With RMI/IIOP, Java applications can interface with the CORBA environments that are popular corporate back-end systems, such as order entry, accounting, and customer management.

■ **Security**   This release supports RSA signatures and X.509 certificates, for Java-based and non-Java-based applications. This enables Java applets and applications to recognize RSA digital signatures and validate signers. Enterprises can now use these security enhancements to protect their computing infrastructure from security breaches.

■ **Applet Caching**   This feature stores deployed applets on the local drive until updated, thereby dramatically improving applet performance while reducing network traffic. Subsequent visits to the host Web page will launch the applet locally, where it remains stored until updated by the system administrators.

▲ **Java Optional Package Installation**   This function enables flexible, mix-and-match installation of the JRE and Java Optional Packages to create customized applications.

Performance and Scalability

Sun has also sought to deliver improved performance and scalability with the latest release of Java. Sun has delivered several features with Java to improve overall performance for the present and the future. Key improvements include:

▼ **A smaller memory footprint**   The application memory footprint has been reduced to make more efficient use of system memory.

■ **Greater scalability**   The server compiler utilizes additional compilation technologies to streamline the code for large-scale, long-running Java applications. The server virtual machine takes full advantage of its multithreaded architecture and capabilities and those of the underlying Solaris OS. All these result in greater scalability across additional processors.

▲ **Better usability**   Many areas of the Java 2 platform have been improved. They include libraries, I/O, networking, graphical components, and others. The result is a Java platform that is more stable and robust.

LINUX

With more administrators willing to roll the dice on a product that didn't come in shrink-wrapped plastic and a code key on the cover, more networks are finding their OS solution in a truly free and open source. The software is so popular, in fact, that according to research from NetCraft, Inc., 29 percent of all public Web servers run on Linux, making it the most popular OS for public Web sites.

Technically speaking, Linux is a variant of the UNIX OS. In 1991, Finnish computer science student Linus Torvalds wrote the first version of the core operating system as a pet project. He added some other tools and named his new operating system after himself: Linux (for Linus's UNIX). Torvalds released the source code so that the system's kernel and utilities are freely available for anyone to use, modify, and redistribute.

The Price is Right

Probably the most unique feature of Linux is the price—it's free. Practically speaking, however, few businesses would install an operating system without a support agreement in place. Seeing that niche, several companies are packaging Linux and including manuals.

Wait a minute, someone is *selling* Linux? Didn't you just say Linux is supposed to be free? It is free, but the money you would spend for a version of Linux from a company like Red Hat isn't for the Linux code; rather, it's for the documentation and support. Table 3-2 lists companies that sell Linux along with documentation and tech support.

If you're savvy enough to install the OS without the need of preprinted instructions, Table 3-3 lists some Web sites where you can download the software free of charge.

The Linux license is free. Even if you buy one copy of Linux from Red Hat, you can install it on every computer in your company. You could copy the CD-ROM and mail it to friends as Christmas cards, if you were so inclined. Now, compare that freedom to the Microsofts and Novells out there. Every computer you use the OS on will require a li-

Vendor	Web Site
Red Hat	www.redhat.com
Caldera	www.calderasystems.com
SuSE	www.suse.com
eLinux	www.elinux.com

Table 3-2.   Vendors Offering Linux, Documentation, and Support Packages

Linux Provider	Web Site
Slackware	www.slackware.com
Debian	www.debian.org
Turbo Linux	ftp.turbolinux.com/pub
Red Hat	www.redhat.com

Table 3-3. Web Sites Offering Linux for Free

cense. As you have more computers requiring the operating system, you'll have to pay more for licenses, as you can see in the following illustration.

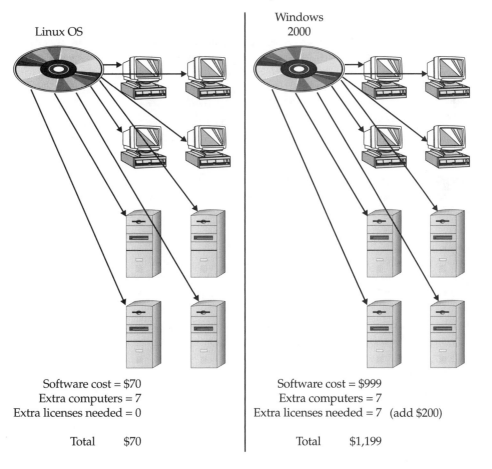

Linux licensing can save a considerable amount of money

Linux OS

Windows 2000

Software cost = $70
Extra computers = 7
Extra licenses needed = 0

Total $70

Software cost = $999
Extra computers = 7
Extra licenses needed = 7 (add $200)

Total $1,199

Here's a great example of cost savings: A couple years ago the Mexican government decided to hook up 140,000 computers in its schools. When it came time to buy operating systems for the computers, the Microsoft Windows price was so high that even with volume discounts they couldn't afford it. By opting for Linux, the Mexicans saved over $124 million just in software costs. The Mexican example shows that, spread over a large network, the savings really add up.

Another licensing issue comes when production systems fail to scale under heavy loads because a piece of software enforces limits on the number of concurrent connections, according to the number of purchased licenses. With Linux, this isn't a problem, because Linux gives you an "unlimited user, unlimited installation" license.

NOTE: Be aware, however, that even though the Linux license is free, any third-party software you add on top of it may be subject to licensing.

Sticking Points

We've given Linux some pats on the back for its cost-friendliness and openness to change, but there are still reasons why it isn't on every computer in the world right now.

Support   The first hurdle is the OS's lack of support. Unless you take the initiative to go out and learn the mechanics of Linux, setting it up has proved to be a bear for novices. Traditionally, Linux users have had to edit configuration files, line-by-line. However, that trend is changing as third-party vendors are offering administration and configuration tools that include centralized, graphical administration. Red Hat's *Linuxconf* and Caldera's *Lizard* (short for Linux Wizard—plus I think they can get a cool little lizard mascot out of it) are two examples of software solutions that can ease the burden of Linux configuration.

Applications? What Applications?   If you want to buy an application for your Windows-based OS, you'll have stacks and stacks of candidates to choose from. Conversely, finding specific software for Linux—with the features you want—can be like finding a needle in a haystack.

On the plus side, more applications are being developed for Linux. The best software availability is for server-side applications. Most major databases are available for Linux with varying levels of support and cost. Also, Internet and Web applications have never been a problem for Linux. Sendmail, a mail transport program, is estimated to deliver 70–80 percent of the world's e-mail.

On the minus side, client-side software is lacking. Though there are applications out there, they don't typically reflect the variety and amount of software that is available for Windows.

But Is It Safe?

One red flag that must pop up in your mind as you read about this open source, free-for-all OS is the sturdiness of its security. After all, if you're counting on Linux to keep your e-business safe from hackers, it's hard to trust something that computer enthusiasts take apart and tweak for fun in their spare time.

Safety   Even though the Linux has been picked apart, once the security systems lock in, they are just as secure as on a conventional commercial release. The key for Linux is that users must be able to use the security features properly for them to work appropriately. For instance, open source firewalls are secure, but they must be configured properly for maximum effectiveness.

Another factor in Linux security is that once security has been penetrated, a fix for the breach is developed and made available to other Linux users within hours. In a closed source system, a fix may never be developed—the breach may never even be admitted to.

International Security   But for an interesting example of how Linux can actually make your network more secure, let's consider companies that reach beyond the North American continent.

Unless your company operates entirely within the United States or Canada or is a bank or financial institution, you cannot implement a truly secure transnational network. This means that if you have operations in London, New York, and Buenos Aires, you can't link those branches together with any encryption software that exceeds 56 bits. U.S. law forbids U.S. companies from selling any encryption software internationally, lest terrorists get their hands on it, build an impenetrable VPN across the Internet, and raise hell.

NOTE: Built into the exportable versions of cryptographic software are "hooks" that prevent a patch from being developed that can beef up the cryptographic software so that it will exceed 56 bits.

If your e-business network reaches customers in other countries, you will be restricted to 56-bit or fewer SSL links. In the U.S. and Canada, SSL links reach 128 bits.

Here's where Linux comes into play. (Will any terrorists reading this book please skip ahead to the next section? Thank you.) Even though you cannot buy 128-bit encryption software, you can get it for free, thanks to Linux.

To get your strong cryptographic server, simply download the Apache Web server, then download a couple patches from any site outside the U.S. When you compile the source code, the patch writes over the Apache source code and installs the 128-bit encryption software.

Since the original Apache source code does not contain any cryptographic code or hooks, this process is clean and legal, and it gives you a strong Web server that will protect your e-business in transnational dealings.

Linux OS 6.2

Now that we've discussed the basics of Linux and what really separates it from its competition in the OS market, let's look at the Linux version you'll be most likely to buy and set up on within your business—Linux OS 6.2.

There are several companies selling their own Linux packages, including Red Hat, Caldera, and SuSE. They all offer more or less the same OS, but the differences lie in the documentation and level of support. For the sake of this discussion, let's consider Red Hat's Linux release.

Red Hat Linux 6.2 offers a graphical interface to ease the software's installation. This version also features increased scalability and reliability, which are especially important for e-business applications.

This version of Linux offers the following attributes that will be helpful for your e-business solution:

▼ Improved, high-availability clustering capabilities

■ A Web-based interface for configuring clusters

■ Beefed-up load balancing technology that improves performance and scalability

▲ A partitionless install on DOS-based systems, which simplifies migration to Linux

As we mentioned earlier, just downloading Linux doesn't give you any technical support. However, by purchasing the software from a company that packages it, you will be entitled to varying levels and amounts of support. Here's what Red Hat offers when you buy their packaging of Linux 6.2 Professional Edition (cost: $180):

▼ 30 days of configuration support for the Apache Web server

■ 180 days of Priority Online Access for software updates

■ 30 days of telephone support and 90 days of e-mail support

▲ Five application CDs with enterprise and Internet software for Linux.

And remember, the license is unlimited, so put it on as many computers as you like.

Apache Web Server

One of the most popular Web servers around is the Apache Web Server—in fact, it runs on about six million Internet servers around the world. The server comes bundled with both Linux and Solaris. The latest version of Apache is version 1.3, and its enhancements over earlier versions include support for Windows NT/9x and support for NetWare 5.

Features

For your e-business solution, Apache offers a number of software features that will enhance operability, security, and functionality. Some of the best elements include:

▼ **DBM databases for authentication**   The databases allow you to set up password-protected pages for large numbers of authorized users.

■ **Virtual hosts**   This allows the server to differentiate between requests made to different IP addresses or names. Apache also offers dynamically configurable mass-virtual hosting.

▲   **Configurable logs**   You can configure Apache to generate logs to track various bits of information about your server's performance.

NOTE: There are two stories about how the name "Apache" came to be. One version says the name was bestowed as a nod to the American Indian tribe of tireless warriors. Another explanation is that "Apache" is a cute name that just stuck. The server was originally cobbled together from some code and a series of patch files, and so it was referred to as "a patchy server."

Issues

As with Linux, since Apache is free, there isn't a lot of built-in help to navigate its technical waters. Also as with Linux, there isn't any official support for Apache. Again, since this is a freebie, there isn't an 800 number to call and there is no warranty. You can get third-party support for Apache, but if you want a do-it-yourself solution, your best bet to troubleshoot problems is by checking the comp.infosystems.www.servers.unix or comp.infosystems.www.servers.ms-windows newsgroups.

NOTE: For more information or to download Apache, visit the Apache Web site at www.apache.org.

NOVELL

Given their products' history, one wouldn't be likely to consider Novell a contender in the e-business arena. The OS is generally known for its print and file capabilities. However, with the release of NetWare 5.1, Novell means to get a slice of the e-business pie.

NetWare 5.1

Novell's latest release of its flagship application is NetWare 5.1. If you already run NetWare in your business, upgrading to NetWare 5.1 will not only bolster your company's computer network, but it will also bring a number of e-business tools to enhance your business.

What's New

As with any new and improved OS, there are things from earlier releases that are beefed up and tweaked out for the new release. As we've mentioned earlier, the biggest improvement in this version of NetWare is its adoption of Web development tools. Specifically, the following features have been jazzed up from NetWare's predecessor:

▼   **SQL Integrator**   This is a tool that allows developers to access any relational data anywhere on the network and combine it with other relational data via a common record.

- ■ **Oracle8***i*   NetWare is bundled with Oracle8*i* and the database is integrated into NDS.
- ■ **NDS 8**   The latest version of NetWare's directory service, which provides scalability to a billion objects, is Web-capable.
- ▲ **Browser-based management tools**   These tools enable managers and network administrators to access all of a network's systems and components from anywhere they can get their hands on an Internet browser.

New Servers

NetWare Web-based network operating systems are enhanced with the addition of several new servers included with NetWare 5.1. The new servers supply a range of services:

- ▼ **Enterprise Web Server**   This server provides content hosting.
- ■ **News Server**   This server enables threaded discussion groups.
- ■ **File Transfer Protocol (FTP) Server**   This server offers simplified file downloads.
- ■ **Multimedia Server**   This server supplies audio and video feeds over a network in .mpg, .ra, .rm, and .wav formats.
- ▲ **Web Search Server**   This server indexes Web sites to simplify searches.

Management

Administrative tasks in NetWare are streamlined and simplified using NetWare Management Portal (NMP). This Web browser–based tool allows you to manage NetWare servers and file systems through a Web browser from any location on your network, rather than having to run to the server room anytime you have to troubleshoot a server problem. Here's a brief look at some of the tasks you can manage with NMP:

- ▼ Mounting and dismounting drives
- ■ Monitoring system resources
- ▲ Browsing the NDS tree

NetWare includes ZENworks and ConsoleOne, two other administrative tools you can use to deploy and manage tools across your network.

WebSphere

In this age of big business mergers, e-commerce isn't being left out. In the case of WebSphere, IBM and Novell haven't combined forces to create their own content. Rather, Novell is including IBM's Java-based WebSphere Application Server 3.0 with NetWare 5.1.

WebSphere is IBM's premiere e-business software suite, which allows application service, web site construction, web site management, and a variety of other tools. It also allows owners to develop e-business sites that will be available to the general public and business partners. We'll talk about WebSphere in more detail in Chapter 4.

The arrangement works well for each party: IBM gets its e-commerce software into the marketplace (NetWare ships about a million servers a year), and Novell makes its OS more competitive by adding e-business tools to its established file and print services.

The meat of what Novell brings to the e-business table within NetWare 5.1 is in WebSphere. NetWare wouldn't be able to offer much in the way of e-business tools if it weren't for the partnership with IBM. These new tools provide an integrated environment, in which you can build, run, and manage Web-based applications. Integration means the applications will run more efficiently and reliably.

The software also includes IBM's WebSphere Studio (Entry Edition). WebSphere Studio provides Java-based tools that will enable site designers and programmers to develop Web sites and applications, then publish them to the WebSphere Application Server.

One of the benefits of this software bundling is that WebSphere Application Server has been integrated with Novell Directory Services. Because of this tight packaging, you are able to establish security for your enterprise's Web applications through the NetWare OS, rather than having to manage security for your network and your Web applications separately.

Beyond streamlining management between two different companies' software, the integration of WebSphere into NetWare allows the WebSphere applications to be secured by Novell Directory Services (NDS). The protection afforded by NDS is considerable, because it employs multiple layers of tough security features. (We talk about NDS in more depth later in this section.)

NOTE: This bundling also gives you a little break when you install the OS. Because WebSphere can be included by checking a little box during NetWare installation, you needn't install the OS, then separately install WebSphere.

NOTE: For more on IBM's WebSphere, visit their Web site at http://www.ibm.com. We also talk about WebSphere in Chapter 4.

NDS eDirectory

Novell's directory-enabled services solution is Novell Directory Services (NDS) eDirectory. It supports more open standards and protocols than the other enabled directories we discussed in this chapter.

Novell is especially proud of eDirectory, because they claim the directory can store a billion pieces of information and perform LDAP searches in less than a second. eDirectory also provides the foundation for such Novell applications as Certificate Server, digitalme, eGuide, iChain, Net Publisher, and Single Sign-on.

Though designed for NetWare, eDirectory will work on the Windows 2000/NT, Solaris, and Linux OSes.

Security

Like Microsoft's Active Directory, eDirectory comes complete with a suite of security components to keep out the bad guys:

1. **Authentication**   The first layer of security asks users to authenticate themselves when they log on. Authentication support ranges from passwords encrypted over SSL to X.509 v3 certificates and smart cards. Additional authentication occurs in the background and is transparent to the user.

2. **Novell International Cryptographic Infrastructure (NICI)**   NICI is a cryptographic tool that developers can use to receive the right level of encryption for their applications without embedding cryptography in the application.

NOTE: The level of encryption is based on which region of the world the application is being used in.

3. **Secure Authentication Services (SAS)**   SAS is a modular authentication framework that provides next-generation authentication services. Currently, it provides SSL v3 support.

Management

Novell includes a host of management tools to help you administer the information in eDirectory. The tools include some that will directly affect your e-business solution (Novell Client) and others that will indirectly affect it (NDS server). Some of the tools included are:

▼ **NDS Server**   Places replicas of eDirectory on primary domain controllers (PDCs) and backup domain controllers (BDCs).

■ **NetWare Administrator and ConsoleOne**   Helps manage network users and resources.

■ **NDS Manager**   Manages partitions, replicas, servers, and the eDirectory schema.

■ **Novell Client**   Gives users access to eDirectory features.

■ **LDAP**   Provides an open infrastructure for applications written to the Internet standard.

▲ **Bulkload Utility**   Adds millions of objects into the directory at once.

Other Features

We're not highlighting all the features of NetWare 5.1 but rather giving you an overview of its features. Here are several additional features that will help your e-business solution.

Novell Storage Services

If yours is a business with lots of storage needs, Novell Storage Services (NSS) can help. NSS relieves limitations on file numbers and sizes and improves volume availability. NSS utilizes a 64-bit indexed storage system and permits a network to handle billions of volumes of directories and file sizes up to eight terabytes while maintaining a small memory footprint.

Java Virtual Machine

The Novell Java Virtual Machine (JVM) is made up of several programs that allow Java applications to run on a NetWare server. Novell JVM allows Java applications to become tailored, NetWare-specific commands. This tool enhances Intranet applications and e-business sites by running servlets, JavaBeans, Java Server Pages, and other Java development tools.

Manage WAN Congestion

WAN Traffic Manager is a Quality of Service (QoS) tool you can use to create policies that will control NDS eDirectory replication traffic over WAN links. Based on eDirectory, WAN Traffic Manager compares input criteria with administrator-established policies. If criteria and policies match, WAN Traffic Manager enforces the policies and allows WAN traffic to either be delayed or proceed. Regulating your WAN traffic reduces costs and congestion usually associated with network traffic.

NOTE: For more information about QoS, see Chapter 8.

COMPARISONS

Over the last couple dozen pages, we've chucked a ton of information at you about the ups, downs, ins, and outs of various OSes. Let's take a look at the features of each OS, compare it to the others, and see how everything shakes down.

One of the problems with this sort of comparison is how much the developers go at each others' throats. According to Microsoft, their OSes are vastly and measurably better than all others. Novell's tests show that every other OS locks up and sets the servers on fire. I won't even tell you what Sun says about its competitors' OSes.

Even more interestingly, they all have the stats to back up their conclusions, which should make you scratch your head and wonder about the validity of those numbers. In an effort to get away from the "benchmarketing" of the companies, we've compiled our own comparisons. Table 3-4 reflects some of the features you want for your e-business and how the OSes stack up against each other.

In this section, we've compared price, features, and what kinds of hardware you'll need for each OS.

Features

Table 3-4 represents a comparison of the four OSes we've been talking about. Listed are a number of the features you'd be likely to use in your e-business solution. We did not, on the other hand, rate the OSes' performance, because performance will differ greatly de-

Product	Windows 2000 Server	Red Hat Linux 6.2 Professional	Sun Solaris 8	Novell NetWare 5.1
Cost	$999, includes 5 licenses	Free or $180 with documentation and support from Red Hat. (Other versions are available that are less expensive.) Unlimited licenses	$75, for 8 CPUs or fewer	$995, includes 5 licenses
Bundled Web server	IIS 5.0	Apache Web Server 1.3.9	Apache Web Server 1.3.9	NetWare Enterprise Web Server
Group user management included?	Yes	Yes	No	Yes
Group management for directory service included?	Yes	Yes	Yes	Yes
Remote administration console?	Yes	Yes	No	Yes
Maximum CPUs per node	4	8	64	1

Table 3-4. Features Comparison of Windows 2000, NetWare 5.1, Linux 6.2, and Solaris 8

Product	Windows 2000 Server	Red Hat Linux 6.2 Professional	Sun Solaris 8	Novell NetWare 5.1
Performance monitor for bytes sent?	Yes	Yes	Yes	Yes
Performance monitor for CGI and other API requests?	Yes	Yes	Yes	Yes
Performance monitor for current connections?	Yes	Yes	Yes	Yes
SMP support?	Yes	Yes	Yes	No
Support for hot patching of software?	No	No	Yes	No
Enabled Directory?	Yes	No	Yes	Yes
Development tool included?	Optional	No	Optional	IBM WebSphere 3.0
Maximum load balanced nodes	32	Unlimited	Unlimited	32
Automatic settings for high-traffic sites?	Yes	No	No	Yes
Support for hot swapping hardware?	Yes	Yes	Yes	Yes
Support application server?	Yes	Yes	No	Yes
Virtual servers?	Yes	Yes	Yes	Yes
Supports ASPs?	Yes	Yes	Yes	Yes

Table 3-4. Features Comparison of Windows 2000, NetWare 5.1, Linux 6.2, and Solaris 8 *(continued)*

Product	Windows 2000 Server	Red Hat Linux 6.2 Professional	Sun Solaris 8	Novell NetWare 5.1
Authoring tools?	Yes	Yes	No	Yes
Search engine included?	Yes	No	No	Yes
DNS server included?	Yes	Yes	No	Yes
IPv6 support?	No	Yes	Yes	No
IPSec support?	Yes	Yes	Yes	No
SSL 3.0?	Yes	Yes	Yes	Yes
Performance monitoring?	Yes	Yes	Yes	Yes
FTP server included?	Yes	Yes	Yes	Yes
GUI Web server setup?	Yes	Yes	No	Yes
Certificate server included?	Yes	No	No	Yes

Table 3-4. Features Comparison of Windows 2000, NetWare 5.1, Linux 6.2, and Solaris 8 (continued)

pending on what kind of processor you use, the speed and size of your network, and a plethora of other variables.

Costs

In a perfect world, a discussion of these operating systems' prices would be irrelevant. However, as you well know, regardless of what features and functions an operating system has, often the deciding factor comes down to a matter of money.

Obviously, one of the operating systems we discussed has the inside track in the pricing game—Linux. The only way Linux can be beaten on cost is if a company offered cash back if you take their system. Don't hold your breath. Solaris comes reasonably priced, as well. They charge $75 for unlimited machines with eight or fewer CPUs and unlimited users.

But once you get outside the world of Linux and Solaris, prices tend to step up. Windows 2000 Server costs $999, and NetWare 5.1 costs $995. For Windows 2000 and

NetWare 5.1, those costs represent the OS with 25 user licenses for Windows and 5 licenses for NetWare. If your company has more users, you'll have to buy additional licenses from the manufacturers. Microsoft will charge $199 for an additional 5 licenses or $799 for a 20-pack. NetWare is heftier with its licensing fees. Five additional licenses will cost $995, and a 25-pack will cost $2,750.

NOTE: Both Microsoft and Novell offer a variety of upgrade packages and licensing options. For more detailed information about licensing their products, visit their Web sites at www.microsoft.com/windows2000 and www.novell.com/products/netware.

Hardware

The OS you buy has requirements of its own; namely, it will only work on machines with specific memory and speed levels. Table 3-5 represents the bare minimums for the systems we've discussed.

Product	Windows 2000 Server	Red Hat Linux 6.2	Sun Solaris 8	Novell NetWare 5.1
Processor	Pentium-class (at least 133 MHz)	Will run on a number of different types of platforms, assuming they are at least i386 or better.	SPARC or Intel platform	Pentium-class
RAM	256MB	8MB	64MB	128MB/256MB for WebSphere
Hard Drive	2GB	850MB for clients/1.7GB for servers	600MB for desktops/1GB for servers	50MB DOS partition. 1.3GB outside the DOS partition for additional products and WebSphere

Table 3-5.   Hardware Requirements for Selected OSes

Since these are the bare minimums, you are encouraged to exceed these levels as often as possible. Performance will increase as these levels are surpassed.

For more information about the OSes that we discussed in this chapter, visit their respective Web sites listed in Table 3-6

Manufacturer	Web Site
Microsoft Windows 2000	www.microsoft.com
Sun Solaris 8	www.sun.com
Red Hat Linux 6.2	www.redhat.com
Novell NetWare 5.1	www.novell.com

Table 3-6.   OS Manufacturers' Web Sites

CHAPTER 4

Configuring an E-Business Server

For all intents and purposes, for e-business to work there need to be two computers—one buying and one selling. The buyers and sellers can be further translated into the world of networking if you think in terms of "servers" and "clients." In this chapter, we'll talk about configuring the computers on the seller's end—the servers. In the next chapter, we'll talk about configuring the client computers.

NOTE: This is one of those instances where computerese and business can create some confusion. When we talk about "client" computers, we aren't always talking about the person buying something. We may be talking about computers that have to hook into the server for maintenance.

E-BUSINESS SERVERS

Servers can manage a plethora of functions in your e-business. From the bare bones of the e-business to payment systems to auctions to databases—there's a server out there for everything.

What They Do

The servers are the machines on your network that control various mission-critical operations. From the point of view of a LAN, servers feed client computers and in large networks govern such functions as file and printing services.

In the realm of e-business, however, servers' functions become even more specialized. Also, depending on the size of your network, you may have several servers—some performing unique functions, others duplicating functions because of the sheer magnitude of the work demanded of them.

Consider the contrasts between the two businesses shown in Figure 4-1.

Since Tinyco.com has a small number of customers, it only needs a couple of servers to handle its Web functions. On the other hand, Giantco.com gets an astronomical number of hits every month and scores thousands of sales every day. Because of the sheer volume of visitors and sales, Giantco.com needs more servers: some replicating functions for the sake of load balancing, and others performing specific, mission-critical functions.

The following servers are common types you will encounter when building your e-business solution and will govern important functions on your network.

Payment

Once customers get to your network and start buying things, you need a way to take their payment information, process it, and get paid. This is where payment servers come into play.

These servers (where they reside on a network is shown in Figure 4-2) take the information about the customers' orders, then get the customers' payment information, transmit the information to the payment processing center, receive the approval, and then complete the order.

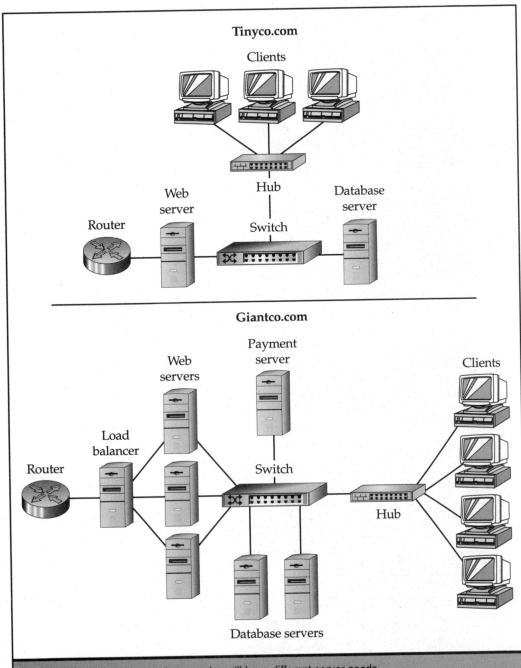

Figure 4-1.   Different-sized companies will have different server needs

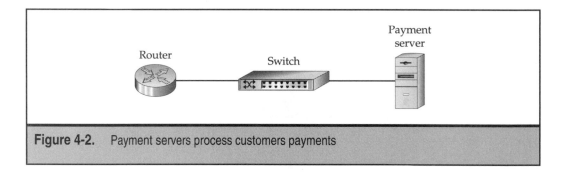

Figure 4-2.   Payment servers process customers payments

There are a couple of reasons why a separate server is necessary for payment processing:

▼ **Security**   With extremely sensitive customer data on file, a breach of security can be a costly, embarrassing mistake. By having a separate server, you can not only beef up its security, but by sheer network layout, you can isolate this server as the most secure part of your network.

▲ **Processing**   By using a separate server for payments, there is less drain on your network as a whole, because the payments are being handled on their own server.

Application Servers

Application servers enable your organization to develop, deploy, and manage business-critical Internet applications. The most important function of application servers is to connect database information (normally coming from a database server) and the end-user or client program (often running a Web browser). Figure 4-3 shows where application servers are located on your network.

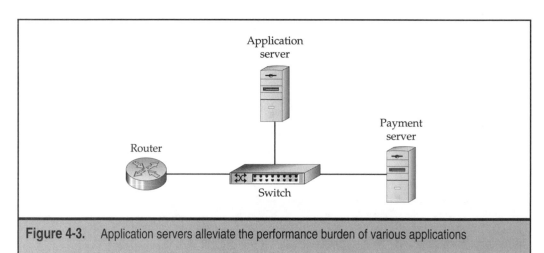

Figure 4-3.   Application servers alleviate the performance burden of various applications

There are a number of reasons for having a middleman in this connection—among other things, the desire to decrease the size and complexity of client programs; the need to cache and control the data flow for better performance; and a requirement to provide security for both data and user traffic.

Application servers don't just have a life in the realm of Internet sales—they are also used for an organization's internal network. When application servers were introduced, it became clear that applications themselves—the programs employees were using to do their work—were becoming bigger and more complex. At the same time, there was more pressure on the applications to be able to share more of their data. More applications either were located on a network or used a good deal of network resources, so it made sense to have a program on the network that would help share application capabilities in an organized and efficient way, thereby making it easier to write, manage, and maintain the applications.

Database

Likely, yours will be an e-business that utilizes a database, which lists your goods and services. A database server serves an important function; it provides a centralized location within your network for your product catalog, customer lists, and any other data needing warehousing. Figure 4-4 shows where a database server sits on your network.

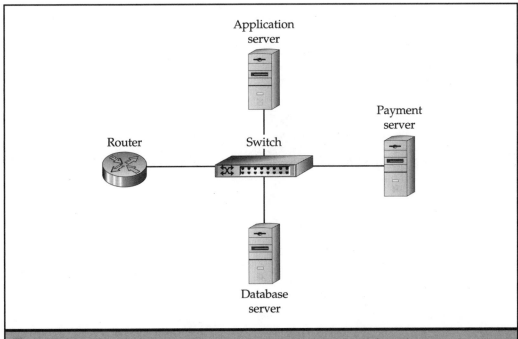

Figure 4-4.   Database servers warehouse your catalog and customer information

These are the servers that consumers and supply-chain partners will access to find your company's catalog. There are important reasons why your databases need their own servers:

▼ **Performance**   When your database is located in a centralized location, customers and partners can have speedy access to it. If this server is located on the same machine as another server, each server will take a hit when the other one is in operation.

▲ **Reliability**   In the unfortunate event of a crash, the last bit of data you want to lose is your database. By housing the database on its own server (or servers), you minimize the chance for loss if there is a catastrophe.

Web servers

Web servers are basically intermediaries between the client's Web browser (such as Microsoft Internet Explorer or Netscape Navigator) and the desired content. When Web servers were first developed, they served simple HTML documents and images. Today, they are frequently used for much more.

A Web server (its location on the network is shown in Figure 4-5) delivers static content to a Web browser at a basic level. This means that the Web server receives a request

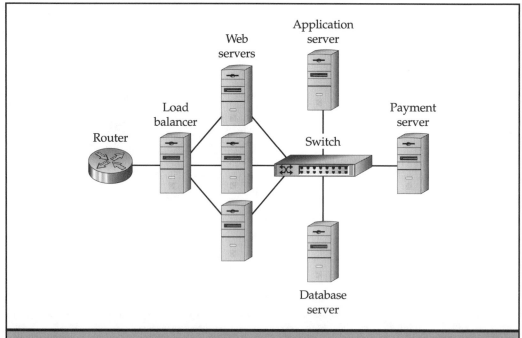

Figure 4-5.   By using several Web servers, you can balance the load of incoming visitors

for a Web page such as http://www.firesummit.com and maps that Uniform Resource Locator (URL) to a local file on the host server. In this case, the Web site's file is somewhere on the host file system. The server then loads this file from disk and serves it out across the network to the user's Web browser.

In a nutshell, that's basic Web server functionality. But as you develop an e-business solution, the roles of Web servers become more and more important. Not only do they have critical roles because of the core job they perform, but they are also important for security and performance.

If, for instance, your e-business becomes very popular, you would add more Web servers to increase availability and relieve bottlenecking. Some organizations, like Microsoft, have thousands of servers dishing out information for their customers.

Server Considerations

There are two things that make your server: hardware and software. Servers are powerful computers that serve specific functions in your network, and how they are configured—both physically and logically—will make all the difference when you configure them.

Let's examine issues related to hardware and software selection and installation to see how you can optimally build the servers for your network.

Hardware

The hardware you select for your various servers is extremely important. Without enough resources, the servers can't do their jobs properly and the end results will be bad news for your organization.

When deciding how fast, how much memory, and the other details associated with a computer purchase, it's necessary to understand what the server will be used for. The computer's role in your network will be extremely important. For instance, if the server will house your database, you'll likely want a machine that has more hard drive space and RAM. On the other hand, if it's the application server, you'll want something with a fair amount of RAM that is also speedy.

Another important consideration is expandability. For instance, let's say you have a database that has grown to the limits of your server's hard drive. Rather than buy an entirely new server, you may well be able to add a larger hard drive and let the database grow on the same machine.

Complicating the server issue even further are size considerations. Servers needn't be the classic "tower" computer that has become the e-business stereotype. Some servers are flat boxes the size of VCRs that plug into a rack full of routers and switches. Other servers are so big that they look more like they were made by Maytag than Hewlett-Packard.

Software

Certainly, hardware comes in all shapes, sizes, and colors. But without specific software telling the servers what to do, all those computers are useless. Selecting which software to use is, at its heart, much like selecting hardware. The most important role of the software is to allow the server to do the job for which it is assigned.

Something you'll have to be mindful of as you buy software is its compatibility with your hardware and operating system. Sure, you could buy a copy of Microsoft's BizTalk Server 2000, but it wouldn't be helpful if yours is a Sun platform. As you read in the preceding chapter, selecting the best OS requires weighing a number of variables on your part. Ultimately, your final OS selection will come down to a hodgepodge of both technical and corporate decisions. You'll have to balance such needs and issues as:

▼ Cost

■ Licensing

■ Will the OS work with the server software we want?

■ Is there an existing OS dominating our organization, and will a new OS be compatible with it?

▲ Support options for your chosen OS

Next, you have to decide the role of the server in your network. Is it a Web server, an application server, a database server, or some other type of server? Naturally, the type of software you buy will be governed by what you need the server to do. Later in this chapter, we'll look at some popular server technologies for specific needs.

Finally, as always, it's important to make sure that the software and OS you buy will work on the machine you bought. It will do you little good if the server software requires a 500 MHz machine with 256MB of RAM and you're trying to shoehorn it into a box running 100 MHz with 32MB RAM.

MAJOR PLAYERS

With so many bits and pieces of software out there managing and controlling everything from online auctions to billing systems, it would be impossible to talk about everything. Forget the fact that software is constantly being revised and repackaged!

Instead, let's take a look at what the biggest players in the tech industry offer for your servers. We'll look at mega-giant Microsoft; iPlanet, the joint venture between Sun Microsystems and Netscape; IBM's WebSphere; and Novell's e-business offerings.

Microsoft

Never ones to miss out on a chance to get in on the latest thing, Microsoft has developed not just a product or two for e-business but a whole fleet of software with a common philosophy and design thread—Windows DNA.

In this section, we'll offer an overview of Windows DNA and then take a closer look at two key DNA components. To build your own e-business solution using Microsoft tools, you need only two products (well, actually it's three if you count Internet Information Services (IIS), which comes prepackaged with Windows 2000). Those two components are SQL Server 2000 and Commerce Server 2000.

Windows DNA

Microsoft offers an all-inclusive approach to e-business. Like iPlanet, they have virtually every angle covered for B2B, B2C, and any other e-business scenario. Microsoft's solution is called Windows DNA. With this series of software products, Microsoft offers a comprehensive set of Web application services, which are fully integrated into the Windows operating system. In other words, the Web application server for Windows DNA is Windows 2000. So what does full integration mean? It means better reliability, better functioning, and better results.

The following features and technologies, which are integrated in all editions of Windows 2000, are the components that make Windows DNA a complete effort:

▼ **Internet Information Services 5.0**   (IIS) These integrated Web services allow users to easily host and manage Web sites to share information; create Web-based business applications; and extend file, print, media, and communication services across the Web.

■ **Active Server Pages**   (ASP) This high-performance Web server-scripting environment is ideal for generating and presenting dynamic Web content.

■ **COM+ Component Services**   Provides easily accessible component services for transactions, thread pooling, object pooling, just-in-time object activation, remote object invocation, and more from a wide array of development languages.

■ **Distributed Transactions**   Provides transaction support for updating two or more networked computer systems in a coordinated fashion.

■ **Microsoft Message Queuing**   Enables guaranteed communication across networks and systems regardless of the current state of the communicating applications and systems.

■ **Role-Based Security**   Enables developers to define security easily at the method, interface, component, or package level.

■ **Network Load Balancing**   Provides scalability and high availability by balancing incoming IP traffic among multinode clusters.

■ **Active Directory Services**   Centralizes administrative information about users, applications, and devices.

▲ **High-Performance XML Support**   Facilitates the creation of applications that exchange XML-formatted data with Microsoft Internet Explorer and XML-enabled server products.

By using these integrated Web application services, developers have a much easier time when they build an e-business infrastructure.

Windows DNA 2000 Components

In addition to Windows 2000 and SQL Server 2000, Windows DNA 2000 contains the following server products:

▼ **Microsoft Application Center 2000**   This server simplifies and eases the deployment and management of Windows DNA solutions within server farms.

■ **Microsoft Commerce Server 2000**   Commerce Server 2000 is Microsoft's premiere tool to deliver B2C e-commerce. It provides all of the personalization, user and product management, marketing, closed loop analysis, and electronic ordering infrastructure necessary for B2C transactions. Commerce Server 2000 is designed for quickly building tailored, scalable e-commerce solutions that provide business managers with real-time analysis and control of their online business. SQL Server 2000 provides data modeling and administration tools for sites built on Commerce Server 2000. These services include user profiling, product catalogs, and Business Internet Analytics, the analysis of customer Web click-stream data to make predictions about customer behavior and drive personalization.

■ **Microsoft BizTalk Server 2000**   This is Microsoft's B2B solution. Taking advantage of Extensible Markup Language (XML), BizTalk Server 2000 provides business process integration within the enterprise and with trading partners across the Internet through the exchange of XML-formatted business documents. SQL Server provides storage and easy-to-schedule transformation capabilities for data from BizTalk Server. SQL Server 2000 and BizTalk Server 2000 support the same XML Data Reduced schema. This allows documents to be transmitted directly between SQL Server and BizTalk Server.

▼ **Microsoft Host Integration Server 2000**   This product provides network, data, and application integration with a variety of legacy hosts. SQL Server 2000 allows developers using Host Integration Server 2000 to store, retrieve, and transform data from legacy systems, as well as enabling bidirectional, heterogeneous replication between those legacy systems and SQL Server 2000.

SQL Server 2000

In spring 2000 Microsoft released the beta version of SQL Server 2000, and it is poised to become the top dog in the database world. In fact, many big e-business companies already use earlier versions of SQL Server as their database of choice. Some SQL Server users include:

▼ 1-800-flowers.com

■ Barnesandnoble.com

■ Buy.com

■ Dell.com

■ Eddiebauer.com

▲ Starbucks.com

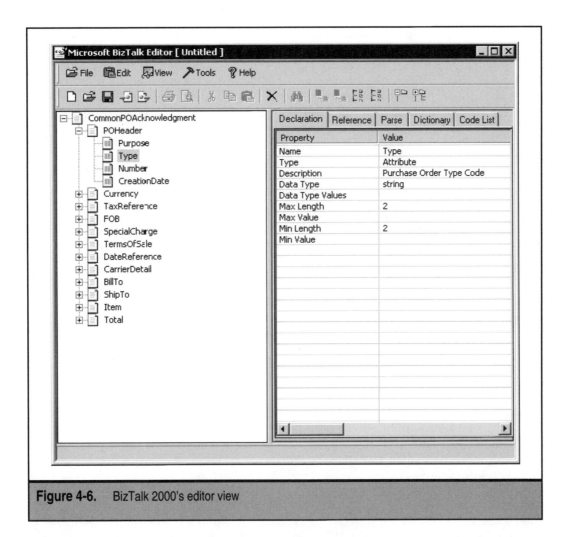

Figure 4-6.   BizTalk 2000's editor view

Right off the bat SQL Server 2000 is a great tool for your e-business. It comes out of the box Web-enabled with end-to-end support for Extensible Markup Language (XML) and a new, integrated data-mining engine which will enable your customers and business partners to find the data they need in a fast, efficient manner.

Features   SQL Server 2000 can make it easier for your organization to conduct business over the Web with customers and supply-chain partners. One of the feathers in SQL Server 2000's cap is its capability to help companies better understand customer behavior on the Web and quickly discover new business opportunities.

Data mining automatically sifts through large volumes of business information, which helps customers find the products and services that they desire. An embedded data-mining engine reduces the complexity of this sophisticated process. Analysis Services includes clustering and decision tree data-mining algorithms and is extensible by third parties via OLE DB for data mining.

SQL Server 2000 Analysis Services includes unique, new features for analyzing Web click-stream data, performing closed-loop analysis, and sharing analysis results across the Web through firewalls. Simplifying access to strategic data resources, SQL Server 2000 English Query allows end users of all skill levels to pose questions in English to the database via the Web. English Query translates a user's question into a proper database query and returns the desired results from the relational store or Analysis Services.

SQL Server 2000 boasts a higher level of reliability and scalability than its predecessors, and, as we've said throughout this book, reliability and scalability are important considerations when deploying an e-business solution. With SQL Server 2000, rather than replacing old systems with bigger, more expensive ones, you can achieve scalability increases through software scale-out simply by adding additional servers to a database cluster. SQL Server 2000 achieves high levels of scalability through several means:

▼ SQL Server 2000 introduces Distributed Partitioned Views, a feature that provides e-commerce customers with unlimited scalability by dividing workload across multiple independent SQL Server–based servers.

■ SQL Server 2000 natively supports high-speed System Area Network (SAN) technology such as GigaNet's cLAN server farm network and Compaq's ServerNet 2.

■ SQL Server 2000 tightly integrates four-node failover clustering and log shipping into its management console and setup wizard.

▲ SQL Server 2000 Analysis Services allows multidimensional queries against dimensions with hundreds of millions of members. SQL Server 2000 also introduces indexed views, a technology enabling high-performance reporting applications against relational databases.

Integration   All this technology is great, but if you need a room full of programmers who live on Mountain Dew and No Doz and still take six months to get your solution online, it does little or no good, especially in a volatile, fast-paced marketplace. SQL Server 2000—which integrates well with Windows 2000—is relatively easy to use. Some of SQL Server 2000's speed and efficiency attributes include these:

▼ The integration between SQL Server 2000 and the Active Directory in Windows 2000 allows SQL Server databases to be managed centrally alongside other enterprise resources, simplifying system management in large organizations.

▲ SQL Server 2000 introduces new security enhancements for safeguarding data inside and outside the firewall. SQL Server 2000 supports role-based security, includes tools for security auditing, and offers file and network encryption.

With new features in SQL Server 2000 Analysis Services (such as custom rollups, flexible dimension architecture, and fine-grained security), it's easier for customers to build high-end, specialized business intelligence solutions for e-businesses as well as the financial services, insurance, retail, and manufacturing sectors.

Commerce Server 2000

The next tool in our Microsoft e-business solution is Commerce Server 2000. This server product provides a comprehensive set of features, which will help you build your business-to-consumer and business-to-business e-business site. In addition to the Web site building tools, Commerce Server 2000 also includes sophisticated business analysis features to uncover business opportunities and refine e-business promotions.

Commerce Server 2000 builds on Microsoft's popular Site Server version 3.0, Commerce Edition (SSCE). Commerce Server includes both enhanced and entirely new features that combine to provide the functionality found in SSCE, while adding extras for the 2000 version.

The heart of Commerce Server 2000 lies in its ease of use along with its tools to analyze and target customers.

Development Tools   Packaged with Commerce Server 2000 are the tools to build and deploy the e-commerce site you want. Right out of the box, you can get a fast start with a variety of helpful tools, including:

▼ **Retail Solution Site**   Jump-start development for any consumer-facing marketing or e-commerce Web site. This tool includes business-to-consumer functionality for personalization, merchandising, catalog search, customer service, and business analytics.

■ **Supplier Solution Site**   Implement key sell-side business-to-business capabilities. The Supplier Solution Site includes secure user authentication and group access permissions, purchase order and requisition handling, XML-based catalog updates and exchange, and trading partner self-service.

■ **Auctions**   Set up and manage your own online auctions with this tool. Auctions can be used with both customers and your supply-chain partners.

■ **Commerce Server Manager**   This Microsoft Management Console snap-in makes it easy to manage Commerce Server resources. Using the Commerce Server Manager, site administrators can manage Global Resources, Commerce Server applications, Site Resources, Sites, and Web Servers. In addition, third-party vendors are building integrated solutions for Commerce Server 2000 that can extend the Commerce Server Manager to include administration capabilities for their value-added components and applications.

▲ **Commerce Server Site Packager**   The Site Packager is a utility that packages and unpackages entire Commerce Server sites and applications into a single file for easy transport between servers. Simplify deployment to test, staging, and production servers or package sites for distribution across disconnected networks. Solution providers and application vendors can also use the Site Packager to package solutions with custom integrated components for out-of-box delivery to customers.

Business Desk   Business managers can also have access and control over analysis and business operations within Commerce Server 2000. More than 20 modules are included to perform common business tasks, including reviewing reports, creating marketing campaigns, updating product data, checking order status, and modifying profiles.

Commerce Server Business Desk provides business managers with Web-based remote access and ensures they can take action at any time and from any location. In addition to the modules created by Microsoft, third-party modules are also available.

Table 4-1 shows some of the modules available for Business Desk.

In addition to these modules, Business Desk also uses role-based security, which enables business users to view and manage only the modules for which they are authorized.

iPlanet

In the spirit of big mergers, Sun Microsystems and Netscape have joined forces to offer their iPlanet fleet of e-business software solutions. Since the software has been developed by Sun, their technological gift to the Internet—Java—features predominantly in all the software solutions.

We'll only look at two of the most popular solutions here, but iPlanet offers a slew of software that handles everything from billing to application service.

iPlanet Application Server 6.0

As you might expect, because iPlanet Application Server (IAS) is a product of Sun, Java is a major component. Java's importance to IAS is both a plus and a minus to the product. Java makes IAS a potentially effective tool; however, only businesses that have sophisticated Java development skills and a commitment to Java will find IAS to be a good buy.

Analysis	Manage business reporting and analysis, including segmentation
Auctions	Manage business reporting and analysis, including segmentation
Campaigns	Manage advertising, discounts, direct marketing, and other campaigns
Catalogs	Design, create, and manage product and custom catalogs
Orders	Manage orders, including status and shipping, handling, and tax processing
Users	Manage information on users and organizations

Table 4-1.   Some Business Desk Modules

For organizations that aren't doing Java development, IAS isn't your best bet. It doesn't support Microsoft's COM (Component Object Model) objects, although COM integration is expected by late 2000 or early 2001. Additionally, C language support has been deprecated in IAS 6.0—C is still supported, but this support won't be updated. This is bad news if yours is an organization that will develop applications in C.

Functions IAS's biggest advantages are its high level of scalability and its fault tolerance. Organizations realize performance gains from IAS through using its capability to scale applications across multiple CPUs and multiple machines. IAS further maximizes Web application performance through connection caching and pooling, results caching, data streaming, optimized Web server communication, and a multithreaded, multiprocessing architecture. iPlanet Application Server also integrates with iPlanet ECXpert software, providing business-to-business integration across a company's value chain.

For organizations that use JavaServer Pages (JSP) in their Web applications, there will be greater motivation to upgrade to version 6.0 because JSP support is significantly enhanced in this release. For instance, version 6.0 now includes failover and load balancing with JSPs.

When it comes time to get the applications onto the Internet, IAS can link with iPlanet Web Server (which is included with IAS); Microsoft's Internet Information Server (IIS); or the Apache Web server.

IAS's development tool, called iPlanet Application Builder (IAB) 6.0 (shown in Figure 4-7), costs $1,295 per seat and includes a development-only version of IAS 6.0. Using IAB, you can edit JSP and HTML files in three views: graphical preview, a tree outline, and text editor. There are also separate command line tools for these tasks, which are also simple to use for those using third-party development tools. IAB includes a number of wizards, which help with application development.

Features Buyers might get a little sticker shock when considering IAS. The server costs $35,000 per CPU on all platforms. This is 50 to 200 percent more expensive than comparable servers. IAS is available for Windows NT 4.0 with Service Pack 5, Solaris 2.6, HP-UX, AIX, and Windows 2000.

Here are some of the main features of IAS 6.0. It:

▼ Complies fully with Java 2 Platform, Enterprise Edition and is J2EE Compatibility Test Suite certified

■ Integrates a transaction monitor for secure distributed transactions across multiple data sources

■ Provides multiple load-balancing options based on response time, server load, weighted round-robin, and intraserver process level

■ Extends load-balancing to JavaServer Pages and rich clients

■ Delivers advanced caching technology to enhance performance for database access and Java Servlet processes

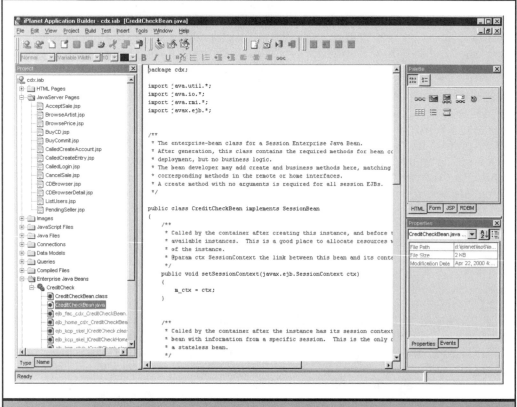

Figure 4-7.   The iPlanet Application Builder

■   Provides clustering and failover to enable continuous uptime and transaction processing in the event of server failure; automatically detects and restarts failed servers or processes

▲   Includes an integrated XML parser and an integrated XSLT engine to facilitate business-to-business integration

iPlanet MerchantXpert

Once you've got your applications online, iPlanet provides a channel to your customers through which you can conduct business. iPlanet MerchantXpert is another component of the iPlanet family of e-commerce applications.

MerchantXpert is particularly suited for enterprises selling to and servicing consumers for hard goods, especially in the technology, automotive, and pharmaceutical industries. Enterprises can use MerchantXpert together with SellerXpert—iPlanet's solution for B2B selling on the Internet—to create online sales channels for both businesses and consumers.

MerchantXpert—which is available only for the Sun Solaris 2.5.1 and 2.6—controls important components of online selling, such as product selection, order tracking, and customer service. MerchantXpert includes a customizable catalog, a search engine, and ample order management and payment services.

A key advantage of the MerchantXpert architecture is its scalability. Its modular components can be partitioned and replicated across a large set of servers to support all users in large enterprises. MerchantXpert is not a one-purchase option, however. In order to run the software, you must also own a Netscape ECXpert license and an Oracle database license.

Some of MerchantXpert's features include:

▼ Customizable templates for storefront creation

■ An interactive product catalog that supports thousands of SKUs

■ Payment processing capability

■ Comprehensive order management, including pricing, taxes, product availability, shipping, and tracking

■ Flexible customer profile management

■ Configurable business logic

■ Multimerchant and multicatalog support

■ Integration with systems using a variety of formats and protocols

▲ Tight integration with existing business systems and partners, utilizing a variety of formats such as EDI (through Netscape ECXpert)

Novell

Novell has really seen the writing on the wall. The world of computers and networking isn't about LANs anymore, it's about the Internet and e-commerce. To play a little catch up and stay in the game, Novell offers a directory service and a B2B solution to provide more functionality with your Novell solution. These two pieces of software work together to deliver e-business functionality.

NDS eDirectory

In the last chapter, you'll remember, we talked about enabled directories like Microsoft's Active Directory and Novell's NDS eDirectory. These types of directory services are particularly useful, especially when designing an e-business solution.

We already talked about eDirectory's features in the last chapter, so let's take a closer look at how eDirectory can benefit your e-business solution. eDirectory can help your enterprise with a wide range of e-business needs. For instance, eDirectory can help you:

▼ Build and manage secure and customized relationships with customers and partners who want to use the Internet as their primary channel for conducting business.

■ Create customer loyalty by offering products and services based on personalized personal profiles and behavior.

▲ Extend your existing network infrastructure to employees, customers, and supply-chain partners.

There are a number of reasons that an enabled directory will help your e-business. Though many of these features will also be found in other enabled directory services, NDS eDirectory provides a solid base for Novell e-business solutions. Some of the business gains include:

▼ **Accelerated e-business deployment**   eDirectory uses Internet standards (like LDAP, PKI, and XML), allowing easier and faster interconnectivity with other applications. Furthermore, when you are connecting to another company with an LDAP-based directory, this compatibility makes for standard access and a standard schema and format, as well as reliable transmission and protection of information that is written to and read from directory services. Figure 4-8 shows how eDirectory uses a schema to track information.

■ **Improved e-relationships**   Relationships don't only exist between people; they certainly exist between businesses. Not only do e-relationships include the trusted relationships between your people, computer systems, and network

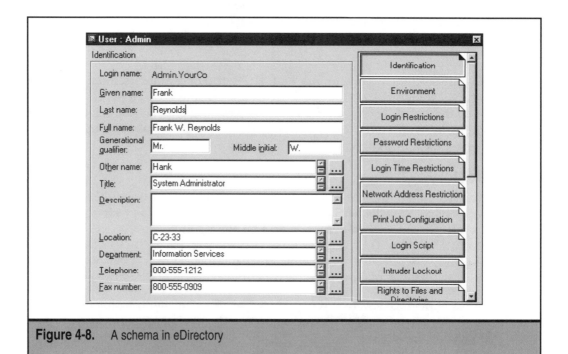

Figure 4-8.   A schema in eDirectory

services, but they also include the online associations of your customers and partners with your online content and services. eDirectory can help find and store identity information about customers, suppliers, and business partners. As a result of this mining and analysis, you can develop highly personalized profiles on everyone who comes in contact with your e-business.

■ **Security** eDirectory uses a standards-based security infrastructure that gives administrators easy, flexible control over your network's security policies. Public Key Infrastructure (PKI), cryptography, and authentication services are integrated within eDirectory, enabling administrators to centrally manage policies and control access across the entire network. eDirectory also supports such authentication as Secure Sockets Layer (SSL), X.509 v3 Certificates, and smart cards. By using Single Sign On services, users need only log onto a network once, but in a secure manner.

■ **Compatibility** eDirectory is able to function in mixed environments where there may be Novell, Windows, and Solaris operating systems in different parts of the company—or even with a business partner with a different operating system.

▲ **Growth** E-business solutions must not only serve the needs of today but also look ahead to what's coming down the road. Every e-relationship that you maintain in your directory is represented by a directory object. For an enterprise managing only internal relationships, 20 or 30 may exist. However, if you link to other businesses, your relationships can grow exponentially. eDirectory comes equipped for future scaling and is able to handle a billion objects.

Not only a capable directory service, eDirectory is crucial to the functioning of Novell's iChain B2B solution, which we'll talk about next.

iChain B2B Solution

If yours is a solution that will require B2B e-commerce, Novell offers its iChain solution. iChain offers business-to-business management, and e-commerce application integration in one package.

iChain is based on NDS eDirectory and provides a handful of features that will benefit any B2B need, for instance:

▼ A hierarchical model with privileged inheritance and a common security model

■ Central profile/policy/identity management

■ Single sign-on

▲ Transaction authorization management

Overview iChain integrates core services—including security, management, and commerce—for conducting B2B activities on the Internet. The iChain platform is built on top of eDirectory, which offers data sharing between separate business entities, such as supply chains. This supplies a secure and controlled infrastructure over which your directories and those of your partners can communicate and update each other. Figure 4-9 shows iChain management from Novell's ConsoleOne.

iChain allows you to extend your information infrastructure so that it can be leveraged by e-commerce and Internet-based B2B operations. It acts as an integration platform, allowing all components of your e-business network to share data and relationships.

iChain Components   The iChain foundation consists of two components: the iChain Proxy Server and the iChain Web Server. These two components utilize the functions and features and storage that NDS eDirectory provides. Let's take a closer look at what each of these components does.

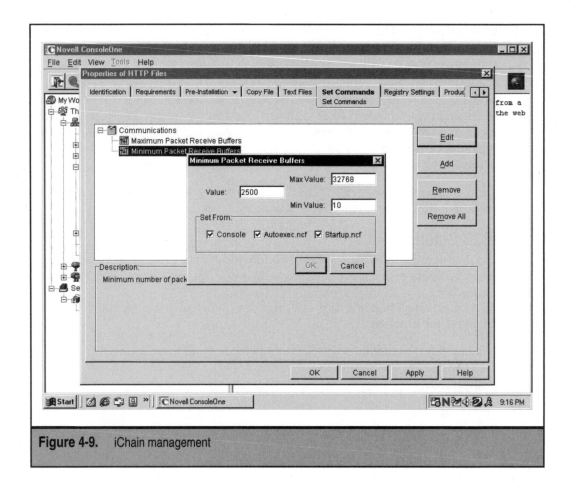

Figure 4-9.   iChain management

▼ **NDS eDirectory** is the underlying data store for iChain. eDirectory is used to store and maintain configuration, access control, and relationship information for users accessing the system. Information about the iChain proxy server, the accessible community membership, access control policies, special features, and personalized user interfaces is stored within eDirectory.

■ **iChain Proxy Server** is the key component of any iChain infrastructure. It acts as a firewall in your network and is the main point of entry for anyone trying to access your network. iChain Proxy Server is a reverse proxy. It provides HTTP acceleration, which allows iChain to delegate this process away from the Web servers so that they can focus on applications tasks.

▲ **iChain Web Server** can be virtually any Web server you choose to use. iChain's infrastructure allows support and integration with most Web servers; however, NetWare 5 Enterprise Web Server is shipped with iChain. The most popular Web servers that will work with iChain include Microsoft IIS, Netscape Web Server, and Apache Web Server.

iChain Functions   By utilizing the aforementioned components of iChain, users are able to extract a number of key functions that are important for e-business. Here are some of those features:

▼ **Extranet access management capability**   Extranet Access Management is the ability of a company to manage and protect its information and its Web site's business transactions over the Internet, while allowing its employees and customers access to the Web site. iChain manages its security by employing a standards-based security infrastructure providing flexible control over a network's security policies, cryptography, and authentication services.

■ **Delegation of authority**   If yours is a large enterprise, it may be impractical for one person to oversee all security issues at all branch and field offices. Therefore, iChain allows you to assign responsibilities to others within your organization.

■ **Security**   iChain employs a number of security features to keep your e-business safe. The application allows for multiple authentication mechanisms, including NDS user ID and password, token-based authentication, and mutual SSL authentication. It also provides virtual private networking (VPN) features and offers its "SSLizer," which provides for full-time data encryption. You can also manage and distribute certificates with Public Key Infrastructure Services and X.509 Certificates.

■ **Policy Management**   iChain provides tools to capture identity information from your customers, suppliers, and business partners. This allows you to create highly personalized profiles about everyone who interacts with your e-business. For instance, iChain can generate marketing data based on customer demographics, buying patterns, product interest, and so on.

■ **Communities**   iChain's Community services allow you to create communities of users and define access policies for those users. This allows you more ease in managing your customers. Community services can also be set up to allow customers—through an online form—to establish which community they should be part of. Also, when users log on, a custom home page or portal can be displayed, showing specific information and links for that specific community.

▲ **Application integration**   iChain's adherence to standards allows you to integrate third-party solutions into iChain. For instance, you can use third-party messaging systems, SQL databases, Web publishing, and LDAP directory support.

IBM

IBM's venture in the e-business server market includes a plethora of robust tools that you can use to develop e-business with a range of functionality. WebSphere is a full line of software solutions that offer everything from Web page design to Web serving. For our purposes, let's look at the two most useful pieces of software that you would use for your e-business: Application Server and Studio.

WebSphere Application Server

IBM WebSphere Application Server is an e-business application deployment environment built on open standards–based technology. WebSphere has been designed to work on a number of platforms, a fact that widens its availability considerably.

The cornerstone of WebSphere is its application offerings and services. The WebSphere Application Server comes in three flavors—Standard Edition, Advanced Edition, and Enterprise Edition. Here's how each version differs from the others.

Standard Edition   The Standard Edition lets you use Java servlets, JavaServer Pages, and XML to quickly transform static Web sites into active, dynamic pages. Geared at Web developers and content authors, the Standard Edition includes:

▼ Usability enhancements throughout, including a Quick Installation that eliminates guesswork

■ Enhanced Java, leveraging Java 2 Software Development Kit V1.2.2 across all supported operating systems

■ Support for JavaServer Pages

■ Support for the Java servlet 2.1 specification, including a graphical interface, automatic user session management, and user state management

- High-speed pooled database access using JDBC for DB2 Universal Database and Oracle

- XML server tools, including a parser and data transformation tools

- IBM HTTP server, which includes an administration graphical user interface and support for LDAP and SNMP connectivity

▲ Integration with IBM VisualAge for Java to help reduce development time by allowing developers to remotely test and debug Web-based applications

Version 3.5 supports Windows NT, Windows 2000, Solaris, AIX, AS/400, and HP-UX. Version 3.02 supports Red Hat Linux, Caldera Linux, OS/390, and Novell NetWare.

Advanced Edition The Advanced Edition is a high-performance EJB server for implementing EJB components that incorporate business logic. Aimed at Web application programmers, the Advanced Edition provides all the features of the Standard Edition, plus:

▼ Improved integration with Lotus Domino, IBM Visual Age for Java, and IBM WebSphere Commerce Suite

- Full support for the Enterprise JavaBeans (EJB) 1.0 specification, including both SessionBeans and EntityBeans (container-managed and bean-managed persistence)

- Deployment support for EJBs, Java servlets, and JSPs with performance and scale improvements

- IBM LDAP Directory, which can be optionally installed

- A DB2 server, which is automatically installed as part of the run-time environment

- Support for distributed transactions and transaction processing

▲ Management and security controls, including user and group level setup and method level policy and control

Version 3.5 supports Windows NT, Windows 2000, Solaris, AIX, AS/400, and HP-UX. Version 3.02 supports Red Hat Linux and Novell NetWare.

Enterprise Edition The Enterprise Edition integrates EJB and CORBA components to build high-transaction, high-volume e-business applications. The Enterprise Edition, which is meant for enterprise e-business application developers and architects, includes all the features of the Advanced Edition, plus:

▼ Full distributed object and business process integration capabilities

- IBM's world-class transactional application environment integration

- Complete object distribution and persistence

- Complete component backup and restore support

■ XML-based team development functions

▲ An integrated Encina application development kit

Version 3.5 supports Windows NT, Solaris, and AIX. Version 3.02 supports OS/390.

WebSphere Studio

To build content for WebSphere, IBM has created WebSphere Studio. It is a suite of tools designed to help build Web content and to help Web development teams to work together smoothly. Studio has features that help Web page designers, graphic artists, programmers, and Webmasters work together so that the right professional can work on the right piece of your e-business puzzle. With WebSphere, organizations can create, assemble, publish, and maintain dynamic interactive Web applications, powered by WebSphere Application Server.

With the integration of Wallop's Built-IT technology (which IBM acquired in the fall of 1998) and the enhancement of its base functions, WebSphere Studio offers the following features you need to create and manage e-business Web sites:

▼ Graphical display of the links between files in a project

■ Automatic update of links whenever files change or move

■ A built-in Page Designer for creating and editing HTML and JSP files

■ Wizards that help create dynamic pages using databases and JavaBeans

▲ Staging and publishing to multiple servers

Additionally, Studio includes several companion tools for your Web development toolkit:

▼ **Applet Designer** A visual authoring tool that makes it easy to build new Java applets

■ **WebArt Designer** A handy tool for creating masthead images, buttons, and other graphics for your page

▲ **AnimatedGif Designer** For assembling GIF animations

In the next section, we'll show you how you can use WebSphere Studio to create content on your Sun and Microsoft servers.

CONFIGURING A SERVER

Would you buy a car without kicking the tires? Probably not, and you probably shouldn't neglect the equivalent steps if you're spending thousands of dollars on a Web server (or servers). In this section, we take a look at two different ways you can install a server. We've chosen two different platforms and two different server solutions to show you how to get your e-business online.

First, we'll take a look at Microsoft's Windows DNA with SQL Server 2000 and Commerce Server 2000. As of this writing, both of these pieces of software are in beta testing, and some of this information is subject to change, but major changes are not likely.

Next, we'll show you how to set up IBM's WebSphere on a Sun Solaris platform. Not that we intend to shovel any more money on that pile in Bill Gates' backyard, but we'll also point out some of the stark differences between a Windows install and a Solaris one.

But before we get started, a word of warning is needed: Setting up an e-business site is not an easy task. The steps that we're going though here are abbreviated and condensed. In many cases, you need to know such information as the location of databases, specific IDs and passwords, and even the overall design of your Web site. We simply don't have the space to talk about all the details and all the issues associated with setting up an e-business Web site.

That having been said, the following two sections should give you a good, basic understanding of what is expected from you when you are developing an e-business solution.

Microsoft

Microsoft has one of the fastest, easiest ways to get your online presence up and running shortly after peeling the plastic wrap off the software. To show you how to set up an e-business solution using Microsoft software, we'll use SQL Server 2000 and Commerce Server 2000. These will be applied on a system running Windows 2000 with Internet Information Services (IIS) 5.0 installed.

NOTE: Remember, IIS 5.0 comes with Windows 2000 Server, so you don't have to pay for extra software to enable a bunch of Web services.

Installation and Configuration

The first step for an install is to ensure that you have the right hardware and software requirements. Commerce Server 2000 has three different components you can install to operate your server. If you choose simply to install the administration tools, but not the server components, you have that option. If the business manager wants the business desk installed on her computer but does not need the other two components, Commerce Server 2000 allows that installation. Table 4-2 shows the hardware and software requirements for each Commerce Server 2000 component.

SQL Server 2000 and Commerce Server 2000 are reasonably straightforward affairs to install. For the most part, it's a matter of double-clicking a "setup" icon and following the on-screen steps.

Before installing SQL Server 2000 on a Windows 2000 computer, you must first download and install a "hotfix." The hotfix is a 743KB file available from Microsoft's Web site. This issue will likely work itself out with the next service pack made available for Windows 2000.

Another issue that warrants mention became apparent on my first effort to download the Commerce Server 2000 beta from Microsoft's Web site. First, I tried downloading it with an option that would install it as it downloaded from the Web site. The install on the 25MB server was extremely slow—bear in mind I was downloading from a high-speed

	Server Components	Administration Tools	Business Desk
Hardware	400 MHz or higher Pentium II-compatible CPU 256MB of RAM minimum recommended 100MB of available hard-disk space to install services; additional space required for site content and databases NTFS-formatted hard-disk volume CD-ROM drive Network adapter card Windows 2000–compatible video graphics adapter	266 MHz or higher Pentium-compatible CPU 128MB of RAM 20MB of available hard-disk space CD-ROM drive Network adapter card Windows 2000–compatible video graphics adapter	166 MHz or higher Pentium-compatible CPU 32–128MB of RAM depending on operating system requirements 5MB of available hard-disk space Network adapter card Windows 2000–compatible video graphics adapter
Software	Microsoft Windows 2000 Server or Windows 2000 Advanced Server operating system Microsoft SQL Server 7.0 or later	Microsoft Windows 2000 Professional, Windows 2000 Server, or Windows 2000 Advanced Server operating system	Microsoft Windows 2000 Professional, Windows 2000 Server or Windows 2000 Advanced Server, Windows NT 4.0 Workstation or Windows NT 4.0 Server, or Windows 98 operating system Microsoft Internet Explorer 5.5 or later

Table 4-2.   Prerequisites for Commerce Server 2000 Components

network, so it wasn't bottlenecking on a dial-in modem. In fact, it was so slow (I waited about 2 hours) that I decided to let it run overnight. I returned almost 24 hours later, and it was still not finished.

My next attempt to install the program involved downloading the entire compressed package, then installing it. This, too, did not work. In fact, the setup program told me that I didn't have the right version of the software. (I did, but it didn't recognize my version of Windows 2000 Advanced Server.) It was only the third attempt (following exactly the same steps, incidentally) that I was successful; then Commerce Server 2000 downloaded smoothly and installed with no problems.

Site Construction

With our Microsoft solution, it's necessary to build and connect to a database, and then you can use included "solution sites" to finish the Web site. For the most part, these are simple, by-the-numbers affairs that require you to provide some information; then the computer will complete the task.

The key tool you'll use for this project is the Microsoft Management Console. This tool provides a centralized location for a number of Windows 2000 tools—in this case, SQL Server and Commerce Server are managed from snap-ins to the MMC.

Database Setup   Site construction requires first setting up a database in SQL Server. This is accomplished by opening the MMC (as shown in Figure 4-10), selecting the SQL servers icon in the left pane, and then creating a new database.

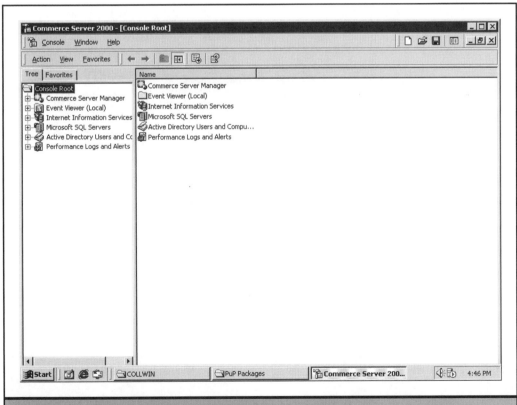

Figure 4-10.   The MMC contains the tools necessary to build your e-commerce solution

NOTE: Because the MMC is a centralized location for all your computer management needs, you can configure an MMC with any tools you want. Included with the install of each server, an MMC is preconfigured for each. If you open the MMC for Commerce Server, it contains the SQL Server controls. By using this MMC, you avoid having to switch back and forth between the managers for each server.

This starts a wizard that creates the database you want to create. As you can see in Figure 4-11, we've created a database for a hat store.

At this stage, the wizard will ask you a number of questions, including:

▼ The database name

■ The size of the database

■ The size of the log file for the database

▲ Whether you want the database to grow automatically or allow you to restrict its size

These can be tricky questions to answer (except for the database name—that one should be pretty easy). As you can see, you'll have to figure out before you start how

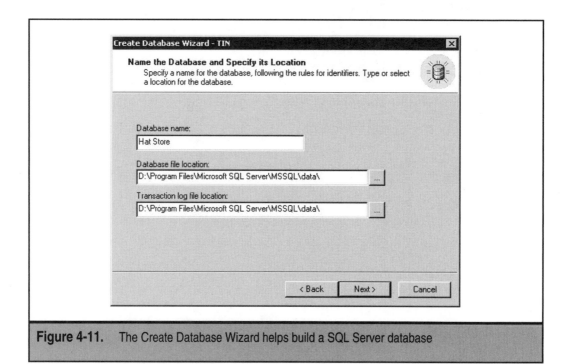

Figure 4-11. The Create Database Wizard helps build a SQL Server database

much database space you'll need; then you'll have to make sure you have enough space, physically, on your server.

When you have successfully completed this task, as shown in Figure 4-12, you should have a newly created database that is ready to link to Commerce Server 2000 and be managed from your MMC.

Next, you must link your database to Commerce Server 2000. This is accomplished, again, with your MMC. Under the "Commerce Server Manager" icon, you can find the tool you need to link your newly created database to Commerce Server 2000.

Setup   Connecting to a database is all well and good, but how can you actually build a Web site?

Solution Sites are packages included with Commerce Server 2000 that contain the resources you need to build a site. After you install Commerce Server, you can unpackage one of these Solution Sites and then use it as a foundation for building your own site.

Commerce Server includes the following Solution Sites:

▼ **Retail**   Contains the Commerce Server resources for building a retail site.

■ **SupplierSQL**   Contains the Commerce Server resources for building a supplier (business-to-business) site.

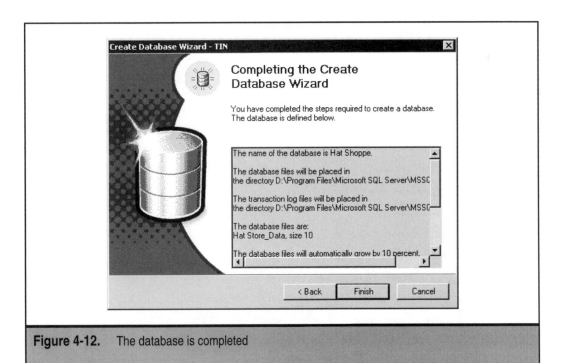

Figure 4-12.   The database is completed

■   **SupplierActiveDirectory**   Contains the Commerce Server resources for building an Active Directory–enabled supplier site.

▲   **Blank**   Contains all the Commerce Server resources for building your own custom site.

When it comes to customizing your site, you can use any HTML editor (like FrontPage, for instance) to give the Web pages your own unique touches.

Once you've developed the look and feel of the Web site, you can tweak out its functionality using Pipeline Editor, which is an application used for editing Commerce Server pipelines. Pipelines are collections of COM-based components that are preconfigured to handle common e-business tasks—like processing a credit card payment.

You can use Pipeline Editor (as shown in Figure 4-13) to edit a pipeline on your local computer or on a computer connected to a LAN. Pipeline Editor displays a pipeline as a pipe, showing the stages of pipe segments. The components used in a stage appear as valves.

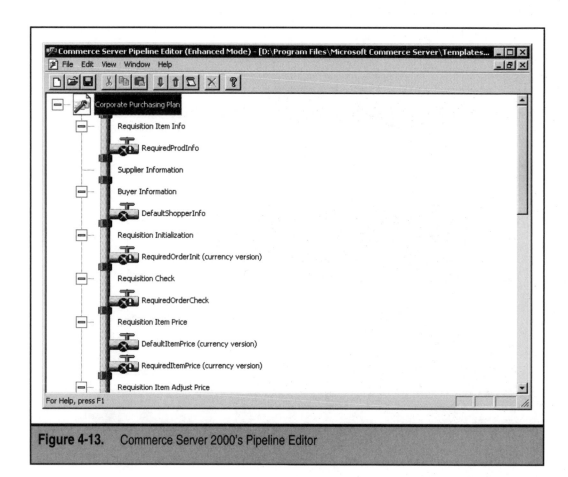

Figure 4-13.   Commerce Server 2000's Pipeline Editor

You can customize a component within the pipeline architecture and add an additional component, such as a payment method, to your site. You can either use one of the preconfigured components that were included with Commerce Server, make your own, or get one from a third-party vendor, such as Cyber Cash (www.cybercash.com) or VeriFone (www.verifone.com).

Commerce Server includes the following types of pipelines:

▼ **Content Selection Pipeline** Selects content to be displayed to users. For example, it determines which advertisements a user should see or which discounts a user should receive, on the basis of the targeting expressions you create using Commerce Server Business Desk, how many advertisements are to be delivered, and other factors.

■ **Event Processing Pipeline** Records events related to the displayed content (for example, a user clicking an ad) and stores them in the Commerce Server databases. This information is then used for reporting purposes, for example, how many users have clicked an ad.

■ **Direct Mailer Pipeline** Constructs and delivers messages for direct mail campaigns. It can construct personalized e-mail messages or messages with static content.

▲ **Order Processing Pipeline** Processes either business-to-consumer (retail) orders or business-to-business (supplier) orders. This pipeline ensures that an order goes through all the necessary stages to be processed appropriately. For example, it retrieves the product description from the catalog, retrieves the shipping address for the user, computes the amount of tax, and computes the total price.

Commerce Server includes the following types of Order Processing Pipelines:

▼ **Product Pipeline** Computes price and discount information for a product.

■ **Plan Pipeline** Verifies the integrity of the order. For example, if the order does not contain any items, then an error is generated.

■ **Purchase Pipeline** Accepts the final purchase of an order form, writes an order to database storage, and, optionally, finalizes a receipt and writes the contents of the order to the receipt database.

■ **Corporate Purchasing Plan Pipeline** Computes the purchase order total for a supplier purchase, including all promotional discounts, taxes, shipping, and handling charges.

▲ **Corporate Purchasing Submit Pipeline** Validates the purchase order or requisition, transfers the purchase order to the vendor, and writes the order to the database.

Once you've completed the site, it's simply a matter of putting it on your Web server (which you already have installed, courtesy of IIS 5.0). Then you're open for business.

Added Functionality A useful feature that comes with Commerce Server 2000 is its site packaging function. A *package* is a specially formatted Commerce Server file; each package is identified with a .pup extension. A package always contains a single site, which includes the resources, their data, and applications for a Commerce site.

In addition to site resources, applications, and the IIS settings that are needed to re-create the Web server configurations, Site Packager also includes the property values from the Administration database. For example, when you package the App Default Config resource, all of the current property values are also packaged. When you unpackage the App Default Config resource, the property values are unpackaged onto the Administration database.

The package includes global resource pointers but not the global resources themselves. Connection strings are packaged without the user name and password fields.

During the application packaging process, Site Packager searches the Internet Information Services (IIS) metabase on your local computer and finds the physical directory that is the root for that application. It then starts at that root directory and packages all the subdirectories below it in the tree into a new file with a .pup extension. Site Packager preserves certain settings in IIS such as authorizations and access permissions.

Site Packager is helpful if you intend to deploy a site across several servers (for load balancing or other needs). Rather than track down every resource and copy the site file by file by file to the server, Site Packager condenses them into one file that can be easily shared between servers.

WebSphere

The computer rules for consumers aren't the same as they are for business. If, for instance, you were to ask 100 people on the street what kind of computer they have, most would say they use a PC. Ask the same question of 100 businesses, and you'll get a different answer—Sun computers.

If yours is an organization that relies on Sun technology, IBM's WebSphere Commerce Suite is a comprehensive solution for your e-business. They are used for a host of e-business needs, including building, maintaining, and hosting stores and malls. In addition to the basic necessity for getting the applications built and offered up online, the suite also provides a range of features and functions for content management, relationship marketing, order management, and payment management for all types of e-businesses.

The commerce suite comes in three flavors:

▼ **Start Edition** Designed to help get entry-level Web sites up and running quickly, this edition helps businesses attract customers and capture sales cost-effectively. Businesses can develop sites with a full range of e-business functionality, including interactive catalogs, order management, flexible shipping and tax support, payment processing, and post sales support.

■ **Pro Edition** The Pro Edition is meant for businesses that want to add more tools and features to their online presence. It comes complete with all of the

Start Edition features, plus it has enhanced catalog technology, personalization features, auction capabilities, and support for a host of platforms.

▲ **Service Provider Edition** The Service Provider Edition allows service providers to set up and operate secure hosted e-commerce services and communities for multiple businesses. A complete suite of software components helps businesses build, maintain, and host full-service stores and malls for multiple sellers.

For our WebSphere solution, we're using the WebSphere Commerce Suite Version 4.1. Among other tools, the package includes:

▼ **WebSphere Commerce Studio** Aids in the design and development of e-business sites.

■ **IBM Commerce Integrator** Connects e-business software applications with existing back-end systems such as ERP, CRM, and supply-chain management.

▲ **IBM WebSphere Catalog Architect** Helps online businesses create, update, and manage product information.

Don't take this to mean that the only way WebSphere technology can work is on a Sun computer. If you'd like to try it on your Microsoft computers, WebSphere would be more than happy to help you out.

Installation and Configuration

The first step for an install is to ensure that you have the right hardware and software requirements. Table 4-3 shows what is needed for the WebSphere Commerce Suite for Windows NT/2000, Sun Solaris, and IBM AIX platforms.

Once you've established that you have the correct software and a sufficiently beefy server, the next step in the install process is to make sure you install the software packages in the proper order. The following are some issues to consider when installing the software:

▼ If you install Commerce Suite and Commerce Studio on the same machine, install Commerce Suite first so that it will be automatically configured. If you install Commerce Suite after Commerce Studio, make sure you follow the instructions in Commerce Studio's online help to configure your system.

▲ If you install Commerce Suite on a different machine than Commerce Studio, you need to configure both Commerce Studio and the Commerce Suite server so that you can publish your stores. The instructions for this task are included in Commerce Studio's online help.

Installation on a Windows NT/2000 is a reasonably straightforward affair. After logging onto the computer with an administrative ID, insert the WebSphere Commerce Suite, Pro Edition CD-ROM and start the setup process. You'll be prompted for the user

	Windows NT/2000	Sun Solaris	IBM AIX
Hardware requirements	A dedicated Pentium 166 MHz (or higher) IBM compatible PC 256MB RAM minimum 500MB free disk space for program files CD-ROM drive	Sun SPARCstation capable of running Sun Solaris 256MB RAM with 320MB swap space 400MB free disk space for program files CD-ROM drive	IBM RS/6000 processor capable of running AIX 256MB RAM minimum 900MB free disk space for program files CD-ROM drive
Software requirements	Microsoft Windows 2000 Server/ Advanced Server *or* Microsoft Windows NT Server, Version 4.0 with Service Pack 4 For Oracle ODBC support, Oracle 8.04 or 8.05 is required	Sun Solaris operating environment Version 2.6 or 2.7 For Oracle ODBC support, Oracle 8.04 or 8.05 is required	IBM AIX, Version 4.3.2 or Version 4.3.3 For Oracle ODBC support, Oracle 8.04 or 8.05 is required

Table 4-3. WebSphere Commerce Suite Prerequisites

ID and password that you just used, then you'll be prompted to insert the rest of the CDs in the following order:

▼ DB2 Universal Database, Enterprise Edition

■ DB2 Universal Database Extenders

■ Net.Data

■ WebSphere Application Server, Advanced Edition

▲ WebSphere Commerce Suite, Pro Edition

However, if you're installing the software on a Sun computer, expect a more challenging installation experience. Where the Windows version was a reasonably straightforward process, installing the software on a Sun is more complicated and can be frustrating.

First, you must log onto the Korn shell as `root`. Next, installation requires that the CD-ROMs be installed in the following order, with the following steps:

▼ **DB2 Universal Database**   Mount the DB2 UD CD-ROM and start the installation process. You're asked to fill in database information for "User

Name," "Group Name," "Password," and "Verify Password." From a command line, use Admintool to change the default shell for your DB2 instance to the Korn shell.

■ **Net.Data**   Mount the Net.Data CD-ROM and start Admintool. Using this tool, install the Net.Data software.

▲ **IBM HTTP Server**   Mount the WebSphere Application Server CD-ROM and using the Admintool, select the following packages to install:

- ■ gskrf301 or gskru 301
- ■ HTTP Server Admin Messages
- ■ HTTP Server LDAP Module
- ■ HTTP Server Manual Pages
- ■ HTTP Server SSL Module
- ■ IBM HTTP Server Documentation Base
- ■ HTTP Server Documentation
- ■ HTTP Server MT Module
- ■ HTTP Server SNMP Module
- ■ HTTP Server Source Code
- ■ HTTP Server SSL Module Common
- ■ HTTP Server Administration (Run-Time)
- ■ HTTP Server Base Run-Time
- ■ IBM LDAP Client

When the session is completed, you must set up the IBM HTTP Server through a series of entries in the command line.

▼ **JDK 1.1.6 and WebSphere Application Server**   Mount the WebSphere Application Server CD, switch to the CDROM directory, and then run the setup program. This component requires you to select a custom installation to install selected software. You'll also be required to enter your USER ID and Password, Database Type, Database Name, User ID, Password, DB Home, and DB URL.

▲ **Commerce Suite**   Mount the WebSphere Application Server CD and, using the Admintool, install the software.

Once you've completed the installation, you'll be asked to reboot the computer and configure your software.

Like the software installation, configuring the Sun solution requires more work and computer science knowledge than does the Windows installation. For instance, configuration on the Sun requires another series of commands at the command line. These will create the application server repository, start the application server, start the HTTP server, and start the configuration manager. This brings you to the location where you will create a database instance.

Conversely, on the Windows machine, you simply click through the Windows screens, start the Configuration Manager, click a few tabs, and then complete the database instance creation as you would on the Sun.

As you can see, the Solaris installation is a much more complicated affair than the relatively easy Microsoft installation. One presumes, however, that if you are utilizing Sun computers in your organization, you have the personnel who are knowledgeable about the installation and operation of Sun computers.

Site Construction

If you made it through the installation phase, you're home free. Once you get the software properly installed, using WebSphere's Commerce Studio will be a stark contrast to the installation phase of the process.

Getting Started   Using Studio is a reasonably easy affair. Studio's main window has a File view on the left side. Its tree architecture represents the directory structure of your source files. You can organize the files and folders any way you like. Figure 4-14 shows a Studio sample project opened in File view.

When you open Studio for the first time, the program asks if you want to create a new project. You are then presented with the new project dialog and asked to provide more information about your first site. As you see in Figure 4-15, this information includes the name of the project, its location on your hard drive or shared file system, and what type of site that you want to create. You can choose a blank site or choose from the precreated templates as a starting point.

If you already have a Web project on your server or file system, you can just choose a blank project, and then add the files you want later on. There are several ways to add those files to your project:

▼   The Studio's Import Wizard can be used to import an entire site. You can access the site using either HTTP or FTP, and there are options for controlling how far to follow links, which domains to access, and what to do when you encounter password-protected pages.

■   The Studio's archive format can be used to archive an entire site in one quick step, creating a single compressed file. This is useful in that if you're transferring sites between different computers, you need only compress them into one file.

▲   You can also use the Insert dialogs for files and folders. When you open the Insert File dialog, it gives you a list of file types that you can import. It contains templates of the most common file types found on Web sites, and you can start your own files from these templates. Any files that you add to the templates folder will also show up in the list, so you can add standard page layouts or other kinds of files that your team needs.

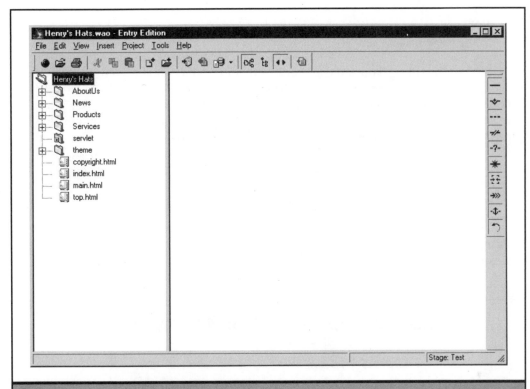

Figure 4-14. WebSphere Commerce Studio's main view

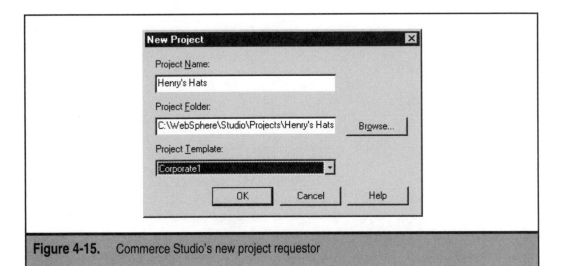

Figure 4-15. Commerce Studio's new project requestor

NOTE: If you are using WebSphere on Windows NT/2000, you can drag and drop files from Windows Explorer onto the tree.

Once you're rolling, you can use Studio's relations view (as shown in Figure 4-16) to get an idea of the structure of the site, and to see which files link to which. If any of the links in your site are broken, they will show up in this diagram as broken lines, so you can find them and fix them directly. Studio also helps you avoid broken links in the first place; whenever you rename or move a file, the links get fixed up for you automatically.

You can move around the diagram by clicking the plus boxes to adjust the view. The diagram shows 10 kinds of links, including inside and outside links, unverified links, anchor links, and others. It also shows source links, which indicate that one file was derived from another one (such as a GIF file that was exported from a Photoshop PSD file), as well as custom links that you define yourself.

Working with Files   To work with the files in your project, you can use the editing tools that come with Studio, or you can register any favorite tools that you already have. For

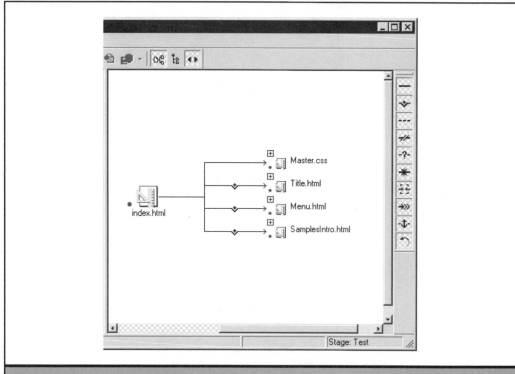

Figure 4-16.   Commerce Studio's relations view

example, you might have a favorite image editing tool that you want to register as the default editor for JPG files. To register tools, or to see what's already been registered, use the "Tool Registration" option under the "Tools" menu.

For editing your HTML and JSP pages, Studio includes the WebSphere Page Designer. Page Designer (as shown in Figure 4-17) has Design, Source, and Preview tabs so that you can either work in a visual mode or edit the tags directly. Page Designer is a full-function HTML editor, supporting all the standard HTML tags, plus JavaServer Pages (JSP) syntax, JavaScript, and DHTML. There's even a built-in editor for cascading style sheets.

A quick and easy way to add artwork to your page is by using the Web Art Designer. The Web Art Designer lets you combine text, background textures, and special effects to make new GIF or JPEG files.

When you work with the Page Designer, Web Art Designer, or Applet Designer, these tools are fully integrated with the Studio environment. For example, when you save your HTML page and go back to Studio, any images or other embedded files are added into the Studio project automatically.

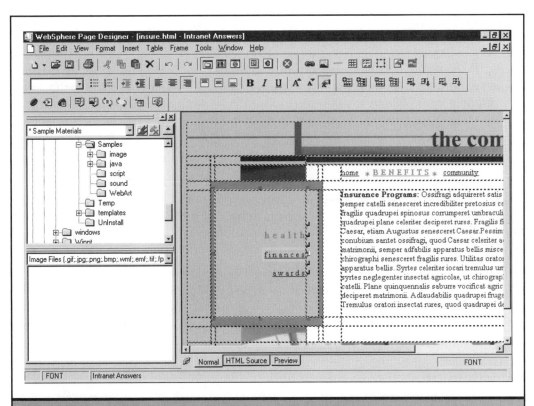

Figure 4-17.   WebSphere Page Designer helps you develop your Web sites, graphically

Publishing and Previewing   When you've constructed your Web site and are ready to get it on the World Wide Web, it's time to preview your work, then publish it to your Web server. Publishing means sending the content to your IBM HTTP server and the WebSphere Application Server (which you installed at the beginning of this process). If these servers are installed and running on your local machine, Studio's installation will detect them and set up default publishing locations automatically.

If you want to verify the publish settings or change the locations to which files will be published, you can switch to the Publish view, which shows all the servers, files, and folder locations for your publishing stages.

The Publish view looks very much like the File view, except that it shows which servers you are publishing to, along with the structure that will be copied to your server's file system. Normally, this matches the structure in your File view, but it doesn't have to match at all. You can move the files around any way to suit your needs. For example, you can define more than one server and divide your files across them.

The term "stage" means the definition of the servers and directories that you want to publish to. Usually, you work in the Test stage, but you can add additional stages for your own testing, combining your work with your team's work, and finally deploying the site to your production servers.

When you're ready to publish, just click the publish button on the toolbar, and the files will be copied to the correct directories on your HTTP server and your application server. During the publish operation, you can make choices for how to fix up the links and set various kinds of prompts and warnings. Once all the files are copied to the server, you can preview the site from any page, such as the home page. If you are previewing and testing a lot, you can turn on the *autopublish* setting, and your files will be published automatically as you make changes. This way, you can just press the Preview button, and you never have to stop to publish the site.

THIRD-PARTY SERVERS

Earlier in this chapter, we talked about the software offerings of some of the industry's heavy hitters. Naturally, they aren't the only options out there, so let's look at some other, specialized pieces of software.

Want to set up your own auction site? Forget eBay, there are ways you can build your own auction site. Obviously, you'll need a way to get your customers' payments. To that end, you'll need some payment processing software to turn those credit card numbers into cold hard cash. Finally, if you're setting up a business-to-business site, we'll talk about a couple pieces of software that will help your solution.

Online Auctions

Who needs eBay when you can do it yourself? All you need is a little gumption and the right application. Even if you don't care to be a conduit between two private citizens to sell their old stuff, auction software can be used to sell surplus materials to other businesses, or for contractors to bid on projects.

Auction software isn't as prevalent as the other server software, but it is out there. First, if you decided to buy WebSphere, auction software is included with it. But if you want to go with another company's software, two of the most popular auction services on the market are Commerce One's Auction Services and Siebel Dynamic Conference.

Commerce One Auction Services

Commerce One Auction Services provides an effective way to reduce procurement costs and increase the return on excess merchandise. Commerce One's solution is targeted at companies that plan to buy millions of dollars worth of supplies, annually. It supports complex business rules and complex procurement practices, yet it is still easy to use.

If you decide to use Commerce One's Auction Services, you must first forward your company logo to Commerce One, order a domain name for the auction site, and obtain a 128-bit digital certificate (see Chapter 12 for more information about digital certificates). Then, you can set up the site using Microsoft Internet Explorer 5.0 or higher or Netscape 5.0 or higher.

Configuration   Configuring your auction site is easy. Site administration is set up hierarchically and can be customized to meet the specific business rules of your enterprise. Administrators have full access to all rights; they can then assign lesser rights to "originators."

Once permissions have been assigned, you simply assign auction categories, bidders, and groups of bidders. At this point, Originators can be given access rights, allowing them to set up and administer auctions, within parameters set by the administrator.

Within categories you establish, you can set up subcategories. For instance, if you set up two categories called "seeds" and "tools," you could establish the subcategories of "okra," "tomatoes," "hoes," and "rakes." Creating a new subcategory entails the simple task of clicking an icon and typing in the name and description.

Auctioning   Setting up an auction can be done two ways—via a form or by following a wizard—both of which are very simple. The application offers two kinds of auctions:

▼   **Forward Auction**   This type of auction is used to liquidate merchandise and follows the typical auction conventions—the highest bidder wins.

▲   **Reverse Auction**   This type of auction is used to solicit bids, and, as opposed to a forward auction, the lowest bidder wins. For instance, if you have contractors bidding on new computer equipment, the one who brings them in at the lowest price gets the contract.

Once you establish what you're selling, you also establish the starting amount and increment amounts. Since Commerce One Auction Services are aimed at multimillion dollar sales, it wouldn't be a bad idea to set up beefy bid increments (like $10,000 or so) to avoid bids that vary by a few arbitrary dollar amounts.

In addition to setting up the basic who, what, where, and how muches of an auction, Commerce One allows you to attach multimedia files to help share information about your products.

Once an auction is set up and in place, bidders within an appropriate group receive e-mail inviting them to the auction. The bidder then logs on and is able to access the auctions to which he's been given permission. Once the bidder wins an auction, a star icon appears on the bidder's screen letting him or her know that he or she won.

Siebel Dynamic Commerce

The latest release of Dynamic Conference from Siebel (formerly know as OpenSite Auction 4.0 until they were acquired by Siebel in early 2000) is designed for any Web site that wants to build an auction. Dynamic Conference is a useful product that contains a multitude of tools to develop and maintain effective auctions.

Setup   OpenSite Auction can be installed on an ISP's remote server or on another server on your organization's network. If you're using Windows NT, you can use a Windows-based graphical installation program; all users have access to a browser-based graphical installation wizard.

If you're building an auction site from scratch, one of your biggest decisions will be choosing between a Windows NT implementation and a UNIX implementation. When it comes to browser-based installation and routine administration and maintenance, there's really no difference between the different operating-system versions. However, the advanced features found in the NT version have some advantages over any UNIX version: only NT users can use Oracle as the database engine (which offers far more flexibility when it comes to third-party reporting and data-management tools).

You can begin building your auction site by using the standard Web pages included with all three versions of Dynamic Conference. If these pages don't do what you need, a visit to the Template Editor lets you edit and preview pages before making them live. If you want to develop a "look" for the auction that coordinates with your organization, a Style Editor lets you create it by applying colors, fonts, layouts, and custom images (such as logos) across all the Web pages on an auction site.

You can offer individual items for auction or a parcel of items where customers can bid on individual items or the entire parcel. Auctions can be closed at a specific time or dynamically, where an *eAuctioneer* monitors an auction and then closes it if there's no bidding after a specific amount of time has elapsed. Customers can get an e-mail message notifying them when new items are added to their favorite auctions.

Features   Some of the features of Dynamic Conference include:

▼ Reverse Auctions (buyers request goods and companies bid in a downward bidding cycle until a final price has been reached) designed for corporate bidding processes.

■ Modified English Auctions, typically used when multiple quantities of the same item are offered for auction. In this type of auction, all winning bidders pay the amount of the lowest winning bid, ensuring that no one pays more for the same items.

■ Sealed Bid Auctions, where bidders are not informed of the winning bid until the auction is completed.

■ Private Auctions, where access can be limited to a small invited set of bidders.

▲ Consignment Auctions, where multiple sellers can sell their goods via the auction site. The administrator runs the auction and then receives a commission.

It's no wonder that Siebel bought this bit of software from OpenSite. It's a comprehensive product that provides a host of functionality. Not to mention, it's one of the biggest-selling pieces of auction software on the market.

B2B

If your e-business solution will have a B2B relationship with another organization, you will have somewhat different needs from those of an organization developing a B2C. Several companies offer server software specifically for B2B transactions. For instance, Microsoft offers its new BizTalk Server 2000 (as of this writing, it's still in beta testing), and iPlanet has its SellerXpert.

Let's take a look at two other offerings for B2B servers—Commerce One's BuySite 6.0 and webMethods B2B servers.

Commerce One BuySite 6.0

BuySite 6.0 Commerce Edition is designed to meet the needs of e-businesses who seek to develop a B2B solution. Aimed specifically at e-procurement, BuySite offers a suite of tools with means to streamline and enhance the task of purchasing.

BuySite handles a plethora of e-procurement tasks, from requisitioning to payment. Its key features and functions include:

▼ **Selection of goods and services via the GlobalLink Content Management Program** The GlobalLink content program is a comprehensive way to acquire goods and services.

■ **Creation and management of requisitions** The casual system user can build a requisition with items selected from a variety of search techniques. In addition, employees can create requisitions with the latest information—such as price, color, and quantity on hand—from suppliers. Professional buyers can also get the functionality of an industrial-strength procurement system to source, track, and manage requisitions made by employees.

■ **Approvals and workflow** BuySite includes a workflow engine that enables organizations to model their internal approval processes for maximum control and leverage their employees' buying behavior.

- **Purchase order creation** Upon approval of the requisition, purchase orders are automatically created and sent to the suppliers for fulfillment. This feature shifts the manual chore of routing purchase orders from the purchasing professional to the suppliers.

- **Status** Users can check the status of their requisitions and purchase orders by accessing a stats screen directly from the home page.

- **Receiving** Users can receive goods and services at their desks via the receiving function. BuySite can also be configured to allow for centralized receiving at a supply dock or mailroom, for instance.

- **Payment initiation and reconciliation** To complete the procurement cycle, BuySite enables payment initiation and reconciliation. This includes configuring specific payment types and terms, such as invoice and procurement card for suppliers or users, and indicating this information on the purchase order. Payment information is then sent in real time to suppliers.

- ▲ **Reporting** BuySite can generate a variety of reports that can be used to monitor spending activity as well as for leverage when negotiating contracts with suppliers.

For more information about BuySite 6.0 Enterprise Edition, visit Commerce One at www.commerceone.com.

webMethods B2B

Written in Java, webMethods B2B is a cross-platform B2B solution. The software platform extends critical business applications and collaborative processes beyond corporate fire-walls, integrating them with the ERP/EDI systems; mainframe applications; databases; and Web sites of customers, suppliers, partners, and marketplaces.

Even within the most diverse trading communities, webMethods B2B automates real-time, bidirectional exchange between disparate applications. Data is exchanged directly between each company's business applications without human intervention, and regardless of existing technology at either end.

Two key components within the webMethods B2B architecture work in unison to create and execute service calls between business applications in use throughout the trading network.

- ▼ **webMethods B2B Developer** is an easy-to-use visual environment that lets users set up their B2Bi infrastructures. It defines B2B services and data transformations necessary to process data in any format. With webMethods B2B Developer, users can define where data comes from and where it goes. They can define and build business rules and processes, as well as auditing and logging rules. And they can take full advantage of the integrated testing and server administration tools that are provided.

▲ **webMethods B2B Server** executes the processes and services defined by the developer. It enables the flow of information between companies, their trading partners, and trading networks. Core services within the server provide the flexibility to handle data in any format; navigate through all protocols, platforms, and standards; work with any business system; and support all business processes and trading relationships.

Some of webMethods' functionality includes:

▼ **Scalability and Performance** The scalable architecture of webMethods B2B can handle thousands of simultaneous trading partner connections and service client requests asynchronously. Optimized for multiprocessor systems, the platform also supports high-volume, server-side processing of business documents. Plus, users can add load balancing and failover capabilities by clustering multiple webMethods B2B integration servers.

■ **Manageability** The administrative function of webMethods B2B simplifies tasks such as updating license keys, adding users, monitoring server activity, and setting configuration options for individual services.

■ **Security** webMethods B2B provides end-to-end security through standard Internet protocols such as HTTPS; LDAP for user and group information; SSL encryption and X.509 digital certificates for security and authentication; and Access Control Lists (ACLs) for fine-grained control over access of services.

▲ **Fast Deployment Through Adapters and Supplier OnRamps** webMethods B2B Adapters eliminate costly and time-consuming custom programming. These add-ons to webMethods B2B provide out-of-the-box integration with major ERP and other systems, reusing existing software and infrastructure.

For more information about webMethods B2B, visit them online at www. webmethods.com.

CHAPTER 5

Connecting Clients

In the computer world, talk about clients is a simple, straightforward matter: we're talking about the computers and terminals that the workforce uses to access the LAN, servers, and network printers. However, when we put it in the context of e-business, talking about clients gets a little hazier. In this framework, clients can mean one of many concepts:

▼ Traditional "client" computers used within your organization

■ A supply chain partner's client computers, which have occasion to connect to your servers

■ A customer's computer, connecting to your business via the Internet

▲ An employee connecting across a VPN or WAN

As you can see, the issue of client computers is a multifaceted one that can mean different things to different organizations. In this chapter, we'll talk about the two primary ways you will need to concern yourself with client connectivity: connecting employee workstations and preparing your Web site with the best resources available.

This chapter isn't a step-by-step procedure explaining how to connect clients. Rather, we'll talk about the issues behind client connectivity and some of the technologies and tools you can use to make your Internet presence as useful and effective as possible.

CLIENT CONNECTIVITY

In this first section, let's talk about the issues associated with connecting client computers that would be operated by employees or supply chain partners and have a trusted level of access to your network. These are the computers that will be in operation in different departments in your organization, as well as operated by sales staff who log into the network remotely.

When you are connecting client computers to your network, it's important to understand how hardware and software needs will dictate how you connect computers. Further, given the rapid expansion of technology (technology gets faster and requires more memory all the time), you'll need to understand the importance of having machines and peripherals properly suited to your organization's needs. But first, let's talk about how your network knows where clients are connected.

IP Addressing

It would be so easy if all you had to do was plug all your computers into a hub, then plug that hub into the network. Client connections done, right? As you can imagine, it's not quite that simple.

In order for everything on a network to know where all the other components are located, they all require an IP Address. IP addresses, which you've probably seen here and there, are four sets of numbers (octets) separated by decimal points, like 10.25.121.10, for example. These numbers tell the other components in your network where individual clients, servers, printers, and other network devices are located, as illustrated in Figure 5-1.

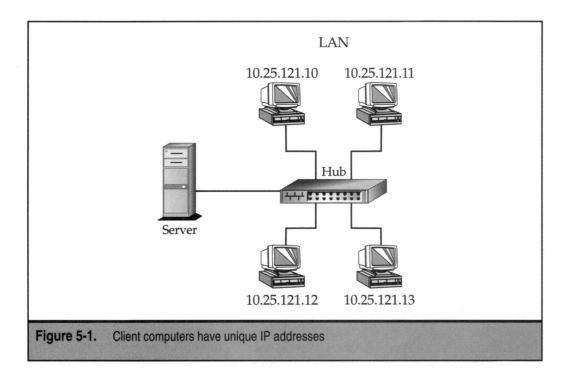

Figure 5-1.   Client computers have unique IP addresses

One of the most critical facets in connecting client computers is ensuring that the correct IP addresses are entered and that they correspond with what the server is expecting them to be.

Basically, there are two methods of setting an IP address: it can be either manually entered or dynamically set. We talk about IP addressing in more detail in Chapter 7.

Hardware Requirements

When you set up client computers, you must ensure that they have the right hardware for the jobs they'll be expected to perform.

One of the first hardware issues to be aware of is what your OS will require. Each OS manufacturer has a different requirement for hard drive space, RAM, and processor speed. For instance, let's look at what Microsoft requires of a Windows 2000 Professional client:

▼   133 MHz or higher Pentium-compatible CPU

■   64MB of RAM as a recommended minimum

▲   2GB hard disk with a minimum of 650MB of free space

Of course, these are just the bare minimums that will allow your clients to function. And the word "function" should be used loosely. If you go with the bare minimums, expect performance to be slow and don't be surprised at a crash here and there.

But the issue of hardware requirements is not limited to what the OS demands. Again, it is necessary to consider your organization's mission and this particular client's function. If, for instance, this client will be accomplishing the graphic design for your Web page, don't expect to get by on a 133 MHz computer with 64MB of RAM. By the same token, you may not want to shell out the $3,000+ for a 1 GHz, 256MB computer if the particular client will be word processing (you'd have the finest word processing system on the planet, however). Figure 5-2 shows how different computers have different hardware needs.

Your best bet is to consider the software applications you'll be using along with the requirements of your OS and ensuring your client computers have at least that much. If you can afford it, it wouldn't hurt to throw a few extra MB of RAM in there, for good measure.

Software Requirements

The software you use to connect client computers will depend, largely, on what kind of operating system you've chosen to use. For optimal reliability and effectiveness, it's best to use the client OS that corresponds with the OS you've selected for your server.

Working with OSes

For instance, if your servers are using Microsoft Windows 2000 Server, then you should install Windows 2000 Professional on your client computers.

Of course a homogenous computer system is not always possible. You may have some stray computers here and there that are running UNIX. There may be a department in your organization that insists on using Macintoshes as well.

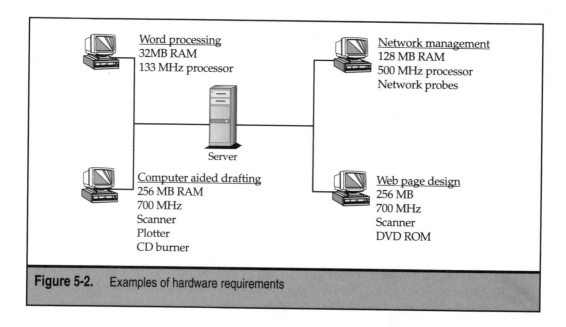

Figure 5-2.   Examples of hardware requirements

Another consideration when outfitting your clients is that you must pay attention to what their roles will be in your organization. The clients that will be performing Web design will need the appropriate design software. The clients that will be responsible for performance and tuning your network will need the right monitoring and performance tools.

If you are in a situation where you have a mixed environment (as shown in Figure 5-3), you'll need to make sure you have the right version of the client software to interface with the server OS. For instance, Novell offers several different flavors of its client software that will make other OS clients compatible.

While Microsoft and many other vendors provide client software for a wide variety of operating systems and network packages, the bidirectional sharing of resources in terms of security and efficiency is not equivalent across all platforms.

The need to integrate multiple platforms in an enterprise environment is certain to arise given that new networks are rarely built from scratch but evolve from existing systems. The "drawbacks" in having to integrate Windows for Workgroups, NetWare, Windows 95, and Macintosh users on the network can be minimized with careful planning. However, you should keep an eye on your resource utilization and, if you can afford it, upgrade hardware and software to reduce the diversity of platforms in the enterprise.

While all these clients can be connected to the network, maintaining or achieving the required level of functionality for these clients may be impossible, because client performance or security is insufficient. For example, a small workgroup with clients that need to access NT, NetWare, and UNIX resources could be configured with the entire collection of standard client protocols to provide these services. Unfortunately, the memory demands of the network drivers would leave the clients without enough memory to run applications.

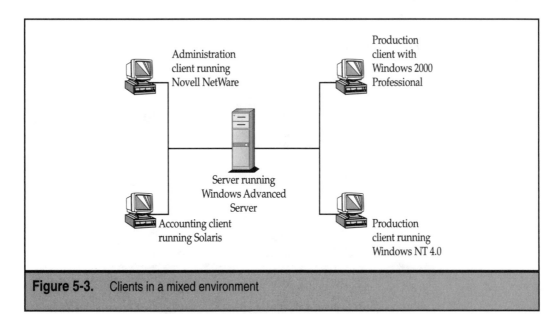

Figure 5-3.   Clients in a mixed environment

The common sense approach suggests implementing upgraded hardware and operating systems whenever financial constraints permit.

Licensing Issues

Complicating the client software issue even more is licensing. You are not allowed to buy one piece of software and then install it on every computer in your organization. Sure, it saves you a whole bunch of money, but the software manufacturers tend to pooh-pooh the practice. Rather, if your organization requires copies of PageMaker on every client, you can buy the piece of software and then buy the number of licenses you will need for the number of clients that will run that software.

But licensing issues don't end there. Now, let's say you want a piece of software for several machines, but you're on a budget. No problem. You can install a piece of licensed software on all of your computers, yet only buy a license for one machine. As Figure 5-4 demonstrates, this doesn't mean you've gotten over on the software company; rather, it means that only one person will be able to use the software at a time. In this example, the company has purchased two licenses for PageWizard. However, with two clients already using the licenses, no one else can use them at that time.

NOTE:　If you decide to buy a limited number of licenses, expect an employee or two to complain, "the software isn't working." In fact, it will work just fine; it's just that all the licenses are being used.

Licensing can be a complicated issue, especially if you have software with expiring licenses. You should also keep the issue in your mind after you've done your initial build-out. In the future, if you add more client computers, make sure you've paid for enough licenses.

So what happens if you don't have licensed software? A couple things. First, if the software is intuitive enough, it may simply not work. On the other hand, if it does work,

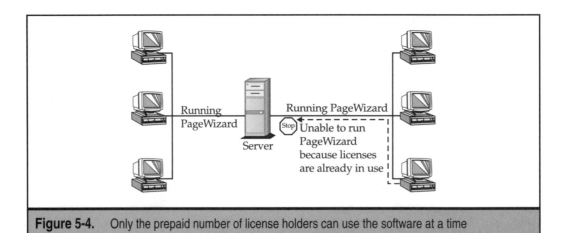

Figure 5-4.　Only the prepaid number of license holders can use the software at a time

you run the risk of facing some serious monetary fines and penalties if you're caught with unauthorized software.

Login and User IDs

When connecting clients, you should make sure that the users who make use of those machines are required to log onto the network using a user name and password. There are some OSes (Windows 95/98 for instance) that don't require user names and passwords. It's best to steer toward OSes like Windows NT/2000, which require the login information.

Using these authentication tools accomplishes a couple things. First, it's a very easy, basic layer of security. It's one of the easiest ways to keep unwanted people out of your network. Also, it can keep users limited to the systems they're authorized to use. This isn't some draconian way to oppress the worker; rather, it's a good way to ensure that people aren't screwing up pieces of your network that they aren't familiar with.

With some OSes, if you have multiple people using the same machine, the login and user ID can generate a customized workspace for each individual. Rather than worry about trashing something that the first shift person is working on, you can create different desktop environments. This can also alleviate any issues that arise if one employee wants Homer Simpson wallpaper and another favors cuddly kittens.

User names and passwords are good things for identification. Especially in an environment where money will be exchanged for goods or services, you'll want to make sure you know who conducted a transaction on your system.

WEB BROWSERS

If yours is an organization that will conduct business directly with the public, there is one type of client that you are most likely to rely upon to get people (and their money) to your business. The Internet has changed the way the world does business (which is why you picked up this book in the first place), and the main way people link with companies is with a Web browser.

Web browsers may seem like simple, nondescript little pieces of software, but understanding how they work and how their bits and pieces function can help you streamline your e-business offerings and bring unique, useful content that will help your business.

In this section, we'll talk about how browsers work, what makes them work, and some of the popular browsers that your customers are likely to be using. But before we get into the nuts and bolts of Web browsers, here's a little Internet history lesson.

Roots

In 1989, CERN computer scientist Tim Berners-Lee proposed a global hypertext project, which would eventually become the World Wide Web. The World Wide Web was originally conceived and developed for large physics collaborations, which demanded immediate information sharing between physicists working in different universities and institutes around the world. The project worked under the assumption that people could work collaboratively by putting information on a Web of hypertext documents.

The World Wide Web is installed on servers, and client software—called a browser—accesses the information stored on the servers. The software locates the information by searching for a link's Uniform Resource Locator (URL).

Next, it uses Hypertext Transfer Protocol (HTTP) to get the document, which is coded in Hypertext Markup Language (HTML). The browser's mission in life is to communicate over the Internet with Web servers using HTTP. When you first open your browser, it follows a link that reads a document written in HTML and then displays it for you in a window. For example, let's say that a customer is visiting your Web site. Your Web page is maintained as a HTML file, and to access this document, your customer's browser has used the HTTP protocol to request this document to the Web server where it is stored. This is illustrated in Figure 5-5.

The Web server then responds to the customer's browser request and by following the HTTP protocol it sends the requested document (your Web site) to the customer's browser. After downloading the requested file, the browser interprets the HTML in the document and displays it on your screen.

From its humble beginnings allowing physicists to share information in a real-time environment, the World Wide Web has gained usefulness and momentum until now it is a household phrase and one of the biggest driving forces in commerce.

Nuts and Bolts

But most of us have really only one frame of reference when looking at the Internet. We see everything through our browser's eyes. It's important to know how browsers have developed and what makes them work so that you can develop the best Web pages that technology allows.

Together with fellow computer scientist Robert Cailliau, Berners-Lee wrote the first World Wide Web client (which ran under NeXTStep) and the first World Wide Web server, along with most of the communications software, defining URLs, HTTP, and HTML. The first browser was a WYSIWYG hypertext browser/editor. The World Wide Web and browser first ran on a NeXt computer in 1990 at CERN and were made available on the Internet the following year.

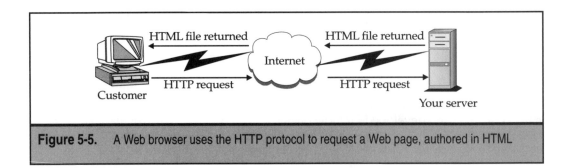

Figure 5-5.   A Web browser uses the HTTP protocol to request a Web page, authored in HTML

The first browser with the point-and-click graphical user interface that we've come to know and love was NCSA Mosaic. If you were one of the first people navigating the World Wide Web with a browser in the early '90s, you'll probably remember visiting NCSA's Web site and downloading Mosaic—for free, no less.

With the exception of some bells, whistles, flashing lights, and gongs that we see on the browsers in use today, the functionality is virtually identical to Mosaic. All the buttons we know and love were there—"Stop," "Forward," "Back," "Refresh." Heck, even the little animation in the upper right-hand corner of the screen showing a busy browser was copied—in some form—by both Netscape and Microsoft. But beyond the surface similarities, Mosaic provided the functional basis for the Web browsers to come.

The core functionality of Web browsers (indeed the World Wide Web, itself) comes from HTML coding. Also, in an e-business setting, it's necessary to provide a secure tunnel through which information can be passed without having to worry about its defense. Let's look at how these mechanisms, HTML and SSL, allow Web browsers to share information across a multitude of platforms and ensure a secure way to exchange sensitive information such as credit card numbers. Web page design gets spiced up when designers use Extensible Markup Language (XML) and CGI scripts, which keep Web pages from being stale.

HTML

Though most computers look the same on the outside (putty-colored box, monitor, keyboard, and mouse), inside they are not the same. Different platforms use different hardware and software. Not to mention that they were developed by different companies with different ideas about how things should work. Because of this, computers can rarely talk to each other without some help.

A Common Language   It helps to think about computers like they are different nations. Like the peoples of different locations in the world, they developed their own customs, their own languages, their own currencies, and so on. Computers are the same way. Natively, they have different ways to talk to their disk drives; their monitors don't talk to the computers the same way; and sometimes the plugs connecting peripherals are shaped differently than other computers'. Again, as with independant nations, that's all fine and well until the two different types of computers have to interact.

Like two different tribesmen meeting to trade beads and feathers for antelope meat, computers need a way to communicate (no one likes to get screwed over on a simple antelope trade). Maybe each trader has learned enough of the other's language to make the transaction. Maybe they use hand signals and gestures to negotiate and haggle. Whatever the means, there is a method to understand the other person.

This is where Hypertext Markup Language (HTML) comes into play. As with our antelope meat-trading friends, a common form of communication is necessary to get any business done. HTML is a language that exists so that computers of any platform can share the information on the World Wide Web. Since it is ridiculous to assume that only one kind of computer would use the Internet, a common language must be used, as shown in Figure 5-6.

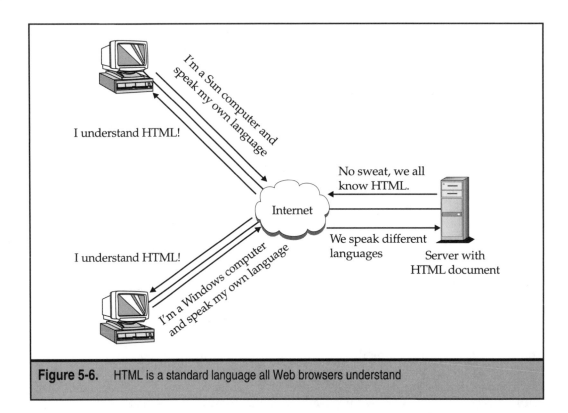

Figure 5-6. HTML is a standard language all Web browsers understand

HTML 4.0 is the latest version of the Web's core markup language. The biggest improvements over earlier versions of HTML come through the definition of new tags and extending old tags to offer more flexibility in working with forms and tables.

> **NOTE:** Tags give specific formatting instructions to your browser that explain how something should be displayed. For instance, a tag will determine in what size, what color, and what font text is displayed.

HTML may be a language that's taken for granted. After all, virtually every Web site works with little or no incident, no matter what version of HTML is running. That's for two reasons: First, no version of HTML will render an older version obsolete. Therefore a certain level of backward compatibility is assured. The worst that can happen is that some funky new capability won't work if a user shows up at an enhanced site with a browser that hasn't yet implemented that function.

Second, browser manufacturers stay on top of developments in markup languages. In the aggressive browser market, browser manufacturers incorporate new tools and functions even before the standards process has been completed.

The Latest Version The most obvious improvement between HTML 4.0 and its predecessor (version 3.2) is the approach to stylistic elements and attributes, particularly the phaseout of certain elements. The idea is to let Web authors separate a document's content and structure from its layout. This becomes more and more important as Web content is downloaded to televisions and personal digital assistants, as well as computers.

The most notable improvements in HTML 4.0 will let you build pages for your organization that are more attractive, animated, interactive, and user-friendly than what you could build in the past. Another boon comes if you use forms on your Web page. HTML 4.0 allows you to create forms that look better, act better, and are easier for users to navigate. Further, even without animation tools, you can make Web pages more exciting by combining the new and extended tags in the HTML 4.0 specification with relatively simple JavaScripts. (We talk about Java in more detail later in this chapter.)

So what's next for HTML? Experts tend to think that HTML has gone about as far as it can with HTML 4.0. The greatest future developments in markup languages are likely to come from XML (Extensible Markup Language), which allows developers to create customized tags.

XML

The newest markup language is XML. XML is useful because a document can be written once and then displayed on many different products: a computer monitor, a cellular-phone display, a device for the blind where it is translated into voice, and so on. Because of this attribute, an XML document can outlive the authoring and display technologies available when it was written.

NOTE: This is, of course, theoretical. Since XML is such a new markup language, it hasn't had a chance to outlive current authoring or display technologies. Take its permanence with a grain of salt. After all, the next great thing may be on its way next year.

XML is expected to have an influence outside the Internet, especially, for example, for people who produce content meant to appear across a variety of media, as shown in Figure 5-7. XML's real strength for Web content is how it interacts with the Document Object Model (DOM), which is an interface that defines how data is accessed in a document. Using the DOM, programmers can write dynamic content in a standardized way. For instance, a piece of text might become underlined when a user rolls a cursor over it.

For all the bells and whistles on the Internet, ultimately what is important is the content available on the Web sites you visit. Unfortunately, content is routinely tied to how the user's browser will display the content. Think about it, how many times have you seen a disclaimer in miniscule writing at the bottom of a Web page reading "Best viewed at 800 x 600"?

XML ameliorates that issue because rather than specifying where on the screen something needs to be displayed, Web builders can specify how the document is structured. For instance, a Web page author can specify the document's title, a table of contents, the author, and so on. Then, any device with an XML browser (a PC-based browser, a palmtop, even—gulp—WebTV) can render the document, tailored to that device's specific settings.

XML's most notable feature, however, is its extensibility. Your organization can use XML for future applications and content needs. XML is also being considered as a

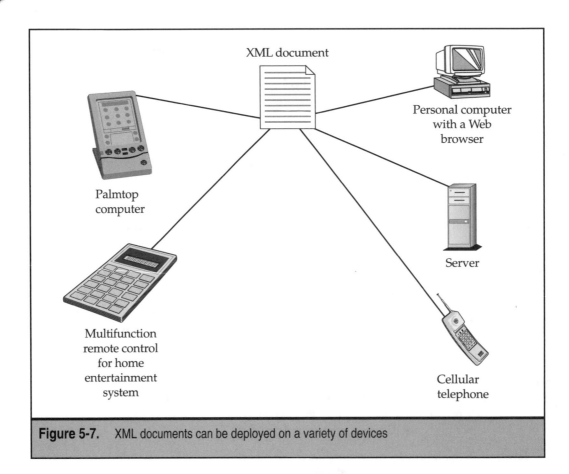

XML document

Personal computer
with a Web
browser

Palmtop
computer

Server

Multifunction
remote control
for home
entertainment
system

Cellular
telephone

Figure 5-7.   XML documents can be deployed on a variety of devices

standard for exchanging data as well as documents. For example, you may find your company sharing your database with a supply-chain partner across the Internet using an XML application.

Acronym Overload   If you're getting acronym overload in this section—and why wouldn't you, because we're talking about HTML, HTTP, XML, WYSIWYG, whatever—let's talk about how XML works with all the other acronyms out there.

Even though HTML 4.0 is a beefier markup language that gives more stylish results than its predecessors, it can't deliver the best goods all by itself. One of the tools that can be used side-by-side with HTML is XML.

HTML 4.0 is the latest permutation of an existing language. XML is an entirely new language with its own set of tags. HTML is a subset of SGML (Standard Generalized Markup Language), which has been used for layout in the print world for years.

XML exists somewhere in between HTML and SGML. XML allows you to create and define your own elements, which are particularly important to large-scale and niche publishers.

Basically, HTML can't be used to define new applications, but XML can. For example, both the Resource Description Format (RDF) and the Channel Description Format (CDF) are applications that were defined using XML. XML and HTML are really more like cousins than siblings.

XML documents can be read by SGML viewing tools. However, XML isn't as intricate as SGML, and as a bonus, it's designed to work across bandwidth-inhibited networks, like the Internet.

Most likely, HTML, SGML, and XML will be used wherever their strengths lie. None is expected to become the do-all and kick the others off the scene. In the future, HTML will likely remain the simplest way to publish most data quickly on the Web. If the data has a longer-term use or requires more structure, Web builders will likely rely on XML.

E-commerce and XML   So does XML work well for e-commerce? You bet it does.

Ideally, XML can be used to exchange information from catalog to catalog, from catalog to payment system, and from payment system to payment system. XML has two goodies to make this goal a reality, and it does it in two important ways:

▼   **Content definition**   One of the tools in the works is a way to define data elements that all businesses would have in common. The so-called Commerce Core would define how to tag things like organization name and address, products, prices, and quantities.

▲   **Information exchange**   Text-based XML is perfect for exchanging transaction data between servers. Common Business Language (CBL) is proposed as a way to describe product- and service-catalog software, data about business rules, and other similar needs.

The long-term goal is for industry groups to use CBL as a common basis for specific tools. Several initiatives have already been announced that will likely enhance e-commerce in the future:

▼   **Open Buying on the Internet** (OBI)   OBI is a standard for international business-to-business purchasing across the Internet. OBI is based on current Internet standards (HTML and SSL, for instance).

■   **Open Trading Protocol** (OTP)   This will allow trading with consumers over the Internet. Rules can range from how to offer items for sale to payment options to product delivery and customer service.

▲   **Internet Content and Exchange** (ICE)   ICE will be used to enable the site-to-site exchange of online assets, whether those are content or applications.

XML is expected to beef up and energize e-commerce. It will let vendors tag products and those items' associated information (such as price, size, or color) in a standard way, making it easy for customers to comparison-shop across the Web.

Meanwhile, Netscape and Microsoft will likely continue to expand XML browser support with more XML applications, style sheet support designed for XML, and XML hyperlinking protocols.

SSL

As with any transaction, the business of e-business is consummated when the buyer forks over some money to the seller. In the flesh and blood world we live in, this is no problem. You buy a CD at a store and pay the clerk with some cash or a credit card. The transaction is usually uneventful, and bandits rarely take your money.

But it's different online.

Unless there is some mechanism in place to shield outside viewers from catching your customers' credit card numbers—or viewing personal or proprietary information—e-business is in danger of corruption. Happily, RSA Data Security Inc. has a solution that has become an Internet standard for security. In fact, if you've ever purchased anything online, you've no doubt used the Secure Sockets Layer (SSL) Protocol.

The root of SSL is *public key encryption,* which is widely used for authentication and encryption. Public key encryption is a technique that uses a pair of asymmetric keys for both encryption and decryption. Each pair of keys consists of two parts:

▼ The *public key* is made public by distributing it freely.

▲ The *private key* is never distributed but always kept secret.

Data that is encrypted with the public key can be decrypted only with the private key. Conversely, data that is encrypted with the private key can only be decrypted with the public key. SSL's asymmetrical nature is what makes it so useful. Encryption is covered in more detail in Chapter 12.

Authentication   On the Internet, you can tell someone that you're the President of the United States and no one would be able to prove that you're not (unless you're talking to the *actual* President, then he'll know for sure you're lying). During the course of normal Web browsing, this isn't such a big deal, but when it comes time for money to change hands, it's clear that you need to know who you're dealing with. This is where *authentication* helps.

Authentication is the process of verifying identity so that one party can be sure that another party is who it claims to be. Figure 5-8 shows how SSL-based authentication works.

Suppose Larry from accounting needs to buy a gross of number two pencils. He goes to Pencilworld.com, places an order, and is ready to enter a secure site, which maintains

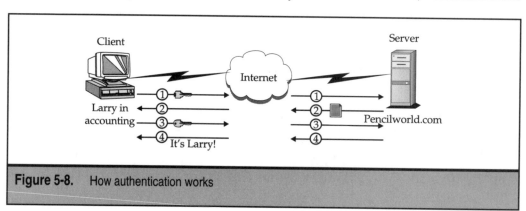

Figure 5-8.   How authentication works

his company's procurement information. But before he types in the number, Larry's computer must prove to Pencilworld.com that he's allowed to order supplies from them. Here's how it works:

1. Pencilworld.com wants to authenticate Larry, who has a pair of keys, one public and one private. Larry sends his public key to Pencilworld.com.

2. Pencilworld.com generates a random message and sends it back to Larry.

3. Larry uses his private key to encrypt the message and returns it to Pencilworld.com.

4. Pencilworld.com receives this message and decrypts it using Larry's previously transmitted public key. Pencilworld.com compares the decrypted message with the one they originally sent to Larry. If they match, Pencilworld.com knows they are talking to Larry.

Using this method, an imposter wouldn't know what Larry's private key is and would be unable to properly encrypt the random message for Pencilworld.com to check.

Certificates   However, the method just described is not foolproof. Someone else can go to Pencilworld.com and say they are Larry in accounting, and then use his own public and private keys to get access to the procurement account. The rapscallion can say he's Larry and then prove it by encrypting something with his private key. Then Pencilworld.com can't tell the bandit isn't Larry.

> **NOTE:**   There are, of course, more checks and means of security in e-business Web sites, especially when money is changing hands. But let's follow this example for the sake of explaining how basic SSL works in a Web browser.

To ameliorate this problem, the standards community has come up with an object called a *certificate.* A certificate contains several components that make it unique to each person, for instance:

▼   The certificate issuer's name

■   The entity for which the certificate is being issued

■   The public key of the subject

▲   A number of time stamps

By using certificates, everybody can examine Larry's certificate to make sure it is genuine. Assuming Larry has maintained tight control over his private key and no one has managed to forge it, Figure 5-9 shows how a certificate is used in negotiating a SSL transaction.

1. Pencilworld.com receives Larry's first message, examines the certificate, and makes sure it belongs to Larry.

2. Pencilworld.com can trust that the public key is, indeed, Larry's and then request Larry prove his identity, following the procedure we outlined.

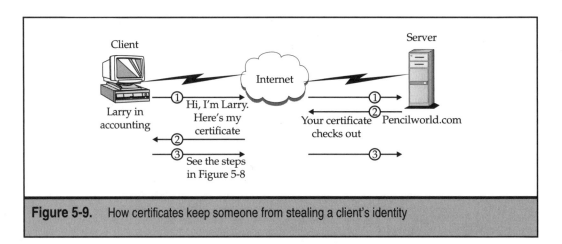

Figure 5-9. How certificates keep someone from stealing a client's identity

This is by no means the definitive tome on World Wide Web security, simply a quick look at the basic tools browsers use to form basic, safe connections. For more detailed information about e-business security, see the chapters in Section 4.

CGI

The Common Gateway Interface (CGI) is a standard for connecting external applications with Web servers. A plain HTML document that your Web browser retrieves is **static**. That means it exists in a constant state: a text file that doesn't change. Conversely, a CGI program is **executed** in real time, so that it can output **dynamic** information. That means the content is plastic and can change.

CGI specifies how to pass arguments to the executing program as part of the HTTP request. The program will generate some HTML code, which will be passed back to the client's browser, but it can also request URL redirection. The CGI program can, for example, access information in a database (like an online catalog) and format the results as HTML. A CGI program can be any program that can accept command line arguments.

The programming language Perl is a common choice for writing CGI scripts. Some Web servers require CGI programs to reside in a special directory, often "/cgi-bin," but better servers provide ways to distinguish CGI programs so that they can be kept in the same directories as the HTML files to which they are related.

Whenever the server receives a CGI execution request, it creates a new process to run the external program. If the process fails to terminate for some reason, or if requests are received faster than the server can respond to them, the server may become swamped with processes.

NOTE: In order to improve performance, Netscape devised NSAPI and Microsoft developed the ISAPI standard, which allows CGI-like tasks to run as part of the main server process, thus avoiding the overhead of creating a new process to handle each CGI invocation.

In essence, here is how CGI works. Let's say that you wanted to put your store's catalog on the World Wide Web. If you use CGI, you create a program that will transmit information to the database engine, then receive the results from the database, then transmit them to the client. This is an example of a gateway, and this is where CGI's roots are.

Since a CGI program is executable on the server side, it is like letting the world run a program on your system, which isn't the safest thing to do. As a result, there are some security precautions you should be mindful of when using CGI programs. The most basic measure that has the greatest impact on the typical Web user is that CGI programs need to reside in a special directory, so that the Web server knows to execute the program rather than just display it to the browser. This directory is usually under direct control of the Webmaster, prohibiting users from creating their own CGI programs (unfortunately, sometimes enthusiastic employees can do more harm than good).

CGI is like one of those little fuzzy animals Greenpeace has on posters, buttons, and tear-jerking commercials. Because of Active Server Pages (which we talk about later in this chapter), CGI is becoming an extinct species. Expect to see more and more Web pages designed and built with ASP and fewer and fewer pages with CGI content.

Microsoft Internet Explorer

If Bill Gates hadn't been so pushy about getting his browser into the hands of every man, woman, child, and dog in the world, he probably wouldn't have clashed horns with the feds. But the truth of the matter is that Internet Explorer is a very useful, competent piece of Web browsing software.

The browser was introduced to take on Netscape Navigator. After not too long, Microsoft's browser had surpassed the popular upstart.

Overview

In the years since its inception, Internet Explorer has been a constantly evolving piece of software. The latest release of the popular browser is version 5.5. Like previous upgrades, it adds more tools that streamline Web browsing and the user's interface with the browser.

The name of the game with Internet Explorer 5.5 (from here out, let's call it IE 5.5 and save a gallon of printer's ink) is simplicity. Compared to earlier versions of the browser, IE 5.5 is a lean, mean browsing machine.

Features

Microsoft makes downloading and customizing IE 5.5 much easier and faster compared to earlier releases of their browser. Its setup routine gives you control over exactly which pieces you want to take the time to download and install.

For instance, if you want Shockwave and DHTML but not Java or Outlook Express, you can make that choice and save your time and hard drive space. Later, if you come across a page that requires one of the features you opted not to install initially, IE 5.5 will let you add it then.

To make browsing less of a head-scratcher, Microsoft has taken away a lot of the techno-cryptic terms that abound on the World Wide Web and confuse normal people (i.e., your customers). For instance, try to pull up a nonexistent Web page and you won't see the familiar "Not Found" message anymore. Rather, you'll see a more soothing message explaining why the page may not be there and offering suggestions on what the problem could be. This feature is nice and fuzzy for the user, and emblematic of a kinder, gentler Microsoft.

One of the browser's nicest features is for those who have a hard time typing things exactly as they need to be. As anyone who has used the Internet knows, one letter or dot out of place, and you're going nowhere. Microsoft helps ease the pains of those with fat fingers or an inability to spell with its AutoCorrect feature. AutoCorrect fixes common typos in Web addresses. Type "http:/," for instance, and it will automatically change your typo to "http://."

The most impressive addition to IE 5.5 is its tweaked-out AutoSearch feature. For instance, if you type common words into IE 4.0's address bar, the browser will take you to Yahoo and find some possible links. IE 5.5's AutoSearch make searching even more refined. Now if you type in common words, IE 5.5 opens a new pane full of possible links, while automatically linking to the most probable site. The Search Assistant on IE 5.5 is more powerful and flexible than in previous versions. In the previous version, you were allowed to pick which default search engine you liked, but that was the extent of it. In IE 5.5, however, clicking the Search button calls up a pane, which allows you to select different search options ("Find a Web page," "Find a person's address," "Find a map," and so on). If you don't like the results you get from the first engine, just click the Next button to pass the same search along to the next engine.

The AutoComplete function has also been improved in IE 5.5. Now, rather than simply completing previously viewed URLs in the Address box—and possibly sending users to the wrong site with similar letters—the new and improved AutoComplete gives you a drop-down list of sites that you can choose from.

The following lists some of the other highlights you'll find in IE 5.5:

▼   FTP sites appear as files and folders, not text lists.

■   Saved Web pages include all graphics. In previous versions of the software, saved Web pages had blank spaces where the GIFs and JPEGs used to be.

■   The Windows Radio allows you to listen to online music and news from Internet radio stations (Microsoft even gives you a list of stations to get your started) while you browse.

■   You can get links associated to the site you're visiting.

■   Your toolbar can be customized. Don't want the History button taking up real estate? Get rid of it. Want Discuss within easy reach? Just add it.

■   The browser supports Profiles, so multiple users can maintain separate accounts on the same computer.

▲   Those who want to see what a Web page looks like before it's sent to the printer will appreciate IE 5.5's print preview mode.

Netscape Navigator

One could argue that the World Wide Web didn't really take off until Netscape Navigator took a lot of the fuss out of connecting. Let's face it, Mosaic was a revolutionary piece of software, but it was a pain in the rear to install and get up and running. Navigator took a lot of the headaches out of installation and made its creator, Mark Andreessen, a very, very wealthy 24-year-old when the company went public.

Like Internet Explorer, Navigator includes buttons and core functionality very much like those of its predecessor, Mosaic.

Overview

Netscape and Microsoft are in a constant state of one-upsmanship. After one company releases the latest version of its browser, the other one responds shortly with the latest, greatest version of its software. Ultimately, the consumer is the winner, because it keeps the two competitive.

Like IE 5.5 (and I'm sure Netscape will appreciate the comparison), Netscape improves browser performance in Navigator 6 by reducing the size of its program and getting Web pages to load faster. And, as in previous releases of the software, a bunch more bells and whistles are added.

Features

To get Navigator's new level of efficiency, Netscape did some work at the heart of the Web browsing beast: the rendering engine. The rendering engine is a piece of software that actually draws the Web page according to the incoming HTML code. Navigator 6 renders its Web pages much faster than its predecessor, all because of a new engine under the hood.

The browser is built on top of Gecko, an open-source rendering engine that is small, fast, and standards-compliant, and that also happens to be highly customizable. It uses XUL, an XML-based user interface language. So what does that mean for the end user? Anyone who knows how to edit XUL files can customize Netscape's entire interface. For example, your organization could alter the browser to conform to your specific corporate needs. You could remove the Preferences settings so that employees can't screw around with security settings. Or you could add buttons to the taskbar that would let supply chain partners come directly to specific pages.

Conformity   Gecko's greatest advantage is its compliance with World Wide Web Consortium standards.

NOTE: The World Wide Web Consortium is the organization that defines World Wide Web standards.

Its full support for technologies like HTML 4.0 means that Web site builders will be able to write smaller, more concise Web pages that work equally well in both Navigator 6, IE 5.5, and any other browsers conforming to the World Wide Web Consortium's standards. Lack of conformity has been one of the biggest problems afflicting Web design. In theory, now that the big boys (Netscape and Microsoft) offer better standards support, more sites will deliver richer, more robust content that makes good use of these new and improved formatting technologies.

Again, Netscape takes its lead from Explorer when it comes to downloading, configuring, and installing the browser. Instead of having to download the entire browser complete with extra features to get Netscape 6, you download a small installer that lets you pick the components you want to install, and then downloads those components into your computer.

Remember the first time you figured out how to change the wallpaper on your desktop or add funny little noises when your computer opened a file, closed a file, or crashed? Netscape picks up the mantle of personalization by adding skins, which can take old, plain Web browsers and give them a little personal kick. Rather than being stuck with the buttons that Netscape predefined for the browser, users can customize their browser to reflect their complex personalities, inasmuch as a Web browser can be used as a form of self-expression.

Security Enhancements   How could something so innocuous sounding as a "cookie" be a safety risk? In the world of Web browsing, cookies—those teensy, tiny pieces of data many Web sites maintain on your hard drive—are usually harmless; like a cute little cocker spaniel named "Peaches." For instance, if you go to a site that offers personalized content, like Amazon.com, cookies are used to identify you so that they can bring you content custom tailored to you (and try to sell you books and DVDs based on what you bought before). But some privacy experts warn that the little cocker spaniel can become a hungry, one-eyed pit bull named "Mauler" if nefarious types use cookies. They worry that companies might use cookies to track users without their knowledge. Netscape 6 addresses that concern with its Cookie Manager.

Another security enhancement is Netscape 6's Password Manager. This tool lets you manage the usernames and passwords you use on various Web sites. When you submit a password on any site, the Password Manager pops up to ask if you'd like to save that password for future use. If you choose to use this feature, the next time you return to a site where you've stored the password, the browser automatically fills out the username and password. But what keeps evildoers away from your password list? Navigator protects your stored passwords with a master password that you create the first time you use Password Manager. Also, Navigator 6 encrypts the password files so that they can't be stolen from your hard drive.

Netscape seems to love Microsoft's terminology, because it introduces a new tool called "My Sidebar." This tool displays Web content on the side of the main browsing window, which is akin to a television's picture-in-picture feature.

My Sidebar exists on the left side of the browser window. Individual tabs, which correspond to Web pages you want to monitor, are clicked to bring Web content to that window. My Sidebar panels come from both Netscape sites and third-party content providers such as the Weather Channel.

JAVA

HTML does a good job of providing basic operations for a Web page. You can show text in different sizes, colors, fonts, and so forth. You can also provide links to other pages and display pictures. But in 1995 Sun Microsystems came up with a new programming language for the Internet that provides more complex tools that deliver more visually and functionally impressive features.

Java Overview

Java is an object-oriented programming language and its main claim to fame is its portability. That means that the same Java program will run on any platform without having to be rewritten or recompiled. Java programs are able to run on PCs, Macs, mainframes, and even consumer products, like PDAs or cellular telephones.

How It Works

Java's portability is achieved because of the way that it is compiled and run. First, the source code is compiled into *bytecode*. Bytecode is not the executable machine language you get when compiling source from other programming languages. Rather, it contains instructions to the Java virtual machine (JVM). The JVM resides on the platform on which the program will run.

The virtual machine serves as an interface between the bytecode and the machine's processor. It interprets the bytecode one instruction at a time and translates it into the machine's native code. The machine's processor then carries out the operation. This is illustrated in Figure 5-10.

Any platform with a virtual machine will run any Java program, using its own instruction set. Most of the major operating systems, such as Windows, UNIX, and Mac, have their own Java virtual machines. The major Web browsers, such as Internet Explorer and Netscape Navigator, have their own virtual machines.

If the upside of Java is its portability, then the downside is its speed. Because Java is interpreted, it does not run as fast as other languages. Also, since Java does its work on the client computer, the clients will take a performance hit.

How You Can Use It

So, given all this information about Java, how can you use it in your organization? There are two types of Java programs that you can write:

▼ **Applications** are stand-alone programs that do not require a browser to execute.

▲ **Applets** are Java programs embedded in HTML documents and run on Web browsers.

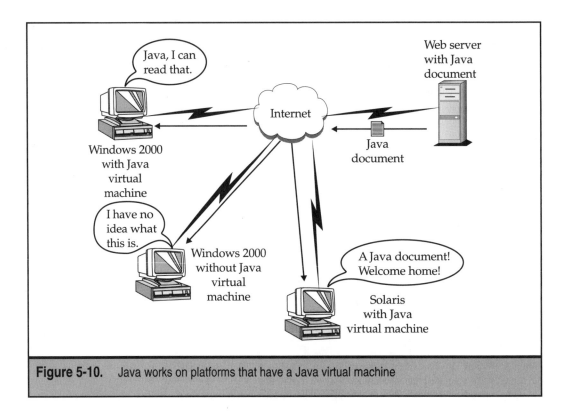

Figure 5-10. Java works on platforms that have a Java virtual machine

When you download a page containing a Java applet, you are actually downloading the bytecode for that applet. The bytecode is interpreted by your Web browser and run on your computer.

Java 2

Since its introduction in 1995, Java has undergone some maturing. The latest permutation of Java is Java 2. Java 2 builds on the foundation that was constructed by Java, plus it adds a number of new features that will enhance application and applet design and construction.

Overview

Rather than introduce one single language, the Sun developers designed Java 2 to work in devices of various sizes that perform varying function. Java 2 comes in three flavors:

▼ **Java 2 Platform, Standard Edition (J2SE)** provides appropriate functionality for the desktop/workstation devices.

■ **Java 2 Platform, Enterprise Edition (J2EE)** has all the functionality required for heavy-duty server systems.

▲ **Java 2 Platform, Micro Edition (J2ME)** is intentionally small to fit reduced memory consumer devices and can distribute functionality, as appropriate, between the resource-constrained client and the server.

Each of the new Java platform editions combines Sun Java virtual machines, the Java programming language, core packages, and optional packages. The new editions share many core packages and the Java programming language to facilitate developer productivity and compatibility. To further refine the target markets for each edition, especially the consumer electronics market addressed by J2ME, Sun will provide sets of application programming interfaces (APIs), called *profiles*, with the specific edition.

A specific profile teamed with a specific edition provides a complete deployment environment for devices in a specific vertical market. Examples of profiles include a wireless profile that spans low-end cellular phones and pagers, or another for handheld devices, such as PDAs and mobile point-of-sale terminals.

Applications on all three editions can be developed using a common application programming model. Applications developed using the programming model will scale upward from systems built with Java 2 Platform, Micro Edition to systems built with Java 2 Platform, Enterprise Edition.

Features

Though we've been talking about Java 2, let's shake your understanding of it up a little. Even though the latest release is, technically, Java 2, Sun complicates the issue of version numbering by identifying its latest release of the software as Java 2, Version 1.3.

Oh, my aching head.

J2SE v 1.3 (did you get all that alphabet soup?) is Sun's first upgrade release of the Java 2 Platform, Standard Edition since its release in December 1998.

The new features of J2SE v 1.3 include:

▼ **Faster performance** The Java HotSpot Client VM and performance-tuned libraries are the fastest versions of Java yet.

■ **Easier Web deployment** New features such as applet caching and Java Optional Package installation through the Java Plug-in technology enhance the speed and flexibility with which Java technology–based applets and applications can be deployed. Java Plug-in technology is a component of the Java 2 Runtime Environment, Standard Edition v 1.3 and enables Java technology–based applets and applications to execute.

■ **Security enhancements** New support for RSA electronic signing, dynamic trust management, X.509 certificates, and verification of Netscape-signed files provide more ways for developers to protect electronic data.

■ **Ease of development** A bunch of new features and development tools in J2SE v 1.3 enables easier and faster development of powerful Web-enabled or stand-alone Java applications.

▲ **Enterprise interoperability** The addition of RMI/IIOP and the Java Naming and Directory Interface (JNDI) to the J2SE 1.3 release enhances enterprise interoperability of the Java 2 Platform, Standard Edition. RMI/IIOP improves connectivity to back-end systems supporting CORBA. JNDI provides access to directories that support the popular Lightweight Directory Access Protocol (LDAP) among others.

JavaBeans

Sun makes Java easier to use by the use of JavaBeans. JavaBeans are software components that can be plugged into or removed from Web pages with relative ease. Software components can be added into applications by people who are skilled in Web page construction, but who are not necessarily skilled in programming. It's easy to understand software components like JavaBeans if you think about a stereo system.

Each system is made up of several separate components: CD player, amplifier, receiver, tape deck, and so on. Each of those components had to be built by skilled electronics engineers using small, complicated parts (integrated circuits, wires, circuit boards, and the like). Additionally, each component has a series of controls on the front that regulate the radio station, track number, volume, and so forth. On the back of each component are various plugs that allow you to connect all the equipment together.

As the stereo's owner, you are expected to understand the controls and figure out which cords plug in where. But that's the extent of what you're expected to know to operate a stereo; you don't need to know how all the gizmos and gadgets inside the individual components interconnect.

Now, compare this to a Web page. An HTML page at an online seller allows you to select an item from the catalog, and then buy it using your credit card. The page must provide a mechanism to accept credit card details, a way to indicate the selected product, and a way to finalize the purchase. The Web page would probably be built by someone who can put together the individual components, not a programmer, as shown in Figure 5-11.

The Web page builder constructs the Web page and includes on it three software components:

▼ One that takes credit card details

■ One that allows a customer to select an item

▲ One that displays a button with the word "buy" on it

The publisher "wires" the components together by interconnecting these three software components. The person who built the Web page doesn't know (or need to know) how the credit card component verifies its details or of how the transaction component processes the request.

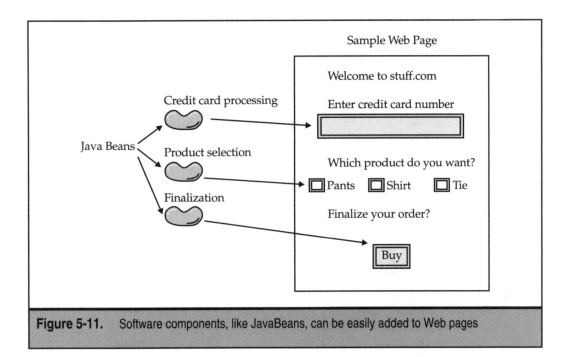

Figure 5-11. Software components, like JavaBeans, can be easily added to Web pages

Why Use JavaBeans

JavaBeans has a number of advantages that set it apart from other component models. The following outlines the highlights of JavaBeans. JavaBeans are:

- ▼ **Portable** They are scripted in Java with no platform-native code.
- ■ **Lightweight** It's possible to use a component as small as a push button or as large as a complete database.
- ■ **Easy to create** Creation should be possible with or without complicated development tools.
- ▲ **Hostable in other component models** JavaBeans should be able to run under ActiveX, OpenDoc, or other components. For instance, a JavaBean contained in an ActiveX container, such as a word processor, will behave exactly as if it were a native component.

Enterprise JavaBeans

There are two types of JavaBeans: those working on the client side and those working on the server side. Enterprise JavaBeans (EJB) work on the server side.

EJB enables software developers to build server-side, reusable business objects. However, EJB takes the notion of reusable objects a step further by providing for attribute-based programming to dynamically define such attributes as lifecycle, transaction, security, and persistence behavior in EJB applications.

For example, using attribute-based techniques, the same enterprise bean can exhibit different transactional behavior in different applications. Additionally, the method of persisting an enterprise bean can be altered during deployment without ever having to recode the enterprise bean.

So what does this mean for you, the e-business owner? If you have a bean created for a specific purpose, like processing credit cards, you can send that bean to a number of different systems. On the other hand, if you have to process a certain type of credit card a particular way, you can use the same bean, but it can be modified to give the functionality you need.

ACTIVE SERVER PAGES

Microsoft developed its own way to provide dynamic content for Web pages. By using Microsoft's Active Server Pages (ASP), customized content can be delivered to customers, partners, or the general public.

With ASP, you can build high-powered, dynamic Web server applications from a development environment that combines HTML, scripts, and ActiveX components on the server. Businesses and organizations can use ASP to put a Web front end on existing e-commerce solutions, or to build entirely new Web-based applications.

ASP Overview

ASP integrates Web scripting and components in Internet Information Services (IIS) 5.0 as shown in Figure 5-12. The pages generated by ASP are HTML files with embedded scripting code that executes on the server and can reference ActiveX Server Components.

Running server-side scripts provides a number of advantages. First, the code is secure from hackers: Because the code executes on the server, the Web client never sees the code; it just sees the results. This is a useful feature that prevents users from examining or swiping your code.

Another advantage of ASP is that your server can better manage expensive resources (database connections, for instance) to support more traffic. ASP supports "apartment model threading," which offers a high level of server scalability and performance.

NOTE: Apartment model threading works by giving each thread a copy of the program and global data; the thread then runs in a protected area or "apartment."

ASP keeps your Web site open and available because the code on the server runs closer to the data and back-end systems. This eliminates a lot of low-bandwidth network traffic.

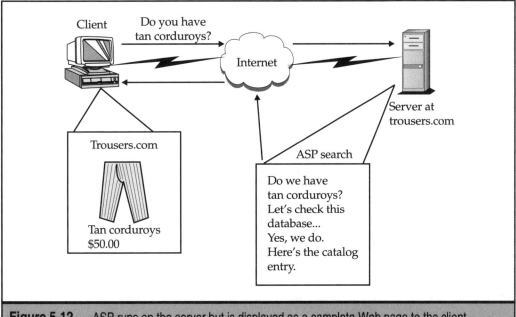

Figure 5-12.   ASP runs on the server but is displayed as a complete Web page to the client

How ASP is Used

ASP is a very useful tool that links your Web pages to a database, for example, providing the content to that page, without having to create its own, unique page. For example, visit your favorite online store. As you search the catalog and browse various items, you'll notice that the basic Web design is the same. The only things different are the products for sale.

This is done because it would be terribly labor intensive, not to mention horribly inefficient, to create an individual Web page for each and every item in the merchant's catalog. But the Web page is there, so where did the content come from?

To generate those pages, a template for every product is used. When customers want to examine items in the catalog, the store's online database is accessed, and the requested information is plugged into the template and displayed as if it were its own, unique Web page. This is shown in Figure 5-13.

ASP is a lot like the popular Common Gateway Interface (CGI), but is easier to use and streamlines the data transfer and sharing process. For instance, ASP accesses information in a form not readable by a client (like a SQL database) and then acts like a gateway between the two to produce information that the client can view and use.

Conversely, using CGI, the server creates as many processes as the number of client requests that are received. The more concurrent requests there are, the more concurrent

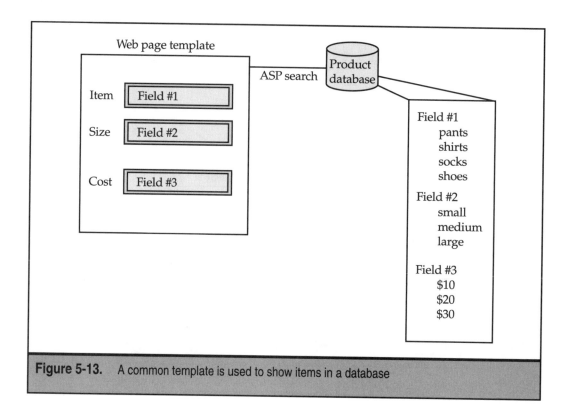

Figure 5-13.   A common template is used to show items in a database

processes created by the server. Creating processes is time consuming and sucks up large amounts of RAM on the server. This can restrict the resources available for sharing from the server application itself, slowing down performance and increasing wait times for connecting clients.

Developing ASP pages

The dynamic content for ASP pages can be developed by Webmasters and programmers who are familiar with HTML and programming languages like Microsoft Visual Basic Scripting Edition, JavaScript, Perl, REXX, or C++.

To develop and use ASP, you'll need IIS 3.0 or better. If you are using a Windows 2000 environment, you already have IIS 5, which comes standard with Windows 2000 servers. If you are running Windows NT, you can download IIS for free from www.microsoft.com/iis.

In order to run ASP, you'll need one of the following Microsoft operating systems:

▼ Windows 2000 Server

■ Windows NT Server 4.0

- Windows NT Workstation 4.0 with Peer Web Services
- Windows 95/98 with Personal Web Server

NOTE: Windows NT 3.51 and Windows NT 4.0 on MIPS will not support ASP.

You can do an awful lot with ASP. Using ActiveX Server Components and any existing applications you've already developed in such languages as C++, Visual Basic, and Java, you can tweak out your site with the content you want. Microsoft included a set of application component objects with IIS 5.0 that incorporate the most commonly requested Web server functions:

- ▼ **Advertisement Rotator**   Will your Web site contain advertising banners at the top of the pages? If so, the Advertisement Rotator will be very helpful. The Advertisement Rotator component automates image presentation. It's perfect for displaying constantly changing advertising, news content, or other images. Individual ASP files use this object to access a list of images: The site administrator simply creates the list and includes image information such as image size, which files to use, and the amount of time to display each file. If you want to track who shows interest in your ads, another management file on the server records the number of times users click the ads.

- ■ **Browser Capabilities**   The Browser Capabilities component identifies the browser type entered in the HTTP header and creates an object with read-only properties conforming to the browser's capabilities (like forms or scripting, for example) that affect your server-side code. The component examines a list of known browsers to get the object's properties. Like the Advertisement Rotator, the feature list is a text file that you can easily maintain as new browsers are developed and introduced.

- ▲ **Content Linking**   Content Linking allows navigation among multiple pages in a long composition, like a long news story. A text file stores a table of filenames: navigating forward or backward retrieves the proceeding or preceding page. This is useful when someone other than a developer needs to maintain the page. When you add, delete, or otherwise modify the pages, this component automatically handles the content linking via the text file, without having to update links in Web pages or scripts.

PLUGINS

Browsers are good at doing what they do best—they browse World Wide Web pages. They don't come, natively, with the tools to watch movies or play music. To add that kind of functionality, they rely on plugins that will let browsers do a number of funky things.

Plugin Overview

Plugins are browser add-ons that are developed by third-party software manufacturers. They can do anything from play video clips to receive Internet radio stations and manage Internet conferencing. There are a slew of plugins out there, so which ones are the most useful?

Unfortunately, that's sort of a loaded question. A plugin's usefulness is a subjective issue. You've probably seen the most common plugins (like Adobe Acrobat and Macromedia's Shockwave and Flash). But how many Web sites have you gone to where a certain featured bit of content can only be viewed with a plugin you've never heard of before? Do you download the plugin and press ahead or do you skip over the plugin and its associated file?

Why Plugins Are Useful

Plugins get somewhat of a bad rap because most people tend to look at plugins as a way to create and propagate cute little online video games or sweet little greeting cards and cartoons. Hardly something you'd want to associate with your e-business, right?

What needs to happen is a little paradigm shift. If you realize that content can be presented in an attractive, slick, appealing way using Flash, rather than simple HTML coding, you might be more inclined to create Web content with that particular plugin.

However, as we alluded to earlier, deciding which plugin to use—if any at all—can be a challenge. You have to decide if your customers will be willing to wait for plugin content to be downloaded to their respective computers. Is what you have to offer important or useful enough to justify the download? Or, will you be able to craft the plugin content not to take hours to download?

By the same token, will you use a plugin that is popular and respected, or roll the dice with a new plugin that hasn't been used anywhere else? Do you think customers will want to download yet another plugin for their browser?

These are all issues you and your IT team will have to hash out. But if you decide to use plugins, there are a number of useful ways they can enhance your online presence.

How Your Business Can Use Them

How you use a plugin is really limited to your own vision. Really, this isn't meant to be some bit of wisdom imparted by Yoda or a self-help guru. The extent of what you can create is guided by your ideas and the physical restrictions of the plugin.

In the subsequent sections, we'll look at three of the top plugins that you can use for your e-business. They provide a range of functionality from displaying static content, like the printed page, to colorful, interactive content that can engage your page visitors.

For instance, using an Acrobat file, your company can publish a catalog that can be downloaded, printed, and referred to offline. Additionally, an Acrobat file can deliver a prospectus without having to clear-cut half a South American rainforest to print the thing.

By using Flash, you can create an interactive catalog with appealing, eye-catching graphics. You can also create more exciting, interesting Web pages without having to learn Java.

Shockwave is a great tool for architects, for instance, who might want to share a set of plans. Using Shockwave, detailed bits and pieces of a blueprint can be embedded within one file for easy review later.

Plugins are really limited to what you want to put out there and how much you want to jump into them. Take a look at what Acrobat, Shockwave, and Flash have to offer, and then you can decide if there are ways you can take advantage of them to deliver content to your clients.

Adobe Acrobat

Even in a dot com world with Java, fantastic interactivity, and features never before conceived by man, there is still great usefulness in the static, printed page. Adobe Acrobat gives you a way to deliver the printed page across the Internet, while keeping all the layout and design attributes stable.

Overview

Adobe Acrobat is a popular way to deliver the written word in the specific layout that the author intended. The latest version of this plugin is version 4.0, which maintains the features that made it popular, while adding a number of much needed improvements.

Features

As compared to its earlier incarnations, Acrobat 4.0 adds a multitude of editing, annotation, and security features. These new tools take Acrobat files where they haven't gone before, allowing users not only to share documents but to collaborate on them as well.

With Acrobat 4.0, you can now highlight or strike through text and draw directly on the page. You can even stamp a page with such messages as "Approved" and "Confidential." Each of these stamps has a corresponding note field, which allows you to add explanations to your stamps.

Acrobat 4.0 doesn't give you a ton of editing tools. It does allow simple text corrections. This may not sound like a big deal, but this mild-mannered feature can be a benefit after a document has been converted into a PDF file. Now, users can fix the typos that have sneaked into the final document without having to regenerate an entire PDF file.

One of the best attributes of Acrobat 4.0 is a feature that has been a long time coming. In the past, if you were reading a PDF file and wanted to copy the information, you'd have to rekey it. With Acrobat 4.0, you can copy entire paragraphs, tables, and images to the Clipboard for use in other programs.

Among the other features of Acrobat 4.0:

▼   Improved use of sticky notes: they're easier to use and organize.

■   You can add voice comments to PDF files.

▲   You can insert applications into PDF documents. For instance, you could embed a database file into a PDF document.

Acrobat 4.0 makes creating PDF files easier than ever before. Now, you can drag files from Explorer into an open Acrobat window, which will start the conversion process. If you use Microsoft Office, Acrobat streamlines the process even further because it inserts a command and a toolbar button that will let you output PDF directly from Microsoft Excel, Word, and PowerPoint.

NOTE: You will not, however, be able to output an Access file directly to PDF.

Acrobat 4.0 also allows you to use the new Web Capture command, which converts HTML pages into PDF files. These files can be read off-line, and you get a better level of reliability when printing off a hard copy. Acrobat maintains all of the hyperlinks in a Web-captured document, so you can simply click the desired link, which will invoke your Web browser.

For more information about Adobe Acrobat, visit Adobe online at www.adobe.com.

Macromedia Flash

Macromedia Flash is all about delivering interactive multimedia over the Web, which is a tricky idea, if you think about it. First, multimedia information requires a lot of bandwidth to download, challenging the throughput capacities of users' analog modems and also other, high-speed connections. Besides, developing, manipulating, and displaying interactive and multimedia information requires a fair amount of sophistication in the authoring and viewing software; it's a sophistication that exceeds HTML editors and Web browsers.

Overview

Macromedia Flash is a tool to deliver resizable and compact full-screen navigation interfaces, technical illustrations, long-form animations, and other eye-candyish effects for your Web site.

Flash allows users to view interactive, animated content that is created not only with the Flash authoring tool, but also with other leading design tools that can export to Macromedia Flash file format.

Features

One of the best features of Flash is that it is included on most Web browsers, since it is included with all copies of Windows 98, Netscape Navigator, America Online, and Macintosh. Thus, 91.8 percent of Web browsers already have the Flash player installed.

For Web surfers who do not already have Flash installed, Macromedia offers the 165KB file—for free—on its Web site, www.macromedia.com.

MSNBC, for instance, uses Flash to create dynamic content that enhances the story and appeals to readers.

Flash uses vector graphics technology. Unlike bitmapped images that are created and ideal for a single, set size, vector images can adapt to all the typical display sizes and resolutions. This is a good tool for showing Web sites uniformly on a variety of devices, from desktop computers, palmtops, or any other Web-browsing device.

Vector images—graphics, charts, maps animations, and so on—fit into files that are smaller than bitmapped GIF and JPG images. The compact files make information transfer much speedier.

Flash content is created with the Macromedia Flash 4 authoring software or Macromedia FreeHand 8 print and Internet design software. Flash 4 allows Web designers to import artwork from their favorite illustration tools, apply transparency, create morphing effects, add interactivity and sound, and animate them over time. The resulting file is saved and published as a Flash Player file.

Flash is an effective way to deliver impressive, catchy content on your Web site, and not just because of its ability to deliver content in much smaller packages (a Flash file is about a quarter the size of a comparable GIF file). Because of Flash's browser saturation, it is a more reliable format than Dynamic HTML, Java, and other advanced Web design formats, because either they are not mutually compatible or they are inconsistent with other browsers.

Shockwave

Like Flash (produced by the same company), Shockwave brings interactive content to your clients across browsers that really weren't designed to dazzle.

Overview

Shockwave's reason for life is about delivering interactive multimedia over the Web, which isn't an easy task. First, multimedia information requires a lot of bandwidth to transfer and taxes the throughput capacities of not only analog modems but also high-speed digital connections. Also, creating and displaying interactive and multimedia information requires a lot of sophistication in the authoring and viewing software.

Shockwave uses a compression technology for integrating multimedia in a Web page for delivery over the Internet or corporate intranets. For example, you can zoom and pan through an illustration and select embedded URL links. You can also interact with net-aware, interactive presentations.

Features

Shockwave may sound a lot like Java, so how do Shockwave and Java stack up against each other? It's an apples to oranges comparison, really.

Java is a good tool for building client/server applications that can contain varying degrees of multimedia. On the other hand, Shockwave is a tool for creating multimedia content that can contain varying degrees of interactivity. Shockwave and Java have some similar capabilities, but each is built for a different task. If you want a Web client/server application, your best bet is to stick with Java. On the other hand, if you want easy-to-create interactive multimedia, Shockwave is a better bet. One of the best things about shocked graphics (*shocking* means that Shockwave has been used on the graphics) is their interactivity. By simply holding down the SPACEBAR, visitors can zoom in (up to 26,500 percent) on a graphic. And by holding down the CTRL key, they can pan around the image with the mouse. The lines in the illustration stay smooth regardless of how far you zoom.

If you decide to develop your own Shockwave content, FreeHand is a useful tool for embedding complex graphics like maps, schematics, or engineering illustrations. You can make these illustrations as detailed as you like. This will let users zoom in on the most important or most interesting aspects. You can link parts of illustrations to other URLs, giving users quick visual access to related information.

To create shocked Web pages, first you create content using some of the same tools you'd use to make Flash content: FreeHand, Authorware, or Director. Then, you "shock" the content with a utility called Afterburner and integrate it into an HTML document.

We've thrown a ton of information at you in this chapter. What you should take from all this is that there are a number of ways that you can configure client computers. Whether you have to set up a computer for Larry in accounting or make sure your Web page will be compliant with most of the browsers out there, a fair amount of planning will be required before a solution is complete.

PART III

Building an E-Business Infrastructure

CHAPTER 6

LANs

If you haven't picked up on it by now, computer-types like to speak in acronyms. You can't just say "random access memory" or "hardware abstraction layer." Instead, you talk about things like RAM and HAL. In planning an e-business solution, one of the acronyms you'll hear repeatedly is "LAN," short for Local Area Network. In this chapter, we talk about LAN basics, how LANs are constructed, and what you'll need for your e-business.

WHAT IS A LAN?

As its name suggests, a LAN is a network that connects local computers, servers, printers, and other components. It is the network that connects your marketing department to accounting. It is the network that connects R&D with the color printer. It's the network that connects your computer with Larry's computer in production.

In fact, your network may be divided into several LANs. For instance, your production, marketing, and administration departments may have their own LANs, which combine to make one large LAN. A *backbone* is a relatively fast LAN interconnecting other LANs.

When the outside world navigates its way through the Internet to your e-business, it will be the LAN that you design and configure that will provide customers and business partners with the content they need. As such, your LAN needs to be designed and maintained so that it runs as fast and efficiently as possible and isn't constantly maxed out and bottlenecked.

LAN ARCHITECTURE

In order for you to design your own LAN—or update an existing one—it's important to understand how LANs work. In this section, we'll talk about both LAN design and function.

Network Topology

The layout of a LAN is referred to as its *topology*. Most hosts—computers, servers, and other components on the LAN—are connected to networks through either hubs or switches (which we will discuss in more depth later in this chapter). Hubs and switches give network administrators more choices in both the physical and logical network topology. They are modular in the sense that devices and hosts can be added without having to change anything on the network backbone. But above all, hubs and switches do away with antiquated topologies that required you to plug all your components into one main line of cabling.

The preferred topology used by network designers is the *star topology,* which breaks the network into easier to manage segments, rather than one overtaxed LAN. Breaking things up into smaller LAN segments makes it easier to meet current needs and still leave room for future change and growth. Network segmentation also improves network performance by isolating traffic. Users within a work group or department are most likely to send messages to one another, so putting them on their own LAN segment means others won't get caught in their traffic.

In a star topology, reliability is enhanced because what happens on one LAN segment doesn't affect the overall network; the fault is isolated within the segment where the trouble started. Also, the modularity of hierarchical networks naturally enhances security and manageability because devices can be grouped in ways that best fit management needs. Figure 6-1 shows common variations on the basic star topology.

In stark contrast to the bad old days of trunk pulling and cable dropping, connecting a host to a network now is as simple as plugging in a phone-style jack.

The topology of a network is, of course, most closely tied to the enterprise's geography: who's on what floor, which server sits where, and so on. But other considerations also come into play. Table 6-1 lists network design factors and how they affect decisions about what to do when designing a network.

OSI Reference Model

One of the key technologies behind LANs and network design comes from a standard established in the late 1970s. The Open Systems Interconnect (OSI) Reference Model was established to provide the standard by which computers could communicate with each other.

The OSI Reference Model has seven functional layers. Each defines a function performed when data is transferred between applications across a network, as illustrated in Figure 6-2. Each protocol communicates with a peer that is an equivalent implementation of the same protocol on a remote system.

For example, the Simple Mail Transfer Protocol (SMTP) is an application layer protocol that communicates with peer e-mail applications on remote systems. The e-mail ap-

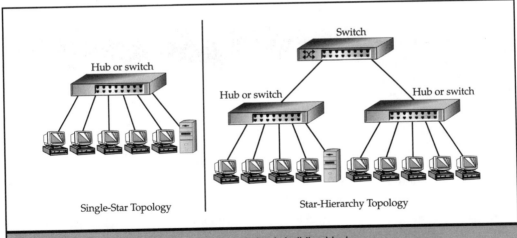

Figure 6-1. The star topology is the network's basic building block

Factor	Network Design Consideration
Preexisting cable plant	To save time and money, network designers frequently try to run networks over wiring already installed in the walls and ceiling spaces of a building. Sometimes they have no choice, and the type of network devices that can be used is dictated by preexisting cabling.
Performance goals	Projected network traffic loads and end-user "need for speed" can influence the class of network devices and cabling plant used.
Platforms	The installed base of network operating systems and computer platforms frequently dictates network design decisions.
Security	Topology layout is often used as a way to help enforce security.

Table 6-1.   Topology Design Factors (Besides Geography)

plications do not care whether or not the physical layer is a serial modem line or a twisted-pair Ethernet connection. They are only concerned with functions within SMTP.

▼ **Layer 1** The *physical layer* deals with the actual transport media that is being used. It defines the electrical and mechanical characteristics of the medium carrying the data signal. Some examples include coaxial cable, fiber optics, twisted-pair cabling, and serial lines.

■ **Layer 2** The *data link layer* governs access to the network and reliable transfer of packets across the network. It controls synchronization of packets transmitted as well as error checking and flow control of transmissions. Token-passing techniques work at this layer.

■ **Layer 3** The *network layer* is concerned with moving data between different networks or subnetworks. It's responsible for finding the destination device for which the data is destined. IP together with IP routing is a function of layer 3 of the OSI model.

■ **Layer 4** The *transport layer* takes care of data transfer, ensuring that data reaches its destination intact and in the proper order. The Transmission Control Protocol (TCP) and User Datagram Protocol (UDP) operate at this layer.

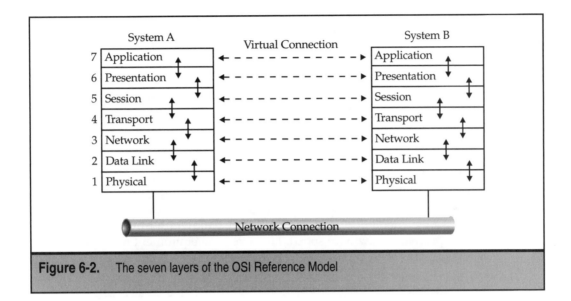

Figure 6-2.   The seven layers of the OSI Reference Model

- ■ **Layer 5**   The *session layer* establishes and terminates connections and arranges sessions between two computers. The Lightweight Directory Access Protocol (LDAP) and Remote Procedure Call (RPC) provide some functions at this layer.

- ■ **Layer 6**   The *presentation layer* is involved in formatting data for the purpose of display or printing. Data encryption and character set translation such as ASCII to EBCDIC are also performed by protocols at this layer. BIOS and file storage methods work on this level.

- ▲ **Layer 7**   The *application layer* defines the protocols to be used between the application programs. Examples of protocols at this layer are protocols for e-mail, HTTP, and FTP.

Datalink Protocols

One might think that getting computers to share information is simple: just plug one into the other and watch the data flow. If only it were that easy. In order for the information to pass back and forth between computers, it's necessary to have protocols in place to act as an intermediary or a messenger service.

Ethernet

The most popular network technology is *Ethernet*, which carries data at a rate of 10 or 100 Mbps.

> **NOTE:** You'll often hear 100-Mbps Ethernet referred to as *Fast* Ethernet.

Ethernet operates by contention. Devices sharing an Ethernet LAN segment listen for traffic being carried over the wire and defer transmitting a message until the medium is clear. If two stations send at about the same time and their packets collide, both transmissions are aborted and the stations back off and wait a random period of time before retransmitting.

Ethernet is inherently less expensive than other technologies, thanks to the random nature of its architecture. In other words, the electronics needed to run Ethernet are easier to manufacture because Ethernet doesn't try to control everything on the LAN.

The obvious disadvantage of Ethernet is that a lot of raw bandwidth is sacrificed to aborted transmissions. Theoretical maximum effective bandwidth from Ethernet is estimated at only 37 percent of raw wire speed. However, the equipment is so inexpensive that Ethernet has always been, on balance, the cheapest form of effective bandwidth.

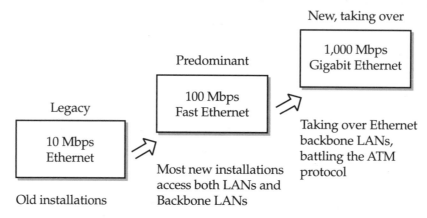

Token Ring

Token Ring is Ethernet's main competition as a LAN standard—or at least it *was*. Token Ring differs sharply from Ethernet in its architectural approach. Token Ring takes its name from the fact that it defines attached hosts into a logical ring. We use *logical* to describe Token Ring here because the LAN segment behaves like a ring by passing signals in a round-robin fashion as if the devices were actually attached to a looped cable. This is shown in Figure 6-3.

Tests show that Token Ring can use up to 75 percent of raw bandwidth, compared to Ethernet's theoretical maximum of about 37 percent. The problem with Token Rings, however, is that for them to pay off and reach maximum efficiency, they must be deployed across large networks.

This is a problem because most LANs tend to be small, since most enterprises are small. Moreover, even big companies have their networks segmented into smaller LANs, which are too petite to realize the benefits of a Token Ring. And, not the least of its issues, Token Ring is rather expensive.

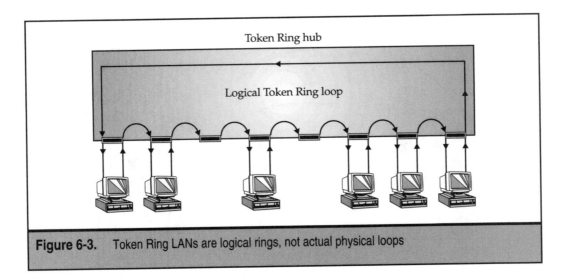

Figure 6-3. Token Ring LANs are logical rings, not actual physical loops

FDDI

Fiber Distributed Data Interface (FDDI) is a 100-Mbps protocol that runs over fiber-optic cable media. Like Token Ring, FDDI uses a token-passing architecture to control media access, yielding high effective bandwidth from its 100-Mbps wire speed.

FDDI's architecture made it attractive for use in backbone LANs, especially for office campuses and other large-area applications. FDDI has started to fade from the scene because ATM and Gigabit Ethernet are usurping it as the backbone technology of choice.

FDDI uses dual rings to provide additional reliability because of their redundant paths. The secondary ring goes into action when the primary ring fails. As Figure 6-4 shows, FDDI isolates the damaged station by wrapping around to the secondary ring and looping back in the other direction, thus keeping the ring intact.

ATM

Asynchronous Transfer Mode (ATM) transmits 53-byte cells instead of the packets used by other protocols. A *cell* is a fixed-length message unit. Like packets, cells are pieces of a message, but the fixed-length format leads to certain characteristics:

▼ **Virtual circuit orientation** Cell-based networks run better in point-to-point mode, where the receiving station is ready to actively receive and process the cells.

■ **Speed** The hardware knows exactly where the header ends and the data starts in every cell, thereby speeding processing operations. ATM networks run at speeds of up to 622 Mbps.

▲ **Quality of Service (QoS)** Predictable throughput rates and virtual circuits enable cell-based networks to better guarantee service levels to types of traffic that are high-priority.

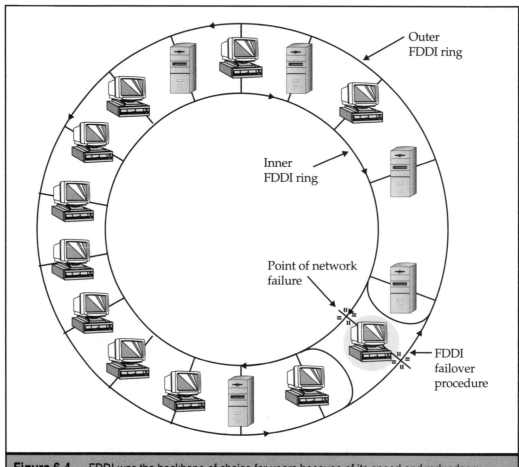

Figure 6-4.   FDDI was the backbone of choice for years because of its speed and redundancy

As with token-passing architectures, ATM's deterministic design yields high effective bandwidth from raw wire speeds. In fact, ATM's effective yield is said to be well above even Token Ring's 75 percent.

If ATM is so much better than other network protocols, why aren't all networks running it? The answer lies in the fact that most traffic is not sensitive to transmission latency. The added expense and complexity of ATM can be hard to justify in the absence of a lot of multimedia traffic, because there is sufficient time to repackage messages at the receiving end. Figure 6-5 shows examples of both types of traffic.

Normal messages aren't particularly sensitive to intermittent delays or the sequence of delivery. For example, an e-mail message with a document attached might be 50KB. The user doesn't care about the order in which various chunks of the message are re-

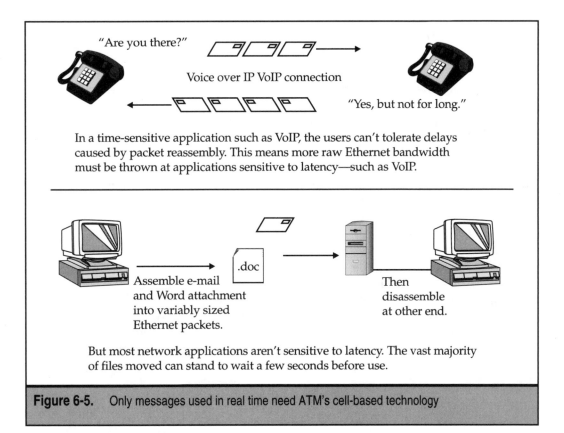

"Are you there?"

Voice over IP VoIP connection

"Yes, but not for long."

In a time-sensitive application such as VoIP, the users can't tolerate delays caused by packet reassembly. This means more raw Ethernet bandwidth must be thrown at applications sensitive to latency—such as VoIP.

.doc

Assemble e-mail and Word attachment into variably sized Ethernet packets.

Then disassemble at other end.

But most network applications aren't sensitive to latency. The vast majority of files moved can stand to wait a few seconds before use.

Figure 6-5.   Only messages used in real time need ATM's cell-based technology

ceived and wouldn't even be aware of any delays. Therefore, the network can deliver the message as it sees fit.

NOTE: Another way to ensure that important packets are arriving to destination computers in an orderly fashion is by making sure you have good QoS tools in place. We talk about QoS in Chapter 8.

Gigabit Ethernet

Gigabit Ethernet is a 1,000-Mbps extension of the Ethernet standard. The push for Gigabit Ethernet is largely motivated by its inherent compatibility with other Ethernet specifications.

Its greatest advantage is familiarity, given that Ethernet is the pervasive technology. Many network managers are biased in favor of Gigabit Ethernet because their staffs are familiar with the technology. Like ATM, Gigabit Ethernet backbones operate over a variety of fiber-optic cable types.

Higher-Level Protocols

In the last section, we talked about the physical media over which networked computers would communicate. But being physically able to talk to each other still doesn't ensure computers will understand what others are saying. For instance, consider the president of the United States picking up the telephone and calling the president of Mexico. The telephone in this example would be the data link layer, like FDDI or Ethernet. However, even though they're on the phone together, they still don't speak the same language. That's where this next set of protocols comes into play. These protocols, which operate at the third level of the OSI Reference Model, can be thought of as the telephone number the president would dial. When we get to the seventh layer—the application layer—of the OSI Reference Model, that would be analogous to the topic of conversation. After all, both presidents need to know what they're talking about.

NetBEUI

NetBIOS Extended User Interface (NetBEUI) locates other devices on the LAN by using NetBIOS machine names, those familiar 15-character computer names. When a computer has data it needs to send to another device on the LAN, it broadcasts onto the LAN looking for a specific NetBIOS name. The simplicity of the NetBEUI protocol makes it very quick on a small network. However, as the network grows, this broadcast methodology can quickly begin to consume more and more of the available bandwidth because of the growing number of broadcasts. NetBEUI is the default networking protocol used by Microsoft.

IPX/SPX

Internetwork Packet Exchange/Sequenced Packet Exchange (IPX/SPX) shares information about its services to network servers and routers by way of the Service Advertising Protocol (SAP). Services in an IPX network use SAP to advertise themselves and their network addresses. Workstations use the information made available through SAP to obtain the network addresses of servers that offer needed services. By default, SAP broadcasts the information onto the network every 60 seconds. This can become a problem as the network grows, and along with it the information in the SAP table being broadcast. IPX/SPX is the default networking protocol used by Novell.

SNA

It seems that almost every large, well-established network has some need for *Systems Network Architecture (SNA)* support. This is because the IBM mainframes it is associated with are prevalent and still in use. SNA was developed to provide networking to the terminals of older mainframes.

In 1974, IBM took the communications out of the applications themselves and provided for shared communication functions for all applications, similar to the modularity of the OSI model. The benefits are the same, achieved by putting the network definitions into a common networking application with common interfaces that all applications can use. Any changes or additions can be made in one place, instead of requiring changes to every application.

LAN COMPONENTS

So far in this chapter we haven't really talked specifically about the parts of your LAN that you can actually touch. Mainly it's been concepts and technologies, but not anything that forms the physical basis of your LAN. In this section, we'll talk about your LAN's hardware—the stuff that you plug into other stuff with flashing lights and power switches. We'll talk about switches, hubs, and routers—the components that direct and control traffic on your LAN.

Switches and Hubs

Hosts need to hook up to networks somehow. Hubs and switches provide local connectivity to hosts; they are the building blocks from which LANs are pieced together. How you configure your network and how you set up your LAN's topology will determine what kind of switch and/or hub you will need.

What Are Switches and Hubs?

Hubs and switches have many similarities, so much so that the technical name for a switch is *switched-hub*. Both contain banks of connection ports into which twisted-pair cables can be plugged (usually with RJ-45 connectors, which are similar to phone jacks). Either hubs or switches can form part of a LAN domain; either can be used to funnel messages into network backbones; and either can support remote management. Figure 6-6 illustrates their similarities.

But the difference between switches and hubs is that switches are "smart." Rather than just passing the information on to every computer plugged into it, like a hub, a switch can decide if the information needs to be passed on to everyone or if it is destined for one particular computer on the LAN. The capability to be selective about where information goes isn't just to vex Larry in production, who thinks everyone is out to get him. Rather, it saves bandwidth and relieves network congestion.

Decisions about what information is passed to a specific computer can be made at an administrative level, then shared with the switch that will implement the change. Figure 6-7 draws out the differences between hubs and switches.

Switches   Switches have more powerful hardware and software capabilities that make it possible to create and manage domains. Switches overcome most of the trade-offs that come with shared media and LAN segmentation. They eliminate unnecessary network delays by letting administrators specify broadcast domains on a case-by-case basis. For these reasons and others, the world is moving from hub-based hierarchical topology networks to switched networks, in which unwanted randomness is removed at minimal cost to connectivity.

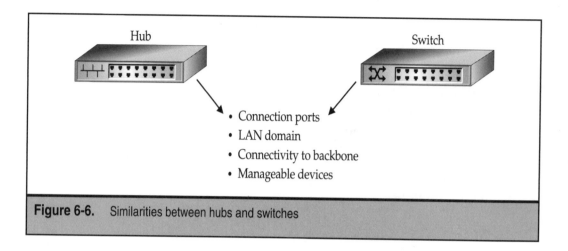

Figure 6-6.   Similarities between hubs and switches

Hubs   But, as Figure 6-8 depicts, the hub's capability to provide cheap and simple device connectivity has carved out a role for it in switched networks. For cost reasons, switched ports are rarely dedicated to a single device, unless that device is a heavily accessed server.

For its part, the hub has gotten smarter and less expensive over the years. Hubs continue to be used for enterprise work groups and small companies. Even computer rooms at the center of sophisticated enterprise networks use hubs as an easy and inexpensive way to make ports available to low-volume servers, administrative PCs, computer room printers, network monitor hosts, and other equipment.

Which to Use and Why   Deciding how to configure a LAN is largely a matter of analyzing network traffic patterns, projecting future need, and deciding whether content can best be delivered shotgun-like with a hub, or more surgically with a switch.

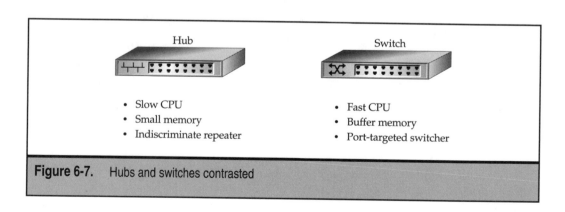

Figure 6-7.   Hubs and switches contrasted

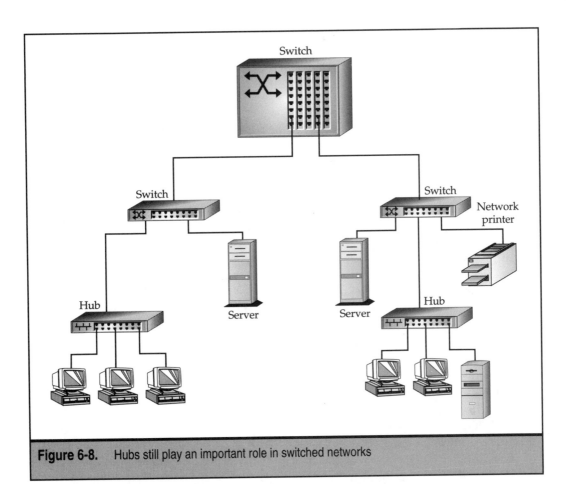

Figure 6-8.   Hubs still play an important role in switched networks

1. The first factor to review is whether the network is performing at sufficient speed. Don't fall into the trap of useless statistics here; measure the LAN's performance at peak periods, say, during month-end accounting closings or seasonal sales peaks.

2. Forecast growth of the user community. Firm up projections to about two years out. If you're a lowly technician, don't be shy about getting well-considered projections from senior management—after all, they'll be the first to howl if the network slows to a crawl a year from now.

3. Project change in the application mix. Are any new computer applications planned that are likely to affect bandwidth consumption? The most likely suspects are video conferencing, computer telephony, and anything graphical. Network planners should take special care if any extranet projects are in the works.

4. Forecast changes in "enterprise geography." The movement of users and resources within the enterprise can strain networks, even in the absence of overall growth. Security, logistics, and network management must respond to organizational flux.

Generally speaking, hub-based networks will suffice if user demand for bandwidth is growing slowly and there are no special security requirements. However, if bandwidth demand, organizational change, or new security and/or network management requirements are on the horizon, serious consideration should be given to using switched networks instead of hubs.

Types of Hubs

Not all hubs are created equal. Different LAN technologies, LAN sizes, and performance levels require different hubs. There are many hub vendors, but their offerings are somewhat similar in price and features. We will focus on Cisco Systems—the largest hardware vendor—in our examples, but refer to Table 6-5 for a more complete list of vendors. To fill varying customers needs, Cisco Systems has a variety of hubs available.

Choosing a Cisco hub model should be a straightforward process. There are three general classes of Cisco hubs, as explained in Table 6-2.

Series	Description
Cisco FastHub 400 Series	High-performance Fast Ethernet 10/100 hubs in both modular and fixed-configuration models, with 12 or 24 ports per module and up to hundreds of ports per stack. All models are stackable in either managed or manageable versions. (Note: As of this writing the FastHub 100, 200, and 300 Series models are being consolidated into the 400 Series.)
Cisco Mirco Hub 1500 Series	Low-cost Fast Ethernet 10/100 hubs in fixed 8-port configuration desktop models for the small office or home office. Both Micro Hub models are stackable; one is managed, the other is manageable.
10BaseT Hub	Developed with Hewlett-Packard, this is a Fast Ethernet 10/100 fixed-configuration managed hub optimized for use with Cisco Catalyst 1900 and 2820 Series switches. It is not stackable but can be cascaded.

Table 6-2.   General Classes of Cisco Hub Products

Switches

Because of the extra duty they do, switches and their roles in your LAN are more complex than hubs. To better understand their role, it's important to consider switched networks and what they bring to the LAN party.

Switched Networking Basics A switched backbone's job is to concentrate on what would otherwise be many hops into a single hop through a single switch. Switched backbones pack large amounts of memory and throughput into a single configuration. While switched backbones aren't absolutely necessary in smaller networks, they are typically in very large ones.

Switched networks operate using MAC addresses. A MAC address, also called a physical address, is a sort of network serial number assigned to a host's NIC. Even if you move a device to the other side of the world, its MAC address remains unchanged.

When a switch is turned on, it begins building a Dynamic Address Table. It does so by examining the source MAC address of each incoming frame and associating it with the port through which it came. In this way, the switch figures out what hosts are attached to each of its ports. Figure 6-9 shows a Dynamic Address Table.

The switch also discovers and maps the surrounding neighborhood, which it uses to locate nearby switches and begin sharing Dynamic Address Table information with them.

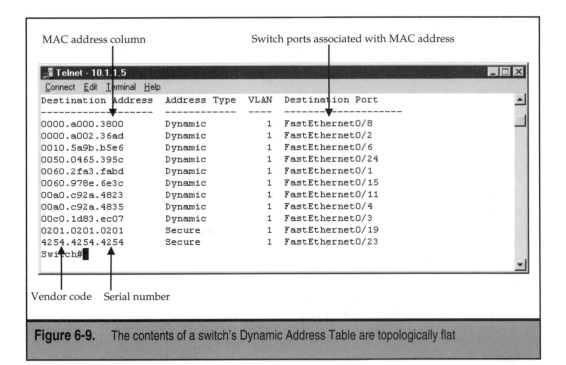

Figure 6-9.   The contents of a switch's Dynamic Address Table are topologically flat

Switch Products   Cisco's product line of switch platforms is divided into two product groups:

▼ **Micro Switches**   This relatively new product family is targeted at the branch office/small-business market niche. Micro Switches are desktop eight-port 10/100 switches designed to deliver high-performance networking in low-cost, simple-to-operate packages.

▲ **Catalyst Switches**   Cisco's main line of switched network solutions is delivered in the form of no less than ten series of products amounting to over twice as many orderable product models.

Table 6-3 outlines the Cisco switch product line, which as this book is being written is composed of 11 product series. Refer to www.cisco.com for catalogs of information on Cisco switches and other products.

Routers

Once your network map gets to a router, that's where your LAN ends. Everything on the other side of the router is part of the Internet, an extranet, a WAN, or another LAN.

Product Series	Description
Micro Switches	Two models with 8 ports of a desktop device designed to create high-performance LANs. The only Cisco switch series with an unmanaged model.
Catalyst 1900 Series	Four-models with 12 or 24 10BaseT ports and 2 uplink ports for 100BaseTX or 100BaseFX. All models have a 1K MAC address cache. Not stackable.
Catalyst 2820 Series	Four-model series designed for aggregating 10BaseT hubs to 100BaseT, FDDI, or ATM backbones or servers. Contains 24 10BaseT ports plus 2 slots to accommodate a choice of high-speed modules (100BaseT, FDDI, or ATM). 1 Gbps backplane. 2K or 8K MAC address cache. Not stackable.
Catalyst 2900 Series	Four models with 12–48 ports for 10/100BaseTX or 100BaseFX with uplinks to 1000BaseX. 1.2 Gbps–2.4 Gbps backplane. Not stackable.
Catalyst 2900XL Series	Five models in two basic packages with 12 100BaseFX or 24 ports for 10/100BaseT and two uplinks to 100BaseFX. Up to 16K MAC address cache. 3.2 Gbps backplane. Not stackable.

Table 6-3.   Cisco's Switch Product Line Consists of Eleven Series

Product Series	Description
Catalyst 3000 Series	Three models of multilayer switches with either 16 or 24 10BaseT ports in fixed configurations. Models differ by having either 1, 2, or 6 expansion slots for modules with ports supporting coaxial cable, twisted-pair cable, or fiber cable types and support for several Ethernet specifications or WAN connectivity. 480-Mbps backplane. Stackable to eight switches in any combination of models.
Catalyst 3900 Series	Two models with 20 fixed Token Ring ports and 2 slots for expansion modules, each with 4 ports for additional Token Ring user ports or 1 ATM OC-3c or 2 100BaseX uplink(s). 520-Mbps backplane. Stackable up to eight switches.
Catalyst 4000 Series	One model with 3-slot modular chassis supporting 10/100/1000 Ethernet. One module has 48 10/100 ports and another 32 10/100 ports with a variety of 1000BaseX uplink options. Powerful 24 Gbps backplane. Not stackable.
Catalyst 5000 Series	Two-series family with five models, with 2–5 slot modular chassis with 48–528 ports supporting 100BaseX, 1000X, ATM, FDDI, or Token Ring. 1.2 Gbps–3.6 Gbps backplane. Not stackable.
Catalyst 6000 Series	Four-model multilayer switch family with 6–9 slots supporting 384 10/100 ports, 192 100BaseFX ports, or 130 1000BaseX ports. 150-Mbps throughput. 32-Gbps backplane scalable to 256 Gbps. Not stackable.
Catalyst 8500 Series	Two models with 5–13 slots supporting multiservice ATM switching, optimized for aggregating multiprotocol traffic. 6–24 Mbps throughput. 10-Gbps or 40-Gbps backplane. Not stackable.

Table 6-3. Cisco's Switch Product Line Consists of Eleven Series *(continued)*

The router is the basic building block of internetworks. Indeed, without the router the Internet as we know it couldn't even exist. This is because of the router's unique and powerful capabilities:

▼ Routers can simultaneously support different protocols (Ethernet, Token Ring, ISDN, and others), effectively making virtually all computers compatible at the internetwork level.

- Routers seamlessly connect LANs to WANs, which makes it feasible to build large-scale internetworks with minimum centralized planning, sort of like Lego blocks.

- Routers filter out unwanted traffic by isolating areas in which messages can be "broadcast" to all users in a network.

- Routers act as security gates by checking traffic against permission access lists.

- Routers assure reliability by providing multiple paths through internetworks.

▲ Routers automatically learn about new paths and select the best ones, eliminating artificial constraints on expanding and improving internetworks.

But there are obstacles to bringing users together on internetworks, whether on a corporate intranet, a virtual private network, or the Internet itself. Figure 6-10 depicts how routing technology is the key to overcoming these obstacles.

Types of Routers

At first glance, routers seem a lot like PCs. They have a CPU, memory, and, on the back, ports and interfaces to hook up peripherals and various communications media. They sometimes even have a monitor to serve as a system console.

But there's one defining difference from a PC: routers are diskless. They don't even have floppy disks. If you think about it, this makes sense. A router exists to do just that:

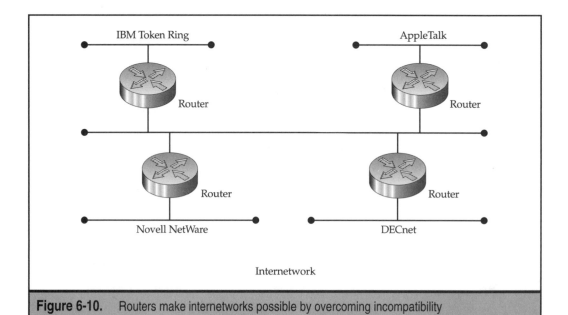

Figure 6-10.   Routers make internetworks possible by overcoming incompatibility

route. Routers have, as their sole mission, the task of processing incoming packets and routing outbound packets to their proper destinations.

Cisco routers use a variety of CPUs, each chosen to fit a particular mission. Cisco 700 Series routers, for example, employ 25-MHz 80386 CPUs (remember those?). Cisco probably made this selection because the 700 Series is designed for small office or home office use, where activity loads are light. The Intel 80386 CPU is reliable, capable of handling the job, and, perhaps most important, inexpensive. Moving up the router product line, Cisco uses progressively more powerful general-purpose processors from Motorola, Silicon Graphics, and other chip makers.

Model Comparison

Table 6-4 summarizes the target market of each series of Cisco routers; the table lists supported technologies and gives a Web address for obtaining additional information.

Hardware Vendors

We've been using Cisco System's product line for examples, but don't feel limited to their hardware. Table 6-5 lists some of the other hardware vendors out there who can supply the hubs, routers, and switches you'll need to build your e-commerce networks.

Series	Market	Fixed Ports	Modules	Comments	http://
700	Home office or small remote office	1 ISDN/BRI; 1 Ethernet	None	Optional 2 analog telephone ports	www.cisco.com/go/700
800	Home office or small remote office	1 ISDN/BRI; up to 4 Ethernet	None	Optional 2 analog telephone ports; advanced security features	www.cisco.com/go/800
1600	Small remote office or small business	Ethernet; 1 serial or ISDN/BRI	1 WAN interface slot	Modular for scalability	www.cisco.com/go/1600
1700	Small to medium business, or mobile or remote user	1 10/100 Ethernet	2 WAN interface slots	Virtual Private Network (VPN) solution	www.cisco.com/go/1700

Table 6-4. Cisco Router Comparison

Series	Market	Fixed Ports	Modules	Comments	http://
2500	Branch offices	Depends on model	Depends on model	Single LAN router; router/hub; access server; high-density router; dual LAN router; single LAN router (modular)	www.cisco.com/go/2500
2600	Small to medium business or remote office	1–2 port Ethernet; Port Token Ring (optional)	2 WAN interface slots; 1 network module slot; 1–2 voice slots	Supports voice/fax over IP	www.cisco.com/go/2600
3600	Medium to large business or remote office	None	2–4 LAN/WAN slots	Supports voice/fax over IP; wide variety of media support	www.cisco.com/go/3600
4000	Medium to large business	None	3 LAN/WAN slots	Modular; high density; wide variety of media support	www.cisco.com/go/4000
7000	Campus backbone	None	2–13 LAN/WAN slots	High performance; high density; wide variety of media support	www.cisco.com/go/7000

Table 6-4. Cisco Router Comparison *(continued)*

Future Components

Unless you've been living on an isolated South Pacific island for the last couple decades, living off coconut milk and slow monkeys, you've no doubt seen how fast technology has accelerated. New processors are introduced every couple months that leave the ones that came just weeks before in the cyberdust. Network technology experiences the same types of development and expansion. In addition to better, cheaper routers, hubs, and switches, there are some other innovations that will help your network, and they're based on fiber.

Company	Web Site	Components
3Com	www.3com.com	Hubs, switches, routers
Extreme Networks	www.extremenetworks.com	Switches
UMAX	www.umax.com	Hubs, switches, routers
Cisco Systems	www.cisco.com	Hubs, switches, routers
Lucent	www.lucent.com	Switches, routers
Intel	www.intel.com	Hubs, switches, routers
Hewlett Packard	www.hp.com	Hubs, switches
Nortel	www.nortel.com	Hubs, switches, routers
Digitan Systems	www.digitan.com	Hubs, routers
AddTron Technology	www.addtron.com	Hubs, switches
Pivotal Networking	www.pivotal.com	Routers
Hawking Technology	www.hawkingtech.com	Hubs, switches, routers

Table 6-5. Some LAN Hardware Manufacturers

Fiber Optics

Optical carriers function under a Synchronous Optical Network (SONET) specification. SONET is a physical layer technology invented by BellCore to operate high-speed fiber-optic backbones.

Now an ANSI standard, SONET is developing at a remarkable rate, having jumped from OC-3 to OC-12 (622 Mbps), then to OC-24 (1.244 Gbps), and now OC-48 (2.488 Gbps). The next push is for an eye-popping 40 Gbps OC-768 in the 2001–2003 timeframe. A 100 Gbps OC level is already running in the labs. These blinding speeds portend the capability to carry very large multimedia files very quickly.

Storage

One of the chief sources of bottlenecks in your system can be a storage shortage. But beyond eliminating bottlenecks, plenty of storage increases efficiency, decreases redundancy, and simplifies management. Two new storage technologies—Network Attached Storage (NAS) and Storage Area Network (SAN)—are providing gobs of storage space.

▼ **NAS** These devices are storage appliances, big servers that you plug into your network that perform one task: They serve up files nice and fast. The capacity of large NAS appliances is in the terabyte range.

▲ **SAN** These are multiserver, multistorage networks that can grow larger than 400TB. A SAN acts as a secondary network to a LAN. Every server that needs access to the SAN has a fiber channel connection. This secondary network relieves the main network of massive data transfer loads because backup traffic occurs between storage devices within the SAN.

The materialization of fiber channel technology is making SANs much easier to implement, which brings new players into the marketplace with offerings such as disk subsystems, switches, interconnects, backup and retrieval systems, CD-ROM libraries, and tape systems.

LAN DESIGN CONSIDERATIONS

When you put together your LAN, there are several inherent traps that you can avoid with a little knowledge and preplanning. Three of the top issues to consider when building your LAN are load balancing, bottlenecks, and clustering.

Load Balancing

Let's say your e-business sells hardware supplies online. You've got lots of traffic to the site, and you anticipated the influx of extra business by adding several additional servers. Unfortunately, you're not selling as many hammers as you anticipated and you've also noticed that your servers aren't responding to client demand as quickly as they should. Upon further inspection, you see that one server is bearing the brunt of all the traffic—sometimes preventing customers from connecting—while the others are sitting quietly, warming up the server room.

Load balancing takes the incoming traffic and evenly distributes it across several servers in an effort to speed transactions and use your resources more efficiently. Devices called load balancers, which are usually specially enabled switches, allow traffic to your e-business to be spread across your network uniformly. Figure 6-11 shows where a load balancer would sit on your LAN.

Load balancing devices allow you to pick from a number of techniques to spread the load across the network. The following are some of the more popular methods to determine where traffic will go when it hits your load balancer:

▼ **Round-robin** The *round-robin* method simply means that each server will be selected in order. It pays no attention to the server's resources.

■ **Least used** The *least used* method sends traffic to the server that has been used the least.

■ **Response time** The *response time* method sends the traffic to the server that responds the quickest to the load balancer's query of availability.

■ **Least connections** The *least connections* method sends traffic to the server with the fewest connections.

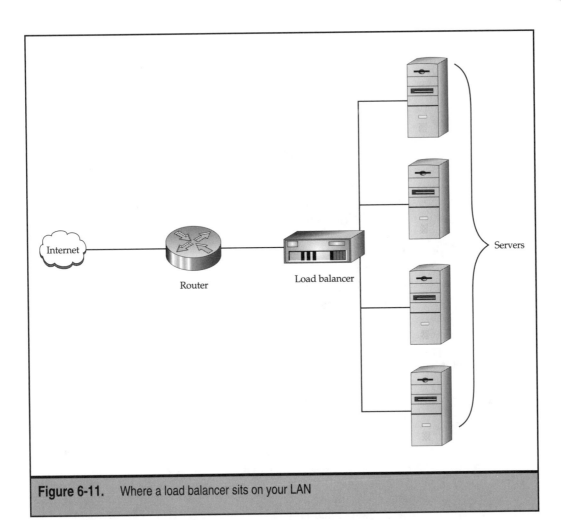

Figure 6-11.   Where a load balancer sits on your LAN

- **Cache-based** By using an algorithm that correlates the number of requests being made on each server or service with the server's cache, the device keeps track of what requests have been made and directs requests for the same file or Web page to the same server. Since that server should still have the page in cache memory, it will be able to respond faster than will another server that would have to load the file from disk.

- **Observed** The device watches the network and correlates the number of connections and response time, then sends traffic to the server with the shortest response time.

- ▲ **Predictive** This method tracks response time and sends requests to the server that is improving and has the highest performance rating, as determined by the load bearing device.

A number of devices out there can help you load-balance your network. One of the easiest ways to provide load balancing is, when buying switches and routers, to pick switches and routers with built-in load balancing capabilities. Let's take a look at three devices that can help balance the load across your LAN.

F5 Labs BIG/ip

The BIG/ip is an industrial PC running a UNIX OS. It provides one internal interface and one external interface, which must then be connected to switches or hubs, one each for the servers and external connections. It also supports a failover connector to a second BIG/ip for redundancy.

The BIG/ip allows rate filtering, which allows the administrator to prioritize incoming traffic according to IP address or network range. It also allows separate and granular control of persistence, supporting SSL persistence, TCP persistence for regular TCP sessions, and UDP persistence for UDP sessions.

HolonTech XP1600 HyperFlow 2 System

The XP1600 HyperFlow not only looks different from the F5 and the Alteon routers, but it *is* quite different. Instead of two telephone-type jacks on the back, it has two rows of eight ports on the front. Redundancy is enhanced with two power supplies, and the unit also supports failover to a hot spare. Clusters can be defined according to IP address or TCP port.

The XP1600 also includes the ability to check back-end servers using CGI scripts to verify the database server that may be supplying data to the Web servers. It includes predefined scripts for specific applications, such as Microsoft SQL server.

Alteon ACEswitch 180 Plus 10/100/1000 Switch

The Alteon ACEswitch 180 Plus is an eight-port 10/100/1000 switch with both telephone-style jacks and fiber optic connectors for each port. Each port can be configured to fail over from the Gigabit connection to the 10/100 connection, and a connection on the back allows for an external redundant power supply.

The switch can provide load balancing for up to 256 servers in up to 256 virtual groups, although that would result in one server per group. It provides a weighted option for configuring load balancing by server. For each server in a group, a load weighting can be assigned that determines how many connections the server must have to be considered equally loaded.

Coyote Point Equalizer

Coyote Point designed its Equalizer to handle pipes as large as a T3 (43 Mbps), an unlimited number of server clusters, and up to two million simultaneous connections.

It also comes preconfigured, which is likely to save you more than a couple headaches. Preconfiguration is excellent for smaller departments with a lot on their plates. To set it up, you simply provide Coyote Point with a list of server and router IP addresses and network masks when placing your order, and Coyote returns the Equalizer, which is ready to plug in and go.

The Equalizer's load balancing responsiveness can be set to provide a slow, medium, or fast response to changing conditions.

Red Hill WebMux

Red Hill Network's WebMux has two ports: one connecting to your LAN's router and one to your LAN's server. The WebMux is also designed so that you can connect another WebMux, which allows hot rollover in the case of failure.

The WebMux can be managed remotely via a secured Web browser. It is also operating system independent—it is not necessary to load software or agents on the Web servers. Another function allows the system administrator to be paged if the WebMux goes down and when it returns online.

Cisco Local Director 430

Cisco's LocalDirector was the first commercially available load balancer in 1996 and is still one of the most popular. It is a stand-alone load balancer that offers support for all common TCP/IP services, including Web, FTP, Telnet, Gopher, and SMTP—all without requiring special software configuration.

LocalDirector supports 64,000 virtual and real servers and offers compatibility with any server operating system, thus allowing administrators to use LocalDirector in mixed environments. LocalDirector also features an integrated security capability, which protects servers from unauthorized access.

Comparison

Table 6-6 shows how the features of each load balancing device stack up against the others. More information on these devices can be found at their respective Web sites. For pricing information, contact the vendor.

Bottlenecks

System bottlenecks exist in every network. When one bottleneck is removed, another pops up. Your server often is only as fast as its slowest link or subcomponent. Even extremely well-equipped servers connected to the network via a single Fast Ethernet segment and equipped with multiple processors, hundreds of MBs of memory, and high-performance disk arrays are susceptible to bottlenecking.

When trying to identify bottlenecks, look at the individual components of the system and how those components are connected.

RAM

When the application needs data, and it is not found in the cache, the CPU must go to main memory. Although memory is cheap and very fast, CPU cache is faster but more expensive. As always, more memory is better.

	F5	XP1600	180 Plus	Equalizer	WebMux	Local Director 430
Ports	2	16	8	2	2	4
Load Balancing Methods	Round-robin Two versions of a weighted round-robin Least Connections Fastest Response Observed Mode (correlates number of connections and response time) Predictive	Round-robin Least Used Response Time Weighted Load	Round-robin Round-robin: Least Connections Two modes for persistent connections	Round robin Weighted round-robin Adaptive Number of active connections Fastest response Least connections	Round robin Weighted round robin Persistent round robin Persistent weighted round robin Least connections Persistent least connections Weighted least connections Persistent weighted least connections	Round robin Fastest Response Fewest Connections
Network Protocol Used	Ethernet	Ethernet	Ethernet	Ethernet	Ethernet	Ethernet
Web Site	www.f5.com	www.holontech.com	www.alteonWEBsystems.com	www.coyotepoint.com	www.redhillnetworks.com	www.cisco.com

Table 6-6.   Some Load Balancing Appliances

Virtual Memory

When the system runs out of free memory, it will become shaky. Virtual memory fools the operating system into believing that there is more memory than really exists. This extra memory is stored on the disk subsystem. When the operating system needs data that is not found in either the CPU cache or main memory, it goes out to the virtual memory file on the disk. However, if the operating system must continually go to disk to get needed data, performance will suffer.

Disk Subsystem

Just a few years ago, 1GB of disk space was a ton of space. Now, you can't even load a kid's video game with 1GB. Several factors affect disk performance. The characteristics of the disks themselves are very important. Your hard disks' rotational speed is a factor to consider. Having a fast rotational rate is great for streaming data such as video or audio. Another factor is the speed of the read/write arm of the disk. The faster that the read/write head can move across the platter to find data, the better.

You should also look at the number of disks that are in use. If you need 60GB of disk space, one 60GB disk is not the best choice in terms of performance and fault tolerance. A better solution would be to get four 20GB disks.

Bottleneck Avoidance

Somewhere in the design of your Web server architecture lies a bottleneck. It is the single reason why your pages don't appear quicker on the clients' computers. Finding the bottleneck can very difficult.

One tool that is quite useful is the Performance Monitor that is built into Windows NT and 2000. You can easily monitor memory usage, disk swapping, network throughput, and processor utilization. See Chapter 10 for more information on how to use the Performance Monitor.

You can also use the Network Monitor tool to check to see if the bottleneck resides on the network connection from your server to your users. If, for example, you are only able to put 500 Kbps onto your T1 connection and everything in your PC indicates that the bottleneck is not in the PC, you should contact your ISP. The bottleneck may be located somewhere on their network.

If, on the other hand, you have purchased high-end equipment and optimized your system only to find that the demand is just too great for it, you should consider adding more machines to serve the Web pages.

Clustering

A *cluster* is defined as a distributed system of two or more computers that can be used as a unified computer resource. In English, this means that you combine the power of several computers to gang up on one task.

This affords improved availability because if one system in the cluster fails, the other can take over the duties of the first. Another advantage of clusters is increased scalability. Clusters make it easy to add components to the collection of computers when the load requires it. You simply take a computer offline to service it while the cluster continues to attend to the workload. Management is also simplified, in theory, because you can manage groups of systems as if they were a single computer.

This is different from load balancing in that each machine in a cluster is working from the same dynamic data store. The cluster appears to be one system, so a change of data on one will change the data on all systems in the cluster.

Types of Clusters

Clustering software comes in two models: the shared disk model and the shared nothing model.

Shared Disk   In the *shared disk* model, any computer or node in the cluster can access any hard drive on any of the other nodes. If there is contention for the disk, a Distributed Lock Manager (DLM) will intervene and control access to the resource. The DLM increases network traffic and puts some additional demand on the CPU resources of the cluster.

Shared Nothing   In the *shared nothing* model, each node uses and owns its own disk resources. If one node requests data belonging to another, it must ask the owner, who in turn passes the desired information back to the requester. In the event of a hardware failure, another node can take ownership of the resources on the failed computer.

Cluster Solutions

Several vendors offer their own clustering applications. Some of the hardware solutions use proprietary hardware, which makes it more difficult to scale later using standard computers. Some of these systems are even packaged in a single box. Table 6-7 lists some cluster solutions for Microsoft-based networks.

Vendor/ Application	Hardware Implementation	Max Number of Nodes	Dynamic Load Balancing	Price (US$)	Contact
Amdahl/Life Keeper	Proprietary	3	No	$30,720–$93,737	www.amdahl.com
Cubix/ RemoteServ/IS	Any	4,094	Yes	$1,875	www.cubix.com
Data General/ NT Cluster in a Box	Proprietary	2	No	$110,000	www.veritas.com
Marathon Technologies/ Endurance 4000	Proprietary	2	No	$24,999, not including hardware	www.marathontech nologies.com
Microsoft/ Cluster Service	Any on HCL	Phase 1: 2 Phase 2: ?	Phase 1: No Phase 2: Yes	Not yet determined	www.microsoft.com
Octopus/ SASO	Any	Unlimited	No	$1,499 for SASO software	www.octopustech.com
Vinca/ StandbyServer	Proprietary	2	No	$3,995	www.vinca.com

Table 6-7.   Third-Party Cluster Solutions

DESIGNING YOUR LAN

The concepts, ideas, and technologies we talked about in the first half of the chapter will pay off now. This is where we will show you how to plan the LAN for your e-business solution. We'll take you through the steps to determine what your LAN will need for an ideal setup.

Capacity Planning

The first step is to understand how much you need. If you go into this blindly, you can expect your servers to get overloaded and problems to follow. Conversely, you can overbuild and spend more than NASA on a low-traffic LAN.

Understanding Existing Internetworks

Few network designs start from scratch. Although it would be nice to work from a blank sheet of paper, most designs must accommodate a preexisting network. Whatever the change, the preexisting infrastructure must be thoroughly analyzed before even considering a purchase.

The next section describes methods for network planning and design. They focus on establishing a baseline of how the network will look upon implementation. To refresh, a *baseline* is a network's starting point, as expressed in traffic volumes, flows, and characteristics. Allowances are made for margins of error and projected growth over and above the baseline.

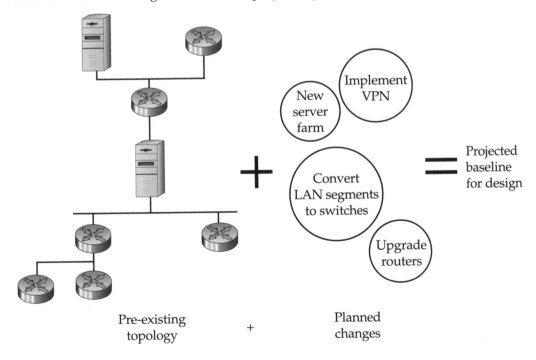

If designing an entirely new network, one must arrive at a design baseline based on well-researched assumptions, often derived from paperwork or other nonnetworked data traffic already in place. If an existing network is being upgraded, the baseline is taken by measuring its characteristics.

Simulating Your Network

As a network evolves, the number and variety of devices and applications it supports will make it a real challenge to understand the system as a whole. It becomes next to impossible to predict with any accuracy how one traffic demand will affect another part of the network. There are simply too many devices, too many routes, and too many conversations going on simultaneously. Since you cannot use the production network as your laboratory, and it's impractical to build an exact replica, it makes sense to make a model of your network and run simulations on it. These simulations subject your "virtual" network to various designs and traffic loads to see how well it functions under those circumstances.

Building a model of your network is a very piecemeal process. To build a model that considers every aspect of the network and the traffic it carries is, essentially, to rebuild your network. Therefore, a model must include certain simplifications and assumptions. The trick is knowing what aspects can be altered without compromising the model. This section outlines the simulation process and helps you understand where to make those important simplifications.

A Simple Simulation

Let's walk through a simple simulation on a lab network we will build from scratch. Figure 6-12 illustrates our test network, which we are simulating on COMNET Predictor by CACI (www.caci.com). Two LAN segments are separated by a WAN link. There is an NT Server and Workstation on each LAN. The network building tools are located in the toolbar on the left side of the screen. Creating a network is as simple as clicking the tool for the network item (such as LAN or Server) and dropping the item into the main window. You connect devices with links and later define their characteristics by choosing from a predefined list or customizing your own specifications.

You can see we have two different models of Cisco routers in our test network. The simulation tool is familiar with the capabilities of most of Cisco's devices and will include those characteristics in the simulation.

Next we'll have to add traffic to the model. Again, in this case, we will keep it simple and create some fictitious traffic demands by hand. In Figure 6-13, you can see five traffic demands that were placed manually. They indicate the origin, destination, application, protocol, and rate for each traffic demand. In a simulation of the production network, thousands of conversations may be listed in this window. These, of course, are imported from the probes.

In this example, we have added traffic demands by hand because the network is so simple. In real life, though, you'll need to capture them with probes and import them into COMNET Predictor.

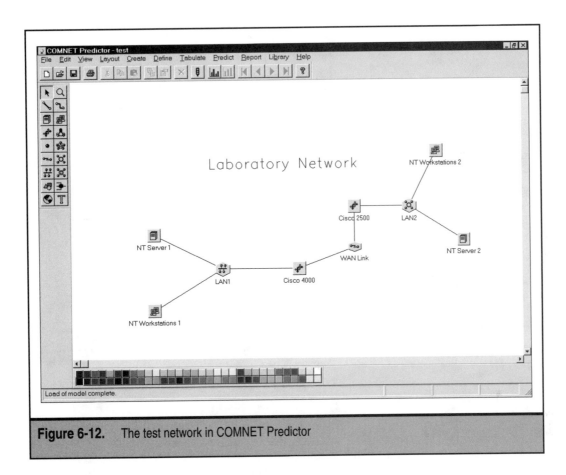

Figure 6-12.   The test network in COMNET Predictor

With the topology and traffic demands in place, we are finally ready to run a simulation. We simply click the Run Simulation icon (the stoplight button near the center of the main toolbar), and the simulation is under way.

Numerous reports can be generated in the COMNET Predictor simulator, to examine utilization, forecasting, and network failures. Figure 6-14 is a report showing the percentage of utilization for each device or LAN in the network. Before we ran the simulation, we told Predictor that we expected a 10 percent growth in traffic each year. Predictor calculated the use of each device or LAN and projected its use for the next two years. From this report, we can see that we might want to keep an eye on our WAN link because it is approaching 40 percent utilization. For further analysis, we could easily change the throughput of the WAN link and run another simulation.

Determining the network traffic you currently experience will form the bedrock of your e-business's foundation. With this baseline established, you can add on with better accuracy and confidence.

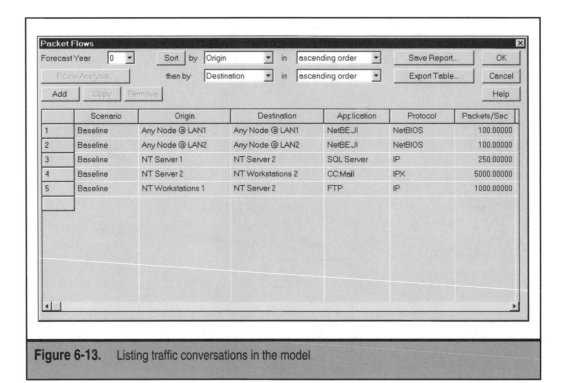

	Scenario	Origin	Destination	Application	Protocol	Packets/Sec
1	Baseline	Any Node @ LAN1	Any Node @ LAN1	NetBEJI	NetBIOS	100.00000
2	Baseline	Any Node @ LAN2	Any Node @ LAN2	NetBEJI	NetBIOS	100.00000
3	Baseline	NT Server 1	NT Server 2	SQL Server	IP	250.00000
4	Baseline	NT Server 2	NT Workstations 2	CC:Mail	IPX	5000.00000
5	Baseline	NT Workstations 1	NT Server 2	FTP	IP	1000.00000

Figure 6-13.   Listing traffic conversations in the model

Building Your LAN

Now that we've talked about the technology and hardware components behind LAN construction, it's time to talk about how it all comes together. Certain pieces must be located in specific locations in your topology. Other pieces will be useless if they're incorrectly placed.

The WAN Link

A LAN works very well on its own, within the four walls of your business and connecting all the divisions of your company. However, when it comes to e-business, you certainly want customers, clients, and partners to have the ability to buy things from you. To that end, you will need some connectivity with the world outside those four walls. This is where a WAN link is important.

One of the crucial factors you should take into consideration is throughput. If you try to connect your e-business solution to the rest of the world on a dial-in line to an Internet service provider, you may want to start thinking about who you want to auction off your office furniture when you go bankrupt. Throughput is critical, because if clients can't get to your servers, you won't sell anything.

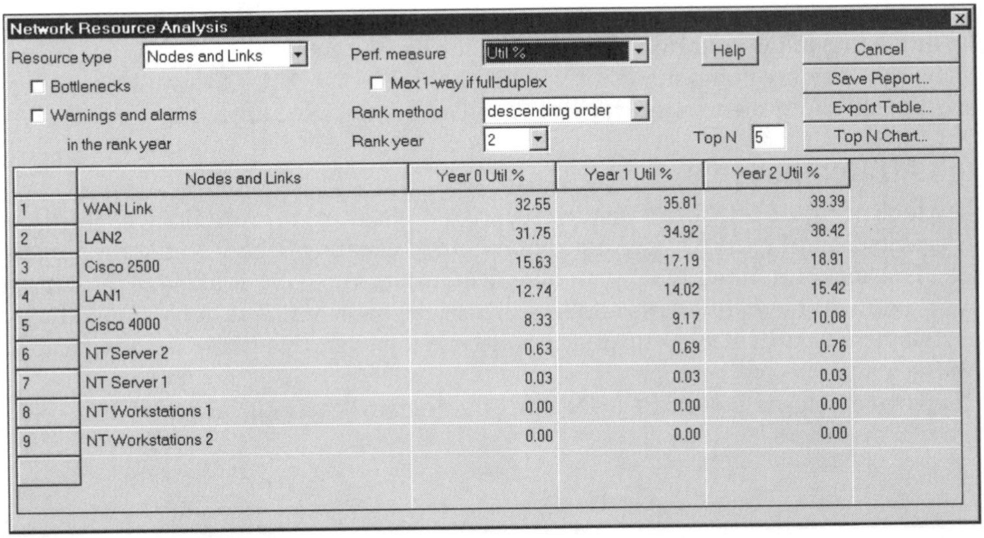

Figure 6-14.   A COMNET Predictor report giving utilization percentages for each network device or link

Even worse, if your WAN link is consistently slow, you'll develop an unfortunate reputation and customers will purposely avoid your e-business in favor of one that's faster and more reliable.

It's good to think about throughput as different widths of pipe. The wider the pipe, the more data can flow through and the less chance for problems. The smaller the pipe, the less data can get through and the more opportunity for trouble. We'll talk more about throughput, comparing the different sizes of pipes, weighing your options, and discussing costs, in Chapter 7.

The Firewall

The next component that your e-business needs is a *firewall*. A firewall sits between your LAN and the outside world. Essentially, the firewall acts as a gatekeeper, allowing in those individuals you approve and keeping everybody else out.

An easy way to think about firewalls in relation to network security is to think of them as like the wall around a castle. The wall has only a few guarded ways in. Someone wanting admittance must identify himself or herself to the satisfaction of the guards. Anyone who tries to get in any other way will be deterred by the ramparts, walls, and moat.

This metaphor applies easily to networking: Before anyone is allowed in the network (the castle), he or she must be identified to a perimeter security force (the guards), which is the firewall.

The people outside the perimeter may be far out on the Internet, or they may be as close as the marketing department. In any event, if they are people you have decided to keep out, a firewall is your network's way to fortify its defenses.

Though they are components of your LAN and WAN, since firewalls are security tools, we talk about them in much more depth and detail in Chapter 11.

The LAN Components

Take a look at Figure 6-15. In the shaded sections of the diagram are topics we will discuss in Chapters 7 and 11, "WAN Configurations" and "Creating Secure Networks," respectively. This diagram shows what your overall e-business network is likely to resemble (of course, you will have different numbers of servers, switches, and hubs, depending on your business's particular needs and topology). However, this figure shows, basically, how everything hooks together.

Let's take a closer look at the LAN side of the network and talk about how the pieces come together there.

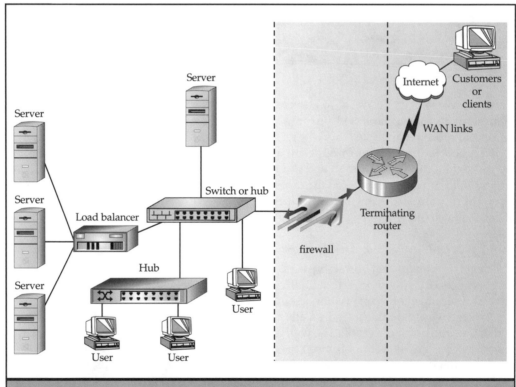

Figure 6-15.   How the pieces of a network fit together

Switches and Hubs   As we said earlier, switches and hubs distribute information and connect network components. In our example, for instance, after the connection terminates the Internet, through a router and the firewall, it gets pumped into a switch or a hub. If none of your servers and clients require their own (unshared) connections to the Internet, a hub will be used to send all information to all users, with only the correct recipient taking the data off the wire.

However, if your components need their own uncontested connection to other devices (or the Internet), this will be a job for a switch. Looking back at our example, we have switches and hubs working on different levels. For instance, let's say the next stop for incoming data (after going through the firewall) is a switch. Based on its programming, the switch would then distribute the information directly to the port where the recipient is. This could be a server, the administrator's PC, a hub, or a load balancer (more on load balancers in a moment). The switch looks at the incoming data and separates the traffic as required. For example, the administrator will need different information than the computers in the server farm, and likewise for the other components.

Hubs and switches can be added further down the chain to distribute data as needed. For instance, the two users at the bottom of Figure 6-15 will share the hub's capacity. However, if these two users had increased data needs—for instance one was taxing the accounting system and another was getting streaming media from another server—then a switch would deliver the best results.

Server Placement   Next, let's consider the placement of servers. In our example, we have four servers: one is the mail server, which receives less network traffic than the other three servers that handle production.

The mail server is only for the use of the company and its employees. It handles the incoming and the outgoing mail and so, comparatively speaking, is much less of a bandwidth burden than the production servers. When mail comes in from the Internet, the switch routes that information directly to the mail server. It would make sense then to place the mail server logically close to the users of that system.

The production servers are located behind a load balancer because they contain the same information and are linked together for reliability and speed. Theirs is a much different role than that of the mail server because they carry a large amount of information, which must be made available as quickly as possible. Moreover, the users of these systems mostly come from the Internet, so they should be close to the Internet connection and not have to contend with other traffic.

Load Balancers   Finally, let's talk about the last component in our example, the load balancer. Here, after the data comes off the Internet, the switch separates it. The content intended for the server farm is sent first to a load balancer, which has been set up so that Web traffic is sent directly to it, so that it can then distribute the traffic evenly across the servers. This allows customers to be connected and served as fast as possible.

The load balancer provides a layer of reliability, as well. For instance, if one of our three servers were to crash, the load balancer would redirect the traffic between the remaining servers. The switchover would be invisible to the customer.

In order to design and build a good LAN (or add on to an existing LAN), there are a number of important design, configuration, and hardware considerations that you must weigh and balance. Remember, the better you design and configure your LAN, the better your e-business solution will function.

CHAPTER 7

WANs

I n the last chapter, we talked about LANs, the networks that connect all your computer components within one centralized area. But when we consider connecting systems that cover great distances, a different form of construction is required.

INTRODUCTION TO WANS

With a LAN, you strung twisted copper wires between computers, servers, switches, and hubs. But once you get outside the four walls of your business, you can't really string miles and miles of copper wire between your office, satellite offices, or partners' offices. Instead, you rely on wide area network (WAN) technology.

WANs don't affect just your connections with other employees of your company. WAN technology is also the technology that—via the Internet—allows customers to visit your Web site and place an order.

What Is a WAN?

In essence, WANs are two LANs that are connected across a great distance. Computers connected to a wide area network are often connected through public networks, such as the telephone system. They can also be connected through leased lines or satellites. The largest WAN in existence is the Internet.

Depending on your needs (and bank account), you can configure a WAN of any of a wide range of sizes and speeds. If simple connectivity is all that is needed, you can hook up easily across the Internet. On the other hand, if yours is a business that will require lots of bandwidth and assured speed, you aren't limited to the Internet and its nonguaranteed speed. Rather, you can lease fast lines across the state, the country, or even the world.

Two branches of your company on opposite sides of the country can use a WAN to provide seamless connection and access to the same data. Also, customers and clients who need to buy your products or services can use a WAN. In this instance, the most likely way customers and clients will come to you is via the Internet.

WANs, E-Business, and You

So, if the Internet is such a convenient WAN, why do you even have to worry about it? After all, the Internet is already in place; you just have to plug in, right? Yes and no. Yes, you can plug in and get started, but it's a good idea to know the major issues before plugging in and writing checks to an Internet service provider.

It's important to understand how information flows across a WAN, and it's important to know your options when it comes to configuring a WAN. After all, you don't want to pay for a T3 line when you could be getting by on a DSL line. On the flip side, you're in for trouble if you have an ISDN connection that's constantly getting clogged up.

You also have a fair amount of flexibility in WAN design and technology. For instance, by using a virtual private network (VPN), you can enable employees who have to travel to connect to your LAN as if they were at the office. Also, Microsoft offers a fine remote access program that will help you connect from afar.

Let's look at the different technologies and strategies that will give you the WAN solution you need.

WAN ARCHITECTURE

WANs really act just like large LANs, separated across a larger distance. Take a look at Figure 7-1. It's the same figure that we referenced in the preceding chapter (and will reference in Chapter 11 when we talk about firewalls). Now, however, we are talking about the components that make up a WAN.

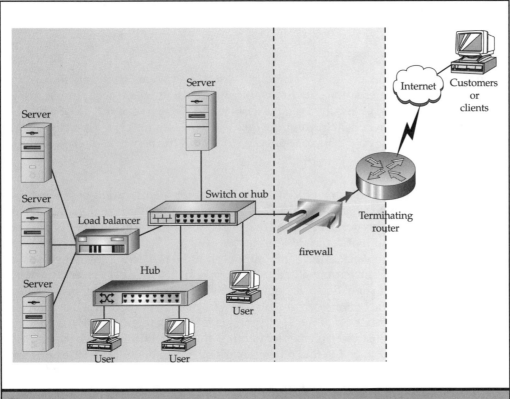

Figure 7-1.   Components in a WAN

Let's start on the easiest portion of the figure first, the client and customer computers. Depending on who will be connecting across your WAN, you may have little to no control over this area. If your WAN is such that the general public will be able to access it across the Internet, then most computer configurations will be entirely out of your hands, and connectivity will rely on your adherence to Internet standards, including TCP/IP (we'll talk about that later). Even if you will be communicating with other businesses and not the general public, it's more than likely that you'll still want to stick with those protocols.

Figure 7-1 next shows a lightning bolt from a cloud representing the Internet. That lightning bolt represents your means of connection. Again, on the client/customer side of the Internet cloud, you'll have absolutely no say in how people connect, but it's critically important that you understand how the lightning bolt on *your* side of the cloud is set up.

Is your connection fast enough? Are you paying too much for a massive connection when a smaller, less expensive one would serve your needs just as well? Are you prepared for the future? These are all considerations you need to address when establishing your *throughput* needs. This, again, is something we'll address in this chapter.

The last stop in Figure 7-1 is the first stop data makes when it comes into your business: the terminating router.

Terminating Routers

When the data stream leaves the WAN and gets into your system, it first goes into a *terminating router*. At this router, the data can be filtered and sent where appropriate. For instance, the router could be set up to send visitors to the Web servers, and those who need access to your LAN can be sent to your firewall. That way, your LAN is protected against the fiercest attacks, but your remote users can still access the network.

What They Do

Terminating routers are like any other routers, except for their location on the network and the added ability to act as firewalls. They also convert low-level protocols, such as a serial connection, to Ethernet. This means that as signals come from your WAN, they are converted into a format that your LAN can understand.

But what about firewalls? Aren't they supposed to be protecting the network? Yes, they are, and they do. But a terminating router supplements your network's security by adding an additional layer of defense. Look at it this way: it's like a burglar breaking into your garage. Even if they manage to get into the garage, they'll discover a deadbolt lock on the door to the house. Even if the hooligan gets into the garage, he still has to worry about getting past the deadbolt. It takes longer for a thug to get through two points of entry and gives you more chance to find out he's working on your network with a crowbar.

Also, if budgeting is a problem, a terminating router can act as a poor man's firewall, staving off unwanted visitors from getting at your network.

NOTE: Terminal routers can be configured to filter out most of the attacks against your system, but your best bet for solid security is to include a firewall, in addition to the terminating router. We talk about firewalls in much greater depth in Chapter 11.

Additionally, terminating routers are effective if you're trying to implement a virtual private network (VPN) or virtual LAN (VLAN) where traffic will be coming across the Internet and accessing the most sensitive parts of your network. Their Quality of Service (QoS) properties ensure that the data needing the fastest delivery is prioritized over the less urgent information. This is especially important if you need to deliver streaming voice or video across a VPN or VLAN.

Models

Several companies offer terminating routers, each including its own levels of features. None of the companies call their products "terminating routers," but all these products provide the same features that you'll need. Cisco and Lucent offer the largest lines of terminating routers. Cisco's product line is their Access Routers, and Lucent's line is its Pipeline family. Table 7-1 represents a few of the terminating routers on the market.

If you are so inclined, you can also set up a Linux box to be a router/firewall. The plus side of this is the cost: the software and configuration are free. However, you'll need to have some knowledge of Linux to get such a system up and running. But if you are on a budget, you can take an old 100–200 Mhz PC and make it a Linux router/firewall.

TCP/IP

Like the LANs protocols we discussed in the last chapter, WANs must also have a common language by which the computers will speak to each other. In the case of WANs, the most predominant protocol is TCP/IP.

The Internet runs over TCP/IP, the Transmission Control Protocol/Internet Protocol. TCP/IP is actually a suite of protocols, each performing a particular role to let computers speak the same language. TCP/IP is universally available and is almost certainly running on the computers you use at work and at home. This is true regardless of LAN protocols, because LAN vendors have implemented TCP/IP compatibility in their products. For example, the latest Novell NetWare product can talk TCP/IP, as can Microsoft Windows 2000.

TCP/IP was designed by the Defense Advanced Research Projects Agency (DARPA) in the 1970s, the design goal being to let dissimilar computers freely communicate regardless of location. Most early TCP/IP work was done on UNIX computers, a fact that contributed to the protocol's popularity as vendors got into the practice of shipping TCP/IP software inside every UNIX computer. As a technology, TCP/IP maps to the OSI reference model, as shown in Figure 7-2.

Looking at Figure 7-2, you can see that TCP/IP focuses on layers 3 and 4 of the OSI reference model. TCP/IP's goal is to move messages through virtually any network technology to set up a connection running virtually any network application.

NOTE: For more information on the OSI Reference Model, flip back to Chapter 6.

	Price	Size	Features	Information
Cisco 1600	$1,500–$2,000	Small office or small business	Modular for scalability and a VPN solution	www.cisco.com/go/1600
Cisco 3600	$3,000–$12,000	Medium to large businesses	VPN solution, supports data, voice, and video over IP	www.cisco.com/go/3600
NetGear RT311 DSL and Cable Modem Internet Gateway Router	$360	10 users	Includes a four-port Ethernet hub running at 10 Mbps and uses Network Address Translation (NAT) as its first line of defense	www.netgear.com
Lucent Pipeline 50 Bridge/ Router	$900	Small offices	Ethernet-to-ISDN router that includes 40-bit IPSec encryption for VPN support; simultaneous IP, IPX, and AppleTalk routing; and multiprotocol bridging	www.lucent.com
LinkSys EtherFast Cable/ DSL Router	$200	253 users	Inexpensive, uses NAT as its first line of defense	www.linksys.com

Table 7-1. A Sampling of Terminating Routers

TCP/IP works because it closely maps to the OSI model at the lowest two levels: the data link and physical layers. This fact lets TCP/IP talk to virtually any networking technology and, indirectly, any type of computer platform. Here are TCP/IP's four abstract layers:

▼ **Network interface** Allows TCP/IP to interact with all modern network technologies by complying with the OSI model.

■ **Internet** Defines how IP directs messages through routers over internetworks such as the Internet and WANs.

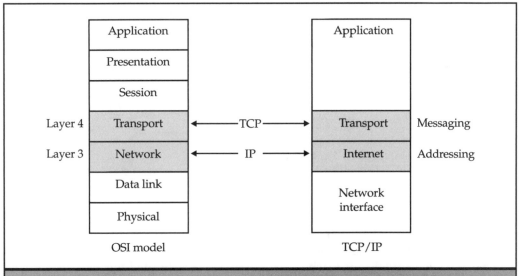

Figure 7-2.   The TCP/IP stack is compliant with the OSI seven-layer reference model

- ■ **Transport**   Defines the mechanics of how messages are exchanged between computers.
- ▲ **Application**   Defines network applications to perform tasks such as file transfer, e-mail, and other useful functions.

TCP/IP is the de facto standard that unifies the Internet; it's why the Internet works. Using it, a computer implementing an OSI-compliant layer network technology (such as Ethernet or Token Ring) overcomes incompatibilities that would otherwise exist between platforms such as Windows, UNIX, Macintosh, IBM mainframes, and the others. We've already covered layers 1 and 2 in our discussion of LAN technologies that connect groups of computers together in a location. Now we'll cover how computers internetwork over the Internet or a WAN.

TCP/IP Messaging

All data that goes over a network must have a format so that devices know how to handle it. TCP/IP's Internet layer, which maps to the OSI model's network layer, is based on a fixed message format called the IP datagram—the bucket that holds the information making up the message. For example, when you download a Web page, the stuff you see on the screen was delivered inside datagrams.

Closely related to the datagram is the packet. Where a *datagram* is a unit of data, a *packet* is a physical message unit entity that passes through the internetwork. People often use the terms interchangeably; the distinction is only important in certain narrow contexts. The key point is that most messages are sent in pieces and reassembled at the receiving end.

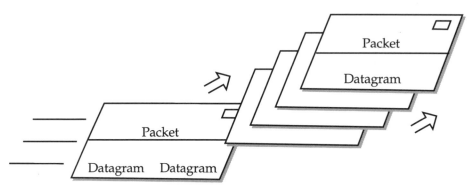

Packet stream

For example, when you send e-mail to someone, it goes over the wire as a stream of packets. A small message might take only ten packets; a big one may be split into thousands. At the opposite extreme, a request-for-service message might take only a single packet.

One advantage of this approach is that if a packet is corrupted during transmission, only that packet need be resent, not the entire message. Another advantage is that no single host is forced to wait an inordinate length of time for another's transmission to complete before being able to transmit its own message.

Establishing a TCP Connection

The TCP connection process is often referred to as the "three-way handshake" because the second step involves the receiving station sending two TCP segments at once. The steps in Figure 7-3 show a couple of the TCP segment fields in action. The first TCP segment's sequence number serves as the initial sequence number, the base number used to keep subsequent packets in proper sequence. The Sequence field is used for reassembling out-of-sequence packets into an understandable message at the receiving end.

Figure 7-3's example shows a PC connecting to a Web server. But any type of end-stations could be talking: a server connecting to another server to perform an e-commerce transaction, two PCs connecting for an IRC chat session, or any connection between two end-stations over an IP network.

IP Addressing

The Internet is a big, big place, holding billions of Web pages—and it's getting bigger every day. Designers had to come up with a way for you to easily find what you want. To that end, IP addresses were developed. These numbers, which you've probably seen here and there, are four sets of digits separated by decimal points, like 220.151.102.10, for example.

IP Addressing Basics

IP addressing solves the problems of Internet organization, and computers can easily keep track of these addresses. We dumb human beings have problems, however, keeping

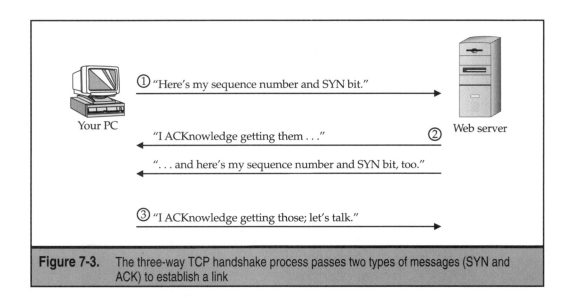

Figure 7-3.   The three-way TCP handshake process passes two types of messages (SYN and ACK) to establish a link

track of really long strings of numbers like 220.151.102.10. So, to make the process easier for us, we use Uniform Resource Locators (URLs), which are then translated back into IP addresses.

To go somewhere on the Internet, you must type a URL into the Address field on your browser. A unique domain name combines with its organization category to form a URL such as velte.com.

URLs only exist to make surfing the Internet easier; they aren't true IP addresses. In other words, if you type the URL "velte.com" into your browser, a query is sent to the nearest Domain Name System (DNS) server to translate the URL to an IP address, as shown in Figure 7-4.

Translation to IP addresses is necessary because the routers and switches that run the Internet don't recognize domain names. Indeed, an IP address must be used just for your query to get as far as the DNS server.

All Internet addresses are IP addresses, issued by the Internet Assigned Numbers Authority (IANA). Domain names are issued by an organization called InterNIC (for Internet Information Center). The primary responsibility of these organizations is to assure that all IP addresses and domain names are unique. For example, velte.com was issued by InterNIC; its IP address, 209.98.208.34, was issued by the ISP, which for its part was issued the IP address from the IANA.

NOTE: A new organization called the Internet Corporation for Assigned Names and Numbers (ICANN) was started in early 1999 to take over assignment duties. ICANN, however, has run into industry resistance and financial difficulties. It remains to be seen whether they'll become the Internet's central registrar.

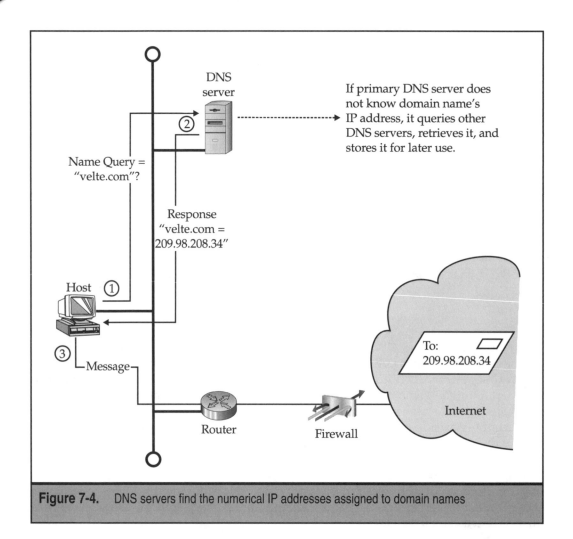

Figure 7-4.   DNS servers find the numerical IP addresses assigned to domain names

The IP Address Format

Every node on the Internet must have an IP address. This includes hosts as well as networks. There's no getting around this rule, because IP addressing is what ties the Internet together. Even stations connected to a LAN with its own addressing system (AppleTalk, for example) must translate to IP in order to enter the Internet.

It's somewhat ironic that, despite the requirement that every IP address be unique to the world, at the same time they all must be in the same format. IP addresses are 32 bits long and divided into four sections, each 8 bits long, called *octets*.

Routers use IP addresses to forward messages through the Internet. Put simply, as the packet hops from router to router, it works its way from left to right across the IP address until it finally reaches the router to which the destination address is attached.

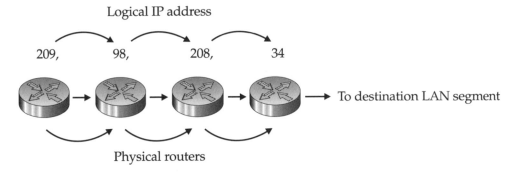

Logical IP address

209,   98,   208,   34

To destination LAN segment

Physical routers

Of course, sometimes a message will go through several router hops before moving closer to its destination. More frequently, messages skip over entire octets and move to the destination LAN segment in just one or two hops.

WAN TECHNOLOGIES

In order for your computers to communicate over a WAN, you can't just stick a piece of cabling in the air and expect instant connectivity (depending on technological developments, maybe in a couple years, but not now). For computers to talk over a WAN, they require various bits and pieces of hardware and software to communicate.

In this section, we'll look at the various technological components that are in play when it comes to WANs. We'll talk about the physical media that will connect your WAN, those media's protocols, and technologies like virtual private networking that will allow you to connect, remotely, to your LAN. We'll also highlight Microsoft's Remote Access Service, which is a highly effective remote access technology built into Windows NT and 2000.

Transports

A *trunk* is any high-capacity point-to-point data link. Trunks can exist within buildings and office campuses, but they're best known as WAN links between buildings, cities, regions, and even continents.

WAN technology has evolved markedly over the past decade, and not just with the Internet boom. For example, Frame Relay packet-switching technology proved dramatically less expensive than dedicated leased WAN lines. We'll briefly review the WAN technologies in use today. They are all dedicated circuits (not dial-in and hang-up) with high bandwidth used to connect locations with many users, as opposed to small office/home office (SOHO) sites with one or two users.

Most companies are replacing leased-line WAN services that share infrastructure services. Their primary motive is to save money, but flexibility is also a big benefit.

T1 and T3 Leased Lines

T1 and T3 are the predominant leased-line technologies in use in North America and Japan today. (There are rough equivalents in Europe called E1 and E3.) Leased-line circuits (or parts of circuits) are reserved for use by the company that rents them and are paid for at a flat monthly rate regardless of how much is used.

Unlike a dial-up connection, a leased line is always active. The fee for the connection is generally a fixed monthly rate primarily determined by the distance between end points and the speed of the circuit. Because the connection doesn't carry anybody else's communications, the carrier can assure a given level of quality.

T1 is the most commonly used digital line technology. It uses a telecommunications technology called time-division multiplexing (TDM) to yield a data rate of about 1.5 Mbps. TDM combines streams of data by assigning each stream a different time slot in a set and repeatedly transmitting a fixed sequence of time slots over a single transmission channel. T1 lines use copper wire, both within and among metropolitan areas. You can purchase a T1 circuit from your local phone carrier or rent a portion of its bandwidth in an arrangement called fractionalized T1. Most Internet service providers (ISPs) are connected to the Internet via T1 circuits or larger.

T3 is the successor to T1. T3 circuits are dedicated phone connections that carry data at 43 Mbps. T3 lines are used mostly by so-called Tier 1 ISPs (ISPs that connect smaller ISPs to the Internet) and by large enterprises. Because of their sheer bandwidth and expense, most T3 lines are leased as fractional T3 lines. T3 lines are often called *DS3* lines.

Frame Relay

Frame Relay switches packets over a shared packet-switching network owned by a carrier such as a regional telephone company, MCI, or AT&T. As depicted in Figure 7-5, Frame Relay uses local phone circuits to link remote locations. The long-distance hauls are over a telecommunications infrastructure owned by the Frame Relay provider, shared among a number of other customers.

The primary benefit of Frame Relay is cost efficiency. Frame Relay takes its name from the fact that it puts data into variable-sized message units called *frames*. It leaves session management and error correction to nodes it operates at various connection points, thereby speeding network performance. Most Frame Relay customers rent so-called permanent virtual circuits, or PVCs. A PVC gives the customer a continuous, dedicated connection without that customer's having to pay for a leased line, which uses dedicated permanent circuits. Frame Relay customers are charged according to level of usage. They also have the option of selecting between service levels, where QoS is programmed according to what priority the customer's frames are given inside the Frame Relay cloud.

Frame Relay networks themselves sit atop T1 or T3 trunks operated by the Frame Relay network operator. Use of Frame Relay makes economic sense when traffic isn't heavy enough to require a dedicated ATM connection.

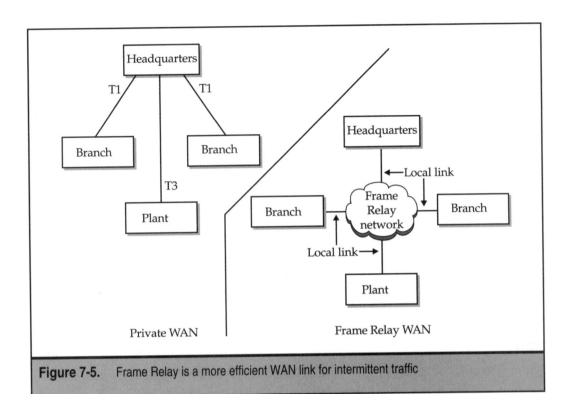

Figure 7-5. Frame Relay is a more efficient WAN link for intermittent traffic

ATM

Asynchronous Transfer Mode (ATM) is a cell-relay-based technology that uses fixed 53-byte cells, which are similar to Frame Relay's frames. Although the industry had been slow to adopt ATM, its popularity has been increasing. ATM can be found in the backbones of larger networks and is being used to build high-capacity WANs. ATM is optimized to handle services on the network that extend beyond standard data services into voice and video applications.

Cisco has shown a considerable interest in ATM and in 1991 cofounded the ATM Forum with Sprint, Net/Adaptive, and Northern Telecom. The ATM forum has been working to ensure that ATM survives and evolves with interoperability in mind. Because of this, ATM has slowly gained wide acceptance and has been implemented by a large number of vendors.

ATM also incorporates advanced QoS mechanisms into its specifications. ATM is built from the ground up to support managed data flows through virtual channels. When applications require higher bandwidth, ATM can throttle other forms of data, allowing data with the higher bandwidth requirements to pass through the network unobstructed.

Besides increased bandwidth, one of the most immediate benefits of ATM is the integration of voice- and LAN-based traffic on a single platform. ATM utilizes LAN Emulation (LANE) to allow Ethernet and Token Ring network devices to use ATM transport by employing Layer 2 MAC encapsulation; in effect, this is *bridging*. These bridged segments are called ELANs. An ATM network can have several ELANs; however, since the ATM network is really just tunneling the traffic, you must still rely on routers outside the ATM network to route traffic between ELANs. For full routing and switching, you must install ATM interface cards on your network devices. In this way, you can begin to realize the full potential of ATM in the traditional network environment.

Protocols

Just as with LANs, computers operating on a WAN need to speak the same language. The following are a couple of common protocols that will keep a solid constant data flow across your LAN.

HDLC

The *High-Level Data Link Control (HDLC)* protocol allows Cisco routers to talk to each other over serial interfaces. This protocol is typically used on point-to-point WAN connections. This is the default encapsulation on a Cisco serial interface, and it supports all of the most common network protocols.

PPP

The *Point-to-Point Protocol (PPP)* supports TCP/IP and IPX. PPP uses the lower-level Link Control Protocol to establish, set up, and maintain the link or line connections. PPP also uses the Network Control Protocol to support IP and IPX. This is used mostly in dial-up connections between routers and other devices. Microsoft clients dialing into a Cisco access server should typically use PPP.

Dial-in Technologies

If yours is a smaller business and you don't need something as beefy as a T1 or T3 line—or if you have satellite offices that need WAN connections, but not at T1 or T3 levels—a couple of plain old telephone system options exist that provide more punch than a 28.8 Kbps modem.

Two technologies have been introduced to bring digital bandwidth into the home and small office: ISDN and DSL. ISDN was introduced in the 1980s, but local telephone carriers have been slow in making it available. DSL is hot new technology, promising even better speeds and wider availability.

Dial-in technologies differ from other WAN media in that connections made using them are temporary. In other words, once the computer user is finished with the session, hanging up the telephone terminates the circuit. To this day, most homes are connected via analog phone circuits. Because normal lines are analog, they require modems at each end to operate, and for that reason they are referred to by some as *analog modem* circuits.

The major problem with analog modem circuits is that they're slow. What slows them down is that the acoustical signals use only a tiny fraction of the raw bandwidth available in copper telephone system cables because they were designed for voice, not data. This is why the state-of-the-art analog home connection is now 56 Kbps—glacially slow compared to 100 Mbps Fast Ethernet now standard inside office buildings.

ISDN

ISDN, which stands for *Integrated Services Digital Network,* was proposed as the first digital service to the home. ISDN requires a special phone circuit from a local telephone carrier and is unavailable in many areas. The key improvement over analog modem lines is that ISDN circuits are digital, and for that reason they use so-called CPEs (customer premise equipment) instead of modems (CPE is an old-time telephony term).

ISDN creates multiple channels over a single line. A *channel* is a data path multiplexed over a single communications medium (*multiplex* means to combine multiple signals over a single line). The basic kind of ISDN circuit is a BRI circuit (for Basic Rate Interface) with two so-called *B,* or bearer, channels for payload data. Figure 7-6 contrasts an analog modem circuit with an ISDN BRI circuit.

Each B-channel runs at 64 Kbps for a total of 128 Kbps payload bandwidth. Having separate B-channels enhances throughput for symmetrical connections, in other words, sessions characterized by the bidirectional simultaneous flow of traffic. A third channel,

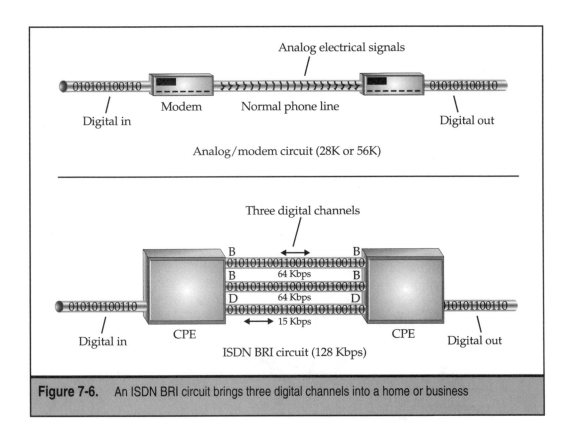

Figure 7-6.   An ISDN BRI circuit brings three digital channels into a home or business

called the *D*, or delta, channel, carries 15 Kbps. The D-channel is dedicated to network control instead of payload data. Separating control overhead signals enhances ISDN's performance and reliability.

A second kind of ISDN circuit is a PRI circuit (for Primary Rate Interface). PRI is basically the same as BRI, except that it packages up to 23 B-channels for up to 1.544 Mbps total payload bandwidth. Small businesses use PRI circuits to connect multiple users, competing at the low end of T1's traditional market niche.

DSL

DSL stands for "digital subscriber line." As the name suggests, DSL also runs digital signals over copper wire. DSL uses sophisticated algorithms to modulate signals in such a way that much more bandwidth can be squeezed from existing last-mile telephone infrastructure.

DSL is an inherently asymmetric telecommunications technology. What this means is that data can be moved much faster downstream (from the local phone carrier to your home) than upstream. There are several types of DSL; two are important to this discussion:

▼ **ADSL**   Asymmetric DSL, a two-way circuit that can handle about 640 Kbps upstream and up to 6 Mbps downstream.

▲ **DSL Lite**   Also called G.Lite, a slower, less expensive technology that can carry data at rates between about 1.5 Mbps and 6 Mbps downstream, and from 128 Kbps to 384 Kbps upstream. The exact speeds depend on the equipment you install.

DSL's inherent asymmetry fits perfectly with the Internet, where most small office/home office users download far more data than they upload.

The key fact to know is that DSL requires a special piece of equipment called a DSL modem to operate. It's the DSL modem that splits signals into upstream and downstream channels. The major difference with DSL Lite is that the splitting is done at the telephone switching station, not in the home or small office. Figure 7-7 depicts this.

Not requiring DSL signal splitting in the home makes DSL much more affordable than ISDN. To use most DSL circuits, you must be located no farther than about four or five miles from the telephone switching station, or Central Office (CO).

Compaq, Microsoft, and Intel are cooperating on future DSL standards in hopes that it will replace ISDN as the last-mile technology of choice. DSL's fat bandwidth is necessary to realize the goal of continuous-transmission video, audio, 3-D animation, and other multimedia applications many envision for the Web.

Virtual Private Networks (VPNs)

WAN connectivity can serve two different types of clients: customers and clients accessing a Web server (for example) or your own employees accessing the most sensitive parts of your network. A typical solution for the former is a basic Web site, but letting employees and others access the heart of your LAN is a little trickier and—from a security standpoint—more nerve-wracking.

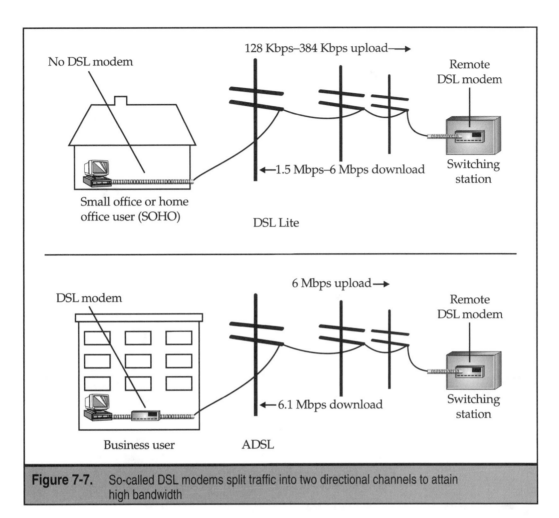

No DSL modem

128 Kbps–384 Kbps upload⟶

Remote
DSL modem

←1.5 Mbps–6 Mbps download

Switching
station

Small office or home
office user (SOHO)

DSL Lite

DSL modem

6 Mbps upload⟶

Remote
DSL modem

←6.1 Mbps download

Switching
station

Business user   ADSL

Figure 7-7. So-called DSL modems split traffic into two directional channels to attain high bandwidth

Virtual private networks (VPN) solve that problem by creating a secure link between your LAN and a computer out in the field somewhere. This is illustrated in Figure 7-8. The connection allows someone in West Virginia to work on the LAN as if they were on-site with the other computers in Arizona, for instance.

A VPN is a private connection between two different locations. This connection is typically encrypted, may employ a tunnel through the Internet, and may have both. The Point-to-Point Protocol (PPP) remote access protocol is often used to encrypt the data passing over the VPN. Once the data is encrypted, it is routed over a dial-up or LAN connection.

IPSec

IPSec is the set of protocols that supports secure exchange of packets at the IP layer. Because IPSec operates at the network layer (layer 3), it can provide secure transport capable of supporting any application that uses IP.

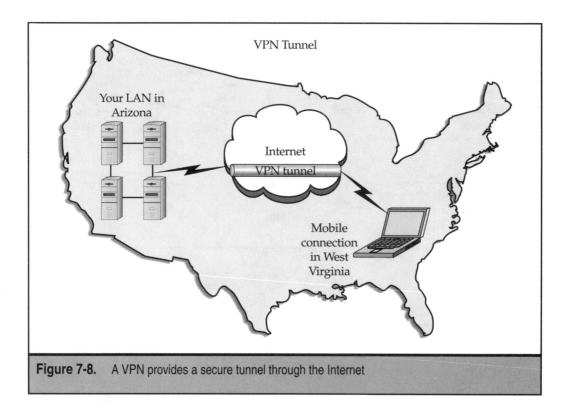

Figure 7-8.   A VPN provides a secure tunnel through the Internet

IPSec provides three main areas of security when transmitting information across a network:

▼   Authentication of packets between the sending and receiving devices

■   Integrity of data when being transmitted

▲   Privacy of data when being transmitted

IPSec operates in two modes—transport and tunnel:

▼   In *transport* mode, Encapsulation Security Protocol (ESP) and Authentication Headers (AH) reside in the original IP packet between the IP header and upper-layer extension header information. For instance, Windows 2000 IPSec uses transport mode to provide security between two end systems, such as a Windows 2000 Professional client and a Windows 2000 Server.

▲   In *tunnel* mode, IPSec places an original IP packet into a new IP packet and inserts the AH or ESP between the IP header of the new packet and the original IP packet. The new IP packet leads to the tunnel endpoint, and the original IP header specifies the packet's destination. You can use tunnel mode between two security gateways, such as tunnel servers, routers, or firewalls.

IPSec tunnel is the most common mode; it works like this:

1. A standard IP packet is sent to the IPSec device with the expectation that the packet will be encrypted and routed to the destination system over the network.

2. The first of the two IPSec devices, which in this case would probably be either a firewall or a router, authenticates with the receiving device.

3. The two IPSec devices negotiate the encryption and authentication algorithms to be used.

4. The IPSec sender encrypts the IP packet containing the data and then places it into another IP packet with an authentication header.

5. The packet is sent across the TCP/IP network.

6. The IPSec receiver reads the IP packet, verifies it, and then unwraps the encrypted payload and decrypts it.

7. The receiver forwards the original packet to its destination.

Point-to-Point Tunneling Protocol (PPTP)

The Point-to-Point Tunneling Protocol (PPTP) enables the secure transfer of data from a remote client to a private enterprise server. PPTP supports multiple network protocols, including IP, IPX, and NetBEUI. You can use PPTP to provide a secure virtual network using dial-up lines, over LANs, over WANs, or across the Internet and other TCP/IP-based networks. In order to establish a PPTP VPN, you must have a PPTP server and a PPTP client. Windows 2000 Client and Server software includes the necessary parameters to configure PPTP communication.

Layer Two Tunneling Protocol (L2TP)

PPTP is a Microsoft technology, which establishes a virtual connection across a public network. PPTP, together with encryption and authentication, provide a private and secure network. Cisco developed a protocol similar to PPTP, Layer Two Forwarding (L2F), but it required Cisco hardware at both ends to support it. Cisco and Microsoft then merged the best features of PPTP and L2F and developed the Layer Two Tunneling Protocol (L2TP). Similar to PPTP, L2TP provides a way for remote users to extend a PPP link across the Internet from the ISP to a corporate site.

VPN Implementation

Virtual private networking allows organizations to use semiprivate and public networks like the Internet as though they are private and secure networks. Although there have been many implementations of VPN technology, those based on IPSec promise to offer interoperability with other vendors. This will allow organizations to establish VPNs between each other without requiring that they use the same brand of firewall or router.

VPNs use encryption and encapsulation technology to create a secure tunnel over a variety of transmission media. VPNs use IP tunneling (encapsulation) that subsequently transports encrypted packets. The encapsulated packets travel through the Internet just like their clear-text siblings. Once they reach their destination, they are decrypted and sent along to the intended recipient. Authentication technology is used to make sure the session between the two devices is authorized. Microsoft's Point-to-Point Tunneling Protocol (PPTP) enables organizations to create dial-up VPNs.

Router vendors have offered products that support the tunneling of data across the Internet and other networks. More recently, they have added various methods for encrypting the contents of the tunneled packets, so that true VPNs can be established. Firewall and router vendors have also integrated tunnels with encryption into their products. All these products are poised to reshape how we use the Internet and free us from the limitations on where we can compute.

Organizations will be able to replace or supplement costly private network bandwidth and perhaps use the bandwidth on the Internet access they already have. With PPTP VPN technology for dial-up access, an organization can outsource the management of modems and dial access equipment to their ISP. If the ISP has a national or international presence, traveling remote users can dial into a local ISP point of presence, avoiding the cost of long distance and 800-number calls. VPNs allow you to reduce network management responsibilities, but remember that you will still need to provide support and management for the VPN software, hardware, and configuration.

Organizations can also use VPNs to link remote LANs across the Internet or any other IP network. VPNs are flexible, multipoint connections that can be set up or closed down quickly. Because firewall vendors plan to include IPSec VPN technology, organizations will be able to set up and tear down VPNs between internal and external organizations on an as-needed basis. These technologies will be instrumental in facilitating rapid deployment of communication channels between individual users and large organizations alike.

Routing and Remote Access Service

One of the most convenient ways to connect to your network across great distances is via Microsoft Windows NT and 2000's Routing and Remote Access Service (RRAS). The tool is a nice piece of standard equipment that comes with either platform and allows you to perform a number of important functions on your network.

Clients and Servers

Windows Routing and Remote Access Service can be divided into two separate components: the client and the server. The client is found in the home or on the road, so it typically dials the server or an Internet service provider (ISP) or private service provider (PSP) to initiate a connection.

Because both the client and the server components of RRAS ship with Windows 2000 and NT and because client packages ship with or are available for Windows 2000, Win 95/98 and Win 3.x, no additional software purchases are necessary to enable basic and secure dial-up services. Also, since most non-Microsoft RRAS clients either include or support software for Microsoft RRAS, dial-up access can be established for little more than

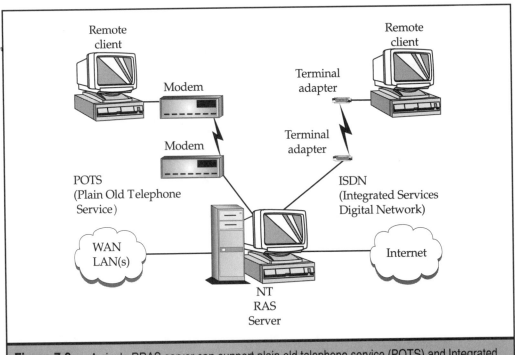

Figure 7-9.   A single RRAS server can support plain old telephone service (POTS) and Integrated Services Digital Network (ISDN) connections

the cost of modem hardware, phone lines, and, of course, your time. Figure 7-9 illustrates a single RRAS server dial-up solution. In this example, an RRAS server can be accessed via a standard phone line or through ISDN. Additionally, the RRAS server has a connection to the LAN/WAN and the Internet.

By purchasing additional hardware (such as modem banks), you can construct larger dial-in facilities using Windows RRAS Server. For even higher-capacity dial-up services, multiple servers can be deployed to allow for a larger number of simultaneous users and to provide a high level of fault tolerance. You might even consider placing RRAS servers in different physical locations as part of a disaster recovery strategy. Figure 7-10 illustrates a multiple RRAS server dial-up solution.

Figure 7-10 shows two RRAS servers entitled East and West. The remote clients have been configured so that they can selectively dial either one. Should one server fail, the other is still available to accept connections. To ensure full availability, each server should be capable of supporting your entire user base at any given time. This means that each server should be running at a maximum of 50 percent capacity during normal operation. Having a backup server is useless if only half of your users can connect—just ask the half who can't connect.

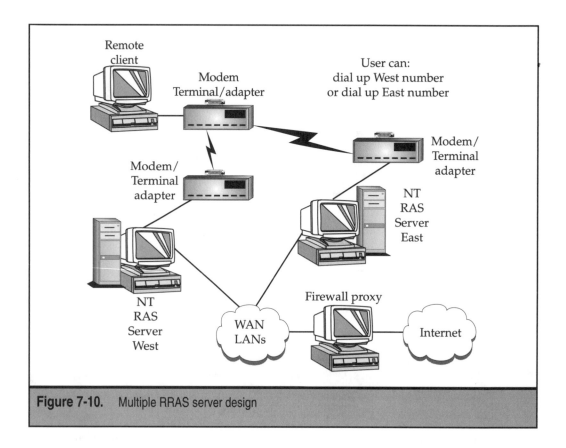

Figure 7-10. Multiple RRAS server design

Office-to-Office Connectivity Using RRAS

Although you can configure RRAS so that multiple users could use a single modem connection, you should be very careful about that type of connectivity because bandwidth is so limited that just a couple of users could easily bring the link to a crawl. In all but the smallest of remote offices, other alternatives, such as small, dedicated routers using ISDN, make more sense than using dial-on-demand RRAS. However, let's take a look at a situation where using dial-on-demand RRAS would be an effective solution to a connectivity problem in a small, remote office.

In this example, the main corporate headquarters of a company is located in the center of the region. Most of the company's regional offices have more than 100 users each, so they use dedicated 56K to T-1–sized circuits (via Cisco 2600 series routers) to establish a 7 × 24 routed WAN back to corporate headquarters.

The problem: Whenever corporate decides to look into a new regional market, they set up a small office in the area staffed with an "advance" team of financial and market analysts (four to seven people), who spend about two to three months in a small office in the area conducting research. They usually move in quickly and need connectivity so that they can exchange e-mail, documents, and spreadsheets with headquarters.

In response to these needs, you set up a small server that acts as a RAS dial-on-demand server as well as a small file and print server in the remote office. Since you already have a few remote access servers at corporate headquarters to support dial-up users, the server is configured to use the same facilities. The remote team gets a rapidly deployable, portable network with WAN access at a reasonable cost. Once the decision has been made to open a regional office, the dial-on-demand solution can be used until staffing has been completed and a more permanent solution can be implemented.

Hardware Scenarios

The best way to begin to develop a RAS solution is to make a back-of-the-envelope calculation of the number of users you expect to be connected at the peak usage and the expected throughput demands of each user. Naturally, the users are limited by the connection type. In all likelihood, users don't use the entire, offered throughput 100 percent of the time.

Next, look at solutions that are in place serving users. You might have another division in the company that has already connected its users with RAS. This is a great place to start trying to gauge your system. Here are some basic guidelines for three different-sized organizations.

Small Sites   In this example, there is a small organizational unit with up to 50 employees. You need to provide dial-up support for a small number of users when they are traveling or working from home. Each might have a 28.8 Kbps modem. Their primary activities are transferring small files and checking their e-mail.

Because you think the site may grow in the future, you should probably start with fast modems connected to an eight-port serial adapter connected to a Pentium 500 MHz machine with at least 64MB of RAM. Because of the slow speeds of the dial-up connections, the data coming from the users is not likely to overload the CPU. In the future, you could double the number of modems to the computer without much worry of having to upgrade the server.

Medium-Sized Sites   For medium-sized sites, we will assume about 500 users. As with all sites, there are a number of users who want to dial up using modems. Additionally, there are your power users who connect via ISDN. The users conduct file transfers, check e-mail, and may run remote access software. They have tremendous fluctuations in their traffic demands, and thus your solution should support the erratic throughput requirements. Let's also assume that your peak concurrent sessions will not exceed 24 POTS dial sessions and 10 ISDN dial sessions in the near future.

At a minimum, you should have one system powered by a Pentium 700 MHz-class processor with 128MB of RAM. You should use multiport serial adapters connected to modem concentrators that support 8–18 modems each. You will also need external BRI ISDN adapters connected to your server by an ISDN interface adapter.

Large Sites   For this exercise, we will assume a large site is 1,000+ users. If your site has many more than 1,000 users, you can scale this paradigm by duplicating the basic system for, perhaps, divisions within the company. You will almost certainly be supporting file and print sharing from servers within the organization. There may be e-mail, Internet access, and the use of applications over the RAS connection.

To support this load, you should use modem pools that can support 60 or more analog connections. Also, you will need PRI ISDN adapters. These devices are typically proprietary devices that have a single, concentrated connection to the computer. The server should be a fast Pentium computer with one to four processors depending on the user load and other duties it may perform. For example, if you also use the RRAS server as a user authentication device, you'll need to take that into account when estimating the necessary processing power. The server should have at least 256MB of RAM.

Once you have purchased a system and put it in place, you should allow a test group of users to try it out. You can closely monitor the usage of the RAS server using Microsoft's Performance Monitor. Some key indicators to watch include:

▼   100 percent of modems used for any length of time

■   100 percent CPU utilization

■   Extensive disk swapping

■   Modem errors such as CRC errors that indicate poor line quality

▲   Serial overrun errors that indicate that the computer can't keep up with the incoming data

Having considered the results from the test group, you should make any necessary changes/additions and test again to make sure problems have been resolved. Then, deploy your solution to the rest of your users and continue to monitor the RAS servers for the previously mentioned problems.

Service Providers

Before you request a semi truck full of servers and equipment so that you can build the ultimate remote access solution, you should consider some of the alternatives that third-party vendors can provide. We will briefly cover the alternatives to buying a truck-load of modems and installing them in your server room.

Using an Internet Service Provider

The first alternative is to consider using an ISP. Contracting with a regional or national ISP can give your users access to hundreds to thousands of modems that you won't have to reset at night. Depending on your needs, an ISP could provide your users with roaming accounts so that they could dial in from Boston on Monday, Minneapolis on Tuesday, and San Francisco on Wednesday.

The infrastructure scenario would look like this: Your ISP provides you with access to modems that allow your users to dial in and connect to the Internet (see Figure 7-11).

Your client machines are configured with Windows 2000 running TCP/IP and the PPTP client software installed and configured using a client installer that you or your ISP wrote. You have a T-1 from your ISP connected to a backbone area on your network. The point of access is protected by a firewall to the PPTP server.

Behind the firewall, you have a Windows 2000 Server with RAS configured as your PPTP server. The server is configured to only accept PPTP VPN traffic; it takes the encrypted traffic originating from the remote client, decrypts it on the inside of your firewall, and sends the traffic on your internal network. Return traffic destined for the remote client is encrypted by the PPTP server and sent out through the firewall, onto the Internet through the encrypted VPN, and back to the remote client.

This scenario allows you to use the Internet as a WAN, while outsourcing your modem headaches to an ISP, although you may still have to manage the firewall and the PPTP server(s) and the associated security.

Using a Private Service Provider

The other option mentioned was the use of a PSP to provision modems and network connectivity back into your network. They provide local-dial modem access throughout the

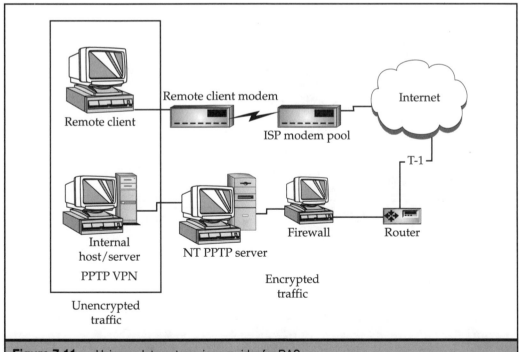

Figure 7-11.   Using an Internet service provider for RAS

world and send your traffic across their switched network to a host or hosts connected to your network. They manage the modems and servers and maintain a help desk for connection-related dial problems. An infrastructure scenario using a PSP would look like Figure 7-12.

In this example, your PSP provides you with access to modems that allow your users to dial in and connect to their private network. Your client machines are configured with Windows 98 running TCP/IP, IPX, or NetBEUI. The client software is installed and configured by an installer program that your PSP prepared for you. You would probably have 512KB of bandwidth using X.25 circuits from your PSP into your facilities. They are connected to four Windows 2000 RAS servers using an Eicon X.25 card. The point of access onto your network is on the Ethernet interface on the RAS server. A firewall stands between the RAS servers and your network. It is configured to allow authorized traffic through and deny all other traffic.

The PSP manages all the circuits and hardware for you, letting you manage the user accounts. The client dials in to a local number and is authenticated once to gain access to the private network; the traffic is then routed across the PSP private network to a specific RAS server. The user is authenticated again, and the traffic is then passed through the RAS server onto the internal network.

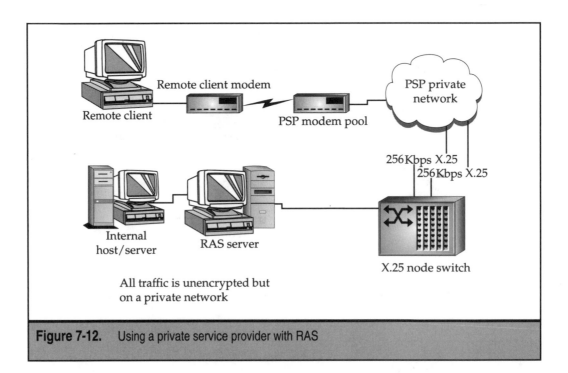

Figure 7-12.   Using a private service provider with RAS

This scenario also allows you to use the PSP network as a wide area network while outsourcing your modem headaches. In addition, you don't have to worry about maintaining the server OS or hardware or monitoring the status of the incoming circuits; they do all of that for you. You are left managing the user accounts and helping with problem resolution when it appears that a remote client problem may be related to the network. The amount of operational overhead can be dramatically reduced, especially in environments where there is a very high volume of RAS traffic.

E-BUSINESS CONSIDERATIONS

Once you've decided how you will build and configure your WAN, there are some other issues you must address. You'll need to decide how much bandwidth you'll need to keep your site up and running. You'll also need to determine how much bandwidth will be enough to cover your administrative needs. Additionally, you'll need to monitor your network and make sure traffic is coming and going to your site as smoothly as possible.

In this section, we'll look at some of the administrative details you should nail down before deciding on a WAN for your e-business.

Management Tools

How do you know how many hits per minute you get, or what users are retrieving from your Web site? You can scour the log files and try to make sense of them, or you can use a management software tool that can do these tasks and much more, such as finding references to nonexistent pages or simulating hits. Some Web management tools for Windows are listed in Table 7-2.

As you can see, there are a number of helpful Web management tools out there. But as more and more business is conducted over the Internet, look for more developers to create tools to help manage your Internet resources.

Product	Contact	Price (US $)
SiteSweeper	www.sitetech.com	$230
net.Analysis Pro 4.5	www.netgenesis.com	$2,500
WebTrends Enterprise Reporting Server	www.webtrends.com	$2,000
EBT DynaBase	www.ebt.com	$2,500

Table 7-2. Web Management Tools Provide Helpful Usage and Server Information

Making the Connection

Implementing complex technologies into a network is always challenging. Introducing new technology into a large-scale enterprise network environment poses additional challenges. The issue of scalability is sure to be among the first to surface. What works well for a dozen nodes doesn't always work well for a hundred, a thousand, or ten thousand nodes.

The complexity in connecting your Web server to the network or Internet is often an overlooked issue. Serious consideration must be given to deciding how to connect your users to your new Internet server. With a myriad of acronyms and choices, it is often confusing to determine what exactly you need. You don't want to put a small pipe in front of your new server, making it useless, but you don't want to pay for extra bandwidth that isn't used.

Connecting to the Internet

We talked about some of the issues regarding ISPs and PSPs earlier in this chapter, but there are some other details that you should satisfy yourself with before writing a check and committing your company. If you do not have an agreement with your ISP for an existing connection to the Internet, you will want to find an ISP that will fit your needs. Some of the questions to ask your prospective ISP are

▼ How many hops are you from a major backbone?

■ What different types of dedicated access do you offer?

■ What is the setup charge for different services?

▲ What are the monthly charges?

The fewer the number of hops the ISP is from a major backbone such as MCI or AT&T, the faster the service and the fewer points of failure between the Internet and your business. It is also important that you pick an ISP that offers connections of greater bandwidth than what you need now. This way, it is relatively easy to upgrade in the future without having to change ISPs. Aside from monthly access charges, be sure to verify the installation charges. They tend to vary wildly from ISP to ISP. For many ISPs, this is where they make a good deal of their money.

Costs for varying connections will vary from area to area. However, Table 7-3 illustrates some of the different connectivity options and their relative costs. The table can also help you ballpark the connection needs of your business. Of course, the number of users that each type of connectivity can support varies tremendously, depending on how active the users are. The relative costs listed in Table 7-3 show a comparison to the cost of a typical 28.8 Kbps connection.

Throughput Requirements

With all these options and the rapid changes in network technologies, it is hard to know exactly what to purchase. It is especially difficult if you haven't had a server up before to

Type	Bandwidth	Estimated # of Users	Relative Cost
Modem	28.8 Kbps	1–5	1
DSL	Typically 256+ Kbps	1–50	2
ISDN	65 Kbps	5–10	3
ISDN	128 Kbps	5–50	5
T1 (DS1)	1.54 Mbps	50–500	10
T3 (DS3)	45 Mbps	4,000+	100
ATM	155–622 Mbps	10,000+	200+

Table 7-3. ISPs Offer Many Different Connection Types

gauge utilization. Nonetheless, there are some back-of-the-envelope calculations you can perform to get a rough estimate of the demand that will be placed on your Web server.

First, you will need to know the size of the data users are going to be pulling from the server. Go to your default Web page, the one that everyone logs onto. Sum up all the items on that page. Do the same for a couple other pages. Add all these together to get your average number of bytes that a typical user is going to request per session. For example, let's say that you have an initial page that contains 200KB and two others have sizes of 300KB and 250KB. Your total, then, is 750KB per session. To give the measure some element of time, pull the pages down yourself and see how long you take to examine the material. If you spend about two minutes pulling down and looking at the pages, you can estimate that an average session takes two minutes and transfers 750KB.

Now you will need to estimate how many users will be accessing the site during its busiest time. In this example, you estimate that there are ten concurrent users at 9 A.M., the busiest time of the day for this server. So your demand is:

$$10 \times 750\text{KB} / 120 \text{ s} = 62.5 \text{ KB/s}$$

This value is in bytes, and since throughput is usually measured in bits, we need to multiply this number by 12 (8 bits in a byte + 4 bits for overhead). Thus, our demand can be expressed as: $62.5 \times 12 = 750$ Kbps.

You might want to consider a T1 line or a fractional T1 line. If this rate of hits is sustained, you certainly want to meet the demand. If this is only a transient peak, you should consider a Frame Relay link that can temporarily burst above the data rate of the line. Other alternatives to consider are reducing the size of each page by using text wherever possible, decreasing the size of your graphics, and reducing the number of loadable modules such as Java applications. Additionally, reorganizing your site to reduce the amount of time it takes for users to find what they need can decrease the download size.

Service Level Agreements

When you decide which ISP or PSP to select, you should be aware of a number of issues and have the answers before you sign on the dotted line.

SLAs—don't sweat it, this has nothing to do with the Symbionese Liberation Army, it means Service Level Agreement—are a great thing to have if you plan to use the Internet to make money. Basically, it works like this: The SLA is a contract between your company and the ISP that specifies minimums for what they will provide. If you have decided that you will need a certain amount of bandwidth at all times, the SLA will bind your ISP to that amount.

The SLA specifies how much traffic the client can send for a certain fee and what will happen to excessive traffic. The essential element of the SLA is the Traffic Conditioning Specification (TCS), which is a technical specification for the treatment of packets.

Be sure to check out your ISP, first. Here are a few of the most important things to look for:

▼ Cost should be secondary to services and quality. Too often companies lazily look at ISPs that are in their price range, then try to piece together an offering from there. The ISP's ability to deliver is the most important thing. If you go with something because it's less expensive, you'll be paying for it in the long run.

■ The ISP should be strategically and financially sound. Don't be afraid to dig around and ask questions. If you're dealing with small firms, a good way to gauge their quality is by how regularly the bills arrive. If they're three months late, they have a problem. On the other hand, with large companies, strategy shifts are a common problem that can inconvenience your e-business.

■ Ask about packet loss and latency figures and even perform "ping" tests, where a packet Internet groper puts intentional stress on the network to test its stability. Be sure to check out network infrastructure, too.

■ Make sure your ISP will be there for you. Round-the-clock service is just as important as performance. If your system goes down, your ISP should be able to get it back up quickly.

■ The ISP should offer the right options. This should be true not only for where your company is today, but for where it wants to be next year and the year after that. An ISP should offer access options such as plenty of points of presence, dedicated access for different speeds, and Frame Relay or ATM networks. It must offer security services that meet your needs, no matter if that means off-the-shelf products or managed firewall servers. It should already have—or at least be developing—service options such as news feeds, network management, intranets, or VPNs.

▲ Talk to your colleagues. Use personal experience, especially from people you know. Most often ISPs are chosen by someone calling a friend in an IS position.

Finding an ISP isn't as easy as opening the Yellow Pages and looking up "ISPs." Certainly, the expanding nature of the Internet makes it tricky to find the latest and most complete list of ISPs out there. However, you can search a list of ISPs by area code by visiting www.isps.com. You can find local ISPs, national ISPs with a local presence, and ISPs with an 800 number you can dial into.

Redundant Connections

Let's consider two companies, Widgetech and CompuGlobal Megaware. Each of these Los Angeles–based companies serves a national customer base on the Internet and receives a fair amount of business. Then, out of the blue, the big earthquake hits, California slides into the drink, and now Arizona offers the best beachfront property in America. Bad news for Widgetech and CompuGlobal Megaware: their offices (and servers) just slid into the ocean.

However, Widgetech was smart enough to place another set of servers, mirroring the content of their Los Angeles–based machines, in Des Moines. After the quake, CompuGlobal Megaware's sales came to a tectonic-plate grinding halt. On the other hand, the Des Moines servers took over, keeping Widgetech in business.

This was, of course, an extreme example of the benefit of redundancy, but it still shows the need for it. Even if the catastrophe is something like a power outage, mirroring your business content on another bank of servers can keep your business on its feet, as is illustrated in Figure 7-13.

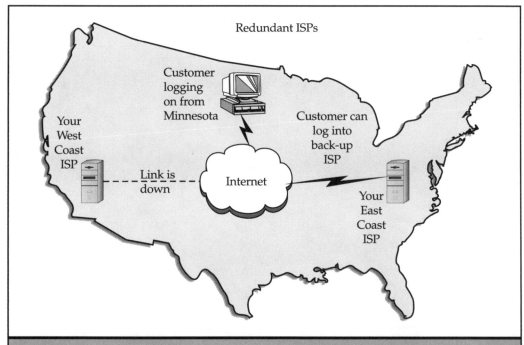

Figure 7-13. A redundant ISP will ensure connectivity in the event of catastrophe

You should also consider the merits of setting up your company on two separate ISPs. In the event that one goes belly-up or has some other catastrophe, it won't be your business that suffers.

It also makes good sense to have a backup system in place just for simple load balancing. If you have a server farm set up in Virginia and another in California, it will be easier for traffic west of the Mississippi to be routed to California, and traffic in the east to Virginia. That'll mean fewer router hops, faster connections for your customers, and an added level of reliability.

CHAPTER 8

Quality of Service

Technology touches business and industry today as it never did before. And because of business's reliance on technology and networking, it's crucial for traffic to get where it's intended, and—sometimes more important—*when* it's intended.

WHAT IS QoS?

In a perfect world, we would have instantaneous access to all the information we wanted with the single click of a mouse. There would be no wait for files to come to us across the Internet. There would be no dialog boxes showing us a percentage of how complete the file is we're downloading.

Back here on Earth, however, things aren't so Utopian. Internetworking did not start with huge, inexpensive, wide-open pipes that everyone can instantaneously transmit data through. And because of the cost and speed issues inherent with modern networking—not to mention the greater and greater demand for bandwidth coming from new technology and applications—there must be a way to send the important data first.

Consider, for example, the blight at college campuses around the nation. With services like Napster offering MP3 digital music files, campus networks are choking because of the students downloading gigabytes of music. With bandwidth being sucked up to download music files, network applications critical to the day-to-day academic and administrative functioning of the colleges are suffering.

Enter Quality of Service.

By utilizing QoS technology and policies, college network administrators can prioritize network traffic. This means that the academic and administrative functions can be given higher priority on the network than the music-hoarding kids.

But what exactly is QoS? Dozens of definitions are being floated, partly because the words "quality" and "service" themselves each have been subjected to such abuse over the years. Join these two trendy words at the hip and confusion can really kick in. But a more serious problem is that QoS is a nascent technology, with the Internet Engineering Task Force (IETF) still in the process of defining technical specifications for many important elements of QoS. Add to this the fact that there are competing commercial agendas for QoS, especially the conflicting needs of ISPs and of corporate intranets.

But QoS is a real technology, and it can be defined. An informative definition might be that *QoS is a collection of run-time processes that actively manage bandwidth to provide committed levels of network service to applications and/or users. QoS implements a framework for service policy and action that extends end-to-end for serviced connections, even across autonomous systems.* From there, a seemingly endless parade of variations ensues, but suffice it to say that QoS is a collection of mechanisms designed to favor some types of traffic over others.

Why Your E-Business Needs QoS

You may not be planning on transmitting movies across your network, but you still must ensure information is flowing swiftly through your pipes—and not getting stuck in any network clogs.

It isn't just video or Internet telephony that relies on QoS. Especially if your business is one that hosts customers, it's important that traffic comes and goes as expeditiously as possible.

Bandwidth Is Not Enough

Until recently, increasing bandwidth solved most network user satisfaction problems. When things slowed down, network managers simply put in a fatter pipe to speed things back up.

But the amount of raw data that can be moved through a network is no longer the only issue. Now, timing and coordination can be just as important as raw throughput to satisfactory service quality. While it's true that most multimedia applications are bandwidth hogs, many also introduce operational requirements new to IP networks. To take an example, packet delay during a voice over IP (VoIP) phone call can cause the speakers to talk out of sequence, robbing the conversation of its coherence.

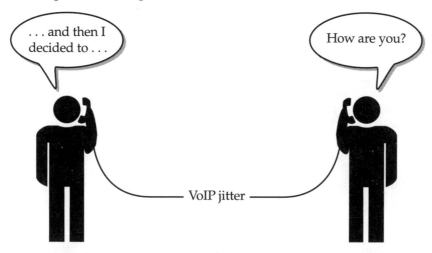

In the parlance, packet delivery delay that causes a signal to lose its timing references is called *jitter*. Because the effects of jitter on VoIP calls are so noticeable to users, it renders them all but useless.

Traditional applications like e-mail, Web browsers, and FTP aren't much affected by jitter or the other by-products of best-effort IP packet delivery. They're "elastic" in that they're not sensitive to timing issues.

Throwing bandwidth at a media application such as VoIP won't necessarily help. Even with a high-bandwidth end-to-end pipe, sudden bursts of traffic would still be manifested as jitter.

Network applications vary in their signal delivery requirements. The more an application's signal pattern is sensitive to delivery delay, the greater difficulty it has with IP's best-effort service approach. (By the way, *delay* is when a message is delivered intact but slowly; in contrast, jitter is where delay harms message integrity.) Table 8-1 outlines various traffic types and their elasticity to packet delay or jitter.

Tolerance to Delay	Traffic Type	Description of Effect of Packet Delay on the Network Application
Very tolerant	Asynchronous	Fully elastic, delay causes no effect
	Synchronous	Delay can cause some effect, usually just slowness
Somewhat tolerant	Interactive	Delay annoys and distracts users, but still functional
	Isochronous	Application is only partially functional
Not tolerant	Mission-critical	Application is functionally disabled

Table 8-1.   Tolerance to Packet Delay (Jitter) Is a Function of the Type of Traffic

Most traditional Internet applications are asynchronous and therefore very tolerant to jitter. For example, a user may not like waiting 30 seconds for a Web page to download (delay), but the HTTP application still works fine from a functional standpoint. Convergence applications aren't so forgiving, although some are more tolerant to the vagaries of IP than others.

Let's put some examples to the categories in Table 8-1:

▼ NetMeeting (nonvideo) is a good example of interactive traffic, where delivery sequence is important but not critical.

■ VoIP is truly isochronous traffic because out-of-sequence speech causes information loss and may even annoy users enough to hang up.

■ Videocasting is another example of isochronous traffic, because each frame must be presented immediately after its predecessor in perfect sequence, and also in quick succession.

▲ The classic example of mission-critical traffic is a process control interrupt instruction to open a safety valve in a nuclear reactor's cooling system.

To take the Internet to the next level, IP must provide more reliable network service levels, and the industry is convinced QoS is the answer.

Changing Business Needs

As bigger, beefier, and more time-sensitive applications become more intertwined with networking technology, it will be even more important to provide crucial services as fast as possible.

A decade ago, no one would have guessed we'd have Jetsons-like video chats across the country on our computer screens. And certainly no one though we'd be able to view interactive online catalogs from our favorite retail stores, or listen to CDs at our desks before we bought them. So, as the Internet and technology changes, so will business offerings and, as a result, network needs.

Whether your mission-critical applications are the bandwidth hogs or your mission-critical applications are affected by the bandwidth hogs, a good QoS solution is important to keep your business traffic (and by extension your income) flowing both now and in the future.

Key QoS Concepts

Before charging ahead into the ups, downs, ins, and outs of the kinds of QoS out there, let's take in some fundamentals. We'll look at some of the concepts behind QoS, how it is applied to a network, and then how QoS is already being delivered.

Existing QoS

The industry has been using a QoS of sorts in WAN links for years. WAN links are costly and have historically been the biggest bottleneck in end-to-end connections. It simply costs more to pull a cable over long distances, across land belonging to others, under streets, and even under oceans. The only way to cut WAN costs is to install faster media, or to spread the cost among more users.

Both problems put intense pressure on the telecom industry to put various QoS mechanisms into their WAN transport technologies, which today are primarily ATM and Frame Relay. These mechanisms now serve as a model for the designers now architecting QoS solutions for the Internet.

Frame Relay   Frame Relay is now the de facto standard technology for dial-up WANs. From the technical standpoint, Frame Relay is a data link layer protocol that uses the High-Level Data Link Control (HDLC) transport protocol for transport. By using HDLC encapsulation, Frame Relay is able to form multiple virtual circuits within a network cloud, making for a fast and reliable network that can be conveniently shared by otherwise unrelated enterprises.

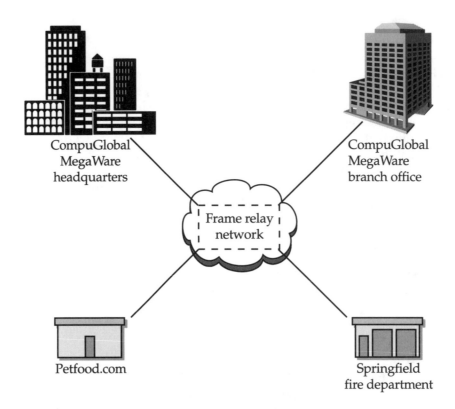

Within Frame Relay, Explicit Congestion Notification (ECN) is a form of flow control accepted by the Frame Relay standards committee as a way of preventing network congestion. ECN consists of two bits that are carried in the frame header. These bits are set by the network in the event of congestion. When congestion occurs, the user device must react by reducing the data rate sent onto the network. It reacts primarily to congestion at the source or destination of the Frame Relay connection.

When the source end of the circuit detects its input buffer filling up, it sets the Forward ECN (FECN) bit. This bit is carried "forward" through the network, toward the frame destination. At the same time, it also sets the Backward ECN (BECN) bit, which is sent back to the transmitting user device. FECN and BECN are worthless in reducing network congestion if the user device does not (or cannot) react to the presence of the FECN and BECN bits.

Frame relay is especially popular for sites with intermittent data traffic. For example, a branch office that needs to talk to the headquarters mainframe in ten-minute spurts several times a day probably couldn't justify the cost of a dedicated link.

ATM Asynchronous Transfer Mode (ATM) has many QoS-enabling features built into it, especially in the form of the fixed-sized, 53-byte cell it uses to transport information.

This gives the hardware in ATM switches a big speed advantage over IP devices, which must process variable-size packets. Those variable-size packets force IP routers and switches to expend extra CPU cycles to figure out exactly where fields begin and end.

ATM switching works by combining multiple virtual circuits (VCs) into a virtual path (VP). Multiple VPs are in turn combined within a physical circuit, usually a fiber-optic cable operated by the Synchronous Optical Network (SONET) protocol at the physical level, as depicted in Figure 8-1.

Each ATM cell identifies itself with a VC identifier and a VP identifier (VCI and VPI) to tell ATM switches how it should be handled. As a cell hops between switches, its VCI and VPI values are rewritten to direct the cell to its next hop, thereby combining path integrity and adaptability.

ATM is at its core uniquely enabled to provide QoS. The primary responsibility of traffic-management mechanisms in ATM is to promote network efficiency and avoid congestion. It is also a critical design objective of ATM that the network utilization imposed by transporting one type of application data does not adversely affect the network's capability to deliver other data.

IP Convergence of the world onto IP for internetworking is a done deal, and the same goes for convergence onto Ethernet as the de facto LAN standard.

But the convergence of virtually all communications media (telephone, television, radio) onto IP is still somewhat problematic because, as discussed, IP by its very nature is antagonistic to the determinism of QoS. The best-effort philosophy of IP is the fundamental result of the Internet Protocol's connectionless nature. When you send a packet, it's left up to IP as to what route will be taken to deliver it to its destination. In addition to its

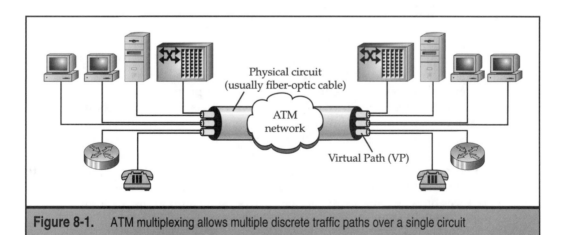

Figure 8-1.   ATM multiplexing allows multiple discrete traffic paths over a single circuit

connectionless, best-effort architecture, IP QoS is a tough engineering proposition for other reasons as well:

▼ Network provisioning is a zero-sum game. Because bandwidth is a finite resource, every bit per second of capacity dedicated to one connection is consumed at the expense of all other simultaneous connections. QoS only finesses bandwidth; it doesn't create it.

■ Users will always take as much bandwidth as they can consume—so long as they don't have to pay extra for it. To be effective, QoS needs a way to authenticate users, and a way to record utilization for billing. These authentication and accounting mechanisms must be unobtrusive and resource efficient.

■ To remain universal, the Internet must be careful to not allocate so much bandwidth to inelastic applications that time-independent applications such as HTTP and FTP become bandwidth-starved.

▲ There is no infrastructure in place to support a run-time QoS environment. ATM and Frame Relay QoS work fairly well because they provide their own internal infrastructures. End-to-end QoS entails operation across a multiprotocol environment, implying an order of magnitude increase in complexity.

QoS Framework

To operate properly, QoS needs a separate policy framework to layer atop IP networks. A service-level agreement (SLA) is a policy, not unlike a network security policy. But an SLA must be propagated to all the devices that are to enforce it, and the policy must somehow be kept uniform across the topology.

Coordinating QoS across large internetworks can get complicated. A communications infrastructure is needed to serve as a framework coordinating QoS policy across the topology. Those familiar with routing protocols or SNMP will understand that a cohesive suite of technical elements—a freestanding subsystem, in other words—must be in place for QoS to work.

Without a framework, it would be necessary to separately maintain each QoS policy on a per-device basis. Forcing administrators to "touch" each device would make QoS within an internetwork both labor-intensive and mistake-prone.

In a typical internetwork, requests for service and changes in operating conditions take place several times a minute. With that kind of dynamism, it follows that network teams will need to tweak fixed QoS policies with some frequency, probably at least weekly.

QoS needs a way to continually account for finite bandwidth resources. Also needed are automated mechanisms to make decisions between competing QoS requests, and to set up and tear down QoS assignments as connections come and go. The mission of a QoS framework takes on high complexity as QoS services span autonomous systems.

ENSURING QoS

Now that you understand what QoS is and what its goals are, the natural question is, "so how do I implement it for my e-business." There are two primary ways to ensure QoS. You can either chop a path through the cyber-jungle by establishing a free path across all the routers between the computers communicating, or you can ensure that the most important packets get priority and are sent across the network first.

In this section, we'll look at the pros and cons of each solution, then we'll talk about which is the best way to approach QoS.

Bandwidth Provisioning

Our first method of ensuring QoS is to clear a path between the two communicating computers. With bandwidth provisioning, a connection is allocated a certain amount of bandwidth negotiated with routers and switches along its path.

As contrasted to bandwidth prioritization (which we'll talk about in the next section), reserved connections are far more complex. Reservation schemes must get all routers along a connection's path to agree on a QoS regimen before transmission can begin. Moreover, the path itself must be defined before the reservations must be made. Reserved path bandwidth may also need to make real-time adjustments to changing operating conditions, further adding to complexity. This process is shown in Figure 8-2.

RSVP

The Resource Reservation Protocol (RSVP) "reserves" certain bandwidth resources along a path connecting source and destination devices to assure a minimum level of QoS. Applications running on IP end systems will use RSVP to indicate the nature of the

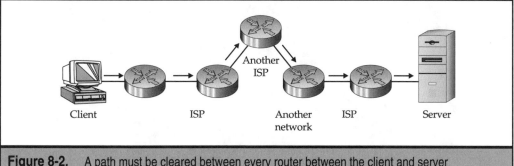

Figure 8-2. A path must be cleared between every router between the client and server

packet streams they want to receive, thereby "reserving" bandwidth that can support the required QoS. This is done by defining parameters for such characteristics as minimum bandwidth, maximum delay jitter, maximum burst, and the like.

RSVP is considered the enabling protocol for what is called *integrated services* QoS architecture, or *IntServ* for short. The "integrated" part comes from the notion that all devices—end hosts and interim devices alike—are integrated into a unitary QoS service regimen to be maintained in both directions for the life of the QoS-serviced flow.

RSVP is complicated. It defines *sender* and *receiver* hosts for each flow of data. The sender sends a so-called *PATH* message downstream to the receiver, with the PATH collecting a roster of devices along the route. Once the PATH message is received, the receiver sends a request called a *RESV* message back upstream along the same path to the RSVP sender. The RESV message specifies parameters for the desired bandwidth characteristics. Once all the interim devices are signed on to support the QoS levels, the session may begin. When the connection is terminated, an explicit tear-down mechanism is used to free up resources on the reserved devices. The RSVP process is depicted in Figure 8-3.

For the reservation to be fully guaranteed, each hop between network hardware must grant the reservation and physically allocate the requested bandwidth. By granting the reservation, the hop commits to providing the requested resources.

If the reservation is denied, the program receives a response that the network cannot support the amount and type of bandwidth or the requested service level. The program determines whether to send the data now using best-effort delivery or to wait and try the request again later.

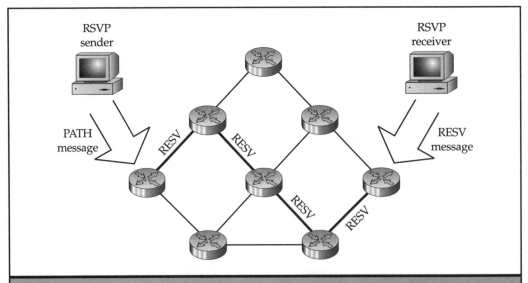

Figure 8-3.   RSVP uses a sophisticated, self-contained messaging system to reserve bandwidth

RSVP is a *soft-state protocol,* which requires the reservation to be refreshed periodically. The reservation information, or *reservation state,* is cached at each hop. If the network routing protocol alters the data path, RSVP automatically installs the reservation state along the new route. If refresh messages are not received, reservations time out and are dropped, and the bandwidth is released.

NOTE: Many legacy routers and switches are not RSVP-compliant. In these cases, the reservation messages pass through each hop. End-to-end and low-delay guarantees for the requested service level are not available.

Route aggregation partially ameliorates RSVP complexity and overhead. For example, if thousands of RSVP receiver hosts were to receive a multicast (say, a Web TV videocast), the RESV messages would be rolled up and combined at aggregation points. Conversely, only one stream would be sent downstream from the videocaster, replicated at aggregation points to worm out to all end-point destinations.

Microsoft's Solution

Owners of the Windows 2000 OS have a QoS leg up over other OSes. Microsoft includes a QoS mechanism with Windows 2000.

Microsoft's QoS solution is based on RSVP-based QoS. Though it is an excellent addition to an OS, people have qualms about *why* Microsoft chose to base its QoS solution on RSVP. We'll get into that later in this section. For the time being, let's look at how Microsoft QoS works.

How It Works   QoS Admission Control is Microsoft's mechanism to apply QoS services in Windows 2000. QoS Admission Control hosts provide a range of QoS functionality, including signaling, policy, marking, and traffic shaping. QoS Admission Control hosts integrate marking and shaping behavior with signaling and policy and present a unified mechanism-independent API to applications.

You can use QoS Admission Control to centrally designate how shared network resources are used. Once you've installed the service, the ACS host controls bandwidth for the subnet to which it is connected. Any host on the subnet can submit priority bandwidth requests to the QoS Admission Control host. The host will determine if there is adequate bandwidth available, based on these criteria:

▼   The current state of resource availability on the subnet

▲   QoS Admission Control user policy settings

A QoS Admission Control host can be set up on any Windows 2000 Server. QoS Admission Control operates at the IP network layer, serving the most common program protocols, including all transport protocols in the TCP/IP protocol suite (TCP, UDP, and RTP).

Figure 8-4 shows clients making reservation requests to the same QoS Admission Control. Each subnet client must pass its reservation request through the QoS Admission Control host.

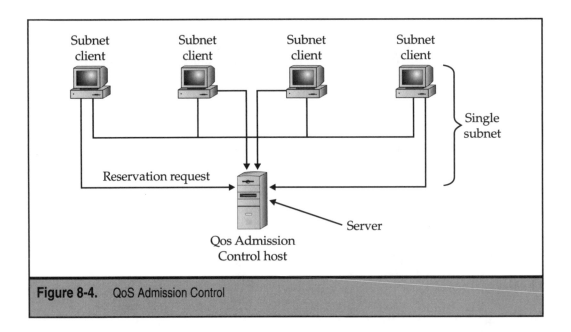

Figure 8-4. QoS Admission Control

The QoS Admission Control host multicasts *beacons* to notify subnet clients that it is available to receive requests. A client will not attempt to send a request to a host that is not sending out beacons.

To avoid losing bandwidth management services, you can install QoS Admission Control on multiple hosts on the same subnet. Only one QoS Admission Control will perform the bandwidth management services at any one time. The other hosts act as backups if the primary QoS Admission Control host stops functioning.

The QoS Admission Control host grants or rejects bandwidth requests from users according to the QoS Admission Control policy rights of each user. The host will reject the request if the user does not have the permission to reserve bandwidth (or the requested amount of bandwidth) on that subnet, or if the subnet itself is simply not capable of handling the bandwidth request.

NOTE: Traffic will never be blocked if a request cannot be granted. Rather, the program is notified and will decide if it wants to wait for a better time to make the request or to immediately send the data using a best-effort level of service.

As the QoS Admission Control server receives each request, the following process is followed:

1. The requesting user identity is verified using the Kerberos security protocol.

2. The QoS Admission Control policy for that user is retrieved from Active Directory.

3. The QoS Admission Control host checks the policy to see if the user has the appropriate rights for the request and then verifies whether network resources are adequate.

4. If a device can accommodate the resource request, it installs a classification state according to the conversation and allocates resources for the conversation.

5. If a device cannot accommodate the resource request, the request at the device is denied and a rejection is sent back to the receiver.

6. RSVP-aware devices may also extract policy information from the request for verification against network policies.

7. The QoS Admission Control host decides whether to approve or deny the request.

Servers and clients running Windows Me, Windows 98, or Windows 2000 are automatically configured to use the QoS Admission Control host to request bandwidth. QoS Admission Control also supports clients using any other operating systems that are running subnet bandwidth management client software.

NOTE: Programs that are not QoS-aware do not interact with the QoS Admission Control but receive best-effort service from the network.

Shortcomings of Microsoft's Solution   Within that last section are some clues about why we're not keen on Microsoft's QoS solution. The main reason is the foundation on which Microsoft builds upon: RSVP. Since RSVP is based on establishing a path across the network, it is inherently weak.

Our biggest grounds for concern with Microsoft's RSVP-based solution are these:

▼ **There are a lot of weak links out there**   In a perfect world, everyone would have brand new network hardware and a homogenous Windows 2000 operating system, complete with Windows 2000 Professional workstations. But in reality, networks tend to be cobbled together from Windows NT and 9x operating systems and use some hardware that's held together with duct tape and a couple stray Post-It Notes that read "Never, EVER, press this button!" It is because of this inevitable combination of new equipment and legacy hardware that RSVP has problems. Though the bandwidth can be established with the QoS-compatible routers, there will probably be a couple in the network that aren't compatible and will provide that weak link in the chain. If that clear path cannot be guaranteed—even at one router—RSVP-based QoS won't work right. And it isn't just the hardware that acts like sugar in the QoS gas tank. A good many applications are not QoS aware yet. All-in-all, the environment is just not suited for an RSVP-based solution.

■ **Lack of scalability**   Because RSVP must reconfigure every router in its path, the onus is on the network to talk to the routers and tell them what to do. RSVP doesn't scale very well, and you're bound to have problems. Conversely, if you use packet prioritization, it really only takes a little extra effort on the part of a client computer to assign precedence to outgoing packets. As they pass through the network infrastructure, they are merely bumped ahead of the other packets that don't have the same level of prioritization. The amount of CPU overhead on the routers is greater for RSVP than for Weighted Fair Queuing, for example.

▲ **Waste of bandwidth**   Since RSVP plows a path across a network, if the reservation space is not used, some RSVP schemes don't allow other applications to use the allocated bandwidth, making the clogged pipe even worse.

Bandwidth Prioritization

The better method—in our opinion—to ensure solid, reliable QoS comes from bandwidth prioritization. Rather than boring a big, wide tunnel through your pipe, bandwidth prioritization takes the packets that are rocketing through the pipe and sends the most important ones off to where they need to go first.

Simple prioritization QoS is packet-based. In other words, the treatment the packet deserves is in one way or another signified inside the packet itself. Although all QoS is priority-driven and operates packet-by-packet, prioritization QoS is distinguishable in that its implementation is constrained to a device inspecting packets. In other words, routers treat prioritization independently of other routers.

If operating conditions are changed when packets from another flow with the same or higher priority enter the same router, the original flow's packets are simply adjusted in its queue. As you'll see, some priority-based QoS mechanisms work by forming multiple output queues.

By contrast, reserving bandwidth requires all devices in the path to converse and collectively arrive at a QoS service-level commitment. Put another way, containing QoS in the packet itself does away with the need to set up and monitor connection flows across routers, across routing areas, and even across autonomous system boundaries. (An *autonomous system* is defined as a collection of routers under a single administrative authority using a common interior gateway routing protocol. For example, an ISP is an autonomous system.)

How It Works

Bandwidth prioritization works so well because it is very simple and it works throughout almost any network.

1. As information is sent onto the network, a software mechanism looks at the information's QoS policies and determines which packets are important and just how important they are.

2. Next, the computer assigns each packet a number ranging from one to seven, depending on their order of importance, as shown in Figure 8-5.

3. At this point, the packets are lined up in the router in seven different queues and wait to be sent.

4. The most important packets (those at level seven) are transmitted first. After the level seven packets are transmitted, for example, the packets in the sixth queue are sent, and so on.

5. This process repeats as long as data is being transmitted.

Why It's Preferred

There are two primary reasons that bandwidth prioritization is the favored solution for QoS, not the least of which is its ability to work with existing technology, a hurdle for any application that works on the Internet. Another important reason bandwidth prioritization is preferable is that it is extremely efficient and wastes no bandwidth, unlike bandwidth provisioning.

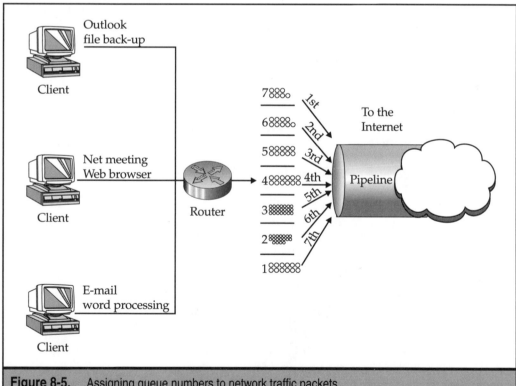

Figure 8-5. Assigning queue numbers to network traffic packets

Used with existing technology   The biggest problem with bandwidth provisioning is that it must use modern, RSVP-capable routers to work. This is fine if you own and control all the routers from end to end. But realistically speaking, you will have control over one router. After that, it's up to the whims of fate.

Routers that will make bandwidth provisioning work are recent models with QoS-specific features. Bandwidth provisioning, on the other hand, works because it operates with all kinds of routers, new and legacy. Bandwidth prioritization relies on sending the packets in a specific, prioritized fashion; the packets don't care what kind of router they go through, because they are guaranteed to go through in a specific, mission critical order. Remember, the most important packets arrive at their destination first because they were the first packets sent.

Efficiency   Delivering QoS through bandwidth prioritization is also the more efficient method, because it uses the bandwidth that's available, without hoarding it from other applications. For a contrast, consider Figure 8-6.

In this figure, you'll see that a decent-sized portion of the pipe has been set aside solely for video conferencing. This is all well and good and does a fine job; however, when no one is video conferencing, that section of the pipe is not being used and going to waste.

Bandwidth prioritization allows the entire pipe to be used; it merely puts the most important traffic first. Consider Figure 8-7.

You can see that all the traffic is getting into the pipe, and when the video conferencing isn't taking place, the next bits of traffic on the prioritization tree are moved up and sent first.

DiffServ

A better-understood prioritization model is called Differentiated Services, or *DiffServ* for short. DiffServ is meant to provide a relatively coarse but simple way to prioritize traffic. DiffServ redefines the original IP ToS field bits into its own scheme, where two of the eight ToS bits are used for congestion notification, and the remaining six bits, for packet

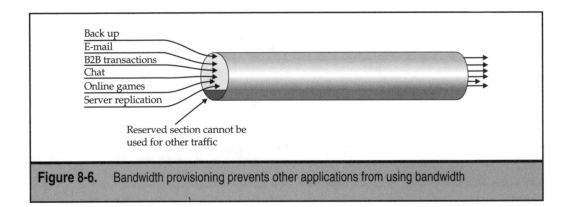

Back up
E-mail
B2B transactions
Chat
Online games
Server replication

Reserved section cannot be
used for other traffic

Figure 8-6.   Bandwidth provisioning prevents other applications from using bandwidth

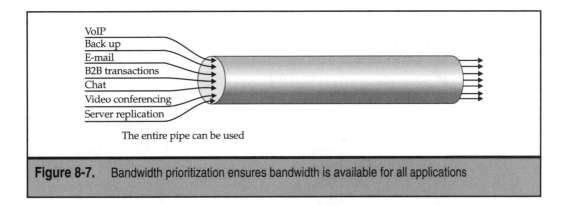

Figure 8-7.   Bandwidth prioritization ensures bandwidth is available for all applications

markings. This new scheme implements so-called *codepoints* within the six-bit marking space. Packets are marked for the DiffServ class as they enter the DiffServ QoS network.

DiffServ attempts only to control so-called "per-hop" behaviors. In other words, policy is defined locally, and DiffServ as a mechanism executes within a device to influence when and where the packet's next hop will be. Once policy is set across a topology, everything takes place in-device. DiffServ supports two service levels (traffic classes):

▼ **Expedited forwarding (EF)**   Minimizes delay and jitter. Packets are dropped if traffic exceeds a maximum load threshold set by local policy.

▲ **Assured forwarding (AF)**   Provides for four subclasses and three drop-precedences within each subclass for a total of 12 codepoints. If traffic load exceeds local policy, excess AF packets are not delivered at the specified priority but are instead demoted to a lower priority (but not dropped). This demotion procedure cascades through any configured drop-precedence codepoints.

QoS for E-Businesses

Nowhere else is QoS more important than in e-business. After all, your customers are relying on the resources of your network and if they can't reliably get at those resources, they can find someone else who will let them.

Consider your own online shopping experiences. How many times have you tried to buy something from a slow Web site? Forget the maddening wait to place your order, think about the times you've been waiting and waiting while your credit card information is bouncing around out there. Think about it in terms of B2B connections. If one of your supply chain partners can't get requested information in a timely manner, it's not just their order that's getting held up, it's the person placing the order and possibly an assembly line full of workers waiting on parts.

With good QoS procedures in place, the aggravation of a slow business connection can be alleviated. This section looks at how businesses can use QoS to ensure safe, reliable, speedy connections.

Networking Scenarios

Research has shown that most QoS implementations done to date are within private (non-ISP) enterprise internetworks. This is somewhat ironic given that ISPs invented the SLA as a way to do business, and the fact that ISPs operate most ATM networks. But it's understandable:

▼ When a packet passes through the ingress router to enter someone else's autonomous system, it becomes less of a priority. Why should they take on the added expense of the processing and administrative overhead needed to assure the packet a QoS service level?

■ Even if another autonomous system wanted to help—say, an ISP that wants to win your business—how can your policies be distributed to, and implemented in, its routers?

▲ If your policy was implemented in another autonomous system, what would assure that it was executed in accordance with a common understanding of which conditions are active and which actions should result?

A lot of Internet gurus are asking these very questions nowadays, and it's a tough nut to crack. As you travel between autonomous systems, you pass through differing policy domains with their own operating styles. Not only would a global policy framework holding uniform criteria be required, a global policy evaluation algorithm would also be needed. Rule sets, bit precedents, policies, and other elements of QoS execution in each autonomous system (AS) must be kept uniform.

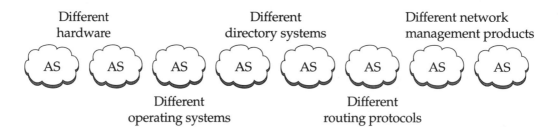

Compounding the problem of inter–autonomous system QoS is the lack of uniform technical infrastructure. Any group of autonomous systems attempting to interoperate QoS are likely to be running a variety of routing protocols, network device hardware, computer platform operating systems, directory technologies, and network management systems. Their existence dictates that a truly interoperable QoS framework be in place in order for end-to-end QoS to work.

QoS works best and can be assured most effectively within the confines of a private or controlled network. Because this network is entirely under your control, you can have the say about how traffic is prioritized. The threat to QoS comes when traffic has to reach out across a public WAN or—worse yet—a public network, like the Internet.

Let's look at how both of these network scenarios play themselves out.

ISPs   The most likely place for network traffic to get congested is when it leaves your router and heads to your ISP, as shown in Figure 8-8.

The biggest problem occurs when traffic leaves the guarantees established by your ISP and hits the Internet proper. Just because the traffic is high priority to you doesn't mean that it's a high priority once it gets outside your ISP.

This is not to suggest that all ISP situations are going to provide choppy service. On the one hand, let's use the example of two companies set up in a B2B arrangement. If the two companies have their own, independent ISPs, then there are many places between each end where network traffic can get bottlenecked.

Let's look at another scenario. Again, let's assume you and a business partner have a B2B e-business solution in place. In this case, however, you're both contracting with the same ISP. You're more likely to be able to have an assured level of QoS, because the traffic will not leave the ISP and have to cross a multitude of routers. It remains within one au-

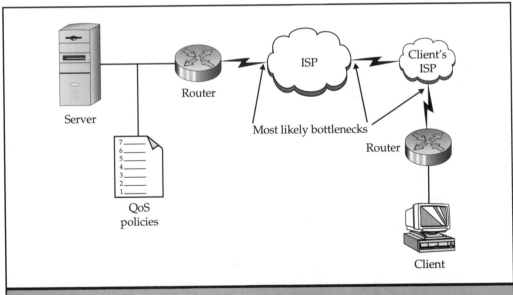

Figure 8-8.   Most bottlenecks occur when traffic enters an ISP

tonomous system. Since most traffic snarls occur when they leave a single ISP, this problem will be mitigated.

Private WANs   The best-case scenario for supplying QoS across a wide area is across a private WAN. As compared to using a public network, this is a more costly option; however (forgive the cliché), you get what you pay for. Take a look at Figure 8-9.

As you can see, there isn't anything in between the two ends to slow down traffic. There's nothing that can reprioritize your critical traffic, and there aren't the bottlenecks that come when you go through an ISP (or worse, two ISPs).

QoS Tools

So what can you do to make your network traffic run smoothly and quickly? There are a few important tools you can use to ensure packets are moving at a nice, brisk pace. Packet shapers, application response tools, and bandwidth monitors are all gear you can use to send packets along, then make sure that they're moving fast enough—and in the right order.

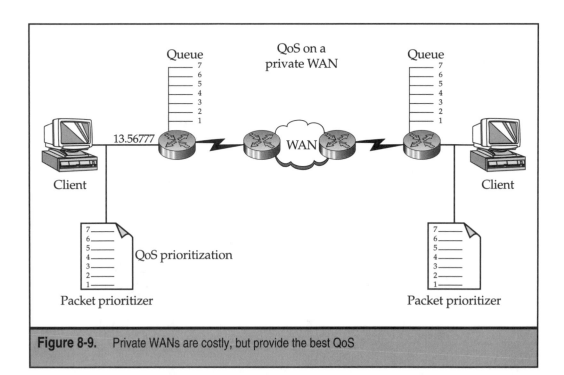

Figure 8-9.   Private WANs are costly, but provide the best QoS

Packet Shapers   Currently, various mechanisms are used to control the characteristics of traffic being allowed into a network. Called "traffic shaping," this method is primarily used at border routers. Network operators are starting to use traffic shaping to condition WAN links for better service quality.

By definition, *traffic shaping* is the practice of controlling the volume of packets entering a network and controlling the rate of transmission in order to make traffic conform to a desired pattern. The name comes from the fact that a traffic flow is said to have been *shaped* when its pattern is changed. The two predominant ways to shape traffic are the "leaky bucket" and "token bucket" mechanisms.

▼ **The Leaky Bucket**   A *leaky bucket* controls the rate at which packets enter a network. This mechanism works by manipulating inbound queues so as to smooth bursty traffic into less variable flows. As mentioned, ATM invented the leaky bucket as a way to control the rate at which ATM cell traffic is transmitted over an ATM link. It has more recently come into use to condition IP packet datagram flows.

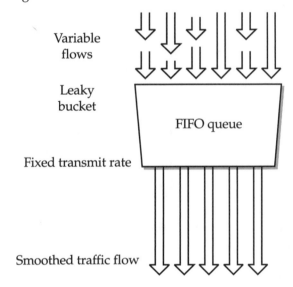

▲ **The Token Bucket Mechanism**   Although the names are similar, the token bucket mechanism is quite different from the leaky bucket. A *token bucket* is the practice of controlling the rate of transmission according to the presence of so-called "tokens" in the bucket. In other words, a *token* is an abstract currency (measured in bytes) that must be available at any instant for the next first-in, first-out (FIFO) packet to exit the network interface. There must be at least as many token bytes available as the number of bytes in the packet to be transmitted.

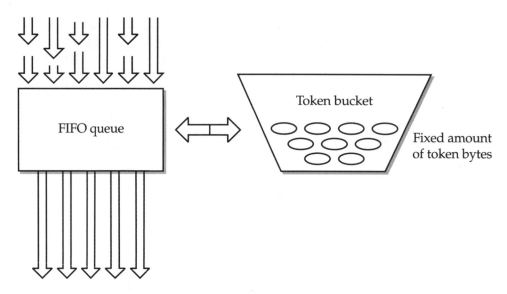

You may want to give consideration to a couple of packet shapers that are on the market. First is the PacketShaper family by Packeteer (www.packeteer.com). PacketShaper is fairly easy to use and is also highly configurable. PacketShaper allows you to set rules and then manipulate how it manages traffic meeting the criteria in a rule. For example, you can adjust the scaling factor on a particular rule to fit a particular traffic pattern.

Another company offering a packet shaping mechanism is Check Point Software (www.checkpoint.com) with its FloodGate-1 software. Running on Solaris and an UltraSparc II, FloodGate-1 emphasizes a system of weights rather than straight guarantees and limits. For instance, if you decide a certain type of traffic is to be given a weight of 10, then traffic granted a weight of 20 gets exactly twice as much precedence. With FloodGate-1, you can set per-connection guarantees and limits, as well as weights for those connections.

Packet shapers have limited use and application. They are best used by organizations with few WAN links, as these hardware devices are required at both ends of every WAN link where you want QoS. Also, they are strategically set, so changes to policy can only be accomplished infrequently.

Application Response　Since the core reason you want to employ QoS is to ensure that specific, important applications are functioning as briskly as possible, you should consider the programs available to monitor your applications and their response times.

These tools are especially important when you're monitoring activity, because you can use them to make sure that the applications that have been given high priority are in fact receiving that priority.

▼　**Network Monitor**　If you are a Windows NT/2000 user, Network Monitor is one such program that can be configured to monitor your applications. It comes standard on both platforms and is a powerful tool that can be used to check a multitude of network statistics.

NOTE: We talk more about Network Monitor in Chapter 10.

- **Ganymede** (www.ganymede.com)   This company offers three products, Chariot, Pegasus, and Application Scanner, that will test applications on your network, both before they are purchased and deployed and after deployment. For instance, Pegasus uses "agents" that are scattered throughout a network to gather application performance information, such as the number of seconds required to complete a transaction. At regularly scheduled intervals, the agents send the statistics to the central console.

- **Application Performance Management** by Tivoli (www.tivoli.com) This product focuses on evaluating end users' experience with application performance by measuring the response time they receive. This information enables network administrators to set and meet service agreements with real end users by using a simple measurement: how long it takes their users to get a response. Tivoli Application Performance Management uses three methods to measure application response time: client capture, transaction simulation, and application instrumentation.

Bandwidth Monitors   Another way to check out your system and make sure everything is flowing as it should is with a bandwidth monitor. These tools are on the market:

- **Enterprise Reporting Server 3.0** by WebTrends (www.webtrends.com) One tool that will monitor (among other e-business-related statistics) bandwidth and application performance.

- **Bandwidth Optimizer** by Elron Software (www.elronsoftware.com) Can pinpoint critical information with a suite of reporting and graphing capabilities. Using these tools, you can find out where your bandwidth is going. Bandwidth Optimizer allows you to discover the breakdown of traffic by service type; when and where spikes in traffic appear; which end users are using the most bandwidth; and how much traffic is mission critical and how much is non–business related.

- **WiseWan Accelerators** by NetReality (www.net-reality.com)   Hardware devices that are physically connected to your WAN. They examine every packet that passes through and send the analyzed traffic to a centralized WanXplorer server. The server stores the data and makes it available for analysis. WiseWan can tell you how applications, servers, users, and clients are using bandwidth and where it's going.

THE FUTURE OF QoS

QoS isn't one simple product that comes in a shrink-wrapped box to cure all your traffic management woes. Rather, it is both a nascent technology and a moving target. It's important to keep a few basics in mind as QoS grows. Also, expect to see more and more QoS solutions popping up, vying for your e-business dollar.

In this section, we'll take a look at what you should keep an eye on as QoS continues to develop. We'll talk about the best way for QoS to be delivered in the future, along with some of the fuzzy features that will ensure you a properly prioritized network.

End-to-End

For QoS to work, it has to be end-to-end. That means that the information coming from the server has to get to the client in the precise order it left and it has to get there in a reasonable amount of time. This relates directly back to the concept of bandwidth provisioning that we talked about earlier in this chapter.

Packets Tagged on Exit

The first feature in the future of QoS is that, for best results, packets must be tagged as they leave their source. For the best QoS, packets must be tagged according to their priority and precedence, and then network devices, such as routers, must place the packets in the correct queue. Once in that queue, they must then be sent out in the correct, prioritized order.

But packet prioritization doesn't end once packets leave the server. In most cases where QoS is important, there is a two-way communication taking place. For instance, VoIP doesn't work going in just one direction. Conversations are a two-way event (unless you're calling your mother), so it's just as important that the packets coming back to the server come back in the correct speed and order.

Services Across the Internet

As you cross the Internet, there's a lot of hardware between your computer and someone else's. Whatever QoS solution you use, it's necessary for every piece of equipment between here and there to pass along your packets in the priority they are received for guaranteed QoS.

Here, again, is where bandwidth provisioning is bad news. All it takes is one misconfigured, old, or obsolete router to become a bottleneck and screw up your QoS mechanism.

As we've mentioned before, the one sure way around that problem is to handle the QoS on the systems you can control. When you choose bandwidth prioritization, the packets will fly across the Internet or WAN in the order of importance. Since there is always a bottleneck between the client and server. QoS must be applied to the bottleneck that is preventing service delivery to the user's satisfaction.

Dynamic

It would be easy enough to set up a QoS solution that will attend to your business needs—today. For instance, if you've established that e-mail packets are the most important things to your business and that traffic must have precedence over all others, that is all well and good, but what about next week? Next month? Next year? What if your priorities change? Will your QoS solution be able to adapt to those changes?

Serve Changing Business Needs

As you well know, the needs and demands on an organization's network can change overnight. You may not be in "the loop" at your organization, and you could find a memo on your desk one morning telling you that all the network's resources must be allocated to financial transactions. If you had just set up the system to accommodate e-mail as the highest priority, and if you didn't have a flexible, dynamic QoS solution, you could be in big trouble.

Another example is a surge in network traffic. Let's say you sell CDs online. As a service to your customers, you have sample clips of music on the Web site that are delivered in a streaming audio format. Because the music is streaming, it needs solid QoS or the music will be choppy. Unfortunately, the recent release from a popular bubblegum band has given your site so much attention that your billing system can't get its data across the network. Given this unexpected data surge, you must be able to tweak your settings so that your network doesn't grind to a spark-producing halt.

As business needs change, so must your QoS response.

Prioritization Based on External Data

As you continue to streamline and beef up your network, you can use information gathered from external sources to govern your QoS policies. For instance, let's use the example of an online stockbroker.

Since you want to keep the money flowing in, you've set a policy that the customers who invest the most money will be given priority above all other customers (no, it's not nice, but this is business after all). This would be simple enough if you knew that there were only five or six big-shot investors among all your customers. You could give their accounts high priority and not worry about it again.

However, there's no way the same set of investors will consistently make the same high amount of trades every day. If you have thousands or tens of thousands of traders, the big rollers will be a moving target and something you can't manage, manually. Therefore, you must rely on some data mining to provide this dynamic information.

Because you use an enabled directory—like NDS eDirectory, for example—you are able to track all your customers, their trades, and the money they're investing. With this database of up-to-the-minute information, you can channel the information about the high rollers to your QoS mechanism and give the big shots priority over the blue-haired ladies selling a stock or two.

Intelligence

Though flexibility is extremely important for a QoS solution, future needs will require QoS not only to accept mission-critical changes but also to be proactive, anticipating problems and dealing with them without having to wait for someone to sit down at a terminal and redirect traffic manually.

Demands at Random Times

For instance, let's say your company runs television commercials on channels around the country, selling ceramic frogs. And every time a commercial is played, your phone bank lights up and operators process scores of orders (these are only the highest-quality ceramic frogs, of course).

Rather than gum up the system when these television commercials run, if yours is an intelligent network, it can remember a list of the commercial times and reprioritize bandwidth accordingly. After the onslaught of ceramic frog freaks subsides, bandwidth can be reallocated back to the rest of the company (such as R&D, where they're working on ceramic puppies).

Cleaning the Pipes

Another problem that can be averted with an intelligent QoS system in place arises when your highest priority traffic is compromised and—even though it's deemed high priority—it stands to clog your network.

For instance, Larry in accounting decides to forward one of those wacky e-mails (that just happen to be about 5MB) to everyone in the company. In an unfortunate twist of fate, the CEO has directed that e-mail traffic be given priority over everything else on the network. By the time Larry finishes his three-page-long CC list, that file has replicated its way into a monster that chokes your network, slows down business transactions, and brings the system to its knees. If your QoS solution is intelligent enough, it can differentiate between the important, mission-critical data and Larry's pipe-clogging blow to your network.

Intelligence will be critical to the future of QoS. You can set strict QoS policies that, logically, your network traffic should follow precisely. However, leave it to the Larrys out there to find a way to screw everything up.

Viziq

Viziq, a new technology from FireSummit, promises to advance QoS to a point years beyond any other product. It delivers your mission-critical information in a timely, efficient, intelligent, and intuitive manner.

Overview

Viziq is a biologically inspired neural-network intelligence engine that automatically adjusts network policies for e-business, service providers, and corporate network applications.

Incorporating intelligence, dynamism, and flexibility in one package, Viziq is a software solution that will work in virtually any network environment to keep the traffic moving. It processes and analyzes the feedback from a number of internal and external sources to alter QoS policies and keep traffic going where it needs to go.

Networking needs   Viziq's development has been driven by four trends in the computer networking industry:

▼   The need to simplify traffic management on increasingly complex networks

■   The emergence of new services, such as multicasting, differentiated service levels, virtual private networks, and voice/video applications

■   The need for businesses to prioritize applications, groups, and individuals using the network

▲   The increasing need for network security

To keep a competitive edge, businesses and organizations must respond quickly to these trends. New services and applications are added, consuming network bandwidth and resulting in poor network performance.

The solutions   Viziq is a policy-based network management system that helps network managers automate device configuration, prioritize applications, and achieve greater control of their networks. It can also help network administrators plan for the future and put the necessary resources in place, stomping out problems before they occur.

Traffic is managed by creating policy-based classes of service, which prioritize the business-critical traffic on your network. Moreover, the system provides real-time network, monitoring, modeling, analysis, and reprioritization to resolve bandwidth contention in cases where the prescribed policy causes an oversubscription of bandwidth for competing applications.

Figure 8-10 shows Viziq's functionality using a Windows 2000 Microsoft Management Console.

This figure demonstrates how Viziq manages a broad range of prioritization information, including policies for specific departments, specific individuals, and a number of specific applications.

Features

Viziq is a robust enterprise solution composed of key policy-based QoS functions, including:

▼   Network monitoring and reporting

■   Enterprise policy management

■   Bandwidth management

▲   Router/switch vendor QoS compatibility

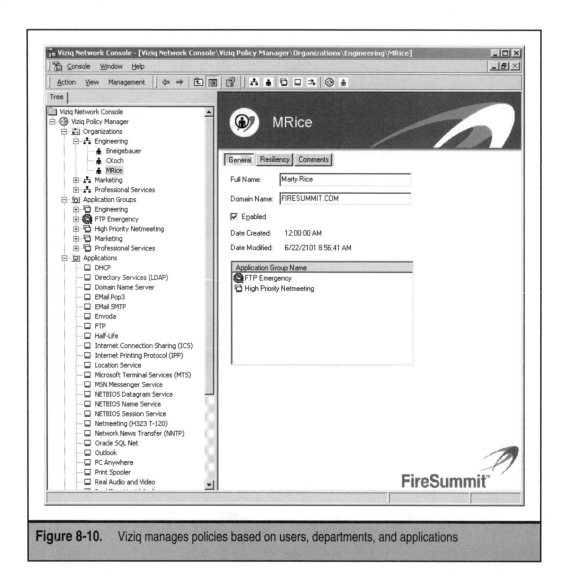

Figure 8-10. Viziq manages policies based on users, departments, and applications

Here's how Viziq works to keep your traffic flowing in a smooth, prioritized manner, as shown in Figure 8-11:

1. A consumer or business attempts to access a server located within another organization. A small, intelligent agent quickly evaluates the request and determines the priority of the traffic by comparing the request to the user's prioritization policy already located on the user's PC. The policy will look at:

   ■ The time of day, day of the week, etc.

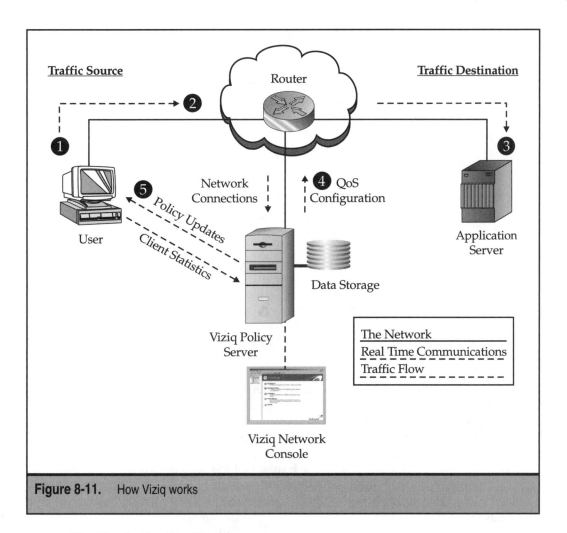

Figure 8-11.   How Viziq works

- The destination IP address
- The destination and source port numbers

2. A network device at the receiving organization has previously been told how to handle certain priorities. Drawing on that information, it forwards the traffic with the correct level of prioritization.

3. The server at the destination receives the request and fulfills it. The Viziq server also analyzes a variety of other information to determine network needs, including:

   - Current network conditions from network devices, such as a router
   - User and environmental information from a Directory Service (such as Active Directory or NDS eDirectory)

■ Historical events from a local database

■ Traffic prioritization policies entered by users

■ Reports output by the Viziq system detailing usage of network resources

4. The Viziq system (or the network administrator) may decide to change how the network devices treat certain levels of prioritization and communicates this policy to the network device.

5. The Viziq system may decide to change the user's policy and communicates that new policy to the user.

Neural Features   The software at the core of Viziq uses brainlike functions, such as learning, memory, and reasoning, in the same way humans do. Though less complex than human brain functionality, those capabilities enable the network software to solve communications problems continuously and to optimize network performance faster and more accurately than can human-managed systems.

The biology of the human nervous system is the inspiration behind Viziq. The system learns through its actions. For instance, like a child who puts its hand on a hot stove, the system incorporates "tetanus stimulation." In other words, serious disruptions to network conditions are better remembered and compensated for than less-serious problems. Similarly, "decay" is written into the code, which enables it to give greater prominence to last week's major problem than last year's.

Viziq also learns through repetition. For instance, Viziq can discover that heavy Web traffic at certain times of day is constraining bandwidth for mission-critical applications. After learning this trait, the software reprioritizes network traffic accordingly.

Though these are "interior" types of learning capabilities, Viziq is augmented by information from a number of "exterior" paths, much the same way humans get information from their own senses.

Viziq monitors its environment, which may include network devices and directory services, for information about how the network resources are being used, how applications are being used, and the rate at which databases are filling and bandwidth is being consumed.

Policy Management   The different people and organizations that come to your network will be there for different reasons. A B2B customer may be placing an order for a certain part; your employees need to use network resources to do their jobs; customers may just be surfing through as they check out your Web page.

Here's how a network administrator would create and deploy individual policies with Viziq:

1. The individual's job and importance within the organization are determined.

2. The applications the user will use are prioritized. If, however, an individual already fits into an existing group of users (he's a member of the engineering department, for example), a predefined set of policies can be applied to that person.

3. Depending on the policies you've established for this user, they are transferred to a prioritization matrix (as shown in Figure 8-12), which is a graphic representation of a user's priority levels, organized by the time of day and day of the week.

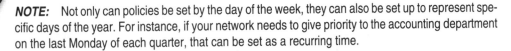

NOTE: Not only can policies be set by the day of the week, they can also be set up to represent specific days of the year. For instance, if your network needs to give priority to the accounting department on the last Monday of each quarter, that can be set as a recurring time.

4. Policies can also be set using IP addresses. For instance, if you need to manage QoS for a specific machine (no matter who is logged on to it), an IP mask allows you that freedom. This is also useful, for instance, if you want to spare network resources by limiting employee Web browsing to certain times of day.

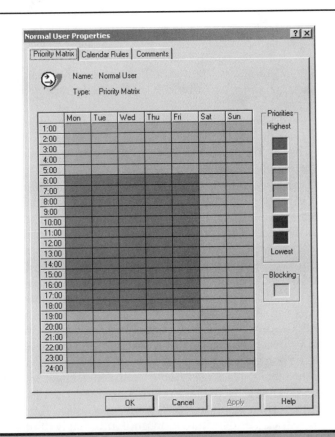

Figure 8-12. Users get their own QoS policies with Viziq

It's important to understand that policies are set as *exceptions.* This means that only the most critical applications are given high priority. After all, if every application used by every user is granted high priority, prioritization won't matter anymore.

Given these different uses and different users, Viziq lets you give different individuals differing levels of your network's resources. And because of Viziq's intelligent infrastructure, policy needs can be intuitively changed to ensure QoS.

Looking at the long term, Viziq employs a user-defined degree of automation in deploying policy changes, allowing the network to reprioritize itself, depending on the current policy and the network's history of management interventions.

In addition to providing QoS based on established business priorities, the network manager can also implement an "emergency network policy" to handle cases where hardware failures cause extreme duress on the network. If there is an emergency event, the network manager can switch to the emergency policy for all clients on the network, causing all nonessential traffic to be dropped and conserve all available bandwidth for the critical network applications. This would be useful, for example, if an e-business Web site loses a T3 line to the Internet and has only an ISDN line as a backup. When the T3 fails, the network manager already has a disaster plan and the tools in place to cope with the outage.

Bandwidth Management   Ultimately, Viziq's intelligence and intuition lead to better management of your resources, namely bandwidth, and optimized performance for your applications.

Viziq's Intelligence Engine ensures QoS is managed to the maximum of available bandwidth using Classes of Service (CoS) to differentiate network traffic. This piece of the architecture acts as the brains of the system, receiving information from multiple sources, including the client computers.

The Intelligence Engine consists of a mathematical model to represent the performance capability and topology of the network. This model is used to establish and maintain performance thresholds and latencies for the routers and clients; represent appropriate queue sizes for differentiated services on the routers; record typical network load; and predict the effect of dynamic priority changes to resolve network congestion for a particular CoS.

Viziq is also useful in controlling denial of service attacks. For instance, if a site places priority on e-mail and a rogue e-mail virus causes a mutation that floods the network with junk e-mail, the system will detect the performance degradation and notify the network manager. The manager can, then, downgrade the traffic to a background effort or shut it down completely until the cause of the problem can be investigated and solved. All of this happens in real time, before the virus has had a chance to cause a network outage.

But lest you worry about a computer that will have so much control that it can take over a network, the software utilizes a Variable Confidence Level Model feature that allows the network manager to vary the amount of automation. As the network manager gains confidence in the software's decision-making capabilities, the software can be assigned larger and larger degrees of automation until, ultimately, it manages 100 percent of the network's traffic flow.

Network Hardware Compatibility   One of the most important features of Viziq is that, unlike other hardware and software applications, it will work on a variety of software platforms and with existing hardware.

It's almost a given that new technology and new applications will require thousands of dollars in upgrades. It's so common, in fact, that either organizations don't seem to mind buying new computers and infrastructure or they hold off on implementing technology they would benefit from because they would have to make a major investment.

Since Viziq uses bandwidth prioritization, which governs the packets being transmitted, not the hardware on each end, legacy equipment can be used without incident.

QoS is a burgeoning technological field. Maybe, one day, when we all wear jet packs to work and have barcodes tattooed on our necks, network pipes will be wide open and super fast. But until that time, you'll need a way to get your important information on the network first.

If you get the right QoS mechanism in place, then once your mission-critical data has been sent where it needs to go, then Larry in accounting can transmit his MP3s to his buddies without messing up your B2B connectivity.

CHAPTER 9

The Thinking Network

A world-class business without a world-class data network is as unthinkable at the beginning of the twenty-first century as a department store without merchandise. As a restaurant without a kitchen. As a skyscraper without elevators.

The previous chapter illustrated the importance and use of Quality of Service for your e-business. We explained some of the key concepts behind QoS along with their use, and we discussed some QoS products you can employ today. In this chapter, we are going to take you to the next level—a glimpse into the future of where networking and e-business is going. We will show you what it's going to take to make a world-class network in the years to come. This vision, called the Thinking Network, builds upon the network infrastructure in place today to raise the bar and make your data network not just necessary but strategic to your e-business.

THE NETWORK CHALLENGE

Until recently, of course, data networks were not viewed as business-critical resources. They were money-saving and labor-saving conveniences, nothing more. Local area networks allowed users of expensive personal computers to share access to even more expensive laser printers. LANs were the home of shared disk space, more convenient than swapping floppy disks and more capacious than a desktop's minute hard drive. E-mail was less prevalent than the interoffice memo. The Internet was known only to a few academic technologists and computer scientists. If "e-business" meant anything, it was Electronic Data Interchange, where vendors' mainframes and midrange systems exchanged information via X.25 communication links.

Life was so much simpler then.

Today, it's rare not to have publicly accessible e-mail for nearly every employee in every business. Customers are outraged if they can't connect to your Web site. If you're not taking orders over the Web, your competitors are—and they will get the order. Every application is a client/server application or is based on an *n*-tiered architecture requiring high-speed Ethernet connections between presentation servers, application servers, and database back-end servers.

When the network slows down, the business slows down. Knowledge workers can't share knowledge effectively. Programmers are less efficient when accessing their code repositories. The quality of real-time communication suffers. Servers can't distribute objects on time. Data synchronization falls behind. Transactions are lost. Employees become less productive. Business slows down. Partners lose money. Customers leave.

In other words, the network is at the heart of the business. And the business's needs and priorities should be at the heart of the network. That's not the case today, however. When it comes to managing the network, administrators strive to ensure that all nodes are "live" with basic connectivity to their resources. Essentially all they are trying to do is to keep the network turned "on." This is about as strategic as just trying to keep your car running without ever putting it in gear to take you places. On the LAN and on the WAN,

Quality of Service is rarely an issue, except when trying to determine when an Internet service provider is meeting its service-level guarantees. Networks are uncontrolled. Employees use as much bandwidth as they want, and employers are powerless to do anything about it. There needs to be a business case for bandwidth use and access.

We have all sorts of tools that tell us what percentage of up time we have, but no tools that tell us how we are really using this expensive yet powerful resource. The next step for networks is to go beyond just keeping them turned on—to take them out of the garage and really apply their usefulness to your core corporate objectives.

Such a binary network—is the network up, or is the network down?—may be fine for old economy enterprises. But next-generation enterprises need more. They need a network that can adapt, at every level, to the demands of the business. They need a network that can use intelligent functions such as learning, memory, and reasoning to solve communications problems and optimize the network's performance in real time. This network will provide dynamically end-to-end service that is required to meet the objectives of the business, as illustrated in Figure 9-1.

No human can manage such a task on his or her own; only automation can do the trick. We call this the Thinking Network: a network that can apply intelligence to automatically tuning its own performance to better meet dynamic business priorities.

Increasing Complexity

Today's LAN and WAN technologies are marvels of performance, reliability, and sophistication. Fast Ethernet to the desktop, gigabit Ethernet backbones. Wire-speed Layer 2 and Layer 3 routers zip information from segment to segment without blocking. Internet access is faster and less expensive than ever, while many major ISPs offer service-level agreements. Web caches make those Internet connections even faster. Virtual private networks over the Internet have replaced Frame Relay and X.25 between branch offices, and dial-up lines run to telecommuters' homes.

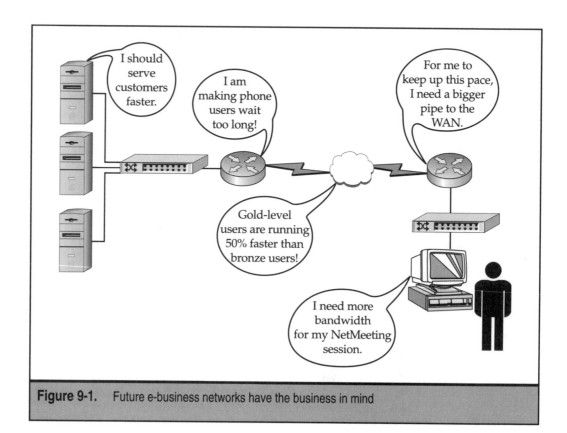

Figure 9-1. Future e-business networks have the business in mind

Traffic Loads

But that's still not good enough. The amount of traffic on the LAN or WAN is increasing rapidly, thanks to new applications such as video conferencing, the use of terminal servers to run programs remotely, and the constant downloading and execution of Java applications rather than storing them locally on workstations. Streaming video, too, is becoming a fixture at many organizations. The network traffic for those applications, unlike simple e-mail or file transfers, is large and very sensitive to jitter and delay.

Adding bandwidth is just a temporary fix. The amount of traffic is increasing faster than the increase in bandwidth made available by new technology. What's more, these new applications are bandwidth pigs, and many are time sensitive. In the past, applications such as e-mail, FTP, or Telnet had relatively low levels of bandwidth consumption or were not very time sensitive. If your e-mail packet took another second or two to reach you, that was alright. New applications demand much higher throughputs to work at all; if your voice packets are delayed by a fraction of a second, the message is unintelligible and worthless.

When driven by today's PCs and servers, with their high-speed PCI buses, it doesn't take much traffic to saturate an aggregated LAN link or overwhelm the WAN or ISP connections. When gigahertz processors and faster system bus technologies like PCI-X become widely available, Fast Ethernet won't be able to keep up with a single PC's demands. What then: Gigabit to the workgroup switch? To the desktop? Even that would be only a temporary remedy.

Traffic Moves Farther

Another growing trend is to increase the distance between you and the information you are retrieving. The old rule stated that 80 percent of the information you request was local to you and you only needed to go the long haul for 20 percent of what you needed. Today that is more than reversed. Nearly all the data that flows to you comes from a distant place. While this greatly increases the amount of data available to you, it increases the complexity and load on the network. The old rule of treating that sort of traffic with best-effort service is going to have to die for us to move forward.

Increased Reliance

It used to be that businesses pretty much had all the data they needed internally. This data was at the ready because it was locally stored and managed. Going off-site was required rarely and usually only in special circumstances. In these cases, dedicated communication lines were provisioned and special contracts were in place for access to this information.

At some point, businesses installed an Internet connection and started using it for some simple information look-ups. As the Internet grew, many other uses for this connection became available and this pipe to the cloud was increased. What has happened is that we have slowly migrated to using our Internet connections for what once was a fast, reliable internal connection. The speed, security, and availability are not what they once were; we have increased our reliance on these external links without increasing the intelligence of the network. We need to realign the network with the business. There must be a better, more intelligent solution.

Not at the Router

Many working groups, standards committees, and vendor consortia are trying to address the bandwidth problem. The bulk of their efforts centers around improvements in three areas: Faster backbones, improvements to the Internet Protocol, and bandwidth reservation/quality of service guarantees.

These efforts are important; there's going to be a lot of traffic to carry, and technologies such as ten-gigabit Ethernet will be essential. The QoS provisions within IPv4's RSVP bandwidth reservation scheme aren't as powerful as ATM's quality of service controls, but they are a step in the right direction. However, reservation schemes break down quickly as the number of devices increases. For example, if a user wished to set up a video conference call with a colleague across the WAN, all the network devices in between the two users would have to be using RSVP and then set aside a reasonable amount of bandwidth for the impending call. This bandwidth can't be used for other traffic if it is reserved, and if any device along the path doesn't use RSVP, the call quality is in jeopardy. It is fairly obvious that beyond a couple routers and a dozen or so users, this solution will cease to function as the routers run out of capacity.

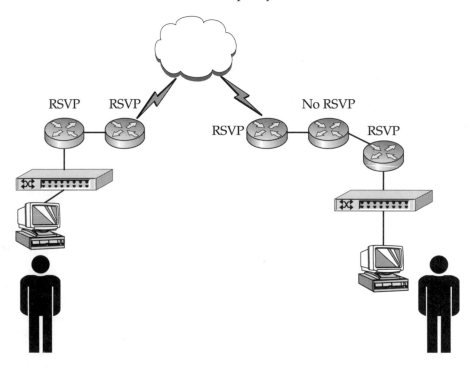

Scalability

The problem is that those solutions are all router- or backbone-based. Yes, it's important to be able to set up high-quality connections between routers. Because a router's focus is on packets, not on applications, any attempts it makes to regulate bandwidth will necessarily be crude, using simple rules based on TCP port number, originating or destination IP address, or other preprogrammed parameters. Even if a router were to attempt to manage the network to that level of precision, there's no way any device could juggle all the combinations of users, applications, priorities, and business rules.

Let's say that you have a business with 100 routers, 10,000 users, and 10 applications. Even these numbers are small for many businesses and certainly minuscule for the Internet, and you can see that you could easily have a rule for each application for each user (100,000 rules). Now remember that you need to change the rules every hour on 100 different devices. Not only is this not feasible, the CPU and memory on the routers would not be able to handle this many entries in a timely fashion. Just looking through all the entries would add so much delay as to defeat the purpose of the entries in the first place.

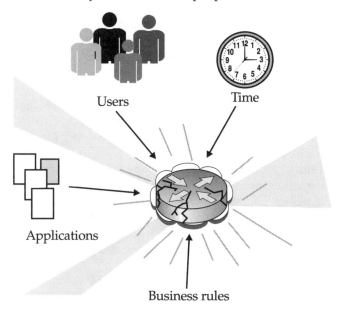

The alternative is to keep the set of rules simple, say by grouping users, by keeping the rules constant over time, and by keeping them static so that you don't have to update all the devices for every change. While this might work, it only provides one percent of where we need to be in terms of turning the network into a strategic tool for your business.

But just as Federal Express can't tell by looking at the boxes which of a business's packages can be delivered in three days, and which must be delivered by 10:30 A.M. tomorrow morning—unless the customer marks the package—so the router can't be trusted to make the fine-grained decisions about traffic priority on its own. The value of a packet or data stream can only be determined at the end-node level—where the traffic originates. Yet it would be a mistake to hand control of traffic prioritization to each workstation or server, letting each choose its own QoS. The end stations don't understand where the bottleneck is between you and your destination. They only know what's going on at the LAN level, and the limiting pipe is often not there. That is why the solution has to apply to more than one WAN connection and has to be dynamic. It will need to apply its medicine to many different parts of the network at different times.

Distributed Marking and Centralized Control

In the Thinking Network, traffic must be coordinated according to business-oriented rules, and prioritized fairly and uniformly; otherwise, anarchy and chaos will reign. Those rules must be applied at every node, at every traffic aggregation device, in real time.

In other words, the network must be intelligent and adaptable, balancing its available bandwidth resources against the needs of end nodes to conduct the business of the company. The architecture calls for each end node to mark the traffic with a certain priority for true end-to-end QoS. The end nodes take direction and traffic-marking policies from a centralized server that understands where the bottlenecks are, the current traffic patterns, and the business-orientated traffic prioritization rules. The centralized server is aware of many links at once, so it can dynamically make changes to individual policies but have a global effect.

The intermediate devices such as routers only need to concern themselves with what priority the incoming traffic is, not the time of day, protocol, destination, and user associated with the traffic. This allows those devices to focus on doing what they do best—route traffic. This architecture is illustrated in Figure 9-2.

Fine-grained control, scalability, and dynamic changes are some of the most important features of this architecture. Because the marking of the traffic takes place at the end node, the finest control can be included in the policies. For example, you could easily have a policy that describes how to tag traffic for a specific user on September 15 at 5 A.M. using a specific type of Oracle transaction to a specific destination. (Trying to get this level of control in each router in a path would be overwhelming.) And because the traffic

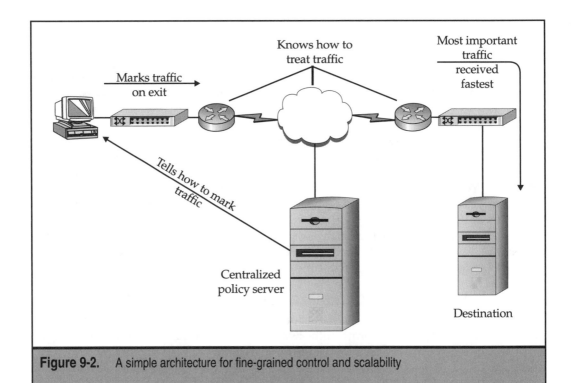

Figure 9-2. A simple architecture for fine-grained control and scalability

prioritization rules are applied at the edge of the network, the system can scale to almost any size. The only limitation is that you may need more centralized policy servers to dole out policies to the end nodes.

> **NOTE:**   Since the end nodes are autonomous once they receive their policy, they do not need to be in constant contact with the policy server. Solutions that require checking in before every use for the network only add latency and network traffic, as well as severely limiting the ability to scale.

THE BUSINESS IMPERATIVE

Businesses have rules that help employees and their service providers determine when something is important, and when it's very important. Most FedEx packages are sent for second-day delivery, except when a manager determines that a package is especially urgent. New business card orders take two weeks, except when business priorities justify the rush charges. Because overtime is expensive, it must be approved in advance. Everyone flies coach unless the flight is more than six hours in duration, in which case an upgrade is justified so that the worker will be productive the next day.

The network is becoming more tightly integrated into vital enterprise processes, becoming a part of the business rather than just another utility like light, air conditioning, and running water. Accordingly, the business rules that govern the network's behavior must be more complex than "be available 99.9 percent of the time, with at least 24 hours notice of planned outages."

As has been shown, demands on the network are increasing to more than fill the available bandwidth. In the Thinking Network, intelligent rules must be in place to determine how that valuable resource is used. We would argue that business managers, not technology managers, must make those rules; the network team should implement those rules—just as the CFO makes the rules about coach-class seats and FedEx, all employees know those rules, and the travel desk and mailroom ensure that those rules are followed.

Business Rules

Which is more important: synchronization of the Notes database across the WAN, or the monthly accounting run? Accounting. Who gets priority access to the e-mail server, users with POP3 connections or those accessing it over the Web? Web users are working in real time and should have higher levels of service. How much priority should be given to video conferencing? Not much when it's linking employees at the same site, more priority when it's spanning multiple locations, but top priority when it involves customers or board meetings. How about incoming requests over the Internet? The e-commerce pages get bandwidth priority over tech support.

Business rules for governing the network's behavior need not be much more complex than those examples, though there must also be clear "default" settings as well as guarantees that all applications will get reasonable attention from the network, and there must be policies for managing conflicts between many applications claiming that they have a high-priority right-of-way. The key is that the rules must be expressed in a language that corporate managers can understand and review. What's more, those rules must be easily translatable into terms that can be implemented by the network management staff, and set as policies that servers, workstations, and infrastructure devices such as switches and routers can all use.

Business rules based on business objectives will bring order out of network chaos. Naturally there will be conflict between business rules in times of very limited bandwidth. The Thinking Network will manage those conflicts dynamically. This turns the network into a strategic business tool.

Challenges to Setting Rules

Why pass the rules all the way down to the workstation level? Because, as with other business rules—like those for long-distance telephone usage, or for when a manager must sign off on a purchase order, or when a customer can have a discount—it's faster and more efficient if the originating user knows the policy and is a participant in its implementation. Certainly bandwidth-aggregation devices like switches and routers provide the resources, but it's the end nodes, the servers and workstations, that carry out the company's business. Therefore, the end nodes should be able to request and receive classes of service from the Thinking Network, not merely based on their domain or IP address range, but based on the business value of the network transactions.

No modern business would dream of having a telephone operator approve every phone call and decide how long it takes to go through, or how good its sound quality should be. No future-looking business should entrust its vital bandwidth-allocation decisions to a backbone router or WAN interface.

Disconnected Managers

One serious problem with today's networks is that there is a large disconnect between those that keep the network running for the business and those running the business. Tools provided to help IT managers are not business orientated. In fact, many of them require advanced technical training and in-depth knowledge of the network. Some of the most useful tools available, such as network modeling software, require such an advanced understanding of networking that many organizations don't have anyone who can run them properly.

Business managers are often so technically inept that they don't understand the ramifications of purchasing a new application for the network such as PeopleSoft. Then the IT manager is left trying to get that behemoth to run over the existing resources while the business manager is saying that it is still too slow. Something has to give for us to move forward.

Deciding Who Rules

Clearly, the goals of the business must be met by its resources, including its e-business infrastructure. So how will businesses turn their objectives into traffic prioritization rules?

The business managers don't get the IT, and the IT managers are not privy to the high-level goals of the business. Moreover, many businesses are divided into separate business units, although they all share the same infrastructure. How will they determine who gets the fastest service?

Organizations are going to have to change the way they treat IT, and IT will have to try to better understand the reason they exist—to move the company closer to its objectives. This paradigm shift will require tremendous work and openness by all those involved. In all likelihood, organizations will have to take a holistic view of their company and seek outside help to determine priorities. This remains one of the biggest hurdles to overcome before businesses can align their technical resources to the success of the company.

Measuring Up

In any business setting, employees are given the rules to help them carry out their jobs. There is also a responsibility on management's part to monitor the rules so as to determine their effectiveness, and help in the creation of new and better rules. Just as the CFO and line-of-business managers review their travel and FedEx charges monthly, so too should they be aware of the effectiveness of their network usage policies.

Any intelligent network should contain the capability to provide meaningful reports to management, along with analysis and recommendations.

Raw data is meaningless. Utilization percentages, counts of dropped packets, average speed of a Web transaction—those numbers won't help business managers make informed decisions about when to add new infrastructure equipment, when to perform system upgrades, when to change the business rules. As with other useful information that managers receive, it must include historical context, comparisons to budget assumptions, and highlights of emerging trends. When rules aren't working, the network is not delivering its greatest value to the business. Managers need to know—and need to know why.

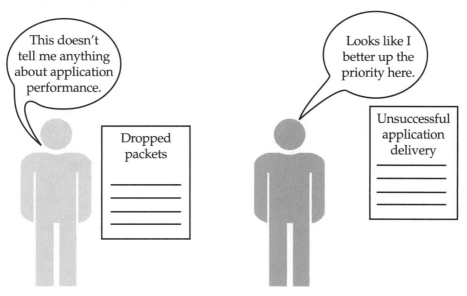

THE THINKING NETWORK

The creation of business rules is only a part—one small part—of the design of the Thinking Network. Rules don't represent intelligence. An ever greater part must be the ability of the Thinking Network to learn by experience how to best deliver service, relying not only on those explicit rules, but also on heuristics and observation of traffic patterns.

The Thinking Network in Action: A Peak into the Future

The Thinking Network will be cognizant of business goals and have a set of rules that can be consulted to make intelligent decisions about traffic priorities. It can consult past events, current network conditions, and user-specific information to dynamically change priorities in your e-business. Here are several examples of how the Thinking Network might work.

PC Boot Up

Consider diskless PCs that boot off the network. Even if there aren't business rules for handling their boot sequence, the Thinking Network might realize that the delivery of an operating system to those devices will get them up and running sooner, so that when it sees the initial handshaking take place between those thin PCs' network interface cards and their BOOTP servers, it might choose to allocate extra bandwidth to that connection. It might even temporarily create a switched virtual LAN containing just the BOOTP server and the thin client, in effect dedicating a communications channel to feeding that thin client with data as fast as it can absorb it.

E-mail May Be Crucial

Here's an example where the dynamic nature and intelligence of the Thinking Network play a role. The business has determined that e-mail traffic is crucial for its functioning and continued high productivity. It has also determined that its e-business traffic is also quite important as well as its control system traffic. These rules are deployed to the end nodes, and everything is running fine until one day a user in a remote office e-mails a large file to the rest of the company.

Shortly, the WAN connection between the remote site and HQ is full of high-priority e-mail traffic. The intelligent system sees this and consults its rules. While e-mail is very important, it should not bring down the network. It decides to dynamically reduce the e-mail priorities of this one e-mail server for a period of time so that the e-business orders and control system traffic can still function. Once the large e-mail has been passed, that server is returned to its highest priority status.

Links Go Down

A large airline takes its online reservation requests over its connection to the Internet. It also uses this link for corporate information transfer over a VPN and for general Web surfing and file transfer. This T-3 is large enough for the airline to use its connection for all these uses, normally.

Then, imagine that the T-3 link fails, and that link switches over to a backup 128 Kbps ISDN connection. That line immediately gets flooded, and virtually no traffic is allowed through. The airline can't take reservations on line. Now, what should the priorities be? Which packets should get priority, which should wait? What is best for the business? The Thinking Network consults its previously determined business rules and quickly sends out a message to reduce the priority on all traffic except the e-business traffic coming in from the Internet. Once the T-3 is back online, the Thinking Network returns users to their previously running policy.

Not There Yet

No solution today offers this level of capability, but the potential clearly exists. Products like FireSummit's Viziq have started down this path, with its ability to prioritize network traffic and adjust network policies in real time for e-commerce and corporate networking applications. However, Viziq's technology only represents the first step on the long road to a true Thinking Network.

More Than Packet Pushing

The Thinking Network can better carry out business rules if it has the flexibility to not only allocate bandwidth but also determine the best routes and devices for delivering end-to-end service between nodes, such as by dynamically creating VLANs or adjusting routing protocol parameters.

Business Values

Taking that concept one step further, if the Thinking Network can extend its reach down into the end nodes themselves, it can better assess the business value of transactions, as well as gauge the real needs and capabilities of those end nodes. Today, a few vendors offer agent-based software that can be installed on servers and monitor the end-to-end performance of their hardware, operating systems, and individual applications such as Lotus Notes, Microsoft Exchange, and Oracle databases. But we need to go where there is very fine-grained control with a global sense of what's going on.

You have an e-business that sells micro-cap stocks to your clients. You place their orders as soon as your system receives them. You also use a database to track the portfolios of your clients. You allow them to look at their own portfolios, and you use the information to better serve your clients. Obviously, your clients are concerned about how fast their transactions can be processed and placed by your systems. You decide to offer the very fastest service to your best customers. You decide that those with the largest trades will get the highest priorities. You instruct the Thinking Network to set users' traffic priorities according to entries in your database. This concept is illustrated in Figure 9-3.

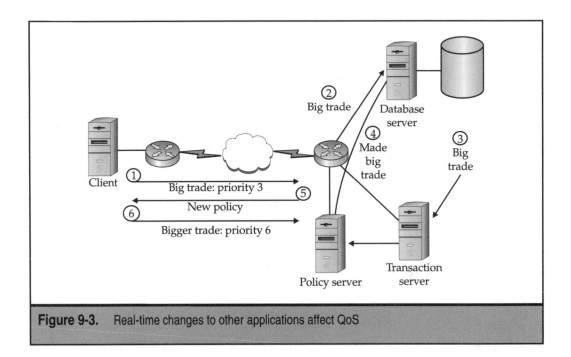

Figure 9-3. Real-time changes to other applications affect QoS

NOTE: Open protocols such as the Lightweight Directory Access Protocol (LDAP) and directory services such as Active Directory or Novell's Directory Service are getting us closer to being able to share information across numerous applications in real time. Networking devices are also opening up and sharing information with Directory Services under the Directory Enabled Networking standard being developed.

Monitoring What Matters

End-to-end performance monitoring is important, but the Thinking Network will measure that performance not in terms of packet throughput or bandwidth utilization, or even of average and peak transaction times, but in terms of business rules. What's more, it needs to be able to adjust those operating systems and applications on the fly. The Thinking Network's agents need to be able to adjust service and daemon thread priorities, to tune operating systems, and to access and change transaction queuing priorities inside applications.

After business rules have been set, the most important value to monitor is the user experience. Saying e-mail is the most important type of traffic and should thus get the fastest service may not be wise even if you have determined that e-mail is the most important type of traffic. You also need to look at the social aspect of the traffic and the people you are prioritizing. For example, when you prioritized e-mail, it moved from a two-second delay to less than a 100 ms delay. This is significant in terms of network latency but probably not in terms of how people use e-mail. If a message pops up in two seconds after it was sent, that is probably good enough.

However, that is not the case with Voice over IP (VoIP). VoIP applications falter if their latency is greater than 140 ms (for spoken English). We know this because we watch people use the application and have determined that it doesn't work with more than 140 ms latency. This is a common-sense example, but an organization can have hundreds of applications/transaction types for which the impact of latency is not clear and probably not put in terms of productivity or financial gain/loss.

Other Considerations to Drive Change

What will drive those changes? Business rules provided by a business rule server, heuristics learned and passed down by the Thinking Network's control center, and intelligent responses to workload and operating conditions determined by the end-node agents themselves. The Thinking Network's central brain can't direct activities to that level; the agents should be able to translate broad goals into the appropriate actions for their hardware and software platform while reporting back to the central brain about important events out at the periphery.

THE VISION AHEAD

The vision of the end-to-end Thinking Network is truly that: end-to-end. It contains a vast number of elements, spanning every connected component in a business network. On the LAN, it includes workstations and servers, and their operating systems and applications. It includes the infrastructure hubs, switches, and routers, as well as shared resources such as print servers, cache servers, storage-area networks and network-attached storage, remote-access servers, firewalls, gateways, and more. On the Internet, the Thinking Network would be pervasive across edge and core routers, traffic and accounting systems, caches, and application service providers.

The Thinking Network Is Ubiquitous

Bear in mind that the Thinking Network need not only serve standard PCs and servers. Cellular telephones, two-way pagers, handheld computers, even embedded systems and Internet appliances are end nodes that could benefit from the careful attention of the Thinking Network's business rules.

It's a big vision, and a big problem—too big for existing tools, and too big for any human administrator to manage. That's why we believe tools like FireSummit's Viziq, though offering immediate and real value today, are only the tips of the iceberg when one considers the true potential of an end-to-end Thinking Network.

To draw an analogy, the Thinking Network is like a big corporation itself. Executives make broad policies: this is what we make, this is what we do, this is our goal. The message is passed out to individual departments and field offices, through managers and supervisors, all the way down to the individual employees—the ones who write, who build, who sell, who support customers. That's where the policies get translated into practice, and the business's value is added, and the user's experience with the network enhanced.

Or to use another analogy: The human brain says, "I want to lift that glass of water." The message is passed through the nervous system to the muscles, who work together, performing the intricate motions and feedback to carry out the brain's instructions. It's a real partnership, spanning the human body's own local area network. Like the human nervous system, the Thinking Network will learn, adapt, and grow.

Using Old Answers to Solve New Problems

The words "learn," "adapt," and "grow" are not typically associated with computer systems. They sound kind of soft and squishy, not hard and machine-like. As you have undoubtedly thought so far while reading this chapter, for the Thinking Network to fly it is going to require some new technologies, not just a simple tweak of what we already have. These words are a good indication of where we are going to get some of these answers: biology.

Complicated Systems

The most complicated systems in our known universe are biological entities that have adapted and evolved over millions of years to successfully survive to today. These systems have had to solve many problems along the way, and scientists have been borrowing answers from biology to solve human-related problems for as long as there have been scientists.

The single most complicated system known to people is the human brain. It has many billions of individual cells (neurons), each of which can simultaneously communicate with thousands of other neurons. Sound like anything else we've been talking about? The parallels between the human nervous system and a global information network are striking.

What Can We Learn?

For almost every problem that developers will face in building the Thinking Network, there has been a similar problem and subsequently a solution found in nature. You just have to know where to look and to be able to extrapolate the solution out to your own problem. A very straightforward example can be seen in learning. Obviously, the Thinking Network must be able to learn from past experiences to be able to predict future needs and outages. Correlations must be made between usage and events that bring an organization closer to or farther away from its optimized state.

People have the same challenge in front of them each day. They must absorb an unbelievable amount of information from many sensory modalities and remember some of it and forget most. They must build a strong correlation to those things that are good for them as well as those that are bad. Think about it. You probably don't remember brushing your teeth 564 days ago, but you probably did it. However, you can certainly remember events that took place years ago. The Thinking Network will do the same. It will be inundated with statistics about usage and a zillion other events. To be functional, it will need to forget data that doesn't correlate strongly to a positive or negative event, but remember data patterns that do correlate strongly to important events. From what we know about how human learning and memory works, we can extrapolate to how data should be stored so as to emulate our own nervous system. The result is a dynamic and powerful system that can mature over time and continue to cope with new stimuli to produce better decisions.

We will require a system like this to successfully move toward the Thinking Network. Although people can deal with an enormous influx of information and manage, people cannot deal with simultaneously being delivered hundreds of megabytes of statistical information about the use of the network. Only computers will be able to do that, because our sensory capabilities and brain are not set up to deal with that sort of information.

Working Together

Realization of the Thinking Network vision will require partnerships, too, as well as standards.

Standards

First, the standards. Imagine the number of components that will need to talk to each other, sharing a common set of business rules, communicating requests for service, receiving reports about real-world network performance. Those components include routers and network interface cards, operating systems and application agents, Wireless Application Protocol telephones, and the Thinking Network control center. For example, today we use VoIP gateways to translate between IP packets and switched phone service. Until all devices use the same protocol (looks like it's going to be IP), we will have to use gateways for translation.

Common Language

In order for the Thinking Network to work, a thin, robust, and common communication protocol—call it STNP, the Simple Thinking Network Protocol—must be able to accommodate all the types of information requests that the components will make today, and tomorrow.

Think of STNP as complementary to SNMP, the Simple Network Management Protocol, in that it's ubiquitous, containing not only primitives but also private data specific to each managed device, capable of both sending events and responding to polling requests. STNP will provide services at a higher level than SNMP, because its primary task is to communicate business rules and to request services, not to exchange very granular metrics and device-control commands. STNP is also complementary with LDAP, the Lightweight Directory Access Protocol, which enables enterprise-wide resource directories.

Partnerships

With such standards comes partnership. As with SNMP, not every device on the Thinking Network must understand or act on STNP requests in order for the network to be intelligent, although every device needs to be able to pass those messages. These devices include PCs, servers, wireless devices, network devices, satellites, and just about any other means of communication. The more STNP-aware devices on the network, the more intelligent and active it will become, and the greater value the entire network will have to the entire business.

Therefore, we envision a virtual partnership, a consensus built around the Thinking Network standards and protocols, ranging from hardware makers to operating system vendors to Internet Protocol carriers to application service providers to application developers. By supporting the vision of the Thinking Network, they will not only add value to their own products and services, but will empower their customers' networks beyond anything available today.

Figure 9-4 illustrates some of the key relationships that must be in place for the Thinking Network. There must be compelling applications and a need to communicate. Initially, these will be voice based, but they will soon encompass video applications, roaming connectivity, unified messaging, and more exotic applications to follow. The second piece is the infrastructure. There must be a means to communicate. This can be wired, as in DSL technology, or wireless, as in the wireless LAN protocol 802.11 specifications. In a global sense, we are only just beginning to see coverage here. The last piece consists of the QoS mechanisms that we have discussed in this and the preceding chapter. A central, intelligent policy server must be in place to orchestrate the whole thing.

We also envision a second partnership, equally as important as the first, between a business's top executives, IT and network managers, and end users. Corporations and other large organizations are often slow to adopt change. We believe that the vision of the Thinking Network is sufficiently compelling to warrant its wholesale adoption by businesses; of course, at first it will be piecemeal, as it will take years for the components of the Thinking Network to come to market. But just as their investment in dual-speed NICs suddenly paid off when Ethernet network hubs were replaced with Fast Ethernet switches, so too the investment in Thinking Network technologies will pay rich dividends for years to come.

The Thinking Network Effect

Bob Metcalfe, inventor of Ethernet and founder of 3Com Corp., postulated what came to be known as Metcalfe's Law: The power of the network increases exponentially by the number of computers connected to it.

We believe that this law applies equally well to our new paradigm: the intelligence, adaptability, and quality of service provided by the Thinking Network increases exponentially by the number of intelligent components connected to it.

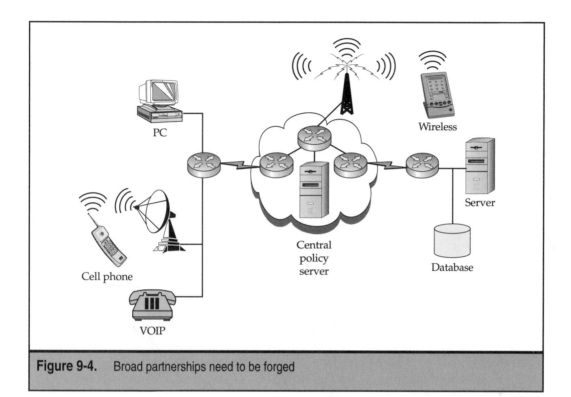

Figure 9-4. Broad partnerships need to be forged

The alternative is a network unable to intelligently match its capabilities and services with the business needs of its users and customers. As the business demands on our technology infrastructure grow, an organization's success is increasingly measured by the quality of its data processing and communications capabilities. One might even say that the network is a strategic part of a business's competitive arsenal. In this new economy, the alternative to the Thinking Network is unthinkable.

CHAPTER 10

Maintaining and Optimizing E-Business Sites

The word "performance" brings to mind a sweet, souped-up race car that can make a grown man cry when it's revved up. But maintaining that piece of machinery isn't done by wrench and tire gauge alone. Rather, it's accomplished through a number of disciplines and approaches. And, like maintaining and tuning a race car, achieving optimal performance for your e-business network will take more than tweaking a couple settings.

In this chapter, we'll talk about the issues related to tuning and optimizing your e-business network. We'll look at a range of issues from the basic and free tasks like stopping network abuse by employees all the way to connecting network probes costing thousands of dollars that collect valuable bits of data.

THE NEED FOR PERFORMANCE

You could buy the biggest, speediest, most expensive computers made by man and link them with blazingly fast network connections. However, even with the best equipment money can buy, if you don't know how to connect and tune your hardware and software, your e-business solution is likely to run into a few problems.

Simply connecting computers together, plugging them into a router, and linking to an ISP isn't the end of your hardware responsibilities. You have to make sure that network traffic is going where it needs to go when it needs to get there. You must know that customers are accessing your network in a fast, efficient manner. You must know when your system is overtaxed and not providing optimal results. If you just connect the computers, bury your head in the sand, and expect results, you're fooling yourself—and wasting thousands of dollars worth of hardware.

Performance will affect your business in virtually every aspect of computer use. Not only will it affect your online business (if shoppers and supply-chain partners are waiting an interminable amount of time to conduct business, they'll go elsewhere), but also such simple tasks as printing something on a network printer or accessing a file on the network will be inhibited.

Luckily, there are a number of ways that you can optimize your network and improve speed. Some of these solutions are cheap or free, whereas others can cost thousands of dollars.

Performance Overview

Tweaking out your system for ideal performance is a multifaceted problem. Enhancing your network's functioning isn't just a matter of fine-tuning your hardware. Nor is software alone the sole culprit for a slow, inefficient network. Rather, network performance comes from balancing hardware and software as well as effectively managing your organization's use of the network.

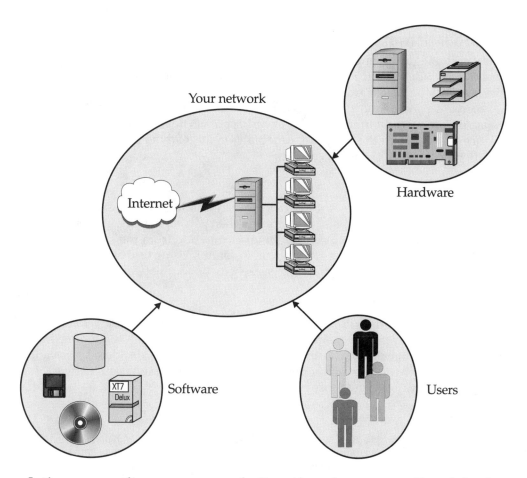

Let's use our earlier race car example. Even if you have a sweet Ferrari that has a 12-cylinder engine, low drag, and a really fantastic paint job, if you put someone behind the wheel who doesn't know how to clutch, the car isn't going anywhere. Also, that Ferrari might as well be up on blocks if you put diesel fuel in the tank. It's the same sort of thing when you think about your network.

If you have the best system money can buy, it matters little if information destined for customers is getting clogged in a bottleneck. Also, if your software isn't ideally configured, packets may be shooting from here to Timbuktu before they get where they need to go.

Best Practices

The meat of this chapter focuses on what tools and techniques you can use to streamline and optimize your network. However, several key areas need to be considered—within your business—before you start tweaking individual network and server components.

Know Your Network

Having accurate documentation of your network—including up-to-date network diagrams that include specific information about network equipment, network topologies, which network protocols are in use, protocol addressing, WAN links, server and user LAN segments, and administrative contact information—is absolutely critical. Without accurate information about the overall network, you will not be effective in keeping performance acceptable in the long run, especially on large, dynamic networks in which there are high levels of change occurring.

Baselining

To get anywhere, you need to know where you are coming from. Baselining your network gives you an important point of reference when you begin to look for opportunities to maximize performance. You can combine information from tools such as network analyzers and server tools such as Performance Monitor. Using the collected information allows you to build a picture of the average capacity of your network.

Keep It Simple, Stupid

Keep your tuning efforts within reasonable and understandable parameters. In enterprise networks, many people are involved in building, maintaining, and tuning the overall network environment. If you must make what would be considered nonstandard changes to your network and server parameters to successfully tune your network, make sure to completely document those customized solutions.

Flat Topology

As larger networks evolve, resist the temptation to hang hubs off of hubs and add additional routers that hang off of user LAN network segments, for example. This nesting of network components creates single points of failure that may not be well documented and are likely to be difficult to manage. You also increase the likelihood that you and others will spend additional time troubleshooting and leave yourself less time to spend planning for the future needs and requirements of your users. There are also security issues associated with allowing "seat of the pants" engineering on the network. An undocumented router hanging off of a remote part of the network can be a wide-open door to unauthorized individuals.

Be a Traffic Cop (a.k.a. Reduce Administrative Traffic)

Keeping the number of protocols in use on your network low is one way to reduce the level of unnecessary traffic on your network. Monitoring "administrative" traffic like SNMP polling, WINS replication, DNS zone transfers, and server-to-server traffic will allow you to make intelligent compromises in the name of tuning. For example, you may need to adjust the SNMP polling intervals of remote equipment so that you can use more of a WAN link for user traffic.

Oppress the Workers (a.k.a. Curtail Network Abuse)

A very important but often overlooked opportunity in tuning the network is to make sure users are not abusing the network. On every network, there are always users (and sometimes administrators) who don't seem to understand that the network is there to support other users who have legitimate business to conduct over the network.

Access to the Internet seems to compound the problem. Inappropriate use of the network can be as simple as users who constantly surf the Web for nonbusiness purposes or initiate large file transfers to download the latest Homer Simpson sound bites during peak business hours. In some cases, your users may not know better. They may not understand the impact of downloading and running that nifty new screen-saver that makes use of streaming content from the Internet to display sports scores. Other abuses may include the occasional Doom or Quake server that appears on the network, but many problems come from the improper placement of legitimate servers on the network. Make sure that file, print, and other servers are given appropriate points of connectivity onto the network so that systems administrators are not tempted to put servers on user segments. You may need to simply inform your users and define usage policies. You can also implement or enable Internet access control using proxy servers or set up filters to restrict access to only those services that support legitimate business needs.

Networking for a Better Network

Always focus on working to identify ways in which users and application developers can more efficiently use the network. Helping your users help you is an ongoing effort that can yield great rewards over time. Create an environment in which users, application developers, workstation and server administrators, and network administrators have an opportunity to communicate on a regular basis.

PHYSICAL CONSIDERATIONS

In the last section, we moved the spotlight from hardware issues to human issues. Make no mistake; the bulk of network performance issues can be resolved by ensuring a properly built network that has been optimally tuned.

In this section, we'll talk about the specific hardware where performance issues are most likely to occur. We'll also talk about some strategies to improve network performance, including network segmentation and planning.

Hardware

The bulk of your network performance problems will come from four places: your servers' memory, processor speeds, disk systems, and network systems. We'll pay more attention to network systems later in the chapter, but let's talk more about the other three suspected performance culprits.

RAM

The first thing to take into consideration when checking performance is how much memory your servers have. Without adequate levels of memory, your network will be sluggish and slow. As a general rule of thumb, you can never have too much memory. Especially now, as RAM is getting cheaper and cheaper, this is an easy, cost-effective way to beef up your system.

Processor

The next place to look for trouble is in your servers' processors. Do you have enough juice in them? Are they running at least 500 megahertz (even more if you've purchased them recently) or are you chugging along on old 66 MHz 486 processors? High-speed microprocessors are extremely important, especially as the role of networking changes. As bigger and beefier files are transmitted across your network and as packets have to get where they're going in a timely manner, you can't get along with a processor that's only slightly faster than an old donkey sporting a little top hat.

But selecting processors can be deceiving. You really have to look into the types of chips you're buying rather than just relying on the processor speed. For instance, a 700 MHz AMD Athlon chip runs faster than a 700 MHz Pentium III. Keep these sorts of issues in mind when buying processors and when deciding which machines you will be swapping out.

Storage

Your computers can't keep everything in their physical RAM. When warehousing files in a mass storage environment, it's important that the servers can get at that information as quickly as possible. Even if the data is there and the computers are trying to get at it, it does little good if you're relying on virtual memory, for instance, which is using a lot of the hard drive's resources.

Make sure you've got hard drives with enough capacity to store your data (like memory, hard drives are inexpensive, so don't hold back). Also, make sure you have a fast enough interface with the servers that will make the requested files come onto the network as fast as possible.

SCSI and Firewire drives are also great hard drives to consider adding to your network. Prices for SCSI drives have come down a great deal and are extremely affordable. Additionally, you experience excellent performance because both SCSI and Firewire are very fast.

Network Segmentation

The easy, kill-a-fly-with-a-sledgehammer approach to increasing network performance is to spend a stack of money and kick your computers' resources up through the roof. That's great and fine, but an easier, more refined way to make things run smoothly is to think out your network and develop the most efficient, logical network possible. One key component of a well-designed network is network segmentation.

Advantages

Segmenting is exactly what its name suggests—separating portions of your network's traffic for increased performance, security, or reliability. To segment your network, generally you would use a bridge, a switch, or a router.

There's a certain level of Zen involved with network segmentation. However, you must also have the insight and wisdom to choose your segmentation points wisely, considering all the devices on your network. To do this right, it's important to understand what kinds of traffic are shooting through your network and the paths they take. Finally, you have to minimize the number of devices between the sources and destinations in your network.

Segmentation via Bridge

A common scenario is to use servers as routers between a network's segments. This is popular because it is relatively inexpensive and easy (adding some network interface cards [NICs] to an existing server is a whole lot simpler than redesigning a network).

Take a look at Figure 10-1, which shows a simple two-server network. Each server has two NICs and two user segments. This is a simplistic example, but many networks

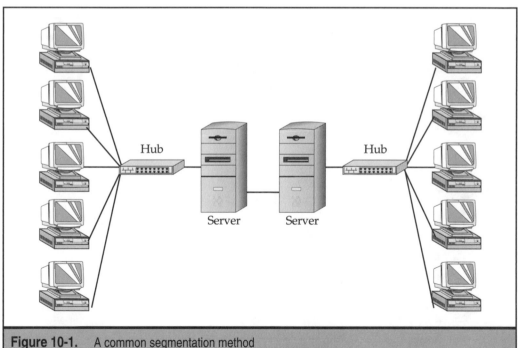

Figure 10-1. A common segmentation method

operate on this same principle, except with hundreds of users. The problem with this segmentation plan is that it places a performance burden on the servers. In addition to providing user services, they must also take on the burden of routing data between the network segments. Both of these servers must also be available for users on one segment to be able to communicate with the other segment. If one server goes down, then users on that server's segment are unable to access both the downed server and network resources on the other segment.

The best way to ameliorate these problems in this scenario is to position a bridge between the two segments, as shown in Figure 10-2.

Now, each server is on the segment it will use most. Since bridges don't retransmit packets that don't need to pass through, this configuration reduces network traffic without adding routing overhead onto the servers. Also, the users in Figure 10-2 won't lose access to the other network segment if one server crashes. In this case, the bridge will continue to route traffic.

Segmentation via Switch

Now, let's say that your network has grown so large that you simply can't keep all your devices on one physical segment. Switches provide an easy way to segment your traffic. This scenario is not too dissimilar to our bridge example. Both switches and bridges act

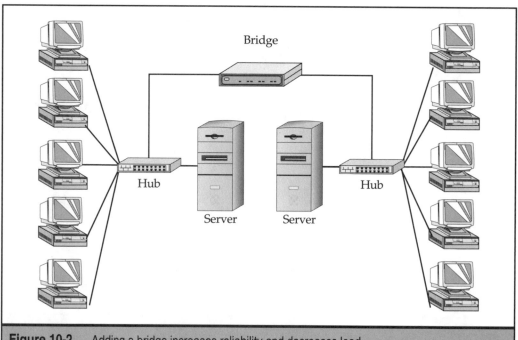

Figure 10-2.   Adding a bridge increases reliability and decreases load

similarly: Data is routed to the port where the destination device resides. The biggest difference between switches and bridges is that switches work on a larger scale. Switches have at least a dozen ports, while bridges have only two. Conversely, a hub transmits packets to all of its active ports.

Each device that connects to a hub has to share its bandwidth with all the other devices connected to the hub. The rub is that if you connect too many hubs, so much bandwidth is shared that client computers cannot use the network effectively.

If you want to design a switching-based network, you should begin with a switch on your network's backbone. This switch then feeds a layer of hubs and more switches. As switches become less and less expensive, this kind of configuration is becoming more and more popular. What's the advantage of this type of layout? A switched environment improves security and performance for each user more than any other segmentation plan. However, this design costs more per port than any other configuration.

The most common configuration you'll find in organizations is based on the preceding design but uses hubs connected to the central switch, rather than another layer of switches. If your organization chooses this option, there are some ways to improve performance. If you are mindful of how traffic flows in your network, you can improve performance in a hub-based network.

Position Devices Together That Communicate Most Often   Keep servers on the same network segment as the servers' most frequent users. For instance, if 80 percent of a server's traffic comes from the production department, placing that server on the production department's segment will reduce traffic on the central switch and cut down the path that the production department's traffic has to travel.

Switch Port Load-Balancing   Conventional thought says 24 to 48 devices can run on the same 10 Mbps network segment. However, a better way to calculate the number of devices on each segment is to look at how much traffic and what kind of traffic each device generates. The production department, for instance, probably uses much more bandwidth than the accounting and administration departments. So rather than putting all three departments on one 24-port hub, buy two 12-port hubs—one for the high-traffic production department and one for the low-traffic accounting and administration departments. This design does little for the administration department but will do a lot for the production department's network performance.

Don't Overload Your Devices   An important reason to use switching on a network is to reduce bottlenecks. Unfortunately, if you don't think out your design completely, segmenting can create a slew of new bottlenecks. The network switch depicted in Figure 10-3 demonstrates how the good intentions of segmentation can have unfortunate results.

The depicted switch has twelve ports. Eight of the ports connect to 10 Mbps hubs, and four ports connect to servers. During peak periods, clients on each of the hubs generate between 2 Mbps to 3 Mbps of bandwidth. This situation would result in a total of 16 Mbps to 24 Mbps of traffic, which is bottlenecking its way right to the servers, which only have

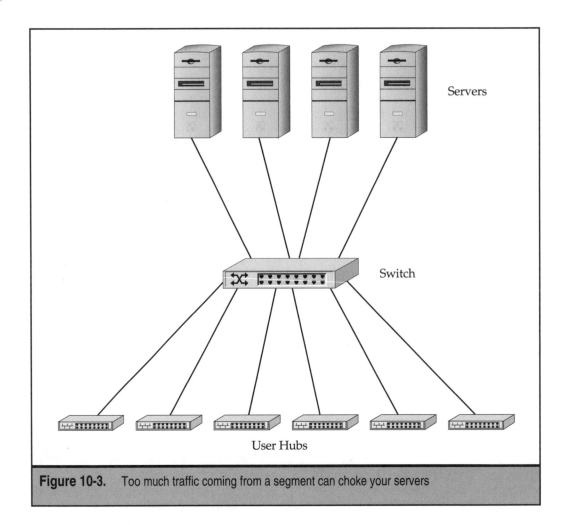

Figure 10-3. Too much traffic coming from a segment can choke your servers

10 Mbps links to the switch. Obviously, this much traffic headed to one server will create a bottleneck and severely impede performance.

Additionally, you don't want to use a switch with Fast Ethernet ports and then have an Ethernet uplink between the switch and the router. Since Fast Ethernet runs at 100 Mbps and Ethernet runs at 10 Mbps, you'll wind up with a nice bottleneck at your link to the backbone.

Segmentation via Router

As you remember from Chapter 8, routers are used to connect networks across vast distances. But they aren't just limited to wide-area concerns; you can use them to segment LANs. The obstacle in using routers is that, since router bandwidth is being used to connect remote offices, bandwidth between routers is limited and expensive. Reducing router traffic is a major performance goal for networks that use routers.

To keep down bandwidth use, routers don't routinely retransmit broadcast packets. However, retransmitting broadcasts can improve the performance of one of the main chores of Windows 2000/NT—name resolution. If you understand how Windows Internet Naming Service (WINS) clients resolve names on your network, you can reduce WAN traffic.

There are four ways WINS can resolve a network device's name:

▼   A device can broadcast a packet that searches for the name of the desired device. If there is a device out there that has a matching name but doesn't respond, then WINS assumes no such device exists on the network.

■   A WINS client asks a WINS server for information about a specific device. If the WINS server knows the IP address of the queried machine, it gives that information to the client.

▲   The remaining two methods WINS uses to resolve NetBIOS names (*mixed mode* and *hybrid mode*) are an amalgamation of the first two methods. The WINS client can broadcast first, then send a packet if the broadcast was unsuccessful. This is known as mixed mode. Or, the client can send a packet first, then broadcast if the packet send was unsuccessful. This is known as hybrid mode.

Unfortunately, broadcast packets don't normally cross routers, so broadcast name resolution won't work if the sought-after device is on another network segment. Directed packets, in this case, are the best way to resolve NetBIOS names on routed networks. On the other hand, broadcasts could be useful in the network shown in Figure 10-4.

Stuffedmonkeys.com has two primary offices (Monterey, California, and Fairfax, Virginia), which connect across a T3 circuit. Stuffedmonkeys.com has two satellite offices (San Angelo, Texas, and Rolla, Missouri), which connect to the network with slower ISDN connections. Monterey and Fairfax house WINS servers that are replication partners. If clients in San Angelo usually only access devices in their own local office, they would have no need to send directed requests to WINS servers to search for devices across the WAN. If clients usually use local devices and don't have a local WINS server, it's best to let them broadcast first to resolve addresses, and then transmit directed packets only if the broadcast fails. Setting clients to mixed mode improves performance by reducing unnecessary communications across the WAN link.

Planning

Before building a car, a house, or a Space Shuttle, planners design their work. They know that without a blueprint from which to work, they'll likely build a shoddy, haphazard mélange of hardware that gets astronauts sucked into outer space because the hatch doesn't seal right. It's clear that a solid design from which to work is important.

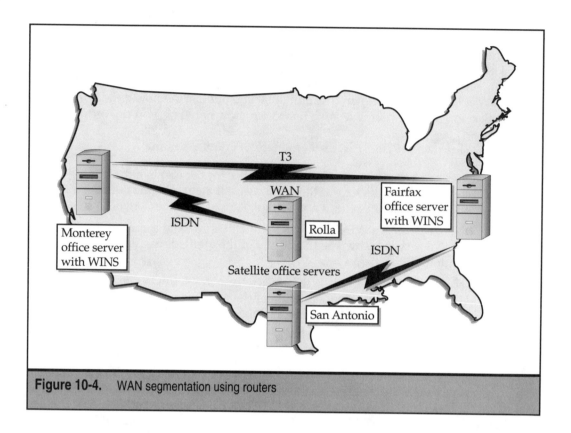

Figure 10-4.   WAN segmentation using routers

I think you know where I'm going with this. If a blueprint is so important with a car, a house, or a Space Shuttle, why not do the same thing with your network? Unfortunately, too many networks are piecemeal designs that could be improved with a modicum of planning and design.

Network Simulation

Network simulation is a fantastic way to ensure that your network is properly constructed. Since networks are dynamic structures (bits and pieces are added all the time), network simulation can show how new devices will affect the whole unit.

Network simulators are pieces of software that allow you to build a test model of your network with different configurations, then apply different loads to see how it behaves. Modeling is important because as your network grows, as routes are transformed, as the topology changes, and as different kinds of devices are introduced, it would be impossible to predict how even the littlest changes would affect the overall network.

A good, solid model of your network will include as many of its details and nuances as possible. Traits to be mindful of include:

▼ Router characteristics

■ Frame relay properties

■ Traffic patterns

▲ Design characteristics

Generally speaking, simulators use two methods to model network traffic: *analytical* and *discrete*. Discrete-event simulation analyzes each packet to determine its behavior. It is slower than the analytical method, which makes more assumptions about network traffic. In spite of the assumptions made by analytical modeling, some performance experts believe that the analytical model is just as accurate as discrete modeling. A good rule of thumb to use is, because of the long simulation time involved in using discrete-event modeling, it is best to use the analytical method when simulating networks with more than 50 routers or switches.

Even on a model of a race car, not every detail can be represented. As much as you would like to include the numbers on the race car's stereo dial, you simply cannot. The same is true when modeling your network. Invariably, there will be some details that have to be simplified. The following items talk about the important items in your network and how you can simplify them for modeling.

Topology   The first step in modeling your network is to create a representation of the network, including its topology and the traffic. The topology is the basic framework of the network; the term refers to both its physical placement and logical configurations. Some of the physical devices that you should include with your representation of the network include:

▼ Routers

■ Computers

■ Switches

■ WAN links

■ LANs

▲ Point-to-point connections

Some of the logical settings you should take into consideration include:

▼ Router interface settings

■ LAN speeds

■ WAN speeds

- Router capabilities
- Routing protocols
▲ Naming conventions

If your eye is starting to twitch over the thought of tracking down all this information, don't worry. You need not enter all this data by hand. There are programs that use SNMP to query your network devices and discover your network's physical and logical settings.

Network Traffic In the last section, we talked about the basic roadmap of your network, so now let's put some traffic on those roads. Just showing where all the expensive pieces of hardware plug into each other is not enough to find out where trouble exists in a network.

It's important to show where the network traffic exists because the traffic generated by existing applications will have a definite impact on the traffic generated by a new application and vice versa. So how do you know where traffic is going and how much is traveling across your network? This is best accomplished by placing network probes where traffic originates and terminates. The downside of using network probes is that they can be very expensive and take a lot of time to set up. Unfortunately, there is no other method to get an accurate look at traffic patterns in your network.

Network probes provide added functionality by gathering information about higher layers in the OSI model; they are usually permanent fixtures in your network. Usually, probes are just PCs with probe software installed on them. Probes can also be pieces of hardware that are smaller than a PC and have no monitor or keyboard. Whichever model you get, they sit quietly and unobtrusively (as shown in Figure 10-5) and gather data from the network.

By the way, they don't give away network probes. These cost upward of $15,000 per probe and can represent a fair investment for your organization. That having been said, the information they gather can be priceless. Table 10-1 lists some vendors for network probes.

Good probes gather information about traffic all the way up to the application layer and generate statistics based on applications. Information you should expect from your probes includes:

▼ Network protocols
- Application name
- Source computer
- Destination computer
- Number of packets in each direction
- Number of bytes in each direction
- Application latency
▲ Conversation duration

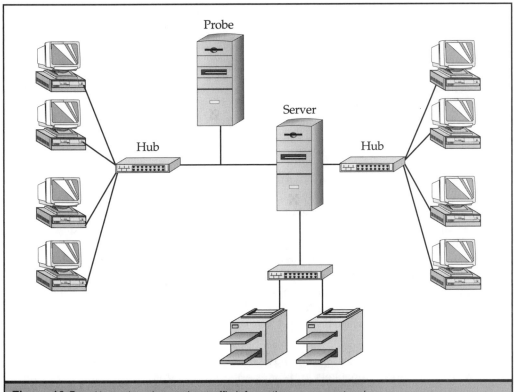

Figure 10-5.   Network probes gather traffic information on your network

Company/Product	Solution Format	Cost	Contact
Nortel Networks/StackProbe	Software and hardware	$5,500–$12,000	www.nortelnetworks.com
Compuware/EcoSCOPE	Software	$3,000–$12,000	www.compuware.com
NetScout/NetScout	Software and hardware	$1,500 for software; $3,000–$15,000 for hardware	www.netscout.com
HP/Network Node Manager	Software	$5,000	www.hp.com/openview

Table 10-1.   Third-Party Network Probes

The main purpose for this information is to build your model of the network, but this information in and of itself is very useful. For instance, you can check application latency to see if the network is meeting a minimum Quality of Service; you can check how much throughput is being used by each application; you can investigate Web usage; and more.

Testing Considerations   When you reach the point where you are ready to run your simulation, testing will take several hours to complete. This is because even in networks with less than 50 routers or switches there are a large number of conversations that will be recorded during the sampling period. To increase the performance of your simulation, you can remove or consolidate traffic conversations.

▼ **Reducing conversations**   Naturally, if you remove conversations from your network, this will artificially reduce the amount of traffic on your network and return skewed results. However, you can still glean useful results after reducing your conversations. When you have a number of probes capturing data at the same time, several probes will pick up the same conversations. Normally, the probes' software will eliminate duplicate conversations, but if the software does not catch them, you should eliminate them manually. Also, conversations with small byte counts have a negligible impact on the network and can be removed without skewing the results. In all likelihood, you can remove about 40 percent of the conversations and lose only three percent of the network traffic.

▲ **Conversation consolidation**   Another way to streamline the process is to consolidate conversations that have the same source and destination and are the same type. All packets and bytes are added to this consolidation, so no traffic load is lost. It's a good idea to define a specific amount of time that both conversations must occur before consolidation. In total, you should enjoy a 40 to 70 percent reduction in the number of conversations by eliminating small conversations and consolidating those remaining.

Running the Simulation   By now, you should have a detailed map of your network's topology and traffic patterns and be ready to run the simulation. To start, you should have a specific question in mind. For example, "If I add an e-mail server to this segment of my network, how will it affect my other applications?"

Basically, you will want to know how performance is affected by changes you plan to make to the network. When you discover performance dropping, some changes you might consider include:

▼ Changing or adding WAN links or LANs

■ Changing or adding routers

■ Changing routing protocols

■ Moving or add servers

■ Moving or add users

▲ Adding or remove an application

Network Simulation Tools

The following third-party vendors offer network simulation tools that will help you model your network. For more information about each of these products, contact the vendor. Their respective Web addresses are listed at the end of each product description.

Hyperformix Strategizer Strategizer is a predictive modeling tool that allows administrators to blueprint an entire customer environment and spot potential flaws, bottlenecks, and weaknesses before the system gets up and running. Strategizer provides a graphical user interface, which allows an administrator to define network topologies and characterize the performance of enterprise networks, including hardware, applications, the Internet, and user behavior.

Strategizer uses its own Application Definition Notation (ADN), which is a C-like programming language allowing software scripting and data model processes. ADN supports object-oriented concepts, which facilitate model reusability and development, debugging, testing, and validation of software models.

Here are some of the most important features of Strategizer:

▼ Its dynamic display allows users to create windows and display run-time messages during the simulation of a model.

■ It interfaces with Hewlett-Packard OpenView and Tivoli NetView and allows the administrator to generate files in XML format that can then be imported into Strategizer as a topology diagram.

■ Experiment Manager allows administrators to perform multiple simulations.

▲ Simulation reports are generated at the end of a model run, and multiple runs can be merged into a single report.

For more information about Hyperformix and their products, visit their Web site at www.hyperformix.com.

NetScout NetScout provides capacity planning by using two of their products in tandem: WebCast and NetScout Server.

WebCast's Web-based user interface and newspaper-style reports help you share application information with others in your organization. Historical trend reports and application usage reports promote capacity planning, policy reinforcement, and business justification of network expenditures.

WebCast delivers a variety of reports, including these:

▼ Daily, weekly, and monthly newspaper-style reports show network conditions and trends, enabling high-level management of mission-critical application flows.

▲ Detailed interactive reports provide up-to-the-minute views of current exceptions, bandwidth hogs, servers, and key applications.

WebCast's features include these:

▼ Access control: WebCast allows you to control access to reports, directing them to the appropriate people at the appropriate time. Access can be assigned by report, alarms, and/or locations.

■ Integration with NetScout Manager Plus, NetScout Server, or Cisco TrafficDirector. Additionally, users can export scheduled reports as GIFs for posting on intranet sites.

▲ Six categories of reports: link, application, flow, performance, baseline, and trend.

NetScout WebCast doesn't work by itself. It relies on information from NetScout Server. NetScout Server aggregates, sorts, and stores traffic statistics collected by NetScout Probes and other data sources, forwarding them as needed to WebCast. NetScout Server is best for large networks that require more data control and is deployed at strategic locations on the network to provide scalable polling, logging, and reporting of network traffic. Working in conjunction with NetScout WebCast, NetScout Server automatically disseminates report information to users, staff, and management.

For more information about NetScout and their line of products and services, visit their Web site at www.netscout.com.

COMNET III COMNET III by Compuware is one of the most popular network simulation tools on the market. Administrators can graphically create a hierarchical model of their proposed network using a drag-and-drop tool palette and libraries of hardware and protocols. Alternatively, COMNET allows administrators to automatically build a model of their network by drawing traffic and topology information from major network management tools, such as Compuware's network probe, EcoSCOPE.

COMNET III can provide analysis about your network in a variety of ways:

▼ With historical information, administrators can set up a network model and experiment with alternatives to gain insight into the interaction of network components and applications.

■ With projected loads, administrators can determine how the current network will handle expected traffic growth and what devices will need to be upgraded.

▲ With proposed networks and applications not already part of the current infrastructure, users can predict network performance.

Some of COMNET's features include:

▼ Simulation of all networks, including LAN, WAN, ATM, frame relay, point-to-point, ISDN, SNA, TCP/IP, POTS, FDDI, and others

■ Prediction of end-to-end delays; throughputs; and utilization of links, buffers, and processors

- Monitoring of peaks and valleys in traffic
- A library of standard protocols and devices to show the effects of swapping out or upgrading devices
- No programming; a drag-and-drop environment simplifies moves, adds, and changes to the existing infrastructure
- ▲ COMNET III's functionality can be expanded by the addition of several different add-on modules

For more information about Compuware, its products and services, visit their Web site at www.compuware.com.

TROUBLESHOOTING

Problems that prevent proper service of your e-business solution can arise from many different areas in the enterprise network. For example, if a client cannot access the data from a server, there could be a problem in any of the following areas:

- ▼ Client computer's network configuration
- User's authentication
- Services failing on the client's computer
- Client software bug or malfunction
- Network hardware, including NICs, cabling, routers, hubs, and switches
- Server's software, services, or network configuration
- ▲ Server's hardware, including processor, memory, power, and hard drives

It is the administrator or support professional's job to resolve issues like this and make sure they don't happen frequently. In this section, we will discuss the general attack strategy and some useful tools you can use to resolve problems in your Windows network.

Because problems can occur at many different levels in the network, it's good to have a procedure to follow so that you can quickly resolve the issue. The following steps can be applied to most network problems.

Define Problem

The first thing any support personnel should do when a user reports a problem is to do their best to define the problem. Very often users will report in very vague statements like, "My program doesn't work" or "The network is down." They do this because they don't fully understand all the components involved with the network or because that is what someone told them the problem was before.

If you are dealing with a naive user, then you must be clever to better define the problem. For example, you may have to ask them to try to run other programs to see if they are affected. You could check with other users to see if they are experiencing similar or different problems.

Once you have exhausted every means possible to define the problem or you think you have a grasp of the situation, you should document the incident for use later.

Locate Problem

This can certainly be the most difficult step because failures can occur anywhere in the network. It is sometimes helpful to start by cutting the network in half and determining in which half the problem resides. For example, if you have a problem between a client and a server, you don't immediately know if the problem resides with the server or the client. You should start by determining this. Can the client use another system to successfully communicate with the server? If so, then you can focus your attention on the client's computer or local segment. In a network, it's a good practice to first examine the problem to see how many users are affected. If we can eliminate the server or the network segment where the server operates, then we can categorize this problem as less critical than if many users were denied service.

To help determine the location of the problem, there are many tools you can use. For example, you could consult with any probes or management stations you may have deployed to see if they are reporting any unusual behavior. You can use a network analyzer to view network traffic. If you find that the problem resides at the level of workstations, then there are numerous applications (such as the Event Viewer with Microsoft Windows 2000/NT) that can pinpoint the problem.

Review Changes

If the system used to work properly (that is, this is not a failure of a new application, feature, or so on), then you can take a shortcut to finding a solution. Review all changes that have taken place since the system was known to function properly. From this information you may be able to determine the cause of the problem. This is where good documentation is so valuable. You might ask:

▼ Was anything added or removed from the network or computer?

■ Is there a new transaction or function you have started using?

■ Were any servers or services (such as DHCP) added to the backbone?

■ Was anybody making changes to applications, systems, or the physical surroundings?

▲ Did you notice the problem at a particular time of the day, week, or month?

Sometimes you'll get lucky and stumble across the answer to your problems right away by checking to see what has changed recently. You might not determine the answer right away, but often these questions might point you in the right direction.

Fix the Problem

By this stage, you have defined the problem and learned of any changes that have taken place recently. Now you need to take action to correct the problem. This might be as simple as replacing a cable or rebooting a system to see if a service restarts properly. It may get quite complicated. You have to replicate the problem in a test network that is separate from the production network. It is often best to change one thing at a time and retest the system. Changing many things may solve the problem but may also introduce new problems.

After several unsuccessful attempts, you may need to return to the first stage or subsequent stages to gather more information. When you believe you have solved the problem, you should test it, perhaps first on the test network, then in the same environment where the problem was first noted.

PERFORMANCE MONITOR

Having the right information about the current state of your systems and the network is critical when conducting performance tuning and troubleshooting problems. In this section, we will take a closer look at the Performance Monitor application included with Windows 2000 and NT.

Though this is not, specifically, a Windows 2000/NT book, the power and usefulness of this OS-based tool are worth highlighting. If you're still considering which OS to use for your network, the functionality and usefulness of Performance Monitor (Perfmon) should add a plus sign to your OS pro and con list.

Perfmon Overview

When tuning your Windows network, you may find it invaluable to have detailed information about the operating system, workstation and server hardware, peripherals, network interfaces, and other software services. Windows 2000 and NT include a mechanism designed to gather statistics based on information provided by various software components running under Windows. The information generated by these components is collected by the Windows Performance Registry. The Registry serves as a mechanism to provide performance data to Win32 applications via the Win32 API. There are standard Windows performance measurements defined and written to the Performance Registry by default. Additionally, programmers can create a DLL that writes performance data for other drivers and services to the Performance Registry. This allows other Win32 applications to read the data. Windows Performance Monitor is a Win32 application that allows you to view the data in the Performance Registry.

> **NOTE:** In Windows 2000, finding and launching Performance Monitor can be a little confusing. You can launch it from the command line (just enter **perfmon**), or you can find it in the Administrative Tools menu under Performance. In either case, Windows 2000 doesn't launch a tool called Performance Monitor; rather, it launches a tool called System Monitor. Don't worry, System Monitor is the Windows 2000 version of Performance Monitor and offers the same functions, features, and operability. For the purposes of this discussion and to alleviate confusion, we'll refer to System Monitor as Performance Monitor.

When Perfmon is first started (Figure 10-6), it is in an inactive state and is thus not monitoring anything. In Windows 2000 the tool is a snap-in to the Microsoft Management Console (MMC). Don't be deceived by its diminutive appearance; Performance Monitor is a very powerful tool. The amount of information that Performance Monitor can access is staggering. A little exploration using the tool can give you information about the state of your machine, helping you to find bottlenecks and tune for performance. This section will provide you with an overview of the tool.

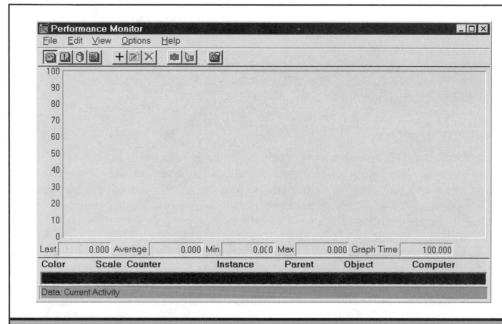

Figure 10-6.   The Performance Monitor default window in NT

The Views

Performance Monitor is best understood by thinking of it as an application with four discrete tools, which are referred to as *views*. These tools allow you to visually display, perform actions on, store, and generate reports on data read from the Performance Registry. These four views are described in Table 10-2.

All these views read information about local and remote systems. The information is organized into computers, objects, instances, and counters:

▼ **Computers**   Represent a local or remote machine on which there are many objects. This distinction allows you to easily view multiple computers with Performance Monitor.

■ **Objects**   Represent a physical, logical, or software component associated with a particular computer. Each object may have more than one instance and contains a number of counters relevant to the object.

■ **Instances (of an object)**   Can be created for each physical, logical, or software component. If there are two processors in the computer, there are two instances of the Processor object. When objects and their associated counters have multiple instances, you can monitor the counters associated with each individual instance separately. In some cases, you have the option of displaying counter data that is based on the total values of all instances.

View	Description
Chart	Displays selected counter data in line graphs or histogram formats. The two display options are referred to as Gallery settings. You can select either display option in the Options | Chart menu.
Alert	Allows you to create alert events based on counter thresholds. Alerts can be set to perform actions according to when a counter exceeds or drops below user-specified values. Actions include network user notification using the Alert and Messenger services; they can also be set to execute an application as defined in the Run Program on Alert box in the Alert Entry and Add to Alert windows.
Log	Allows you to create or open an existing log file and write object data to the file. You can use the log to create reports in the Report view. You can also export the log in .tsv and .csv text formats (tab- or comma-separated values) for use in applications such as Excel.
Report	Allows you to list Objects and their associated counter data in a report using values derived from current activity or from a log file.

Table 10-2.   Performance Monitor Views

▲ **Counters**   Represent meaningful and measurable information defined within an object. For example, the Processor object has several counters, one of which is %Processor Time (the %Processor Time counter represents the percentage of time the processor is busy executing nonidle threads). Another is Interrupts/sec (the number of device interrupts the processor is handling per second). There may be many counters defined within an object.

You can view computers, objects, and counters in any of the four views when selecting the counters you want to read. After selecting a computer, you will see a list of objects available on that computer. Figure 10-7 shows a portion of the drop-down object list for the computer TOONCES.

Some of the objects in the list were added when particular programs were installed on the computer. Others can be added through a manual process. In addition, Windows has a number of objects that are available by default; these are listed in Table 10-3.

To get started with Performance Monitor, we will create a chart that will display some useful information about three different computers on the network. We will point out some of the Performance Monitor features along the way.

Chart View

In Figure 10-8 we have selected the Chart view and clicked Add on the toolbar to bring up the Add to Chart dialog box. We then selected TOONCES and selected the highlighted

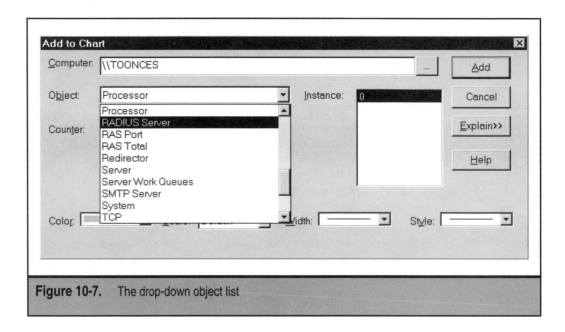

Figure 10-7.   The drop-down object list

Object	Function/Description
Cache	File system memory cache information including cache hits.
LogicalDisk	Logical drive information including disk read/write times, transfer rates, and free space measured in megabytes.
Memory	Physical memory information including committed bytes in use and page reads/writes.
Objects	Software objects that provide information about OS events, processes, semaphores, threads, etc.
PagingFile	Page file usage and usage peaks.
PhysicalDisk	Physical disk information including disk read/write times, transfer rates, and disk queue length.
Process	A software object that allows you to set counters to monitor the behavior of selected applications or the total of all running applications.
Processor	Hardware processor information.
Redirector	Network redirector information including bytes received/sent, connections, file reads/writes, packet data, and network errors.
System	Includes counters that provide general system information including Registry quotas in use, total processor time, systems calls, and system uptime.
Thread	Provides information about threads as a total or within a particular process.

Table 10-3.   Some Default Objects

Processor object. We kept the default %Processor Time Counter and chose a bar/line color of black. The Scale was left at the default of 1.0, and we increased the line Width one notch thicker to be more visible and kept the line Style at the default solid line. Since TOONCES only has one processor, instance 0 is the only instance we can select. If TOONCES had two processors, we could select between instances 0 and 1. Before clicking Add to add this counter to the chart, we clicked Explain to get a detailed description of the highlighted counter—%Processor Time.

We continued to add two more %Processor Time counters, one for a computer called ALPHA and another for a computer called WWW, so we could get a look at the processor

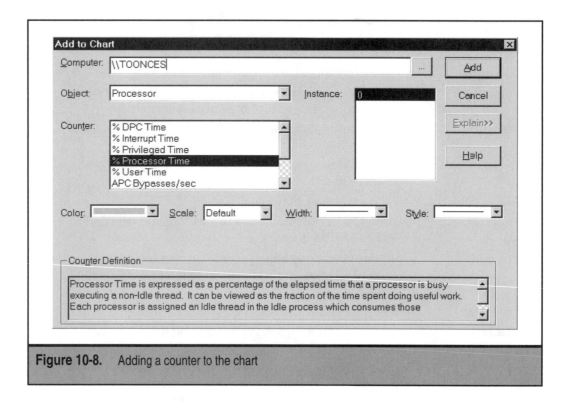

Figure 10-8. Adding a counter to the chart

utilization of three computers on the same chart. After letting Performance Monitor run for a while, we had a comparison of the processor utilization of the three computers as shown in Figure 10-9.

To change the Gallery view of the display from a line graph to a histogram, open the Chart Options dialog box by selecting Options | Chart from the menu, or by clicking Options located on the right-hand side of the toolbar. In Windows 2000, an icon at the top of the Performance Monitor window makes changing the Chart Options a one-click process.

In addition to allowing you to change how the chart is displayed, Chart Options lets you select whether or not you want the Legend, Value Bar, Grids, and Labels to be displayed. You can also define the Vertical Maximum number to be displayed on the left-hand side of the chart. Additionally, you can change the Update interval time or set it to manual if you want to take attended readings.

As with the other views, Chart view can be set up for a wide variety of counters that can be read in real time or from previously saved log files. The uses for the Chart view range from quick performance spot-checks to long-term analysis of data. The information bar below the graphs provides Last, Average, Minimum, and Maximum data on the selected counter. When captured to a log file, this information is stored and can be read later.

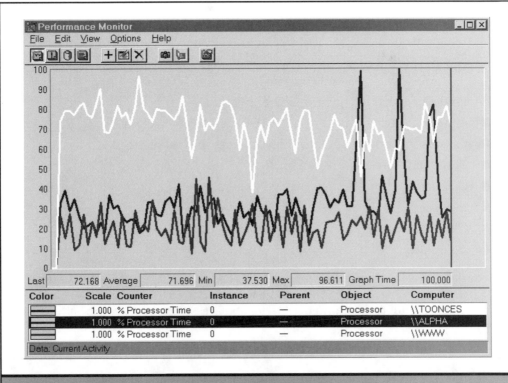

Figure 10-9.   Chart view of %Processor Time counters

Alert View

Alert view is helpful when you want to monitor specific counters but don't want to sit and watch a graph all day. You can set thresholds and have Performance Monitor send you a message if the threshold is either over or under a predefined value. For example, you might monitor the free space on a logical disk and have an alert sent if the free space falls below a specific value. You can also specify a command line executable that will be run if the monitored counter falls above or below the predefined threshold.

Adding alert counters is done in the same way as it was in the Chart view. Click Add Counter or select Edit | Add To Alert from the menu. In Windows 2000, look for the Alert view in the left pane of the MMC while running the Performance Monitor snap-in.

Figure 10-10 illustrates three alerts defined in the Alert Legend. The Value column lists the counter threshold that needs to be exceeded before triggering an alert event. Note that the greater than symbol (>) to the left of each value indicates that the counter value must be greater than the value listed. If the less than symbol (<) were there, it would indicate that the alert counter is configured so that the counter value must fall below the value listed before an alert event would be triggered.

The remainder of the Alert view display is dedicated to the Alert Log. Every time a threshold is exceeded, an entry is displayed in the log view listing that includes the following information:

▼ Predefined alert that generated the entry

■ Time of the alert

■ Counter value with a greater than or less than symbol

■ Threshold value

■ Counter

■ Instance

■ Object

▲ Computer

In order to have Performance Monitor send an alert message, it must be configured to do so. You should note that for the message to be delivered, the defined Net Name must be a registered NetBIOS name and the Alerter and Messenger services (on an NT system)

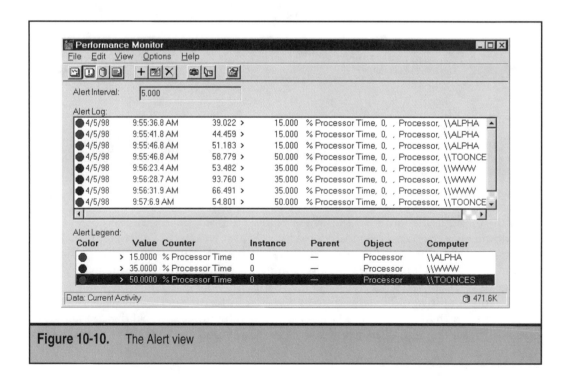

Figure 10-10. The Alert view

or WinPopUp (on Win 95 and WFWG systems) must be running . You can register a NetBIOS name at a specific computer such as "bobalert" by entering **net name bobalert /add** at the computer's command prompt. Once the name is registered, the alerts will be displayed on that computer.

The General, Action, and Schedule tabs within the Alert Properties dialog box (Figure 10-11) are used to define several settings, including the options of having:

▼ The view switch back to the Alert view when an alert event has occurred.

■ The alert event logged into the Application Log so that it can be read in the Event Viewer.

■ The alert event send a network message to a specific network name listed in the Net Name dialog box.

▲ The Update Time set to Manual Update or Periodic Update at a defined interval.

Log View

The Log view allows you to capture object data at specified intervals for review and analysis at a later time. Any of the other views can read the log file and perform their specific

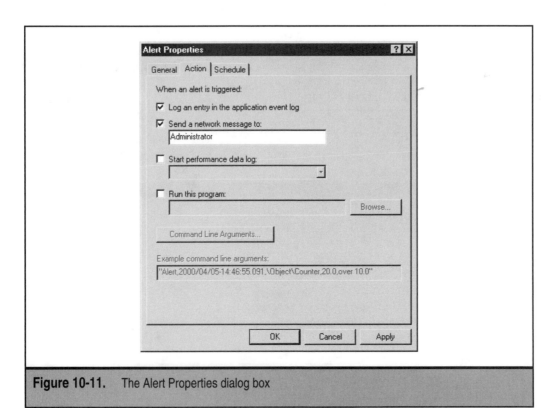

Figure 10-11. The Alert Properties dialog box

functions as if the logged data were happening in real time. For each object selected, all the counters associated with the object are written to the log. To write data to a log, you need to add objects to the Log view. This can be accomplished by selecting Edit | Add To Log from the menu when in the Log view. In Windows 2000, Log view can be easily selected from a row of icons at the top of the window.

This action will bring up the Add To Log dialog box, which will allow you to select computers and objects to log. Once you have added the objects you want to log, open the Log Options dialog box and specify a location, log file, and update time settings.

Be careful when setting the interval—some objects can generate a large amount of data in a very short time. If the interval is short and the object is writing a large amount of data to the log, you might be out of hard drive space in a matter of minutes. Once these parameters are set, click Save and then click Start Log and close the Log Options dialog box. At this time, the Performance Monitor will begin capturing data for all the displayed objects (Figure 10-12) and will allow you to monitor the log file size.

To stop the log, open the Options dialog box and click Stop Log. To view the logged data, select one of the other views (Chart, Alert, or Report), select Options | Data From, and select the path and filename of the log file. Each tool reads the data as if it were being collected in real time.

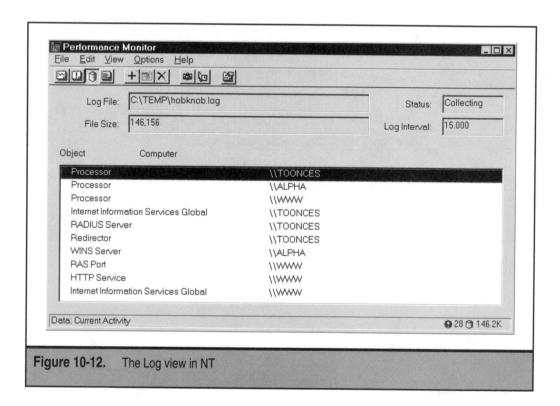

Figure 10-12.   The Log view in NT

Report View

The Report view is similar to the Chart view in that its function is to display counter information. It differs in that it displays the information in a tabular list organized by computers with objects and counters listed below each server. The values are aligned on the right-hand side of the report with multiple instances in successive columns to the right. Counters are added as in the Chart view. Figure 10-13 illustrates the layout for one computer.

The Report view Options dialog box has only one option. You can define a specific update interval or select Manual Update. You cannot print your reports from the application, but you can export them to a file and open them in a spreadsheet application such as Excel. From there, you can print the report or further manipulate the data. With a little bit of tinkering, it is possible to generate some attractive and meaningful charts and graphs.

What to Monitor

Perfmon can track thousands of bits of information. This powerful tool can track and report on every statistic you can think of, and hundreds more that would never have occurred to you. As much as you might appreciate the breadth of the statistics you can

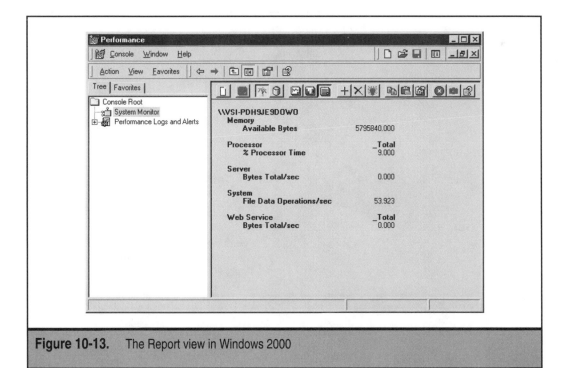

Figure 10-13. The Report view in Windows 2000

gather, sometimes you can get information overload. With all the details Perfmon can keep an eye on, what are the most important things to monitor?

The best plan is to monitor the four most common bottlenecks:

- ▼ Memory
- ■ Processor
- ■ Disk subsystem
- ▲ Network subsystem

In addition to these common bottlenecks, it is also important to watch the resources that affect the way a particular server functions in your network. For instance, you might have a Windows 2000 server configured to handle file and print sharing, application sharing, domain controlling, or running the Web server. How that server is used in your organization should dictate what other details you monitor.

For instance, the servers shown in Figure 10-14 are the network's Web and print servers. Here, it's more important to monitor the network subsystem on the Web server than on the print server. Devising a monitoring scheme that includes the four common contributors as well as the resources pertaining to the server's functions will greatly increase your network's performance.

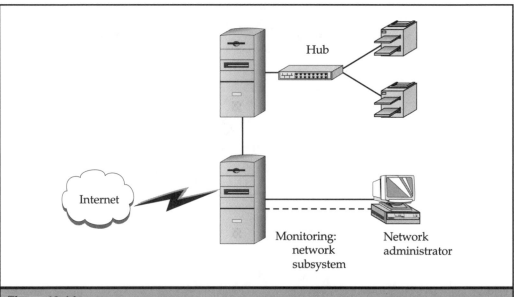

Figure 10-14.   It's more important to monitor the network subsystem on the Web server than on the print server

RAM

The two main memory counters you should monitor are Page Faults/sec and Pages/sec. Used in tandem, they can tell you if the system is configured with enough RAM. More specifically, they show the amount of paging activity within the system. In order to trick your computer into thinking it has more RAM, Windows computers use something called *virtual memory*. Virtual memory creates a paging file on a hard drive that acts as the additional memory. Even though virtual memory is stored on a disk and accessed actively by the OS, the active applications have no idea that they aren't getting physical memory.

Because Page Faults/sec includes both hard and soft faults, an acceptable level will be much higher that that for the Pages/sec counter. Most systems can tolerate Page Faults/sec levels of about 250 before system performance starts to drag. Pages/sec routinely above 20, however, show that the system is not configured with enough RAM. Once Pages/sec values start topping 10, you should start thinking about adding more memory.

Two other counters you might want to keep an eye on are the Commit Limit and the Committed Bytes counters. These counters work together, so you need to look at both sets of readings to determine whether the system is using virtual memory efficiently. The Commit Limit counter shows the total available virtual memory in the system. This is the sum of the physical RAM and the maximum paging file size. The Committed Bytes counter shows the total amount of virtual memory that the system has already committed from its resources (the Commit Limit value). When the size of the Committed Bytes counter approaches the Commit Limit value, the system is close to running out of virtual memory.

So what should the minimum and maximum paging file sizes be? Microsoft recommends the minimum paging file to be the amount of physical RAM plus 11MB (for instance, if you've got 128MB RAM, then you should have 139MB in virtual memory). A better way to determine what you need is to figure out the typical usage requirements of the paging file for a particular system, then specify that value as the minimum (unless that number falls below the Microsoft formula).

NOTE: Windows 2000/NT allows you to let the computer decide how big the paging file should be. However, if you decide to let the computer do that, you'll take a performance hit. It's best to set the size of the paging file manually.

The maximum size of the paging file should be the highest value you ever expect the paging file to grow. Yes, that's fantastically ambiguous, so a good rule of thumb is to set the maximum value to 150 percent of the minimum value.

Processor

The critical counter to use in watching the computer's processor is %Processor. This counter shows the amount of time that the processor is doing *useful* work. This means the amount of time the processor is executing nonidle threads or servicing interrupts. Each instance of %Processor should not exceed 50 percent use. If this counter consistently approaches or exceeds 50 percent, the first step should be to check whether the Interrupts/sec counter is 3,500 or more. If the system is experiencing 3,500 or more interrupts per second, a device or device driver may be to blame for the high processor use.

Disk Subsystem

The first counters to watch in the disk subsystem are %Disk Time and Disk Queue Length from either the LogicalDisk or the PhysicalDisk object. The values you're looking for here are less than 55 percent and less than 2, respectively.

NOTE: The drivers needed to monitor disk performance are disabled, by default, to avoid the overhead of the process. To gather hard disk statistics, load the monitoring drivers by typing **DISKPERF –Y** at the command prompt. When you're done monitoring, enter the command **DISKPERF –N** at the command prompt to disable the drivers.

An important consideration in monitoring the disk subsystem involves its relationship with physical memory. A system that is not configured with the right amount of memory can cause an incredible amount of disk activity, because the system is trying to compensate for the lack of memory by paging. If you notice excessive disk activity and it is supported by unacceptable %Disk Time and Disk Queue Length values, check to see if the paging file is properly configured and the system has enough RAM.

Network Subsystem

The network subsystem is the most difficult system to optimize and troubleshoot because of the complexity of interactions among the components. The operating system, network applications, network interface cards, protocols, and topologies all play important roles in determining how well the network performs. That having been said, the two most important counters to watch are Server: Bytes Total/sec and Network Segment: % Network Utilization.

The Server: Bytes Total/sec counter shows the amount of network activity experienced by the server. An acceptable value for this counter is 0.8 Mbps for Ethernet-based networks and 0.5 Mbps on 16-Mbps Token Ring networks. If values exceed this threshold, chances increase that the network will become bogged down.

For the %Network Utilization counter, there are two acceptable values: *theoretical* and *actual*. In theory, an Ethernet network should be able to use as much bandwidth as possible and sustain levels of 70 percent and higher. However, as the saturation level approaches 30 percent, the rate of collisions increases. As collisions increase, Ethernet begins to use network bandwidth less efficiently. For this reason, %Network Utilization should always be kept under 30 percent.

If you are regularly exceeding this level, you should consider segmenting the network, increasing your network speed, or using switches instead of hubs.

E-Business Considerations

In addition to your memory, processors, disks, and network, you must also keep an eye on some other important statistics that will directly affect your e-business. For instance, Perfmon can monitor your Active Server Pages (ASP) and keep track of any problems. Perfmon can track almost three dozen different ASP attributes, including:

- ▼ **Debugging requests**   The number of requests you receive to debug a document
- ■ **Errors/Sec**   The number of errors that occur each second
- ■ **Request Execution Time**   The amount of time (in milliseconds) that it took to execute the most recent request
- ■ **Requests Executing**   The number of requests currently executing
- ▲ **Requests Timed Out**   The number of requests that timed out before completion

NOTE: For more information about ASP, see Chapter 5.

If your e-business will use the File Transfer Protocol (FTP), Perfmon has 15 different tools you can use to monitor and evaluate your FTP server's performance. Counters include:

- ▼ **Bytes Received/Sec**   The rate that data is received by the FTP service
- ■ **Bytes Sent/Sec**   The rate that data is being transmitted by the FTP service
- ■ **Current Connection**   The current number of connections established with the FTP service
- ▲ **Total Files Transferred**   The total number of files that have been sent and received by the FTP service

One of the most used and useful Perfmon objects is Internet Information Services (IIS) Global. These 12 counters collect a bevy of information about your Web server's cache and how it's behaving. Some of the counters include:

▼ **Cache Flushes** The number of times a portion of the memory cache has expired due to file or directory changes in an IIS directory tree

■ **Cache Hits** The total number of times a file open, directory listing, or service-specific object request was found in the cache

▲ **Total Allowed Asynch I/O Requests** The total number of requests allowed by bandwidth throttling settings (counted since the service startup)

But the most worthwhile object for Perfmon in an e-business is the Web Service object. This object can track 54 different statistics ranging from how many bytes are being sent to how many Common Gateway Interface (CGI) requests are being processed by the Web server. Some of the counters you may find yourself using to optimize your e-business include:

▼ **Anonymous Users/Sec** The rate at which users are making anonymous connections to your Web server

■ **Current Blocked Async I/O Requests** The number of current requests that are being blocked due to bandwidth throttling

■ **Files Sent/Sec** The rate at which files are being sent by the Web server

▲ **Total CGI Requests** The number of CGI requests that are being run on your server

Perfmon is a mighty tool that can track the most important bits and pieces of your e-business. By carefully tracking your system and its resources, you can tune and optimize your network to deliver peak efficiency.

NETWORK MANAGEMENT TOOLS

Once you've designed and built your e-business network, you have to manage it. You must understand where the bandwidth is going, why it's going there, and if you need to make any changes. Luckily, there are a number of tools out there that will help you manage your e-business LAN.

Network management can be confusing. By its nature, the field involves a daunting list of tasks. Networks must be planned, modeled, budgeted, designed, configured, purchased, installed, tested, mapped, documented, operated, monitored, analyzed, optimized, adjusted, expanded, updated, and fixed. The following tools can help you get a handle on the intricate task of network management.

OS-Based Tools

In Chapter 4, we talked about different OSes and what they brought to the e-business party. Now is our chance to talk about what they bring to network management. Each one contains different tools for managing network resources, so let's give each one a quick look.

Microsoft Management Console (MMC)

Microsoft kicked up its NT software when it developed its Microsoft Management Console (MMC) for Windows 2000. The MMC is featured in all versions of Windows 2000 and gives users a consistent environment for managing Windows and network resources. Using the MMC, administrators can select from a variety of tools and snap them into a customized console.

> **NOTE:**   A version of the MMC is available for Windows NT. It can be downloaded at www.microsoft.com.

Solaris Resource Manager

The Solaris Resource Manager is a tool that offers resource management through a common graphical user interface and allows administrators to balance loads across both system and network resources for better availability and Quality of Service.

Solaris Resource Manager lets you assign more system resources to those applications or users that require it. By being able to allocate and distribute resources when they're needed most, you can consolidate multiple applications or services onto a single server. And since you control how and where resources are assigned, you can make the most out of what you have while still ensuring consistent levels of service for each and every user.

NetWare Management Portal

Administrative tasks in NetWare are streamlined and simplified using NetWare Management Portal (NMP). This Web browser–based tool enables you to manage NetWare servers and file systems through a Web browser from any location on your network—rather than having to run to the server room anytime you have to troubleshoot a server problem.

NetWare includes ZENworks and ConsoleOne, two other administrative tools you can use to deploy and manage tools across your network.

SNMP

Almost all modern network management suites are built atop the Simple Network Management Protocol (SNMP). Although SNMP can be directly operated through the command line, it's almost always used through a management application that uses the SNMP communications channel to monitor and control networks. As Figure 10-15 shows, SNMP has two basic components: a Network Management Station (NMS) and agents.

Agents are small software modules that reside on managed devices. They can be configured to collect specific pieces of information on device operations. Most of the information consists of totals: total bytes, total packets, total errors, and the like. Agents can be deployed on the panoply of devices:

- ▼ Routers
- ■ Switches
- ■ Access servers
- ■ Hubs
- ■ Servers (Windows 2000, UNIX, Linux, etc.)
- ■ Workstations (PCs, Macs, and UNIX desktops)
- ■ Printers
- ▲ UPS power backup systems

The idea is to place agents on all network devices and manage things according to the status information sent back. A piece of equipment with an SNMP agent loaded onto it is referred to as a *managed device* (also called *network element*).

The NMS is the internetwork's control center. Usually there's just one NMS for an autonomous system, although many large internetworks use more than one NMS, usually arranged in a hierarchy. Most NMSs today run on dedicated UNIX or Microsoft servers.

RMON

RMON (short for remote monitoring) is a separate but related management standard that complements SNMP. RMON is similar to SNMP in several ways: it is an open standard administered by the IETF, it uses SMI data types, and it collects device data and reports it to an NMS. But RMON differs from normal SNMP in these fundamental ways:

- ▼ RMON is instrument-based; it uses specialized hardware to operate.
- ■ RMON proactively sends data instead of waiting to be polled, making it bandwidth efficient and more responsive to network events.
- ▲ RMON allows much more detailed data to be collected.

RMON instrumentation is more powerful than SNMP, but more expensive. Consequently, RMON probes tend to be placed on critical links such as network backbones

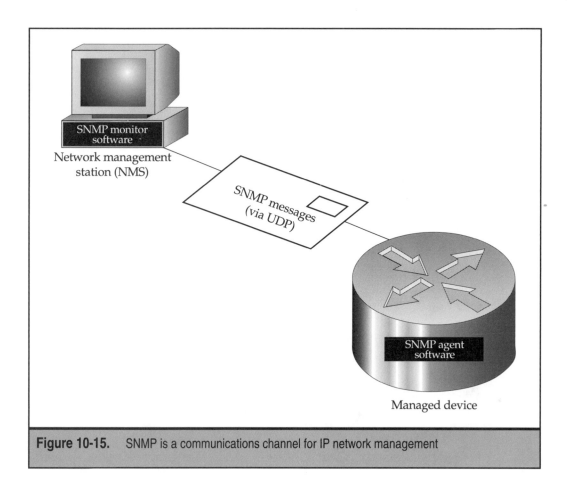

Figure 10-15. SNMP is a communications channel for IP network management

and important servers. Figure 10-16 shows how RMON probes provide management visibility by being situated throughout the network.

RMONs replace expensive network analyzer devices that must be physically attached to the approximate area of a network problem. RMON probes come in different forms, depending on the size and type of device to be monitored:

▼ A specialized module inserted into a slot within the monitored device

■ A probe built for a specific purpose externally attached to one or more monitored devices

▲ A dedicated PC attached to one or more monitored devices

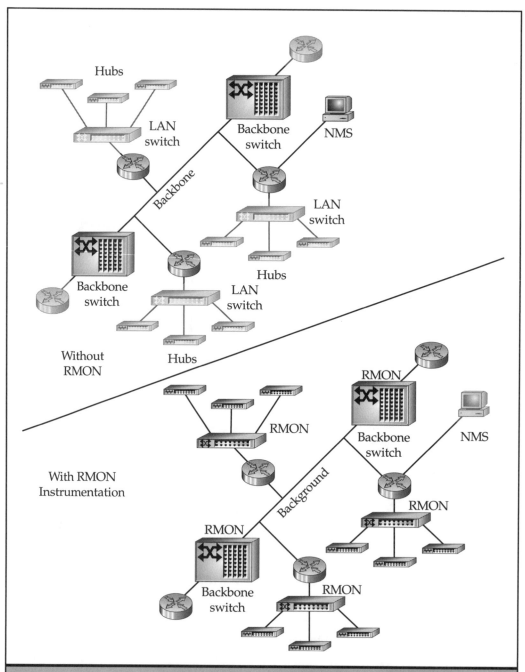

Figure 10-16.   RMON probes provide management visibility across switched networks

The problem with RMON is that it's expensive. It takes extra hardware to store and analyze packets in real time, and that costs money. Consequently, RMON is being used to manage links that are mission-critical or otherwise expensive.

Network Monitor

Windows NT and 2000 ship with a nifty tool called Network Monitor. Network Monitor consists of two components—Network Monitor Agent and Network Monitor Tool. Running the agents on other systems allows a server to collect data from the agent's network segment as if it were physically connected to it. This means you don't have to physically bring an analyzer to every segment as long as the analyzer is already set up.

Network Monitor is a powerful tool. It can track information up to the network layer, perform filters on stations or protocols, and conduct packet analysis.

Network Monitor on NT is shown in Figure 10-17.

CiscoWorks2000

CiscoWorks2000 is a product family, not a point product. In other words, it's a common software platform that serves as a framework from which optional applications can be

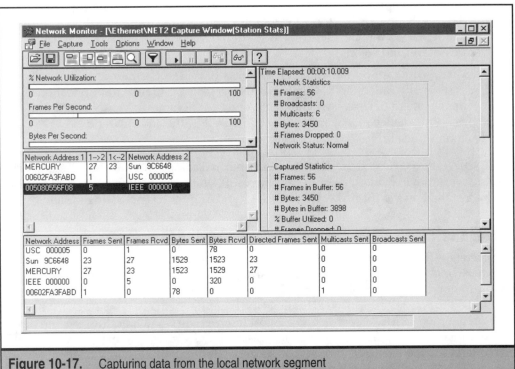

Figure 10-17.   Capturing data from the local network segment

operated. Some call the applications that plug into a suite *snap-ins.* The goal of product suites is to integrate snap-in applications by letting them share data. The suite's infrastructure shares a database and various background processes such as SNMP polling and configuration checking. CiscoWorks2000 can import data from HP OpenView, IBM NetView, and Sun Microsystem's SunNet, to name a few.

Browser	Windows	
Essentials	CiscoView	CWSI Campus
Device inventory database		

CiscoWorks2000, released in 1999, is a full-fledged management environment, which is so big that it would take a veteran network administrator weeks to learn all its applications. Two of the most important tools included with CiscoWorks2000 are:

▼ **Resource Manager Essentials**   Called Essentials for short, these are the foundation applications for monitoring, controlling, and managing Cisco devices. Essentials has tools for remote device installation, SNMP monitoring, configuration management, software deployment, path analysis, device inventory, and so on.

▲ **CiscoWorks for Switched Internetworks (CWSI)**   Pronounced "swizee" and usually called CWSI Campus, this is a suite of integrated applications for management of Cisco switched networks. CWSI handles VLAN configuration, real-time device management, RMON-based traffic analysis, and ATM connection and performance management.

CiscoWorks2000 installs and operates on a normal computer platform—not a specialized network device. In addition to the Microsoft Windows platform, CiscoWorks2000 can be installed on the IBM AIX, HP PA-RISC, and Sun Solaris operating systems.

NetSys Baseliner

Cisco Netsys Baseliner is a network modeling application used to design and analyze internetworks. Baselines are used as a starting point from which to model proposed configuration changes. Baselining tools have become popular because configurations can be checked for mistakes prior to actually implementing them.

Baseliner uses RMON probes and Cisco's Internetworking Operating System device accounting to instrument network traffic. This enables features to help understand traffic characteristics. For example, reports can be generated identifying high-traffic locations, host pairs that generate the most traffic, and other information. Thanks to its detailed configuration database and heavy instrumentation, Baseliner is able to monitor information at a level not possible using other CiscoWorks2000 applications.

A key benefit of this is that Baseliner can perform integrity checking. It compares the configuration files and validates their consistency as a whole, and it looks for any internal inconsistencies within config files. Baseliner's software targets the common configuration mistakes, greatly reducing the time it takes to isolate and fix problems.

THIRD-PARTY MONITORING TOOLS

If you don't want to just rely on what comes prepackaged with your OS software, there are a number of third-party vendors who will be happy to take your money and provide you with network monitoring tools.

The following tools are but a sampling of the many tools out there that will help you keep your eye on your network. For more information about each of these tools, visit their respective Web sites, as listed at the ends of the product descriptions.

WebTrends Enterprise Suite

Enterprise Suite analyzes the log files generated by your Web servers and creates customizable, professional-looking reports containing a wealth of information, allowing your company to more effectively manage its Web investments.

Enterprise Suite consists of several modules, each of which can analyze different aspects of your Web infrastructure. For example, you can discover who has visited your Web site, how long they stayed, and how many pages they viewed. You can even find out information such as the browser version and operating system used, the referring Web site, and the IP address of the browsing computer. Enterprise Suite supports more than 30 log formats, and you can export reports to HTML, Microsoft Word, Excel, or ASCII text files.

You start by creating a profile in which you specify configuration information and filters for narrowing the scope of your reports. Analysis is speedy, and the data is displayed in your browser window. Enterprise Suite also includes a scheduler, so reports can be generated at specified intervals and automatically e-mailed to relevant personnel.

The WebTrends Enterprise Suite includes the following analysis modules:

▼ **Web Server Traffic Analysis**   Provide detailed Web site analysis, and traffic reporting to others in your organization.

■ **Streaming Media Server Analysis**   Understand the details of streaming media usage on your site, including the most popular clips, stops, starts, replays, and more.

■ **Proxy Server Analysis**   Track the usage trends of your intranet and better understand your users' productivity.

■ **Link Analysis and Quality Control**   Improve the quality, performance, and integrity of your Web site.

- ■ **Site Manager**   Gain a visual understanding of your Web site's structure and layout.

- ■ **Monitoring, Alerting, and Recovery**   Keep your Web site up and running at all times.

- ■ **ClusterTrends Server Cluster Add-On**   Accurately analyze Web site traffic and technical performance across clusters of local or geographically dispersed servers.

- ■ **DBTrends technology**   Correlate information from existing ODBC databases with results from WebTrends data analysis.

- ▲ **FastTrends ODBC technology**   Export results from WebTrends FastTrends database to high-end Oracle, Microsoft SQL, Sybase, Informix, and other ODBC-compliant databases for further data analysis.

One of the newest features in the latest version (3.6) of WebTrends is the ability to monitor streaming-media servers, such as Microsoft NetShow and Real Networks' RealPlayer. Enterprise Suite can report how long customers played a specific media clip, the versions of the player used, and the speed at which the content was transferred.

For more information about WebTrends, their products and services, visit their Web site at www.webtrends.com.

EcoSCOPE 4.1

The EcoSCOPE 4.1 application performance monitor brings some impressive analysis tools, which will allow network administrators to ferret out hard-to-see, troubling traffic trends. EcoSCOPE automatically discovers and identifies thousands of applications while tracking and spotting trends in bandwidth utilization based on time of day, day of the week, type of application, and virtually any other factor.

Many features that are well suited for an enterprise environment are present in EcoSCOPE. Administrators can set alert thresholds based on a slew of measured events. For example, you can set an alarm to signal whenever video game traffic exceeds five percent of the network traffic.

Because its performance charts are based on your network's traffic, EcoSCOPE generates topology maps that show the traffic patterns of specific applications. Administrators can use EcoSCOPE to precisely track transaction times and eliminate bottlenecks quickly. EcoSCOPE also lets administrators capture baseline performance information that can be used to compare daily performance and to serve as a basis for estimates about when to expand network bandwidth capacity.

One of EcoSCOPE's greatest qualities is its capability to integrate with other network management tools, allowing easier and more effective capacity planning and providing a better network management environment.

The software's user interface automatically displays the client, server, and applica-tion that have the highest traffic, along with a "user impact" number; the product of multiplying the number of users by the response delay to calculate the total user delay, this reference number makes it a snap to identify which performance problems are the biggest time wasters.

For more information about EcoSCOPE, and other products and services of the Compuware Corporation, visit their Web site at www.compuware.com.

Netuitive 5.0

Netuitive 5.0 uses a statistical correlation that will learn the patterns in your systems' performance data and will automatically predict when and where problems will occur. Using this method, say the manufacturers, you will get advance notice up to 24 hours before a problem arises, rather than right as it is occurring.

Netuitive 5.0 runs on a Windows NT or Windows 2000 server. It uses MS SQL Server 7.0 or Oracle 8 to store its data, predictions, and alerts. It can collect performance indicators from any type of applications system via performance monitor counters, SNMP, or database integration. It includes a Windows-based reporting package and a Web-based dashboard.

Netuitive uses the Adaptive Correlation Engine (ACE), which continually learns from a network's e-business data, predicting future performance and notifying you only when problems are likely to occur. Netuitive continually analyzes and learns about your network and application data streams. New data streams are analyzed automatically as often as every five minutes.

Netuitive 5.0 defines thresholds based on time of day, type of day (weekday or weekend/holiday), and recent data behavior, and it recalculates performance thresholds automatically.

Netuitive will offers the following features:

▼ You can spot system degradation problems and disasters, before they happen.

■ Netuitive is designed to run offline from production systems, which avoids complex overhead or taxing processing power.

▲ Scalability. As you add servers and applications to your configuration, Netuitive can automatically incorporate these into the predictive performance model.

For more information about Netuitive, visit its Web site at www.netuitive.com.

NetworkIT

NetworkIT by Computer Associates is another solution that relies on neural technology to improve network performance. NetworkIT monitors network performance from the end-user and system perspectives. This helps administrators to manage the environment by providing an accurate picture of the network's performance.

NetworkIT is available for UNIX and Windows 2000/NT platforms and supports standard protocols including TCP/IP, IPX, SNA, and DECnet. It also discovers and classifies networked devices and assets, then builds an intuitive topology map based on the results of this self-discovery and classification.

The highlight of NetworkIT is its predictive management, which uses Computer Associates' Performance Neugents. Neugents use neural networks to learn, adapt to change over time, and predict. Neural networks mimic the structure of the human brain to learn from experiences. Using sophisticated algorithms to detect patterns in multiple data dimensions, they can determine which factors are the most important in determining events and can make predictions of future outcomes based on the collected and analyzed data.

By using Neugents, NetworkIT can manage and predict problems in advance. This ability helps prevent router outages and maximizes network performance. Other features of NetworkIT include:

▼ **Application Performance** NetworkIT monitors network-centric performance thresholds such as bandwidth utilization and node response times. Application-related performance information is also monitored and reported. For instance, the software can track the end-to-end response times for a user accessing an application, report the delays on each of the network components between the user and the application, and provide a breakdown of the flow of application traffic.

■ **Programmable responses** NetworkIT enables any number of automated actions to be defined for selected events. This allows you to create sophisticated responses to problems that occur in the network.

▲ **Root Cause Analysis** The program's advanced root analysis employs an event correlation system to determine the root cause of a network problem. This shows the core problem and eliminates multiple events that can confuse the troubleshooting process.

For more information about Computer Associates, NetworkIT, and Neugents, visit their Web site at www.ca.com.

Maintaining and optimizing your network is anything but a simple issue. There are a multitude of areas that you should pay particular attention to in order to increase your network's performance. Tuning and maintenance aren't just a hardware issue—they are a war that must be fought on many fronts. In addition to your system's hardware, it's necessary to make sure your software is operating correctly and that your employees are doing what they are supposed to. If you take all these factors into consideration, your highly tuned, super-fast race car will no doubt win the race.

PART IV

Securing E-Commerce Environments

CHAPTER 11

Creating Secure Networks

The security options available today can seem endless, confusing, and a little scary. This chapter will clearly explain what security solutions are necessary to support a successful e-business by investigating the different types of attacks that can be made on a network and how these attacks can be prevented. Furthermore, we will determine which security solution will work best for your company's particular e-business interests, and we will explain why this solution best fits your overall needs. Subsequent chapters in this section will delve into more detail about network security and the nuances that have made networks more secure.

NETWORK SECURITY

We have established in earlier chapters that the Internet can open up a vast number of business opportunities by enabling access to endless resources. Unfortunately, with all the additional opportunities comes additional risk. If your company's network can access the Internet, anyone on the Internet may have the ability to access your company's network. The decisions that you as a network administrator make for network security are the most important decisions for the overall care of your network.

In very general terms, *network security* can be defined as protecting a network from any harm. Because this definition is general, people rarely realize the true depth of all that is included in the task of designing a security task. The truth of the matter is that security may be the most time-consuming part of maintaining any network, and especially an e-business network, because network security issues are constantly changing.

A useful mental image of the task at hand is to think of network security as a teeter-totter where on one side is the company's network, on the other side is the rest of the online world, and security stands in the middle balancing the load. It logically follows, therefore, that any time a change is made to either side of that teeter-totter, the security in the middle needs to change to maintain the balance. It doesn't take a rocket scientist to figure out that with technology changing so fast, there is hardly a point at which one side or another isn't changing.

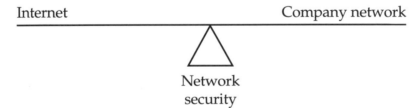

Creating a Network Security Plan

So, with all the changing information, the most commonly asked question is, where do we even start? Before we even consider the wealth of information available on network security, it is important to create a list of the company's priorities for a security system. There is no one simple answer to the network security dilemma. Each security solution has clear advantages and disadvantages, and every company's network has a different list of needs and a different order of priorities. Therefore, each security solution must fit the individual network it will be protecting.

Balancing Security with Accessibility

The security option that will best fit the network balances a combination of key concerns that the company deems important. The top three concerns for an e-business network are the levels of security, simplicity, and cost efficiency.

As networks become more complex, a wider spectrum of options opens up for levels of security a company can implement. Some companies feel that making sure each and every bit of data is totally protected is a top priority. Some companies feel that, although protecting their confidential data is important, it is also important to make their network user-friendly. By minimizing the number of times and places everyday users have to enter their usernames and passwords, such a company achieves greater simplicity at the cost of less security. Finally, most companies are forced to keep in mind the cost of any security they implement. Purchasing security hardware and software is expensive, but so is the time spent managing this security and the time wasted while users try to figure out how to access the network.

Obviously security, simplicity, and cost efficiency overlap in many areas when used in the context of network security, and that is why a list of priorities is the best way to start a security plan. Often direct conflicts are evident between security, simplicity, and cost.

For example, a high level of security will make it very difficult to access data and applications, a fact that is excellent when it comes to thwarting attacks but inconvenient and frustrating for users who needs these resources to do their everyday tasks. Additionally, higher security is more expensive because of the added complexity in configuring and maintaining the network. Time is money in today's business world. If your network administrator is constantly occupied with your network security, you will have one very upset network administrator, and it is not an efficient use of your resources.

The greatest challenge with e-business network security is to find this balance between making your network accessible and easy for those you want to use it, not accessible or easy for those who wish to abuse it, and at a price that your company can afford.

An Overview of Network Security

Once a list of priorities has been established, it is time to move on to a general understanding of network security. A network can be harmed intentionally or unintentionally, from the inside or the outside. In order to cover the great variety of risks, network security operates at two levels, the user-based level and the traffic flow level. A successful security solution most often uses a combination of both user-based security and traffic-based security to control the network. We will be investigating all security options and how they can be used together.

Traffic-Based Security

Traffic-based security regulates the flow of traffic across the network. The major function of this level of security is to stop attackers from outside the network from gaining access into the network, where they could access confidential information or use the network in a way in which the company's integrity would be compromised. Security at a traffic-based level can also be used as a form of maintenance control because it notifies network administrators when anything out of the ordinary occurs at an application level. Traffic-based security is the security that goes on in the background of a network. For example, everyday users don't have much conscious interaction with this level of security and don't normally know anything about it.

User-Based Security

As opposed to traffic-based security, user-based security is the security level that all users are very aware exists. *User-based security* is the security in place that forces users to log on using a username and password.

As strange as it might seem, a network has to be protected from the users that work with it daily. This means making sure that each user has only the ability to use the resources that that user's daily tasks require him or her to use. For example, that might include access to different applications depending on whether the user is in accounting or working in the mailroom. This level of security also allows the network administrator to control what data the users have the ability to see and change. These precautions greatly reduce the possibility that an uneducated or disgruntled user could cause damage to any data or system operations.

WHY HAVE SECURITY

The media have provided enough recent horror stories to scare most companies into considering their security options. However, it is important to understand what the network security risks really are for your company. Once you know what information you are protecting, and what you are protecting it against, it is easier to set up a security plan.

When a network connects to the Internet, it is connected to millions of other networks. This connection allows an immeasurable amount of information to be shared between companies. The problem is that every company's network has information that must be kept confidential and not shared with the rest of the world. However, that very same sharing capability opens opportunities for attackers to share in your company's information. Unfortunately, the knowledge and tools to break into networks are readily available.

The goal of any security solution is to prevent anyone from stealing, corrupting, or otherwise tampering with sensitive information. A company's security worries are really twofold: confidential information and integrity. In other words, a security system is used to prevent an attacker from stealing or damaging the data found on a network, and to stop an attacker from using the network itself to compromise the company's reputation.

Confidential Information

The protection of confidential information seems like an obvious security objective, but the task is often underestimated. For example, confidential information includes both the actual data stored on the network and the network itself.

Making Sure Data Is Confidential

It is important for all your users to know, and be confident in the fact, that the information on your network is secure. All the everyday workings of your company are stored in the form of data on your system. This includes everything from the employee information referenced in Human Resources, such as social security numbers for all employees and payroll figures, to financial information such as banking documentation used in the Accounting department.

Any well-implemented security system needs to ensure that three different things never happen to this confidential data. First, this data must be secure from outside attacks. It is easy to see the problems that would occur if a competitor were able to intercept and read all incoming invoices. Second, confidential data needs to be restricted within the company. For example, it would be equally as bad if everyone within the company were able to access the payroll files. Finally, network security has to ensure that everyday use of the network does not inadvertently destroy saved data.

Keeping the Network Confidential

Just as important as a company's physical data, stored on the network, is the security of the network configuration itself. The biggest reason for this level of security is that lack of control over the network could lead to more security gaps. Network confidentiality acts as damage control. If an attacker gains access to your network, some measure of security must be in place to ensure that the attacker does not have a road map giving detailed directions to confidential information, or to other configuration details that could be accessed or destroyed.

Network security also ensures that any technical problems or malfunctions will be caught early. For example, if network security software is searching for things that are out of the ordinary within the functioning of the network, technical malfunctions are going to be detected as well. Security software can act as a warning system to alert network administrators to configuration problems or system failures before they become widespread problems. Network security can also aid in troubleshooting and fixing problems without bringing down the whole network as well.

How Big Is the Risk?

It has become obvious that companies need to protect confidential data stored on their networks. Unfortunately, when a company connects to the Internet, an attacker has a number of ways to attempt to break into a private network and seize confidential data. An important step in protecting against confidential data attacks stems from understanding exactly how an attacker may attempt to break into a network.

Packet Sniffers   One way an outside party could gain access to a private network is by intercepting and reading *network packets,* which are bundles of data that are passed rapidly one after another, forming a chain-like formation that is read like a long sentence and allows networked computers to communicate. Much as with a pass in football, if the wrong people intercept these packets, bad things can happen.

Although the word "attacker" suggests an outside person trying to break in, it is important to remember that most security breaches come from internal users. This is particularly true in the case of packet sniffers. The attacker must find a way to have a direct connection to the data as it passes between sources in order for a packet sniffer to be able to intercept this information. It is often referred to as "listening on the wire."

Most networks send packets in similar patterns, making it easy for the packets to be read if they are intercepted. The most common pieces of information taken from these stolen packets are passwords or user account names, which provide the attacker with an additional avenue through which to access the network.

Once an attack has been made in this way, it is often difficult to detect or stop. Users are infamous for using the same username and password for as many applications as possible in order to reduce the number of things they have to remember. Having a "key" that fits multiple locks opens up many doors to the attacker operating under the guise of a legitimate user. Equally troublesome is the packet sniffer attack itself, which is hard to detect because network administrators often use the same sort of sniffers to find or fix problems within their own network.

IP Spoofing   IP spoofing is another way an attacker can gain access to a network. An IP spoof occurs when an outside source poses as an internal IP address. The network then becomes confused and sends packets to the wrong IP address. Again, if these packets are not encrypted, they could easily be read, providing confidential information to an outside party. Once again, in a worst-case scenario, the attacker could receive username and password information.

Access to Confidential Information   Most parties attempting to view confidential information are users who already have a valid connection to the network. Any user who is disgruntled, curious, or uneducated is a possible threat. Because these users have authorized access to the network, an attack can be unsuspected and go unnoticed. While an angry user would be the most likely suspect to damage or steal sensitive information, any user who simply doesn't know any better could open doors for future attacks or place sensitive company data on easily accessible drives or computers.

Protecting the Company's Integrity

Protecting a company's sensitive information is often the first concern when establishing a security plan because it seems most obvious. However, protecting the integrity of the company, though often overlooked, is just as important. Any activity that occurs on your network should stand up to the company's polices and standards. The network activity reflects the integrity of the company that manages it. Anyone who compromises that integrity, whether internally or externally, is a security threat.

Maintaining a Creditable Reputation

As mentioned, a company's reputation can stand or fall with its network. For example, the Internet hosts a number of activities that could compromise a business reputation. Again, the theory that "whatever a business can access on the Internet has the capabilities of accessing the business" applies here. As an extreme example, any association, even an accidental association, with one of many illegal operations found on the Internet would reflect poorly on a company. With no security, any network could be used to help disguise illegal activities. A more practical example of the problem of maintaining a creditable reputation is that of restricting access to Web sites of questionable character so that employees cannot view or even download inappropriate material.

Protecting the Physical Network

In the absence of security, an outsider user could gain access to your network and appear to be someone in authority. As a worst-case example, this user could send e-mail from the CEO's account to clients saying anything the user pleases. Inside the company, you also want your network to have a good reputation. You want your users to feel comfortable and secure. Finally, an unknown user could physically harm your network. Interference with network performance can be costly and frustrating.

What Are the Risks?

Again, it is important to know how the integrity of your company could be jeopardized. Knowing how and when an attacker may strike can help you determine what type of security would best fit the situation.

Network Packet Spoofing   Network packet spoofing is mainly used to provide information that an attacker might find useful. For example, as we discussed earlier packet spoofing can provide usernames and passwords. It can tell an attacker other critical information about your network, such as network size or authorization rights. If an attacker can read network packets, chances are that attacker has the ability to change the packets as well.

If an attacker has the ability to change the network packets, it means that the attacker could create an account of his or her own to use at any time. Once a username and a password are created, the attacker would have a legitimate disguise when entering the network. Once in the network, the attacker could change any information in company databases and it would appear to have been changed by an employee.

Posing as an Internal IP Address   Sometimes an attacker is able to pose as an internal IP address and intercept network packets. Once again, if an attacker can get into a network and read someone's user ID and password, the effects can be devastating. If an attacker has the ability to assume an authorized user's identify, the attacker has a great deal of freedom inside the network and may use it to alter information or programs.

Denial-of-Service Attacks   Sometimes when an attacker finds a way to get access to a company's network, the attacker uses the information captured to compromise the applications found on that network. One example is a denial-of-service attack. Denial-of-service attacks are just what their name describes, attacks that lock authorized users out of applications or resources on their own network. These attacks are designed and used to disrupt the normal flow of business for users. As anyone who works with computers knows, lack of access to an application frustrates users and may cost a great deal in lost productivity.

Application-Layer Attacks   Another way an intruder might disrupt the network is at an application level. The attacker preys on software that has widely known weaknesses and exploits them. When an attack occurs at the application layer, it is very difficult to detect as an attack rather than an application malfunction. A very obvious example is an e-mail virus that causes the e-mail application to do things, such as sending e-mail messages, that it shouldn't do on its own. Again, this type of attack is aimed at frustrating users and slowing down productivity.

TRAFFIC-BASED SECURITY

Now that we have discussed some of the attacks that might be made on a network, let's look at what can be done to prevent them. Traffic-based security, as we discussed earlier, is the security implemented over an entire network as a whole at the traffic level. Again the idea of balance comes into the security picture. A good network uses a balance of traffic-based and user-based security. Traffic-based security calls for a good overall idea of what is going on throughout every aspect of the network. The most common form of traffic-based security is the firewall, which will be the focus of this chapter.

Creating a Traffic-Based Security Plan

Now that it is clear why security is needed, it is time to look at how to implement a good security system. The first step in setting up traffic-based security is to create a plan. The main objective of a security policy will be to monitor and control network usage. It is important to preserve balance in creating this policy. You will naturally want the most secure network possible, but you will have to balance that desire against the reality that security is inconvenient. The more security in place, the more difficult it is for even legitimate users to utilize their own network. Security also has to be maintainable by network administrators. The plan that is created must incorporate some give and take to yield a balanced system.

Placement of Traffic-Based Security

A good way to balance security is with strategic placement of security systems at different locations on the network. By focusing on specific locations, you can implement security where it is most needed and easiest to monitor. By defining specific locations, you can also layer security. Three points on a network are commonly defined as possible placements for traffic-based security measures: the outermost perimeter, the internal perimeter, and the innermost perimeter. These boundaries act like imaginary lines dividing the network.

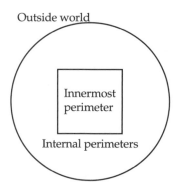

Outermost Perimeter

The *outermost perimeter* is the line between your company's network and the outside world. Most often, this point is at a router or some other hardware such as a firewall that connects your network to the Internet. The most important thing to remember about this location is that you have control over everything on your side of the network, but you have no control over anything beyond this point. The outermost perimeter is an obvious location to provide security, since it is the most likely area to be attacked.

Internal Perimeters

Internal perimeters are defined by the actual locations where your network has security measures. For example, any firewalls or routers inside the actual network or acting as barriers between the outside and the inside of your network are internal perimeters. Security at this placement works to sort out data and direct it to where it needs to go. Routers are often used at these points to direct network traffic. This security is more focused on internal affairs than outside attackers, although it is another good checkpoint on the network to search for unusual behavior.

Innermost Perimeter

The *innermost perimeter* is the very heart of your network, the part of the network that users interact with on an everyday basis. This innermost perimeter is the location of user-based security that ensures that the users are authorized members of the company and are accessing only information they are entitled to see.

As you decide exactly where security should be placed on a network, you should also bear in mind the connections between networks. As far as security is concerned, there are only three different kinds of networks: trusted networks, untrusted networks, and unknown networks.

Trusted Networks   *Trusted networks* are the networks over which you have control or that you are in charge of securing. For example, anything within the innermost perimeter of the network is considered a trusted network. With appropriate security, nothing is going to happen within this realm of the network that the company would disapprove of. It makes little sense to put major security measures between trusted networks, since the same company operates both systems. However, these boundaries are good places for items like routers that can act as traffic control devices and implement a relatively low level of user security as well.

Untrusted Networks   *Untrusted networks* are the networks that your company has no control over. They are the networks that a company would like to connect to in order to share data, but these same networks are potential security risks. Any company wants to share only certain information. Again, untrusted networks force the issue of a balanced security plan; a company wants to communicate but not be vulnerable to these untrusted networks.

Any boundary between a trusted network and an untrusted network is a good place for network security. Security at this level can serve an important filtering function. This location is ideal for ensuring that confidential data does not leave a company's controlled network and that only appropriate connections are made between the two networks. Security between these two networks is a good example of internal perimeter security.

Unknown Networks   *Unknown networks* are all the networks that are not under your company's control and are not precisely noted in your company's security system. They are all the millions of networks that exist that you don't know anything about but are connected to when accessing the Internet. It is the unknown networks that pose the biggest threat to network security.

Any boundary between unknown networks and trusted networks is another obvious place for network security. At such an interaction point, security is less a matter of monitoring communications (as it was between trusted and untrusted networks) than of making sure that no attacks of any sort are made on the trusted network.

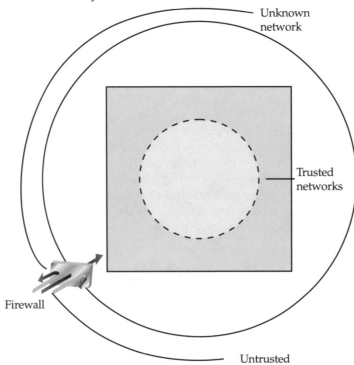

Firewall Security Options

Once you have determined where to place security, it is time to focus on the most essential form of security software, the firewall. A firewall is software that enforces the boundaries between networks. In other words, it is the software that handles traffic-based network security. There are four different kinds of firewalls, but they share one primary function: to narrow the entrance to the network to a single point and then monitor the information that goes in and out of the network.

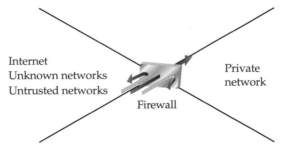

Internet
Unknown networks
Untrusted networks

Firewall

Private
network

Once again, your choice of firewall depends on the balance you want to strike between security and access. Each type of firewall is better at some aspects of security than others. Finding the correct software for the situation is the hardest part of establishing the overall security plan.

NOTE: Some people argue that there are software firewalls and then there are hardware firewalls. In reality, all firewalls are software. In the discussion that follows, all the firewalls described are software; however, some may need additional hardware.

Packet Filter Firewalls

A *packet filter firewall* examines network traffic at the packet level, as the name suggests. As a packet is sent across the network, it is closely examined and is either allowed to pass through or rejected in accordance with the general rules and regulations that have been programmed into the firewall. These preprogrammed qualifications are often referred to as the "permit or deny" orders. Each packet must fit one of two specific qualifications. Either the packet must be on a list of packets to be accepted, in which case it will be allowed in, or it must be on a list of packets to be rejected, in which case it won't be allowed in. The packet filter firewall belongs to the first generation of firewalls.

Objects for Packet Filter Firewalls   There are a number of different objects against which a packet filter firewall checks each and every packet. By evaluating the packet in question against these objectives, the firewall decides if it should let the information through or reject it. A packet must meet each one of these qualifications, or it is rejected.

This firewall can check both or either outbound or inbound packages. The firewall checks the arrival and distention of both incoming and outgoing packets.

▼ The firewall determines whether the physical network interface the packet arrives on is a known and trusted interface.

- It next checks the packet's IP address to see if the packet is coming from somewhere inside the trusted network.

- Once the interface and arrival location have been established, the packet filter firewall checks the IP address to which the packet is being sent to verify that it is a known and accepted destination.

- If the destination checks out okay, the packet filter firewall then makes sure the transport layer is acceptable.

▲ Finally the source port the packet came from and destination port it is heading to are looked at to completely verify the sender and the receiver of the packet.

The Advantages of the Packet Filter Firewall   The packet filer firewall belongs to the first generation of firewalls but is often still used because of its many advantages. This firewall is ideal for light security needs because it is fast and easy to implement. Because the network traffic is processed at a packet level, it is processed fast. The system simply either denies or permits each packet, so the security processing itself is rather fast as well. The packet filter firewall is also easy to configure. One rule can protect the whole network by preventing a connection. One other advantage of this system is that it shields internal IP addresses.

Disadvantages of the Packet Filter Firewall   The biggest criticism of this firewall is that it is not the most secure firewall. Because it operates at a packet level, this firewall doesn't have the capability to manipulate information. It only permits packets to continue through the system or denies them the right to do so. The other two disadvantages to note deal with the administrative aspect of this firewall. The packet firewall does not keep an audit trail of what goes in and out making it difficult to track any potential problems. It is also difficult to test from a network administrator's perspective because it is hard to differentiate between the individual accept and reject objectives.

Circuit-Level Firewalls

The circuit-level firewall is a second-generation firewall. Like the packet filter firewall, it reads information at a packet level. However, the circuit-level firewall identifies each packet as either a request for a connection or a packet belonging to an already established connection. The security focuses on the connection request. If the connection matches the valid connection criteria, the firewall allows its packets through.

Valid Connection Criteria   Much like the filter packet firewall, the circuit-level firewall examines each packet and decides to accept or reject the packet in accordance with a set of objectives. If the connecting packet meets all the valid connection criteria, the connection is permitted; if not, the packet is rejected and a connection is never made.

▼ The circuit-level firewall first checks to see if the packet is trying to connect, transfer data, or close a session.

- It then checks the sequencing information to see if it is all acceptable as well.

- Then, like the packet filter firewall, the circuit-level firewall checks the IP addresses of both the sending party and the receiving party.

▲ Finally, the physical interface over which the data is sent and received must pass inspection as well.

Drawing on all this information, the firewall decides whether the PC has permission to send or receive that data.

Advantages of the Circuit-Level Firewall   The biggest advantage of the circuit-level firewall is its speed. It is the fastest of all security firewalls. Like the packet filter firewall, it can protect the whole network because it will reject an entire connection if it finds it objectionable. It also makes outgoing packets appear to have been generated at the firewall instead of an inside source, so the IP address of the source is shielded. This shielding mechanism, referred to as Network Address Translation (NAT), translates IP addresses from private IP address (from within the network) to IP addresses that will not be dropped by the Internet.

NOTE: Private IP addresses include 10.0.0.0, 192.168.0.0, and 172.16.0.0.

Disadvantages of the Circuit-Level Firewall   The disadvantages of the circuit-level firewall are similar to those of the first-generation firewalls. Again, this firewall functions at a packet level, so it doesn't have the capability to manipulate data within the packet. The packets are either accepted or denied. It also doesn't generate an event log, and it is difficult to test.

Application-Layer Firewalls

Firewalls of the third generation evaluate network packets at the application level, as their name suggests. Because of the focus at the application level, this is the most complex kind of firewall. It tracks all connection information and has the capability to manipulate the data to give parcel permission.

Most application-level firewalls have proxy services as part of their security. This software acts as a liaison between the inside networks and the outside Internet. The proxy server is a bit like an agent who tells his clients who they can and cannot talk to and how much they should say when they do talk. The proxy server also acts as an interpreter. The firewall never really allows direct connections but communicates through a proxy server.

Advantages and Disadvantages of the Application-Layer Firewall   Because this firewall works at the application layer, it is able to manipulate contents of packets. It keeps a detailed record of what information passes through the proxy servers so that Network administrators are able to track possible security risks.

However, all these fancy manipulations slow down the whole filtering process. Application-layer firewalls are the slowest of all firewalls. The negatives are pressures thrown on the people who use and maintain this network. The application-layer firewall is slow because of the complex processes through which it checks the data. It also demands its own server. Because it evaluates at an application level, a lot of processing is involved in identifying all applications. There is also a client-based configuration step so that the proxy client can communicate. Finally, there may be an additional step for users, who have to identify themselves when they log in.

Dynamic Packet Filters

The dynamic packet filter is the fourth generation of firewalls. This firewall is very similar to the packet filter firewall with the notable exception that the network administrator can change the accept/deny rules at any time. It also has a sense of where the packets originated and will accept response packets sent back to the same address.

This firewall again provides limited security. It is fast, however, and it has the added advantage of allowing a response even from an untrusted network.

Table 11-1 lists some firewall vendors that you may wish to contact when planning a security solution.

USER-BASED SECURITY

Now that we have gained a basic concept of traffic-based security, it is time to turn our attention to security measures that may be taken within the network at a people-based level. These internal security measures are referred to as *user-based security*. There are two basic levels of user-based security.

▼ The end user's username and password, which, when used correctly, grant that user access to the company's servers

▲ The network administrator's username and password, which, when used together correctly, grant that administrator access to the network devices for monitoring and maintenance purposes

3COM	www.3com.com
Cisco	www.cisco.com
Novell	www.novell.com
Microsoft	www.microsoft.com
Checkpoint	www.checkpoint.com
Bay	www.nortel.com

Table 11-1. Firewall Venders

We are going to focus our attention on the end user–based security; however, the same general policies apply to network administrators as well.

> **NOTE:**   Remember, if an attacker can gain access with a network administrator's ID, the authorization will be much broader. In addition to having virtually free access to the network, that attacker can also gain access directly to servers or even firewalls.

Why Implement User-Based Security?

As we have discussed, it is possible for outside users to gain access to your network using a number of attack methods. If a traffic level of security fails, though, an attacker can still be stopped through user-based security. Although an attacker may be able to get inside a company's network, that attacker can still be prevented from traveling freely within the network. User-based security is also important for the basic management of a network. It provides network administrators a way to control what each individual user is able to do without standing behind users and watching.

With user-based security, each user is individually identified, authorized, and controlled. For example, each user has a password that is connected to his or her username. Both the username and the password must be provided correctly for a legitimate connection to be made. Once that connection is made, the user has limited privileges. Collectively, the process of user security that connects the username to the password and allows a user access to the network is called *authentication, authorization, and accounting,* or *AAA.*

Authentication

Authentication is the process of verifying who the user requesting access to the network is, and deciding if that user should be given access. Each user has a unique username and password. When the user enters this username and password pair correctly, it is verified and the user is given access to the network. This security measure forces anyone who wants access to the network to know a specific username and password.

Authorization

Authorization is the list of permissions given to a user to access a specific application on the network. Because authorization is distributed by username, not all users have the same access to all applications. This limitation helps secure the network from outside users. It also keeps users out of applications they shouldn't be using, helping keep workers on task and stopping them from messing up the network. Authorization also allows users to connect from different locations and still see their specific network. Within a particular scope of authorization, user groups can be established to give groups of users different rights within a network.

Accounting

Accounting is the record-keeping portion of user-based security. Accounting keeps track of who is logged in from where and for how long. Using these records, the network administrators can keep an eye on users and what they do when connected to the network. This tracking system provides managers with an idea of what their employees do and for how long. It also is used as an intruder alert mechanism for the network administrator, who can use the tracking capabilities to map suspicious behavior.

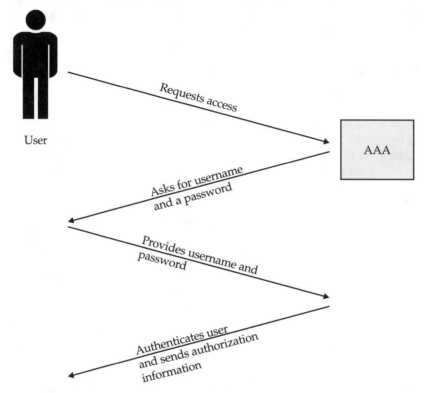

Disadvantages of AAA

Altogether, AAA provides a great source of network security. However, there are disadvantages to this user-based security as well. For example, user-based security can be complex and cumbersome to configure and update. In most situations, each application or server has to be configured individually. Also, user-based security, when used as the only form of security, is very limited. Once an intruder has one user's name and password, that intruder can pass freely throughout the system.

RADIUS Solution

Software is available that makes the management of user-based security much easier by controlling the AAA information in a user database that can be accessed by a number of different servers and applications. One example of such a protocol is RADIUS. RADIUS, which stands for Remote Authentication Dial-In User Service, is a security protocol that mainly focuses on authenticating users and maintaining accounting information for them. RADIUS, which is a protocol that was developed by Livingston Enterprises, Inc., helps manage the authentication, authorization, and accounting for multiple applications and servers at the same time.

How RADIUS Operates

When a user tries to log on to the network, the RADIUS client asks for that user's username and password. The first thing that the RADIUS server does is make sure that the client asking for permission is valid. If the client checks out, the response is then sent to the designated RADIUS server, where a database is searched for the corresponding matching pair. The RADIUS server then decides to accept, reject, or challenge the user's name and password. At this time, RADIUS might also choose to challenge the user to make sure that he or she is valid. RADIUS may send this challenge in the form of text that the user must respond to with additional information. If RADIUS decides to accept the username and password pair, it also sends back a list of authorizations connected to that pair dictating what the user can access. All the information about the user's session is also recorded by RADIUS.

RADIUS uses UDP as a transport protocol, and this constitutes a major difference between RADIUS and the TACACS+ protocol described next, which uses TCP. This choice of protocols is defended by RADIUS supporters as necessary because of complicated technical advantages it offers. In the simplest terms, UDP allows RADIUS to be more flexible in the way in which it communicates with other servers.

Advantages of RADIUS

RADIUS obviously saves time and money by controlling AAA security at an overall level. It also encrypts all password information, making it very difficult for intruders to intercept and read that confidential information. Another key advantage is that the RADIUS client and server communicate in such a way that encrypted information is never actually sent over the network. The accounting features of RADIUS are also impressive in that they can be used independently of the authentication and authorization aspects, because RADIUS records the start and stop of every session. RADIUS is the most used protocol because it is fast and takes up less memory than other protocols.

Disadvantages of RADIUS

The main disadvantage of RADIUS is the possible holes it leaves in security. Although RADIUS does encrypt the password, it does not encrypt the username, the authorizations granted, and the accounting information it records. An intruder might be able to access this information and thus gain access to confidential resources.

The TACACS+ Solution

Like RADIUS, TACACS+ provides the services of authentication, authorization, and accounting all on one server that can manage all the user-based security. TACACS+ was developed by Cisco Systems and is highly regarded as a form of user-based security for access to network devices. (The term TACACS+ stands for Terminal Access Controller

Access Control System Plus.) TACACS+ is best known for its capability to separate the processes of authentication, authorization, and accounting.

How TACACS+ Operates

TACACS+ operates in a similar fashion to RADIUS. TACACS+ sends the username and password information to the access list server, which in return sends the information about which applications the user should be granted permission to. TACACS+ sends information about authentication, authorization, and accounting all separately, however. That way, both authorization and accounting information can be dynamic and ongoing.

TACACS+ operates at a TCP protocol level. The major advantage of this level of protocol is that it ensures that a connection has been established and that the information being sent is received.

There are many benefits of TACACS+. For example, TACACS+ allows the same username and password to work for multiple protocols, greatly simplifying user-based security for the people who use the company network every day. The users save time logging into the network in the morning and are less frustrated than they would be if they had to log in to each application individually.

TACACS+ has very thorough and secure accounting capabilities. The username, the user address, the service attempted, the protocol used, the times started and stopped, and the date are all recorded for each session. This collected information can be used to track any possible security breaks throughout the system.

You need not choose between the TACACS+ and RADIUS protocols. In fact, most of the time the two protocols are used in cooperation with each other. Table 11-2 shows RADIUS and TACACS+ side by side.

	Creator	Encryption	Speed	AAA Management	Transport Protocol
RADIUS	Livingston Enterprises	Only the password	Faster	Combines authorization and accounting	UDP
TACACS+	Cisco	Entire packet	Slower	Separates authentication, authorization, and accounting	TPC

Table 11-2.   TACACS+ and RADIUS Side-by-Side

Final Thoughts on User-Based Security

Overall, the most important thing you can do for user-based network security is let the users know what network security solution you have invested in and why. After all, users who have access to the network are the biggest security threat, but they are also your greatest ally. Users have direct contact with the security solution and most often report their interactions with it as frustrating. If users know why the security is in place, they are more likely to understand why they have to go through the extra steps of entering their name and passwords. It is also reassuring to users to know what security is in place so that they feel confident that their correspondence and confidential information are secure. Users can also be additional watchdogs and notify network administrators of suspicious activity within their personal network accounts.

SECURITY CASE STUDIES

We have covered a wealth of security information that might still seem a little overwhelming. However, when you make a detailed plan of your objectives ahead of time, the security solution seems almost to present itself. I would like you to look at three different security solutions that show three ways that the same security objectives can be met in accordance with your company's main priorities.

As we discussed at the beginning of this chapter, creating the list of priorities is the most important first step. The three biggest things to consider are security, simplicity, and cost efficiency.

Objectives

There are four objectives that we are going to meet with our security solution for each one of these case studies. The objectives I have chosen are the basic objectives that are important for any e-business, but all pose possible security risks.

- ▼ Objective 1: Provide Internet access for employees.
- ■ Objective 2: Provide e-mail services for employees.
- ■ Objective 3: Provide access to the company Web site.
- ▲ Objective 4: Allow remote access to a secure network.

All of these objectives present possible security risks.

Case Study 1

The first company decided that their priorities are low cost and simplicity and that they are willing to compromise the level of security implemented to meet those two priorities. The security solution that best meets the company's needs can be studied in Figure 11-1.

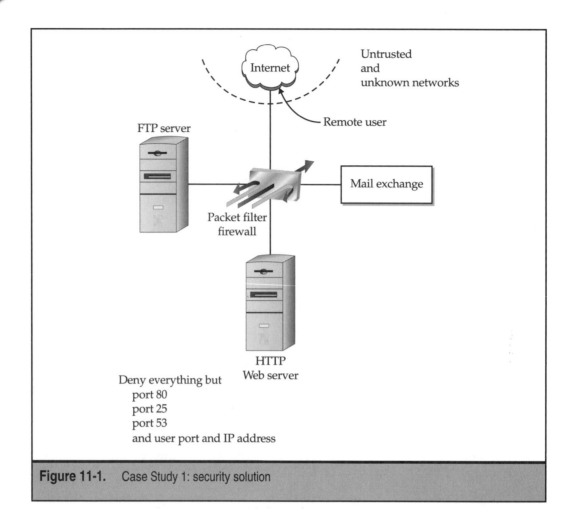

Figure 11-1.   Case Study 1: security solution

This security solution consists of a firewall that acts as a filter between the Internet and the company's HTTP or Web server, FTP server, and mail exchange server. In this case, the firewall is a packet filter firewall examining all the packets that pass between the network and the Internet.

If you remember, a packet filter firewall works by either accepting or rejecting each packet in accordance with a set of programmed objectives. In this situation, the company would configure the firewall to deny all packets except for packets sent to or received from TCP port 80 (the Web server), TCP port 25 (the mail server), and TCP port 53 (the DNS server). Any possible remote users will have to be individually entered into the firewall to allow their specific IP addresses to be accepted as source addresses, and specific source and destination ports must be designated as well.

Advantages of Case Study 1

This security solution is one of the most inexpensive solutions available. The only software needed is the packet filter firewall software. It is also a very simple security setup. There is one firewall and everything is connected into it. The configuration of the firewall is also quite easy. This firewall can only process packets, so all that needs to be entered are the access or reject objectives. However, if a number of remote users dial into the network, each destination or source IP address and port has to be individually entered.

Disadvantages of Case Study 1

Obviously, in the struggle for simplicity and a lower cost, the level of security suffers. For example, an attack can be made on the network as long as it comes through one of the designated ports. Also, this security model provides no user-based security at all. Once inside the firewall, an intruder has a great deal of freedom. Likewise, end users have access to anything on the network as well as anything on the Internet.

Case Study 2

The company in case study 2 was willing to spend a little more money on security and invest a little more time in configuring their security solution in order to have a higher level of security implemented. Figure 11-2 depicts their security solution.

This case study includes two levels of security between the trusted network and the Internet. Again, there is a packet filter firewall, but behind it there is a proxy server (a server that would run protocols such as RADIUS and TACACS+). The firewall filters everything at the packet level, and then the proxy server operates on an application level. The proxy server manages the authentication, authorization, and accounting services for user-based security. Another feature that is added to this firewall is Network Address Translation (NAT), which acts as a shield, keeping the internal IP addresses secret by translating them as they pass through the firewall.

Advantages of Case Study 2

Obviously, with the proxy server adding user-based security and NAT hiding the IP address, there is more security with this solution. The users are no longer free to access everything on the network. Restrictions are set for each user regarding what data and applications that user can and cannot access. The proxy server also restricts users from accessing certain Internet sites. NAT provides additional security. In fact, NAT is sometimes referred to as a natural firewall because the source and destination IP addresses are unreadable.

Disadvantages in Case Study 2

One disadvantage of this security solution is that it is more complicated. There are two different pieces to configure (the firewall and the proxy server). It is also quite a bit more expensive when you consider both the purchase price of the software and the time it takes a network administrator to configure and manage the system.

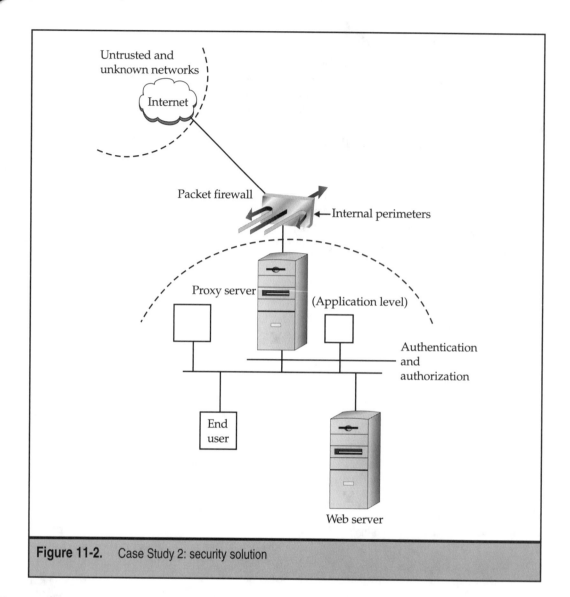

Figure 11-2.   Case Study 2: security solution

Case Study 3

The last company decided that security was the highest priority despite cost and complexity. They wanted to create the most secure network realistically possible. Figure 11-3 diagrams this very secure solution.

In this security solution, two different networks are hidden behind the firewall. One network, which houses the Web server, mail exchange server, and FTP server, is referred to as the DMZ or *demilitarized zone*. One the other side, a proxy server leads to the innermost perimeter, holding the end users and the data.

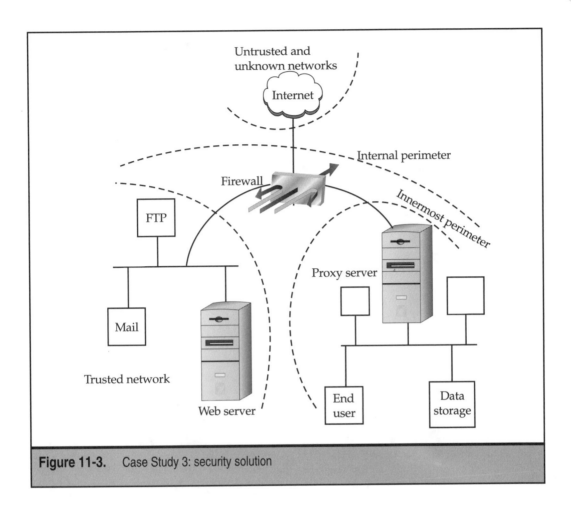

Figure 11-3. Case Study 3: security solution

Advantages of Case Study 3

The biggest advantage in this model is the level of security. As in case study 2, a proxy server controls the user-based security. However, in addition to navigating the proxy server, end-user traffic has to travel through the actual firewall in order to get to the Web, mail, or FTP server. The advantage to this method is that it creates a situation in which an outside user can access a company's Web site without ever being on the same network as the company's confidential data.

Disadvantages of Case Study 3

The disadvantages of case study 3 are obviously going to be cost and complexity. It is going to take a lot more time and effort to manage this security system. It is also going to be more complicated for the users to get to the resources that they need.

FINAL CONSIDERATIONS IN NETWORK SECURITY

As the case studies help point out, you have a number of points to consider when designing a network security solution. The best starting point is to make a list of priorities your company has for its security solution. It is also important to keep in mind what aspects of your company's network are in need of security, and in what ways that security might be compromised. Finally, as you consider the overall network security picture, remember that it is imperative to balance security, simplicity, and cost.

On the practical implementation level of network security, keep in mind that the best security options use a combination of traffic-based security and user-based security. A number of options are available for both traffic-based and user-based security in today's market. Remember that each company's security system is unique and created to serve that company's needs.

CHAPTER 12

Public Key Infrastructure

This chapter will focus on the technology behind securing business transactions outside the private network and how people who never see each other face-to-face can establish a level of trust that will enable them to do business.

A DIFFERENT KIND OF SECURITY

Once companies are confident in the safety of their personal networks, they need to focus on the safety of any transactions that enter or leave their network. As technology continues to open many new avenues for e-businesses, more and more companies are using the Internet as their prime method of communication because of the convenience of speed and access. However, as we have seen throughout this book, with the advancement of technology comes a new security need, in this case, the need to protect confidential information outside the private network.

What Needs to Be Protected

All communications over the Internet need some level of protection. A good basic measuring tool is that the level of confidentiality of a transaction should determine the level of security needed. Most business transactions in general require some level of security. For example, any contracts between your company and your customers are highly confidential and obviously need to be very secure. Confidential e-mail messages are another good example of something that can contain sensitive information and should be protected.

The expansion of e-business opens up opportunities for both customers and businesses; it increases the convenience of doing business but creates a number of new security risks. The transfer of money electronically is an example of an e-business-specific transaction that requires special security measures. When customers can feel comfortable searching a Web site, finding an item or service to purchase, and then sending their credit card numbers and social security numbers over the Internet, business is successful.

Why Secure Transactions Are Important

Secure transactions are important because they establish trust. In any business communication, there are four things that must be verified in order to establish trust:

▼ The identity of each party communicating

■ The guaranteed confidentiality of the transaction

■ The assurance that the transaction has not be modified

▲ The irrefutability of the fact that the transaction occurred

In the past, business communications concerning confidential information were safe and secure because they were done face-to-face. There was no reason to have mistrust if you personally verified the trust concerns just listed. There is something innately believable and trustworthy about something that you can see.

For example, in the past you knew who you were communicating with because you were actually there and could look your business partner in the eyes. You knew that the transaction was confidential and that it couldn't be modified because you were the only two people involved. There was also no question that the communication took place. Whether the transaction was signing a contract, purchasing a product, or transferring money in the bank, security was not an issue when it was done face-to-face.

In today's world, however, it is highly unrealistic to expect all business transactions to occur face-to-face. The Internet opens a huge world of opportunities. Companies can do business with people that they have never met much less seen face-to-face. The down side to the introduction of the Internet is that the trust that used to be taken for granted surrounding business transactions is greatly reduced. For example, a great many people that you would not trust could potentially be introduced into the business transaction equation.

Present Day Transactions Between Companies

There are four major threats to Internet transactions: eavesdropping, stealing of confidential information, forging of messages and transactions, and fraudulent businesses. All four threats must be dealt with to gain the trust of clients and partners and ensure the success of any e-business. All four undermine the trust in a business relationship.

Confidentiality

Ensuring confidentiality is the most important basic security measure any company should take while engaging in business transactions over the Internet. After all, the Internet is a public place much like a large restaurant where people gather for enjoyment, business purposes, dating opportunities, and even to just cause trouble. When you send an e-mail message over the Internet, it is like having a loud conversation in this public restaurant. Can you image yelling out the confidential details of an upcoming business merger in a crowded restaurant?

In order to ensure confidentiality during Internet transactions, companies need to find a way to make their conversations private. One way to regain a sense of confidentiality is to hide or encode the information companies send to each other so that anyone who might intercept the message is unable to read it.

Verify Identity

It does you no good to have confidential Internet communications if you don't know who you are communicating with. Knowing who you are doing business with is the second essential step in building trust in an Internet business relationship. For example, it is a fact of life that in any business relationship privileged information is passed between parties. In reality, the person or business you are dealing with could be anyone over the Internet. In order to ensure that the confidential information only gets to the intended party, it is important to be able to verify who that intended party is.

Transactions Not Modified

Once you have established the identity of the person you are taking to and that your communications are confidential, it is time to ensure that the communication is not intercepted and modified in any fashion. It is easy to picture the confusion that would follow if an order placed over the Internet were maliciously modified and the buyer ended up with only half the materials needed to complete a project. Just as disturbing is the thought of the warranty or even product price sent from the retailer being modified and the loss of business that could follow.

Nonrepudiation

Finally, in any business setting it is important to have a way to prove that transactions took place. *Nonrepudiation* is a term that refers to a company's or individual's inability to deny that a transaction took place. Any good security measure will legally prove that a transaction did in fact occur and what exactly was communicated in that transaction.

PKI

The *Public Key Infrastructure* is a security framework that ensures that transactions over the Web can be as trusted as face-to-face interactions once were. PKI is the overall name that refers to the individual security measures that ensure that transactions will be confidential, force business partners to prove their identity, prevent any modification or tampering with transactions, and legally enforce nonrepudiation. In short, PKI reinstates the trust companies can place in Internet transactions.

PKI is made up of four different parts that all work together to create the security framework:

▼ Public key encryption
■ The digital signature
■ The Certificate Authority (CA)
▲ The Registration Authority (RA)

In examining each aspect of PKI, we will identify how each one does its part to enabled PKI as a whole to meet the four qualifications of establishing trust and thus develop a good business relationship over the Internet.

How to Protect Confidential Transactions

The problem of confidentially has always been a problem when messages are sent between people or businesses when the two parties can't meet face-to-face. If the message is intercepted, it can be read and the information made public.

The Use of Encryption

Ever since information was first transferred, the idea of encryption or code was implemented to secure the message. If the message is written in code, it will be secure even if intercepted. Humans throughout the centuries have known and counted on that fact.

The present system of sending secure messages over the Internet is based on the same general idea of code that has been used for centuries, with one very notable improvement.

The difference between the past and present forms of code lies in the key that decrypts the code. In the past, the receiver, in order to transform the message back into a readable form, needed the key to the secret code. This system worked fine for the most part, because at some point the two parties met face-to-face and could exchange the code key, making sure it was kept top secret. If a face-to-face meeting wasn't possible, the two parties ran the risk of the secret code being intercepted and copied.

However, working with transactions over the Internet, you never see the person's face. The secret key would have to be sent by the same method as the message you wished to send in code. If you were worried about the original message being intercepted and read, you would obviously feel it was an insecure communication or you wouldn't be considering the need to use code in the first place. When it comes to the Internet, a different system of code is needed.

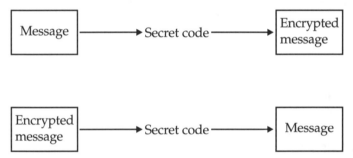

Public Key Cryptography

The basic groundwork for PKI is based on a technology called public key cryptography. *Public key cryptography* is the technological solution to the problem of people eavesdropping on confidential messages sent over the Internet. It is a mathematical secret code in which each letter is changed to a different letter, number, or symbol, creating a page of nonsense and preventing the message from being read even if it is intercepted.

Public key cryptography is different from the historical secret code concept and usable over the Internet because it has two keys. It is created from a mathematical code that is based on an algorithm and a value, with a complementary algorithm and value. The brilliance of this system is that one algorithm can encrypt the message and the other one will decrypt the message. Therefore, one of the algorithms can be made public while the other algorithm is kept totally private. It is impossible for an individual to decode the private key from the public key or vice versa. With this code system, it doesn't matter if the code is intercepted and read because it is made public. The only code that can decrypt the coded messages is the one that remained private.

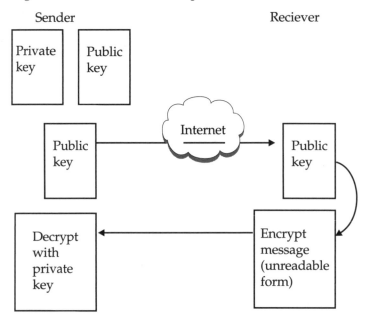

NOTE: Both the private key and the public key can be used to encrypt or decrypt the message. With this system, either party can send or receive the message.

Practical Notices About Public Key Encryption

Public key encryption is a wonderful advancement in securing communication over the Internet. However, because it is still a relatively new concept, there are a few bugs with practical implications that should be noted. For example, encrypting something with a public key takes a lot longer than it would with a secret code because the algorithms have to be a lot more complex to avoid being decoded with their counterparts.

Because of the time required to encrypt and decrypt a message, an alternative practice has started where one encrypts the message itself with a secret code and then sends the secret code encrypted with a public key code. The secret code itself is usually a lot shorter to encode and speeds up the process.

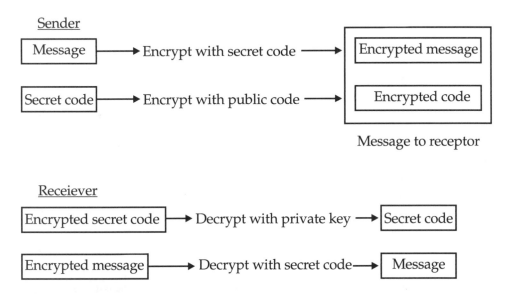

Additional Confidentially Precautions

Having a public code allows multiple people to send your company secure encrypted messages, thus solving the problems of confidentially over the Internet. However, it is important to keep in mind that public key encryption is only as secure as the private key. Obviously the private key should never travel over the Internet. It should be kept on a safe, private server that is not accessible from the network. It is also important to consider the security of the facilities that the private key is stored in. If the server or PC that the key is stored on is physically accessible, the key is less secure that it would be in a locked room. The private key is like a password; the fewer people who know about it, the safer it will remain.

How to Verify the Identity

Once you have established a safe method of communicating over the Internet, you can focus on the identity of the party you are communicating with. After all, public key encryption does no good if the public key is sent to or intercepted by the wrong person and used to send messages in an assumed name. Another huge security breach would result if an individual stole a copy of a company's private key and there were no way to verify the true identity of the sender.

Certificates

It is extremely easy to hide your identity when sending messages over the Internet. Anyone who has ever been in a chat room or signed up for an anonymous e-mail address knows first-hand how easy it is to pretend to be someone else. Assuming a different name or identity is perfectly acceptable in a chat room, but it is unacceptable when it comes to business transactions. *Certificates* are the technical devices that ensure the identity of the sender and thus further establish trust between communicating parties on the Internet. A certificate is composed of two parts, the public key, which we have already discussed, and the digital signature, which we will discuss now.

The format of the certificate is important to note. The certificate must be compatible with all the software and applications that it might encounter. Just because a certificate works for your company doesn't mean that it works for your clients. The International Organization for Standardization (ISO) has stepped in and developed a certificate standard called X.509. This format is defined in terms of fields that servers search for information for compatibility.

Identifying Certificates   There are three different types of certificates. The first type of certificate is the most common. It is an *identifying certificate,* which means that it formally ties the sender of the certificate to that sender's public key. The certificate also verifies the identity of the sender. All this information is sent in an electronic message from the CA to the person identified on the certificate.

Authorizing Certificates   An *authoring certificate* provides the message receiver with more verified information about the individual who is sending the message. For example, an authorizing certificate may include information about the sender's address, age, and company. If the authorizing certificate is for an entire company, it might also include information about the company's corporate standings, past customers, or corporate memberships. All the information contained on an authoring certificate has to be carefully researched by the CA because it is legally binding.

Authorizing certificates came into existence in order for senders to prove certain information about themselves. For example, if a doctor contacts a hospital and requests information on certain medications, the hospital will want to be assured that the individual really is a doctor and not an imposter who would misuse such information. Another example is an individual purchasing a product that is illegal to possess in certain locations. It would be important for the business providing the product to know the address of the individual requesting the merchandise.

Transactional Certificates   The final kind of certificate that is available is a transactional certificate. A *transactional certificate* provides the message receiver with information about the actual transaction itself. For example, a transactional certificate can prove that someone made a change or signed a document in the presence of someone else. This type of certificate is only good for a one-time use.

This type of certificate would be created with a combination of a public key and a private key. For example, if a legal document needs to be signed in the presence of a lawyer, the individual can sign the document and provide a copy of his or her personal public key, and then have the lawyer encrypt the entire message with the lawyer's private key. As you can see, this type of certificate is primarily used for legal purposes.

The three different types of certificates with the information that each certificate provides are summarized in Table 12-1.

Digital Signatures

Digital signatures are one of the key attributes of PKI that makes transactions more secure over the Internet. They are the identity stamp that travels with the Internet message. Much like a hand signature on a legal document, such a signature serves to identify its originator. A digital signature contains the verified identity of the subject, with such attributes as the name, employer, or address. Another very important piece of information that is contained in the digital signature is the party that issued the certificate, as we will discuss.

This digital signature is legally binding if used correctly and can be used with confidence. For example, the government accepts contracts signed correctly in this manner. The National Institute for Standards and Technology (NIST) has also ruled that a digital signature is legal. However, one needs to keep in mind that there have been no court cases to date that have ruled on what specifications need to be in place for the signatures to stand up in court. In general, digital signatures that use an encryption key and verify the identity of the party are legally binding. There are speculations that digital signatures may someday replace hand signatures on important documents because not only do they prove that the two parties agree on the document, but they prove what exactly the document said at the time it was signed. Thanks to encryption the document can't be decrypted if it is changed in any way so there is no chance of forgery after the document has been signed.

Type of Certificate	Information Provided
Identification	The sender's verified identity, including name and company
Authorization	The sender's name, address, age, company, special permits, or qualifications
Transactional	Proof that the sender signed or modified the message in the presence of a legal authority

Table 12-1.   Three Types of Certificates

One way to verify identity when considering the digital signature is to rely on the principle that only the private key can decode the public key. Therefore, if you are confident that the person you wish to communicate with is the only person who has access to the private key, it follows that decryption of the message proves identity. Based on this assumption, the digital signature is simply the sender's identity, company name, and address sent in code. If it is truly sent by the person with the private key, only the public key will decrypt the information.

However, in most business situations the ability to encrypt and decrypt is not enough in itself. A person or company can send a message and their public key requesting confidential information using the name of another company. In short, just because the public key decrypts the code doesn't mean the company you wish to communicate with sent you the code in the first place.

Certification Authorities

Somewhere along the line of Internet communication you have to trust someone completely. An extremely important part of PKI, what enables our preceding discussion of encryption to even take place, is the certificate authority. A *certificate authority (CA)* is a third party who acts as a trusted source proving the identities of the parties trying to communicate.

A CA is an authority much like the one that issues our licenses or passports. These are official documents that ensure to others that the certificate holder is truly a certain person. The CA issues and manages digital certificates.

Jobs and Management Responsibilities   The first responsibility of a CA is to verify the identity of an individual using traditional forms of identification such as certified licenses or ID and company records. Once an identity has been established, it is the CA who issues a digital certificate that designates a public key and a private key to an individual. Thus it is the CA that finally ensures that the person you are communicating with is indeed the person that you believe him or her to be on the basis of who owns the public and private key pair.

Once the digital certificate is in the possession of the verified individual, the CA will ensure the identity only for a certain amount of time or until anything on the certificate changes, such as the person's name, position, or employer. If a change occurs or the time limit is reached, the certificate will expire and the CA will place the certificate on a list of expired certificates. The management of certificates is the most important job of the CA. The system by which certificates expire with time or upon changes greatly tightens security.

When a certificate expires, the CA adds it to the expired certificate list, which is published quarterly, much like an expired credit card number report. It is up to the individual party to check incoming certificates for validity. The most common problem that arises with this system is that one cannot learn what certificates have expired and are therefore no longer certified until the next report. Because of this possible security problem, a number of CAs have implemented a continuously updated database that is accessible to the public. In general, the more recently the certificate was issued, the greater the confidence that can be placed in it.

Some General CA Precautions   Because PKI is still young and the system of CAs has not been totally perfected, there are a number of issues to consider when selecting a CA. First of all, there are questions about the trustworthiness of the CA itself. Both parties need to be confident that the CA is honest and has been doing the needed background checks to ensure identity. For example, a company or individual who wishes to gain access to your private messages may pose as a CA in order to have a copy of the decryption key.

To protect companies from false CAs and to ensure the quality of the CA, most CAs have a certificate authority of their own. This second party can be contacted for addition verification. Obviously, you must then trust the CA who is reporting on the CA you want to work with. The process could go on forever. A root system is being established that finally says "this is the last level of CAs there is"; it is the final authority. Some people have argued that this final layer should be the government; at this time, however, there is no official structure in place.

Most companies seek CAs that have a known and trusted reputation either for their personal CA or to verify the CA that they choose. For example, since traditional business transactions that could not be face-to-face were sent through the U.S. Postal Service, businesses often trust the Post Office as a root CA.

Root certificate authority

When the CA grants a digital signature, it will issue a *certificate practice statement*, which is a legal document that explains in detail the identity of the user, when the certificate was issued, what the CA ensures with this certificate, and when the certificate expires. This documentation is often used as a guide for companies to decide to what degree they can trust a CA.

The CA will also publish a *general certificate policy* that is sent with the digital signature. This policy helps a company to determine the amount of trust they can place in someone else's digital signature and CA. The CP lists the limitations and possible conditions behind the digital signature.

Registration Authorities

Registration authorities are companies separate from the CAs that are used to register or set up new users in PKI. In other words, the RA is the go-between that receives the request for certificates from the user, does the legwork behind verifying the identity of the user, and then contacts the CA. The RA cannot give out digital signatures.

There are some good reasons to use a RA. First of all, the RA is usually a stand-alone company that acts as a liaison between you and the CA. That means that although the CA that is behind the actual digital signature may be in a totally different country, the RA can be right across town. This allows your company easy interaction with the RA, which can include face-to-face interaction to ensure identity.

Another distinct advantage is that the actions of applying for and verifying the identity can be totally separated from those of issuing the certificate. Again, this is just another security step that separates the private information from the actual certificate.

Finally, use of the RA frees up the time of the CA. The background checks on the company's or individual's identity are by far the most time-consuming aspect of PKI. Eliminating that task from the labors of the CA allows the CA to focus on the other aspects of managing PKI.

How to Ensure the Transaction Is Not Modified

The third aspect in establishing trust is the ability to ensure that the message has not been modified in any fashion on its way across the Internet. The digital signature, which verifies the identity of the sender, can also be used as a tracking mechanism to detect any manipulation of the message.

Ensuring the authenticity of the message relies on the same theory as verifying the identity. If you can identify the user who owns the private key that matches the public key you are encrypting with, you can ensure that only that person can read the message. In much the same way, if anything is added or removed from the encrypted message as it is transferred over the Internet, the decryption key will not work. The two keys only work with each other and only work if nothing has been changed between encryption and decryption.

How to Prove Nonrepudiation

PKI also allows a company to prove that a transaction took place. Again, the same technology that verifies the identity and ensures confidentiality provides for nonrepudiation. A company or individual cannot deny sending a message if the digital signature on the message verifies that sender's identity.

PKI also has a feature option that can prove that a message had been created on a certain date and time. This function is called a *digital stamp*. Often in business transactions it is important to show that messages or notices were created and sent by a certain specified time. The easiest way to do this is to send a copy of the message in a form that is unreadable to the CA. The CA can then send a copy of the unreadable message to the party that should receive the message. The CA will also send a certificate that says that they received this message on such-and-such a date at such-and-such a time.

A REAL-LIFE EXAMPLE

PKI is easiest to understand with the use of a step-by-step example of how a company would go about using the security system. In this example two individuals, Matthew and Ryan, want to have secure business transactions and make sure that Jeremy doesn't steal their top secret information.

Matthew contacts his local RA and puts in a request for PKI. The RA verifies Matthew's identity using traditional forms of identification such as face-to-face meetings, a driver's license, and notarized company records. Once the RA has done a thorough background check on Matthew, they send his information and their approval to the internationally based CA.

The CA creates a certificate for Matthew stating his name, his address, and the company that he works for. They attach a copy of Matthew's designated public key, a reference link to the conditions under which this certificate is good, and their personal qualifications for issuing this certificate. They send Matthew a copy of this certificate and a copy of his private key.

Matthew then sends Ryan an e-mail message over the Internet with a copy of his certificate encrypted with his private key and a copy of his public key. The encrypted certificate is now a digital signature from Matthew proving his identity. Upon receiving the message, Ryan can decrypt the digital signature with the public key provided. Because the CA has ensured that the public key was given to Matthew, and the RA has verified that Matthew is indeed Matthew, Ryan knows that this code is not only going to keep the information he sends private, but that the person he is communicating with is actually Matthew. Because all these steps were taken, Ryan can feel assured that he is not communicating with Jeremy impersonating Matthew and sending a second public code. Ryan does one final security check on the certificate by accessing the CA's database of out-of-date certificates. Ryan verifies that Matthew's certificate is good, and now Matthew and Ryan are ready to communicate.

Matthew can send Ryan messages encrypted with his private key, and Ryan can decrypt them with the public key previously provided on Matthew's digital signature. Ryan can read the message, respond, and encrypt his message with the public key before sending it to Matthew. When Matthew receives the message, he uses the same private key he used to encrypt his message to Ryan to decrypt the message Ryan sends to him.

SPECIFIC INTERNET SALES SECURITY

In the case of e-business, companies often want to make their products and services available over the Internet. In this situation the business transaction takes place without the two parties ever meeting or even speaking directly to each other. Internet sales are business transactions like any others, and it is important to establish trust in this situation as well. PKI services also apply to Internet sales situations.

Internet Commerce from the Provider's Point of View

If your business provides goods and services over the Internet, there are three things that your company would realistically want to ensure before they partake in the business transaction. Those three factors are the buyer's identity, nonrepudiation, and the assurance of payment.

Authorizing the Buyer

In past forms of sale such as face-to-face sales and telephone sales, it was much easier to prove identity. Obviously, face-to-face contact made one's identity clear, and the buyer was not going to protest at the time of payment that the buyer was really someone else. In the case of telephone sales and catalog sales, someone has to place the call, leaving a number trail to the buyer. In Internet commerce, we have already addressed the problem of assumed identities.

The exchange of an authorizing certificate would obviously provide the merchant with all the needed information and proof of identity. However, obtaining a certificate is time-consuming and cumbersome. It may discourage buyers from purchasing.

In the real world, most companies don't require the use of a certificate for minor purchases, because it detracts from sales. In the case of major purchases, however, a certificate might be required. A certificate might also be requested if the product being sold is illegal in some areas or requires a permit of some kind. In the end, it is a personal decision for the company.

Most consumers who do a great deal of business over the Internet have their own public keys and identification certificates. In the end, having these safety features greatly benefits and protects the consumers and is in their best interest.

Non-Repudiation and Assurance of Payment

When it comes to sales over the Internet, the verification of payment and the concept of nonrepudiation work together. Most companies don't require proof of identity if they have an assurance of payment. The exchange of money over the Internet is most often done with the use of credit cards.

The credit card number is not processed immediately, because the cost of accessing every card number as it is entered would be huge. However, when buyers enter credit card numbers, they are in a sense identifying themselves. It is easy to trace a credit card number back to the individual who owns it. It is also hard for someone to deny having purchased something if the merchant has the consumer's credit card number.

Internet Commerce from the Consumer's Point of View

Just as the merchant has concerns about the transactions that occur when purchasing a product on a Web site, the consumer also has trust issues. Because it is the goal of any e-business to sell its goods and services, it is incredibly important that the consumer have trust in the merchant. The three concerns the consumer has are very similar to those of the merchants: authorization of the company, nonrepudiation, and confidentiality.

Authorization of the Merchant and Nonrepudiation

When consumers are sending credit card numbers across the Internet, the most important thing they want to ensure is the identity of the company they are sending the information to. The verification of the company's identity also helps assure consumers that the goods or services they are purchasing are exactly what they want and will be of good quality.

The first way to establish trust with a consumer is with the visual logos on your Web site. If the Web site looks like it is official, the consumer will be much more at ease. The second way a consumer can verify the identity of the merchant is with the credit card trail. The consumer can track the merchant in the same way the merchant could track the consumer. The credit card tracking also helps the consumer prove that the transaction took place. Finally, as was mentioned, most consumers who do a great deal of business on the Internet have their own PKI security already in place.

Confidentiality

The biggest concern of new customers who are purchasing on the Internet for the first time is the issue of confidentiality. People fear the interception of their credit card numbers. In reality, this is not a legitimate issue. Credit card numbers are easier to steal off receipts that are thrown away outside of stores or by eavesdropping on phone calls. Again, if consumers are overly concerned about confidentiality, they will invest in a public key and send the information encrypted.

PKI OPTIONS FOR YOUR COMPANY

When it comes to PKI, your company has many options in today's market. Because PKI can be broken up into so many different little pieces, there are a number of different PKI solutions that can be implemented. In the end, the choice needs to be based on what PKI solution you can place the greatest trust in.

How to Shop

As with other security solutions, it is important to have a plan when you start shopping for PKI solutions. Take a good look at the types of transactions your company makes over the Internet, how secure those transactions need to be, and the level of trust your company and your customers can place on the security of those transactions.

Interoperability

Realistically, interoperability is the biggest issue with PKI today. Because it is a new technology, there are few standards, and thus there are problems. Most companies have complex networks that rely on a number of different software and hardware solutions to provide the needed transaction technology over the Internet. The PKI solution that your company settles on needs to be able to work with all the different media your network contains.

The PKI solution you choose also needs to be big enough to encompass all your company's varied needs. For example, it is especially important for an e-business to ensure that the PKI solution also extend to the users of the company's Web site. The PKI must be flexible enough not only to cover these clients when they are working on your Web site, but to work with their systems, including other PKI systems, in ensuring security for other forms of communication, such as e-mail. Most CAs have a detailed report that can be accessed, which provides their individual interoperability capabilities.

Thankfully, a great deal of software available today already comes with PKI capability. For example, both Netscape Messenger and Microsoft Outlook come with a feature that enables users to add their digital signatures with a simple click of a button. Most companies can also use other PKI-ready software to automatically cover their Web sites so that those buying products off the site or sending money to the company are assured of security.

Assess the Need for PKI

Another important step in choosing a PKI solution is assessing your company's need for PKI. In e-business, there is little question that a company needs to look into a PKI solution. Whenever confidential information is communicated outside a trusted network, it is important to secure that information. Security comes down to trust. It is important for potential customers to trust your company and its security. If customers are purchasing items off your Internet site, they want to be assured that any confidential information they enter will really be going straight to your company without any eavesdropping or modifications. Customers also need to be assured that any transmissions of their confidential information within the company will be handled in a secure fashion. Finally, both you and your customers need to make sure that their transactions can be traced and verified so that neither side can back out of the business deal.

Accessibility

The PKI solution that your company settles on must also be simple enough that people use it. PKI is a confusing topic, and the solution put in place has to be easy to use and explained to both people within your company and customers in a fashion that is understandable. Customers and company employees should be made aware of the advantages of having PKI and the new level of trust they can place in Internet transactions.

Where to Shop

There are many PKI providers in the market these days. The best place to find providers is on the Internet. Many companies shop by sticking to the bigger names in the industry. Again, your company needs to make a decision based on its individual needs. Table 12-2 lists a number of the big CAs and their Web addresses.

Company Name	Web Site
Verisign	www.verisign.com
Cybertrust	www.cybertrust.com
Entrust	www.entrust.com
Xcert	www.xcert.com
IBM	www.internet.ibm.com/commercepoint

Table 12-2.   Certificate Authorities and Their Web Sites

Outsourcing versus Management

The final major decision you will have to make while creating a PKI plan concerns how much you trust this important piece of security to be in other people's hands. There are really three different ways to set up PKI for your company: you can run all of the PKI in-house, you can bring a CA in-house to manage that aspect of your PKI, or you can totally outsource every aspect of your PKI.

Run Your Own PKI

One option for your company is to totally run your own PKI. This option implies that you will run both the CA and the RA aspects of PKI for yourself. It obligates you to do all the background checks for individuals who wish to communicate over your PKI system, issuing public and private keys, and ensuring that the digital signatures are legal and binding.

The biggest advantage of totally running your own PKI is that you don't have to trust anyone else. The system is as secure as you make it. The biggest disadvantage is that it is difficult to manage. It takes a number of people and many hours of work to implement and maintain a PKI system run totally in-house. Every new individual who applies for a certificate must be thoroughly verified. And it is not only new individuals that you have to worry about; as mentioned earlier, the certificates have a life span. In the most secure PKI plan, the certificates expire often. There is a lot of legwork involved in running your own PKI.

Hire a CA to Run PKI Within Your Company

Another PKI option is to hire a CA to manage your certificates but hire them to work in-house. With this setup, the burden of actually doing the legwork for verifying users and keeping up with certificates falls on the shoulders of the CA. The CA is already trained to work with PKI and can step right in and start implementing the solution from day one. A great deal of time and money is saved in training. Another advantage to having the CA in-house is that your company still has a great deal of control over the whole process. The security is again what your company chooses to make it based on the general guidance of the hired professionals.

Outsourcing PKI

The last option is to outsource the whole PKI package. The obvious advantage to this method is that no burden of extra work is placed on your company and all the work is done by professionals that already know the material and don't have to be trained. The disadvantage of totally outsourcing the PKI is the trust factor and cost. Your company has to decide how much it trusts the CA and the RA. For example, do they do detailed enough background checks? If they do, are their facilities secure so that no one can break in and access the private keys that are stored in-house? Make sure you do a very close background check to ensure that the CA you are considering is a reputable CA and not just another way for illegitimate companies to gain access to private documentation.

In general, the decision of outsourcing PKI always balances on the issue of trust. Your company has to have trust in the PKI solution so that your customers can have trust in you. Whatever solution your company invests in, implementing PKI will greatly improve the security of Internet transactions.

The most important aspect of building a good working business relationship over the Internet is to establish trust between the two communicating parties. The way to establish trust is to verify the identity, the confidentiality, the authenticity, and the fact that the transaction took place. Companies can verify all of the preceding trust factors by implementing a PKI solution.

CHAPTER 13

Securing
E-Commerce Servers

After you've created a plan to secure your private network, and a method by which to secure transactions between your private network and your business partners, it is time to focus on the weak link that connects the entities you control to the rest of the world: the Web server.

This chapter takes a closer look at the risks surrounding having a Web server. We discuss the vulnerabilities of a Web server in general and how it creates opportunities for intruders to access your private network. We also take a closer look at transactions that occur over the Internet in coordination with your company's Web site and some specific tips for extra protection against hackers.

WEB SERVER SECURITY

The server that connects your company to the Internet and the Internet to your company is in constant danger. It is important to have a clear idea about what the dangers are surrounding that server and what security measures can be taken to protect it.

Why Web Server Security Is Needed

The term "hackers" sends a chill down any e-business network administrator's spine if only because of widely published media stories that surface again and again in the form of computer legends. Although most of the hype can be attributed to paranoia, there is a lot to worry about when it comes to securing Web servers.

In chapter 11 we outlined basic network security and noted that the Web server is the biggest possible security threat to the private network. Users in your company can access the endless resources of the Internet through that server. It is true that the Internet has opened the doors to business opportunities that would never even have been imagined 50 years ago. It is also true that that same server provides an opening to your company's private network to anyone on the Internet with malicious intent.

Unlike assaults on private network security, where many problems occur because of accidental user error, attacks on the Web server are done with clear purpose. For example, there are millions of personal computers accessing the Internet, and just like a server any one of those computers has the possibility of being broken into. However, it is very rare for cases of personal computer hacking ever to make it into the media, because no one cares if a personal computer gets broken into. The information isn't of importance to anyone but the owner. Most attackers search for servers to hack into precisely because there is always information of value on the servers. Whether the server is attacked for a specific reason, or just because it is a server, when someone hacks into a server, it is never an accident.

Attacks on Web servers are done for two reasons. The first reason is that an attack of that sort can give the intruder vital information that can be used in the future to gain access to a private network. The second possible objective behind a Web server attack is to gain access to the Internet interface itself and change the information that is posted on the Internet.

Protection of Confidential Data

As we have discussed before, if an intruder gains access to your private network, there are a number of immediate security problems. From within the network, intruders can steal usernames and passwords or even create their own network account granting them access to internal servers under the guise of an authorized user. If an attacker has access to a private network with a username and password, that attacker has the ability to manipulate applications, causing access problems for employees who should have the authority to use those applications. This intruder also would have the ability to steal confidential data or change data already stored on the network, compromising the company's confidentiality. Finally, the intruder could also send this confidential or changed information to customers or other companies, who are all under the impression that it is coming from a legitimate user inside the breached company.

Protection of the Web Site

The second sort of attack that your company needs to be wary about is an attack on your Web server itself. Some attackers are not trying to steal sensitive information from your company, or even get into your private network. Some hackers are just invading for the challenge of hacking into a server. Perhaps your company is well known and gets a lot of hits on its Web site, making it a good target for hackers who want to break into a Web server and then leave their mark, proving their hacking skills. Or perhaps a hacker feels strongly about something advertised or published on your Web page and breaks into your Web server to alter your site under the guise of protest. Whatever the case may be, it is important to protect the integrity of your actual Web site and ensure that the information you post does not get manipulated.

The reasons behind securing your Web site are fairly obvious. If your Web server is broken into and a hacker is able to change the information on your Web site, your information can be replaced by an obscene parody or offensive material. Customers who might be offended by your site will not purchase anything, or even stay at your site long enough to discover the truth behind your company. Furthermore, customers and business partners can also be intimidated simply by the fact that a hacker could access your Web server and change your Internet site. If people feel your company lacks security, they are not going to purchase anything from your site, nor will they feel comfortable with any other business-related Internet-based transactions. Finally, any down time that your site undergoes due to reconstruction is costly both in loss in business and productivity.

An Example for Warning

Despite all the warnings being issued by security expects, hackers do break into Web servers and change the faces of Web sites all the time. If you need convincing of the need to protect your company's image by securing your Web site, consider what happened to a CIA site in 1996. A hacker broke into the Web server that hosts that Web site and made some basic changes to voice a personal opinion about the agency. Needless to say, the site was down for reconstruction early the next morning.

Protecting Your Web Server and Site

You can use a *Web server security plan* to secure your Web server from hackers, preventing access to your private network and manipulation of your Web site. A well-developed Web server security plan takes into account the network you currently have, the Internet technology you would like to implement, and the level of security you will need considering the confidentiality of the communications. Given those qualifications, the plan focuses on a way to protect the Web server and to protect communications to and from the Web server.

Now that we have identified the problems that can occur if your server is hacked into, it is time to look at the security measures that can be put in place to stop such an attack. There are many different ways to increase the security of the Web server itself.

Policy

Web server security is another complex security topic that is best handled through organization. In fact, the most important thing you can do for your server and your site is to establish a clear policy about Web security. A clear plan aids the security process in a number of ways:

▼ A policy plan helps outline in your mind what is and what is not allowed. As strange as it seems, it might be nice to have guidelines as to whether a violation has occurred.

■ A written policy will also help others understand what the security measures are and why you are enforcing them. This internal security measure will not only keep people from within your own company from breaking policies, but it will help them to identify other possible violations.

▲ A written policy can be used as a guide for the people who use your site. This helps to establish trust, which is essential to business. A written policy can also act as a public warning against policy violations and help to support you legally against attackers.

The more clearly you can explain your policy and the reasons behind it, the easier implementing the system will be for yourself and users.

When creating this written policy, you need not follow any rigid format; however, some key things should always be included:

▼ Permissions covering who is allowed to use the system, when they are allowed to use the system, and what they are allowed to do within the system

■ What is appropriate versus inappropriate conduct on the system

■ The procedures you follow for adding or removing users' access from the system

■ What the local and remote login methods are

▲ What the monitoring procedures are and what is done if a security breach is found

Choosing a Server

Once your company has developed a policy, it is time to take a look at the actual hardware that will be involved in the system. As silly as it may seem, your choice of server will affect your Internet security efforts. In the long run, taking preventive measures is a lot less costly then being unprepared.

One of the easiest ways to tighten server security is to remember that the more basic the features of the server, the more difficult it is to break into the server. For example, specialty servers are the hardest to break into. The reasoning behind this solution is that the fewer functions the server is running, the fewer holes hackers can find that may be used to gain entrance. Keep in mind, however, that running a server with little on it means, well, running a server with little on it. Most companies need and want the performance advantages of having a server that is capable of running many different things, thus having a simple server is unrealistic. If a basic server is unrealistic for your company, another useful tip is that if you don't need an application that is running on your Web server, disable it. Your server may still have a number of different applications running, but at least it doesn't have excess functions.

A number of different platforms, or security software options, are available for Web servers. No one software package has a clear advantage over the others. Each option entails individual risks. In general, it is wise to choose a software company that stays up to date with new patches and solutions for any new security holes that might be discovered.

Server Location

The Web server is the key to the Internet. That server is the way in which all users in your company can access the Web. It is also the way in which all other personal computers on the Internet can access your company.

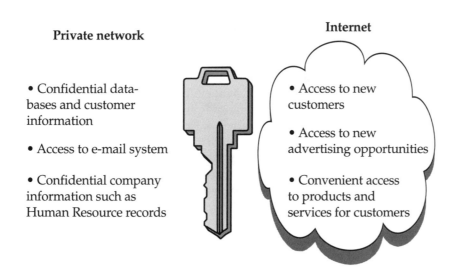

Private network

Internet

- Confidential databases and customer information

- Access to e-mail system

- Confidential company information such as Human Resource records

- Access to new customers

- Access to new advertising opportunities

- Convenient access to products and services for customers

Because this server is such a pivotal point, it is very important to consider where the server will be placed in your network. The Web server, like any server, is obviously at risk from viruses and attacks. Most of the time, servers are protected behind a firewall, which acts as a filter, keeping a close eye on what and who accesses the server. However, there are dangerous implications to placing a Web server behind the firewall.

If the Web server is behind the firewall, then everyone who accesses it is automatically allowed access behind the firewall and thus to the private network. If the firewall is the agent acting to keep all intruders out of the private network, then an internal Web server would defeat the purpose of the firewall. Most people feel that it is less complicated to watch the Web server for possible attacks or security risks and deal with the consequence as they occur than to have to run maintenance and search for attacks on the entire private network. It is also much more cost-effective to fix the Web server than it would be to deal with the aftermath of a private network security breach.

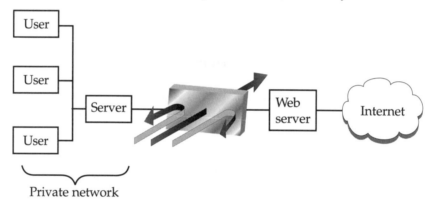

Private network

There is a happy medium between sacrificing your whole private network and having to constantly run maintenance on your Web server. Most companies that have struggled with this problem place their Web servers in the DMZ in an effort to protect their private network. A DMZ, or *demilitarized zone*, acts like its own little network. It is created when the Web server is set apart from the private network but is still behind the firewall. This tiny network is totally separate from the private network, as illustrated in Figure 13-1.

The DMZ setup uses a proxy server to divide the network into two totally separate halves. On one side there is the private network, including all the users and the private databases. On the other side of the network, directly behind the firewall, are the Web servers and sometimes mail servers. In this model, anyone seeking to access the Web server must pass through the firewall in order to do so. However, users accessing the Web server still do not have free rein on the private network. In fact, they have to get through the proxy server to get to the private network. The proxy server in this case acts like another little firewall, dictating who and what may pass to and from the private network.

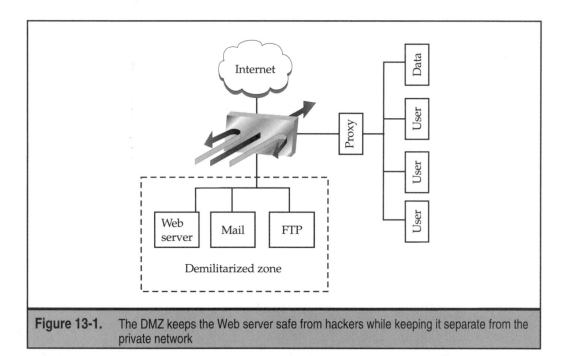

Figure 13-1.   The DMZ keeps the Web server safe from hackers while keeping it separate from the private network

There are some definite advantages to the DMZ setup. First of all, the DMZ separates the private network from the Web server while still allowing the Web server the safety of a firewall. The firewall, as seen in Chapter 11, filters the information passing through and decides what will and will not be allowed. The public network is never associated with the Web server, so if there is some sort of break-in, the private network remains safe. Finally, this setup also helps to monitor the internal use of the Web server. All the internal users have to go through the proxy server to gain access to the Web server. The proxy server can be used to authenticate and authorize employee access to the Internet.

The disadvantage of this setup is, obviously, cost. The more hardware that is put into use, the more expensive the implementation costs are. However, the benefits of a secure Web server can readily justify the money spent up front. Down time, loss of Internet access, reconfiguration, and cleanup after an attack can be more costly and may happen more than once.

Configured Web Server Restrictions

A Web server can be configured to restrict certain connections according to prepro- grammed information. The server may be programmed to reject the connection altogether or to limit the connection to certain files. The two major restrictions are normally IP address or domain name restrictions and user and password restrictions. Once again, this security measure is effective because it gives the network administrator more control over the Web server. The server cannot be accessed freely by anyone but is "locked down" by certain restrictions. Although restrictions are a good way to control access and traffic, they should not be used as the only method of security, since even these security precautions can be overcome.

IP Address or Domain Restrictions   IP address or domain name restrictions are most often put into place to allow a user to connect to the Web server in the first place. These restrictions are configured so that they won't allow connections from certain IP addresses. This restriction mechanism isn't a fool-proof security method for a number of reasons. First of all, an experienced hacker can "spoof" the IP address that he is coming from to make it appear to the server that the IP address is allowed. Not to mention the fact that if someone physically breaks into a PC that is not restricted, that person can reach the server as well. Restrictions can also lead to problems for users who are actually allowed access according to the way their IP address appears after it goes through the proxy server.

Name and Password Restrictions   Some files on a Web server may be subject to access only after a user enters a name and a password. For example, you might be able to connect to a Web site, but in order to see the information you want to view, you have to register or become a member. In other words, locks are set up on certain files. The user has to provide the server with personal information in order to get a username and password that will grant him or her access.

However, much like the restriction by IP address, name and password restrictions also have security problems. One problem that decreases the security is that there are actual programs that can help determine passwords, making it easy for a hacker to figure out a password and gain access. More often, however, the security risks are simply caused by user error. Most users choose passwords that are easy to guess, such as their names or birth dates. Plus, users often use the same passwords for multiple applications, some of which are easy to break into and identify the passwords. Finally, users have also been know to write their passwords down and tape them to their PCs, making it extremely easy to break in.

Hotfixes

No matter what format you choose to run on your Web server, there are going to be security holes. New ways to break in or side-step security are invented every day. When these new hacking methods surface, the companies that produce Web server software create a quick fix. Most of the time the fix is a simple, quick addition to the software called a *hotfix*. Hotfixes are usually small patches that fix specific problems with the security software. These hotfixes are most often found on a Web page run by the security software providers and are free downloads. Network administrators should be aware of what the newest update is for the security software and what security hole it fixes.

Just Generally Be Aware

The last security tip is just to be aware of what is going on both on your Web site and on your Web server. If you notice any activity that looks suspicious, look into it. It is much easier to find a problem or an intruder early and take care of it than it is to deal with the problems they might cause. A good place to check is your access error log files. If you see any system commands that start with "rm," "login," "/bin/sh," or "perl," there is a good chance you have an intruder trying to break in. Also, keep an eye out for very long lines that appear in URL requests; that is often a sign of someone trying to guess a password.

VIRUS PROTECTION

Virus protection is another important risk factor that any company should consider when it will be connecting to the Internet. In the past, viruses were restricted to moving about on disks. Most often, users would receive a disk from another company or from an untrustworthy source and it would contain a virus. This virus would then harm their personal computers and then move through the network. These days, viruses have become more widespread, thanks for the most part to the Internet.

What You Should Be Protecting From

It is important to know about viruses and how they might affect your network. Not only can a programmed threat cause damage to your network itself, but it can open doors to many other intruders. No security measures can compensate for open doors created by special programmed threats. Like any other security threat, the best protection comes from learning about the possible attacks and having a plan of action to deal with any possible threats.

▼ A *virus* is a block of code that is not complete within itself but that can attach to another program and then reproduce within that program. Viruses can have a number of different harmful effects on a network. Some viruses take over the program and make that program unavailable for users. Other viruses corrupt an aspect of a program causing the program to malfunction. Finally, viruses also work by bogging a system down so that performance falters. They can take over resources and restrict access to users that normally can access applications, and sometimes viruses can damage data directly as well.

■ A *worm* is a complete and independent program in and of itself, which copies itself and spreads over a network. Much like a virus, the worm can do damage to the data it interacts with, but it is most dangerous because of its ability to take over a network, restrict resources, or even shut a whole network down.

▲ A *Trojan horse* is an application that appears to be useful and safe but that has another program within it that can cause damage to the PC or network. The Trojan horse is like a worm in that it is an independent, self-contained program. It can have the same effects as a worm as well.

How to Protect Your Servers

Virus protection tools are the best protection against these programs. These antivirus programs can be purchased both on- and offline and can be installed directly to individual PCs or to servers. Virus protection programs scan your system searching for and then destroying any programmed threats before they become a problem. It is important to keep all virus software up to date because new security threats are created every day. The best policy is to search the Internet often for information and virus scans. Table 13-1 lists some quick tips for protecting your network from viruses.

Antivirus software is an important part of preventing viruses. There are many different antivirus software vendors and well as many different software options. The best idea is to get a software package that searches for a number of different signs of viruses. When choosing a vendor, keep in mind that you will want software that is easily upgraded, since viruses change constantly. A vendor should be willing to help explain the different upgrades, have the upgrades easily accessible, and be a reputable company. For example, you don't want to spend a large chunk of time and money installing virus software from a company that will be going out of business and thus have no upgrades. Table 13-2 lists a number of virus software companies and their Web addresses.

Tips	Reasoning
Search the Internet often to find new virus updates	New information comes out daily. Network security is constantly being compromised and then improved.
Keep your virus scanning software offline	If a virus gets onto your network, it can damage your virus scanning software just as easily as any other application. A copy offline is your best protection.
Keep users trained to identify possible programmed threats	Viruses most often enter networks through users' individual PCs. For example, users open programs or documents on infected disks, open corrupt e-mail messages, or download programs from the Internet that expose the network to viruses.
Download new virus software as it becomes available	Because viruses change every time they encounter new virus scans, it is important to keep your virus software as up to date as possible.

Table 13-1. Quick Virus Tips

Virus Scan Company	Web Address
SecureNet Technologies	www.securenet.org
SafetyNet	www.safetynet.com/default.asp
Network Associates (McAfee)	www.nai.com
Cybersoft, Inc	www.cyber.com
ChekWARE	www.chekware.com
Central Command	www.avp.com
Alwil Software	www.alwil.com/en/default.asp

Table 13-2.   Virus Scan Company Information

INTERNET TRANSACTION SECURITY

Once security for the actual Web server is in place, it is time to change the focus to the transactions that take place between your Web server and all the other PCs connected to the Internet. We cannot overstress the fact that if customers and business partners feel insecure about Internet transactions, they will not use your Web site. The better understood and documented your security policies are, the more comfortable customers will be in doing business with your company.

Internet Protocol Security

Internet Protocol security, or IPSec, is the framework for the security of Internet transactions that are implemented at a protocol level. It is IPSec that ensures that transactions to and from your Web server are secure. For example, if someone logs on to your Web site and tries to send an order, IPSec is the security applied to that transaction that ensures it arrives unchanged, unread, and from the person who claims to be sending it.

What Does IPSec Do?

In the simplest terms, the IPSec framework secures by enclosing the packet of information that is being sent in another packet before it is sent over the Internet. On the receiver's end, the packet is decrypted and read by a device that the sender has specified.

IPSec is composed of three different security mechanisms: the authentication header, the encapsulating security payload, and key management. The three mechanisms are used in coordination with each other for the best security results.

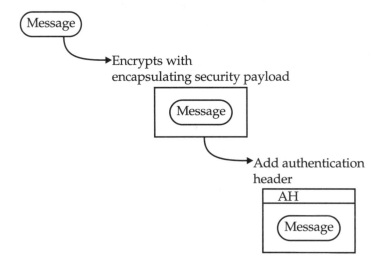

Authentication Header   The first mechanism is the *authentication header (AH)*. The AH focuses on authenticating the individual who sent the information and assuring that it hasn't been tampered with along the way. The AH is inserted after the IP header but before the other information that is going to be authenticated.

Encapsulating Security Payload   The second security mechanism is the *encapsulating security payload (ESP)*. ESP also authenticates the identity of the user, but it supports the encryption of data as well. There are different levels of ESP that can be adapted for each situation.

In the use of AH and ESP, the sender and the receiver have to agree upon an encryption key, a decryption key, an authentication method, and session guidelines. In general, the ESP is applied to the transfer layer first in preparation to send a message. Then the AH is added to the top of that so that the first thing that is read by the receiver is the AH.

Internet Key Management Protocol   Internet Key Management Protocol is said to be the core of IPSec. This mechanism allows the two parties to exchange their public keys and set up a secure session. After the public keys are exchanged, a session identifier is defined. A *session identifier* is the definition of the Internet relationship the two parties share. For example, a session identifier verifies the party you are talking to and then allows specific instructions you may have set up for this relationship. For example, if you have a casual business relationship with another company, the session identifier for any IP addresses inside that company might run an encryption that is shorter than the public key encryption used for other customers. This will speed up communication between these two parties while still keeping it very secure.

There are two different ways that keys can be exchanged between two different parties. The first way is manual key exchange. This method requires users to manually enter the key that they wish to use to communicate along with the keys of all the other people that they plan to communicate with. Although this method is very time-consuming, it is the most widely used method. It works very well in small environments where there are few parties communicating. The other method in which keys can be exchanged is referred to as ISAKMP. This key management tool does not establish session keys, but when used with different establishing tools, it can be used to establish a connection and exchange keys without users' having to add each one individually. Although ISAKMP is more complex, it also saves a great deal of time and can be just as secure.

Why Do You Need ISPec?

ISPec is much like PKI in the way that it establishes trust between parties. As an overall framework, IPSec provides three very important security features for Internet transactions: confidentiality, integrity, and authentication.

Confidentiality   IPSec ensures that all transactions are confidential in much the same way as the PKI mechanism does. The ESP function encrypts the packets before they are sent over the Internet. Once the transaction is encrypted, it can only be decrypted by the Web server. Thus, even if the information were to go astray, it would be undecipherable.

Integrity   The receiver, in this case the Web server, can also make sure that the data has not been tampered with or changed in any way. Because the transaction is encrypted before it is sent, it will only decrypt if the message was not tampered with. Thus, if there is any change to the message, it will not translate to readable material when it reaches the Web server. The IPSec has a function that also provides this service by attaching itself to the encrypted data. If there is a problem with the authentication header, it means that the data located under it could have been manipulated as well.

Authentication   The receiver can also authenticate the source from which the packets came, because of the information provided in the header. Authentication is one of the most important aspects of any security system. It doesn't matter how tight your controls are to prevent interception of the message when you don't know who is sending it to you in the first place.

Differences from PKI

Although IPsec sounds very similar to the PKI approach we discussed in the last chapter, there are a couple of important differences to point out from the very beginning. The other transaction security measures we have looked at function on the application level, whereas IPSec operates at the protocol level. This makes IPSec easier to use because the applications of the two communicating parties do not have to be compatible. Additionally, IPSec allows users to authenticate and communicate through a session instead of by individual messages. PKI is a wonderful security measure for e-mail messages; IPSec is more appropriate for Internet use.

Other Benefits of IPSec

The obvious benefits of IPSec are that Internet transactions gain a measure of confidentiality, integrity, and authenticity. However, simplicity is the biggest advantage that a company gains by choosing IPSec over other security measures. Because IPSec is integrated at the infrastructure level, there are no changes to the individual applications or personal computers running on the private network. This setup obviously saves a great deal of time and money. Because IPSec is not used on the individual level, it doesn't require training all users. In fact, the users need not deal with IPSec at all.

Remote Users　Another great advantage IPSec offers companies is that it provides a way for people who are not in the office to reach important but confidential materials. IPSec creates a wonderful solution for remote users, who can create a tunnel back to the private network using IPSec through the Internet. This cuts down on the cost of private lines and the worry about other security measures for remote users. For example, instead of having to purchase and secure a great number of modems for use in-house, the company can arrange for the remote user to dial locally into the Internet provider and still access the private network. The security of IPSec is much greater than that of individual dial-up lines. Table 13-3 lists the features of IPSec and the benefits that they offer.

Feature	Benefit
AH and ESP	Offer confidentiality, integrity, and authenticity
Internet Key Management Protocol	Connects sessions without users having to worry about configuration of individual communications
Session Identifier	Allows certain communications to use different encryption keys to vary the level of security and thus speed up some transactions
Works on protocol level	Allows security solutions to be implemented without having to configure individual PCs or applications
Standard solution	IPSec is compatible with many different PCs, applications, and other technology, making it easy for all to use

Table 13-3.　Features and Benefits of IPSec

As we have seen through the last three chapters, security is by far the most challenging and time-consuming aspect of configuring a network. The security that is implemented for your Web server and on the Web page itself is no exception. However, much as with the other security solutions we have examined, the implementation will go smoothly if the solution is well thought-out and follows a predetermined plan and keeps the company's objectives clear.

Connecting your company to the Internet might seem overly complex and increasingly risky. The benefits greatly outweigh the risks, however. The Internet is quickly becoming the most successful business tool in today's industry. Use of the Internet and other technology simply forces you to be cautious and aware. With adequate preparations, insight, and planning, e-business security will be the backbone of your e-business.

PART IV

Implementing
E-Business Systems

CHAPTER 14

Connecting E-Business Solutions

In a perfect world, you'd be able to buy a slew of new servers and clients, hook up an ultra-fast network, and open your e-business's virtual doors. However, this is rarely ever the case as finances and existing infrastructure force organizations to build around the technological foundation that is already in place. This is especially the case if your organization is to use electronic data interchange (EDI) to communicate with other businesses. Though EDI has traditionally been the province of big companies, the Internet is bringing it to smaller businesses as a means to streamline B2B communications.

In this chapter, we'll describe how EDI has traditionally fit into business models and outline the issues that surround EDI. Then, we'll talk about how the Internet is making EDI more accessible to small and mid-sized companies and what tools are available to implement EDI. Additionally, we'll talk about how you can integrate your organization (no matter how big it is) into an EDI system and how to integrate new e-business applications into an existing system.

EDI

Businesses today transact with trading partners in one of two basic ways:

1. The majority of businesses use nonautomated means of communicating commerce-related information with trading partners, like mail, telephone, and fax.

2. A small number of primarily the largest companies in the world—fewer than 50,000—conduct a significant portion of their transactions in an automated fashion such as EDI.

In the past, EDI was conducted via leased lines or, more commonly, through value-added networks (VANs). These media were costly and complex, keeping them out of the reach of smaller businesses. The Internet brings radical change to automation in trading. As shown in Figure 14-1, by providing an ever-present public network and standards for communication, the Internet will help businesses lower costs in EDI transactions.

More important, the Internet will make it easier for small and medium-sized businesses to participate in automated commerce transactions. Many businesses—small, medium, and large—can send and receive the majority of their purchase orders and invoices over the Internet.

EDI can best be described as the transmission and reception of documents between computers in a machine-readable form. EDI transactions are very popular because they have high integrity, are highly secure, and can scale to very large operations. These transactions routinely transport mission-critical data between cooperating organizations. In a traditional scenario, companies use VANs to transmit EDI transactions, but the growing popularity of the Internet is rapidly changing EDI.

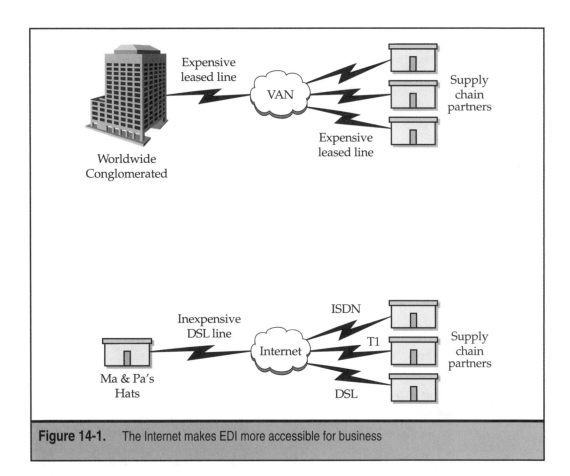

Figure 14-1. The Internet makes EDI more accessible for business

What Is EDI?

EDI is a simple technology that maps the information from a database on one computer to the database information on a different computer. Big deal, you may be thinking, but this is what computers and B2B transactions are all about. What makes it interesting is that EDI has been used for B2B transactions since its development in the 1960s—decades before the Internet made e-business a commonplace activity.

Early electronic transfers were based on proprietary formats that were agreed upon between two trading partners. Because of differing document formats, it was difficult for a company to exchange data electronically with different trading partners. To solve this problem, a standard format was needed.

Roots

In the 1960s, a cooperative effort between industry groups produced the first attempt at developing these standards. Since these were the first efforts, the formats were only for purchasing, transportation, and finance data. Further, they were used primarily for intraindustry transactions. It was not until the late 1970s that efforts began for national EDI standards that extend into the EDI we know today.

At that time, both users and vendors gave their input for standards that:

▼ Were hardware independent

■ Were able to be used by all trading partners

■ Reduced the labor-intensive tasks of exchanging data (data reentry, for instance)

▲ Allowed the sender of the data to manage the transmission, which included knowing if and when the transmission was received

Companies traditionally use VANs, such as GE Information Services, the IBM Advantis Network, or AT&T, for EDI. Further, the VANs don't necessarily just need to connect two organizations. Some VANs can get pretty big (for instance, GE Information Services has 40,000 subscribers). To pay for access to the VAN, organizations generally pay according to how much data has been transmitted across the VAN.

NOTE: Billing for VAN usage is based on kilocharacters, or multiples of 1,000 characters. Obviously, the less data sent across a VAN, the cheaper the VAN bill.

Benefits

The benefits of EDI are seemingly endless. EDI includes electronic order placement, electronic shipping notification, electronic invoicing, and many other business transactions that computers can actually perform faster and more efficiently than people.

EDI is beneficial for several reasons. It:

▼ Improves accuracy and speed of information exchanged between companies

■ Reduces operational costs for customers, suppliers, and your organization

■ Helps organizations reduce cycle time to manufacture and deliver product

■ Improves customer service

▲ Moves customers, suppliers, and your organization toward a "paperless" environment

Furthermore, your customers may demand that you use EDI, because that's how they do business. Some customers have been known to charge a $50 fee per paper purchase order. With some companies, not using EDI in their supply chains can add thousands of dollars in costs each year. In the worst case, some businesses may simply refuse to do business with you if you don't use EDI.

EDI and the "Traditional" Business Model

EDI is an important component in the working business model of many industries. EDI cuts down on mistakes, transmission times, and the amount of staff required to process the transactions. For instance, as shown in Figure 14-2, a store can use EDI to adjust inventory levels every time a cashier scans the barcode on an item. Using this information, the store can pass on stocking levels to its suppliers, thereby shifting the burden of stocking shelves to its suppliers, and can pay its suppliers based on how quickly their products sell at the store. By using EDI, the suppliers get instant feedback about how well their products are doing. This allows the supplier to develop a closer working relationship with their large retail customers.

Retailers often use EDI in conjunction with electronic funds transfer (EFT) so that they can credit money to a supplier as soon as that supplier's new product arrives. EFT is a type of EDI using proprietary file formats that send payment transactions between banks.

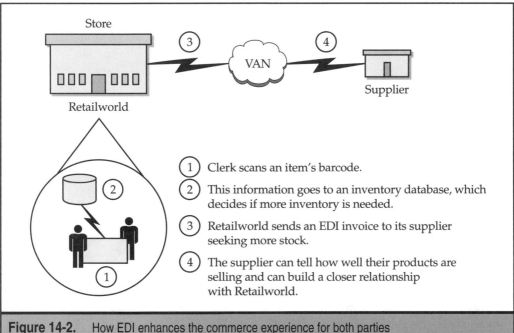

Figure 14-2.   How EDI enhances the commerce experience for both parties

NOTE: Using EFT doesn't assure that the money will immediately be available to the supplier. The banks involved in the transactions have their own rules governing deposits and fund transfers.

Just as retailers rely on EDI to keep their shelves stocked, car makers use EDI as a key part of their business models to apply just-in-time (JIT) manufacturing. Each car maker gets thousands of parts from several hundred suppliers, and an assembly line might stock only two or three days' worth of inventory. Because of the routinely low level of inventory, it would be disastrous to rely on paper invoices to keep all these parts in stock. The suppliers receive paperless EDI purchase orders from the manufacturer, and then provide parts as needed. This arrangement, like the one in the retail shop example, shifts the inventory burden from the store onto the supplier. The car maker pays its suppliers for the inventory the manufacturer uses on its assembly line, thereby shifting inventory issues to the suppliers.

Big Businesses

As you can probably construe from all this, EDI in its traditional form is best suited to big business. After all, the transmission form standards for an industry are largely created by whichever company is the first to need a particular form. Further, the costs related to EDI can be rather high and are only suited for larger businesses.

The ability to streamline the procurement process and reduce inventory saves large organizations millions of dollars each year. Furthermore, items can be ordered, constructed, and shipped in a fraction of the time that it would take in an organization mired down in paperwork.

Small Businesses

In the traditional functioning of EDI, small and medium-sized businesses were ill suited for EDI. The greatest hurdle was that the cost of EDI was prohibitive for virtually every small business. But beyond the cost, manpower issues kept EDI out of small and medium-sized businesses' reach. Large companies maintain full-time EDI staff for the ongoing management of translation systems and auditing of the operation. EDI VAN-based systems, because of their complexity and cost, exclude small and medium-sized businesses from participation in automated trading communities.

But the Internet changes all that. Not only is it an omnipresent network that provides inexpensive connectivity, but EDI functions are being packaged in a large number of B2B software applications. This means that paperless, inventory-friendly ordering and supply management is within the grasp of any business—no matter how large or how small.

The Rough Side of EDI

As nice an arrangement as EDI represents, it isn't the cure-all for every business. EDI in its traditional form is truly aimed at large organizations that have the resources to manage it. Although EDI is great at reducing staffing levels, it requires its own, specialized staff for unique duties, such as:

▼   Managing transactions

■   Negotiating the communications standards with partner organizations

▲   Building and maintaining the EDI infrastructure

But the biggest wall to EDI may be its cost. An EDI hub costs about $1 million to create, and its spokes cost about $45,000 each. Clearly, EDI will not garner any revenue savings in the short term, nor is it geared toward the small or mid-sized business.

The Details

As much time as EDI saves on the back end, a considerable amount of time is spent developing and implementing your EDI solution. You can spend several months getting communications between you and your EDI partner up to speed. Another key issue is that there are many different proprietary and general forms of EDI transactions. Mappings between business partners can be unique and won't necessarily work with any other partner. Though EDI has grown more standardized in recent years, many proprietary forms still exist.

NOTE: We talk more about EDI standards later in this chapter.

Other Issues

As with so many aspects of marrying business with technology, the day-to-day functions and operations are not solely the responsibility of the IT department. Sending EDI transactions between organizations is typically a business function. For a successful EDI implementation, business managers must be involved and knowledgeable about the project. Technically speaking, EDI isn't especially complex or convoluted, but many EDI projects fail when responsibility is thrust wholly on the IT staff.

EDI can be a good solution for big businesses that can afford the investment. However, the emergence of the Internet is making paperless invoicing a much easier process to grasp.

The Internet, EDI, and Modern Business

Though VANs represented a considerable expense for an organization, the Internet provides a low-cost, far-reaching network for your EDI solution. As such, it is changing the established model traditionally used for EDI. Because of these worldwide technology enhancements, the Internet offers businesses exciting new opportunities to communicate with their partners.

More Availability for Small and Medium Businesses

EDI over the Internet makes EDI more accessible to small and mid-sized businesses, but it isn't likely that EDI will displace existing VANs. VANs are used to exchange high-volume information. Unfortunately, as we discussed earlier in this book, the Internet proper can't guarantee sufficient bandwidth for organizations to exchange high-volume EDI traffic. Further, you can't always predict exactly when data sent across the Internet will arrive, so auditing and verification systems are needed. A mechanism is also needed to ensure good Quality of Service (QoS) across your EDI network (for more information about QoS, see Chapters 8 and 9). Table 14-1 shows the trade-offs between VANs and Internet connections.

In the past, EDI development was largely in the hands of the businesses developing their respective EDI solutions. In the Internet era, however, the Electronic Data Interchange-Internet Integration (EDIINT) working group, which is part of the Internet Engineering Task Force (IETF), is developing technology for implementing Internet EDI. EDIINT is addressing concerns including:

▼ Internet message integrity

■ Confidentiality

■ Digital signatures

▲ Nonrepudiation of data transfer

In the coming years, the traditional model of EDI is expected to represent only a small part of the business conducted across the Internet. The EDI market is expected to reach $1.9 billion by the end of 2000, and the total of B2B commerce over the Internet is expected to reach $134 billion. Both of these markets were at about the same size ($1 billion) in 1996. As you can see, Internet commerce is expanding at a much greater rate than EDI, and the greatest potential for growth in EDI is over the Internet.

Developing an EDI solution across the Internet can be as simple and straightforward as creating Web-based forms for supply-chain partners to access and enter data. When a partner submits the form, it's a simple matter to translate the data into EDI output. The translation application is built into the software, so the only thing you need is a Web browser. The benefit of this approach to EDI is that it eliminates the need to learn and maintain complex software and the need to subscribe to a private network that is expensive and that a small or medium-sized business would use only occasionally.

For large companies, the growing popularity of the Internet is causing organizations to create Web-based EDI transactions, while leaving their legacy VAN-based EDI traffic

	Cost	Immediacy
VAN	High	Yes
Internet	Low	No

Table 14-1.   The Pros and Cons of VANs Versus the Internet

intact. Most companies starting from scratch are implementing linked intranets that support both Internet and VAN traffic.

EDI in Action

One company enabling a new way to conduct EDI business transactions is Commerce One. With its Global Trading Web—a joint venture with several international telecom companies—access is created to worldwide markets, allowing any subscribing business to buy from any other subscribing business, any time and anywhere. Trading takes place across the network and via Web browsers, which enables trading on a multitude of platforms and from any location.

The Global Trading Web is composed of many interoperating e-marketplaces, which run on Commerce One's MarketSite Portal solution. Each e-business marketplace is independently owned and operated by a leading business in a region or industry. The companies use the sites for their own purchases and offer the service to their customers. The standardization of trading procedures enables the companies to interact more easily as they further develop their procurement sites.

The members share an average of $1 U.S. for each transaction conducted through the portals. The Global Trading Web can be used by a variety of buying and selling applications, including Commerce One's BuySite or applications from Oracle, Intershop, RightWorks, and SAP AG.

One example of the Commerce One network in action is with computer manufacturer Compaq. The Commerce One MarketSite Global Trading Portal service enables e-business functions from purchasing to auctions.

In addition to Compaq's B2B needs, the company also will resell Commerce One's BuySite Enterprise Edition application for customers requiring an internal buying application. The arrangement also allows customers to browse, order, receive, and customize Compaq's commercial desktops, notebooks, servers, and storage methods through a single site. Further, the arrangement also allows supplier catalog content and auction services to be provided through the portal, enabling Compaq's customers to purchase products and services from hundreds of existing and future suppliers.

VPNs

Using a VAN is not cheap, but one of the key advantages is that the VAN can be used to secure EDI transmissions, and your supply-chain partners can encrypt and authenticate the traffic. Conversely, sending EDI transmissions across the Internet is inexpensive, but the packets are more vulnerable for a bandit to intercept and examine. To secure this information as it is sent across the Internet, many organizations encrypt and digitally sign EDI traffic.

One approach to securing EDI traffic is to send it across a virtual private network (VPN). As shown in Figure 14-3, VPNs may use point-to-point tunneling to stave off attackers and eliminate data interception.

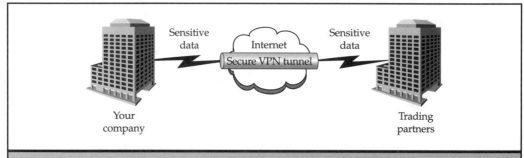

Figure 14-3. VPNs provide a secure tunnel through the insecure Internet

When using a VPN, you compress and encrypt your transmitted and received data. In essence, you create a tunnel between yourself and your supply-chain partner by opening a named IP port at the receiver, but only for the duration of the transmission.

NOTE: For more information about VPNs, flip back to Chapter 7.

What's Next for EDI?

If yours is an organization that wants to pursue EDI, you'll find that many third-party vendors (among them Microsoft, iPlanet, and webMethods) are incorporating EDI tools into e-business packages. Further, many organizations are creating EDI traffic that crosses the Internet. Because of the Internet's bandwidth limitations, VANs will likely be with us for quite a while, especially in established organizations. However, Internet commerce applications that support EDI are likely to afford the greatest future growth for document interchange, especially for low-volume traffic that small and mid-sized businesses would need.

DATA SHARING

At the heart of all EDI transactions is the ability to share data between two different computer systems. As Figure 14-4 shows, your individual hardware is irrelevant. Whether you have a Sun workstation and your supply-chain partner uses a PC is immaterial—communications can still work if the computers are speaking the same language. By the same token, you could both be using PCs, but if they're not speaking the same language, your efforts to share business information are stymied.

In this section, we'll talk about the different ways that your computers can talk with other computers under the umbrella of EDI. The most basic way to communicate is

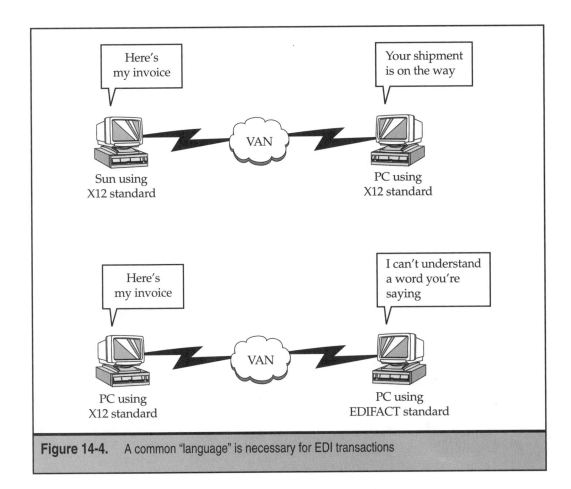

Figure 14-4. A common "language" is necessary for EDI transactions

through a set of standards. These standards were developed decades ago but remain the cornerstone of EDI communications. However, a popular new Internet technology called Extensible Markup Language (XML) is making the process of interbusiness communication more accessible. Let's look at how standards and XML affect EDI communications.

Standards

For years, business data has been exchanged electronically in a number of ways, including via tapes and disks and across computer networks. And, as companies have realized the time and money savings from exchanging computer data instead of reams of requisition forms, electronic transactions between customer and supplier have become more and more popular.

As serendipitous as this arrangement seems, simply transmitting a request to a supplier is complicated. Though the end result is of mutual benefit (one sells something and another gets needed inventory), each organization has different document needs and different computer and communications media.

The obvious solution is that electronic communications needed to be standardized. To that end, there are two different standards sets that are prominent in EDI: X12 and UN/EDIFACT.

X12

You may be thinking, "Wasn't the X12 what Chuck Yeager used to break the sound barrier?" Actually, that was the X1. X12, on the other hand, is the most common standard used in EDI transmissions.

In 1979, the American National Standards Institute (ANSI) asked the Accredited Standards Committee (ASC) X12 to create a set of standards that would assist the electronic exchange of business information. These standards define the data formats and encoding rules required for a multitude of business transactions, including:

▼ Order placement and processing

■ Shipping and receiving

■ Invoicing

▲ Payment

The core of the X12 standards is the simple data element dictionary. A simple data element represents the smallest named item in the X12 standards. It can identify a qualifier, a value, or a description. Examples of simple data elements include:

▼ Invoice date

■ Weight

■ Color

■ Hazardous material classification

▲ A unit of measurement (pounds, dozens, cubic feet, gallons, and so on)

Industries tend to adopt a general standard such as X12 and add appropriate descriptors, unless a standard already exists. Some industries even implement several different EDI transaction sets to meet various customer demands. As of 1997, for example, Hewlett-Packard was transmitting one million EDI transactions per month with 1,000 suppliers. Companies transmitting this many transactions can contract this administrative work to another company that specializes in EDI, but many companies perform this work internally.

Most industries use a subset of the X12 standards. Table 14-2 lists some of the major industry X12 subsets.

In America, X12 is the prevailing standard. Most likely, when you're developing an EDI solution, the standard you will use is a subset of X12.

X12 Subset	Industry
AFPA	Paper industry
CIDX	Chemical industry
WINS	Warehouse industry
TDCC	Transportation industry
VICS	Retail industry

Table 14-2.   X12 Standard Subsets for a Sampling of Industries

UN/EDIFACT

Just as you can't go to Canada or Europe and drive in miles per hour, international EDI transactions have their own standards. I suspect this is just another way to inconvenience Americans (like the metric system), but the official story is that it was developed to respond to European needs.

In an effort to create a single international EDI format, the United Nations Economic Commission for Europe Working Party on Facilitation of International Trade Procedures (you can take a breath now) drew concepts from X12 and other formats to create the UN/EDIFACT family of standards. The EDIFACT standard was adopted by the International Organization for Standardization (ISO) in 1987.

X12 and its "metric" cousin EDIFACT are very similar in the functions they perform. For instance, both define a purchase order. Although X12 is a more mature format and provides functions not present in EDIFACT (such as acknowledgments and security), many of these functions are likely to be upgraded in a future EDIFACT standard.

X12 and EDIFACT differ in their underlying structures. There is no one-to-one correlation between the X12 and EDIFACT data elements to aid translation. Often, multiple X12 data elements are needed to represent one EDIFACT data element. The differences between X12 and EDIFACT formats make interoperation difficult, if not impossible.

NOTE: Rather than attempt some sort of technical synchronicity between the diffuse standards, the ASC X12 has decided to vote every three years whether to move toward the EDIFACT format and standards.

XML

Another approach for opening EDI standards is using XML. The XML/EDI project was proposed in mid-1998 and is picking up steam across all industries that use EDI. Because EDI depends on being able to exchange pricing and product information along a supply chain, the Extensible Markup Language (XML) is well suited for the task, since XML was designed to send data that is translated and applied to specific machines and devices—not unlike Java.

Cross-Platform Operability

As with Java, one of XML's greatest traits is its ability to work on a variety of platforms. XML is useful because a document can be written once and then displayed on many different computer systems.

XML is also designed so that the content can be displayed on a variety of products, such as a cellular-phone display or a device for the blind (where it is translated into voice). This isn't currently a means of EDI interaction, but never say never when technology is concerned.

But the immediate benefit of XML is its capability to work on a variety of machines, as shown in Figure 14-5. XML was created so that richly structured documents—like those used in an EDI transaction—could be used over the Internet. The only viable alternatives—Hypertext Markup Language (HTML) and Standard Generalized Markup Language (SGML)—are simply not robust enough to provide this functionality.

XML would not have been feasible five years ago because the processing power of computer systems was not sufficient to deal with the current sizes of data. One of the

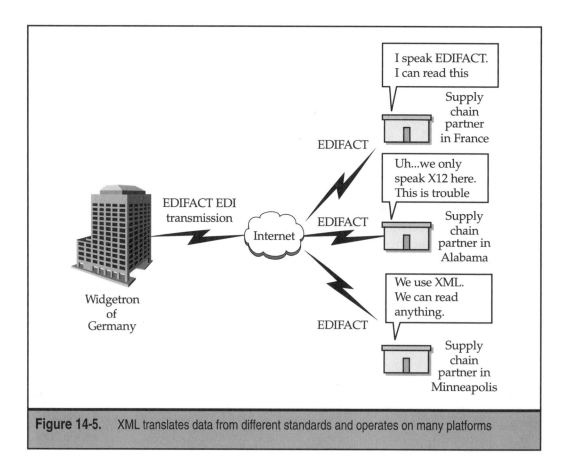

Figure 14-5.   XML translates data from different standards and operates on many platforms

biggest advantages of XML is the low cost to smaller businesses. Where an EDI solution can be very expensive, the arrival of XML makes it possible for a larger company to deliver its business transactions in traditional EDI and XML formats, where XML formats can be targeted to those suppliers who cannot handle EDI.

Elimination of Standards

Since specific data elements can be ferreted out by using document type definitions, the elements that are used to describe a supply-chain partner's product, size, color, or other attributes could be gleaned without first having to agree on mutually acceptable format.

Proprietary standards, including X12 and EDIFACT, could not use this kind of impromptu partnership. At best, an industry might define a subset of an EDI format or forms for specific kinds of transactions. Typically, these standards are created—out of necessity—by the largest organization in that industry. This newly created form becomes the de facto standard.

Combining the existing elements of EDI within an XML framework also makes complex e-business activities possible. Writing some agents (small software applications located on a client computer) in Java makes it possible for a transaction to have intricate behaviors depending on a multitude of desired outcomes. For example, an agent might use the structural information gleaned from the EDI catalogs of several different vendors to purchase larger amounts of a product if a price dips below a particular threshold.

Further, XML/EDI also uses the concept of a global dynamic repository. The repository serves as a dictionary that defines the rules of the terms used in a transaction. That repository would also be used to hold common document type definitions under the XML/EDI proposal.

In Practice

XML is already taking off across many different industries. One example of where XML is making EDI more effective is in the oil and gas industry. One of the XML initiatives undertaken by the Petrotechnical Open Software Corporation (POSC), along with Oilware and Wallace Burnett International, is an XML schema for the exchange of digital well log data. The result of that project is WellLogML. Version 1.0 of the WellLogML specification was published in April 2000 after extensive review by the oil and gas industry.

The following example is a piece of code from WellLogML version 1.0. This code snippet is used to group all of the nonmeasurement bits of information about a particular well. To get a better understanding of the code, the following key explains the variables:

- ▼ **(operatorName**   The name of the company that operates the well
- ■ **partnerName***   The name of a company that is a partner in the well
- ■ **wellName+**   One of the well's names
- ■ **wellPurpose?**   The initial purpose for drilling the well
- ■ **fieldName?**   The name of the field the well is located in
- ■ **WellLocation+**   The surface location of the well

■ **serviceCompanyName**   The name of the service company that generated the
well log data

▲ **comment?)**   A text remark, which applies in the context of its parent element

```
<!--=========================================================================-->
<!--                         WellInformation::WellInfo Section               -->
<!--=========================================================================-->
<!ELEMENT WellInfo (operatorName, partnerName*, wellName+, wellPurpose?,
  fieldName?, WellLocation+, serviceCompanyName, comment?)>

<!ELEMENT operatorName (#PCDATA)>

<!ELEMENT partnerName (#PCDATA)>

<!ELEMENT wellName (wellId, comment?)>
<!ATTLIST wellName
  type          (%wellNameType;)        #REQUIRED>

<!ELEMENT wellId (#PCDATA)>

<!ELEMENT wellPurpose (comment?)>
<!ATTLIST wellPurpose
  type          (%wellPurpose;)#REQUIRED>

<!ELEMENT fieldName (#PCDATA)>
```

XML is an exciting way to make sure that EDI transmissions can be sent across any
medium. It's especially useful for more and more businesses who want to enter into B2B
arrangements across the Internet.

MAKE YOUR EXISTING SOLUTION WORK WITH NEW TECHNOLOGY

Most organizations already have a computer network in place. Therefore, integrating
new components and software into your e-business solution will likely depend on what
you're already using. It's simply not cost effective—nor logical—to scrap everything and
start with a brand new network.

In this section, we talk about some of the issues related to melding your existing network with new e-business-oriented hardware and software. We'll talk about the hardware and software issues related to integration, along with how you can develop future
applications to work with an Internet-based EDI solution.

The Old with the New

Merging new hardware and software into an existing system can be daunting, but it isn't impossible. By the same token, don't take for granted that the process will be a smooth, effortless one.

Unless you have very recent equipment, it is likely that some components just won't work with the new system. One of the biggest issues that will dictate what kind of equipment you keep and which components you have to buy new is the software that you will be running.

If your organization requires a new operating system (OS), this is a prime example where your current system may need to be replaced with a new system.

On the other hand, if you intend to stick with your existing setup—for instance, if your organization uses a Windows NT environment—you are likely to look for software that would work with NT. This approach greatly reduces your integration problems, because you shouldn't have to buy new computers and change the way the entire organization does business. At most, you would want to upgrade to a Windows 2000 environment, which closely mirrors the NT system. By contrast, if you decided you wanted to put in a Sun solution, you would have to scrap your PCs and servers and replace them with Sun machines.

As you know, different operating systems and different applications require different platforms, different amounts of memory, and different processor speeds. If your organization is in a position where more memory is the only upgrade needed, it is easy enough to plug in another memory stick. If you're low on hard drive space, you can either add an additional hard drive or swap out the old drive and transfer the data to the new drive.

Figure 14-6 gives an example of what an existing computer network might need.

The larger problems occur when you have to add a different OS, or your computers, servers, or network infrastructure are so antiquated that performance and logistics demand that new equipment be purchased.

Migration

If you decide to move to a new computer system, you'll need to bring your data with you. This process is called *migration*. Migration can be either an easy process or a hard one. The difficulty comes when one has to migrate from one OS to a completely different OS. Individual OS vendors make migrating from an earlier version of their OS to the latest an easy process. After all, if they want to sell you their software, they want to make sure you can keep your old data.

But whatever OS you are converting to, there are some simple steps that can ameliorate some major migration problems:

▼   Standardize your entire network on the TCP/IP protocol. This is important because TCP/IP is the protocol of the Internet. By getting everyone on this protocol now, you will be ready when your system goes online.

■ Get an evaluation copy of the OS you're migrating to. Most companies have evaluation versions you can buy for a few bucks that will expire in a couple months. Set that OS up in a lab and test out your hardware and software on it. Depending on what happens, you'll know if the migration is worth your while and if your applications are going to work.

▲ Flatten out your topology. If your network is a huge, multitiered monster, see if there aren't any places where you can combine domains so that the relationships between domains aren't so complex. Doing so will allow you the most flexibility when you create your new domain.

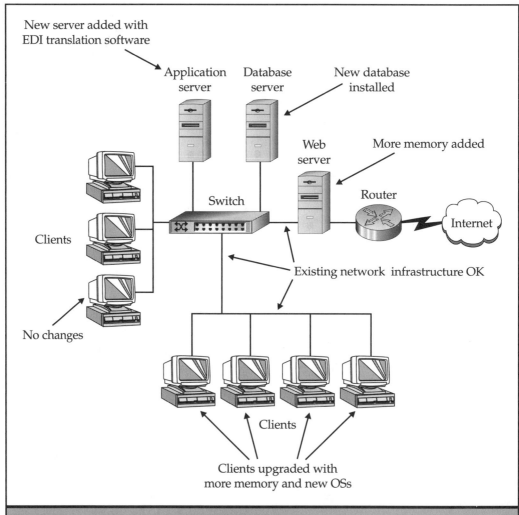

Figure 14-6.   Upgrading an existing computer system

Migration can be a hassle, but it is necessary if you are upgrading to a better OS. To avoid future migration pains, it wouldn't hurt to try to look ahead at the state of the industry and try to determine which OS will hang in there the longest. That way, if you stick with one type of OS, future migrations won't be so disruptive.

Also, it's important to decide if it is *really* important to upgrade to a new OS. It is ideal to work in a pure OS setting, but sometimes that's just not feasible, especially if you have computers that perform unique tasks that cannot be accomplished on another OS. Often, you can upgrade components of your network that will still work with the existing OS. In this mixed setting, you are likely to lose some functionality, but if it helps you retain more important tools and features, you may want to make that decision.

Interconnection

When you do decide to integrate your new e-business system into your legacy system, you have some important factors to consider. One of the most important factors, if you intend to keep your legacy equipment, is ensuring that the old and the new systems will be compatible. There's little use in buying new hardware and software with the intention of merging them with an existing network if they simply won't work together.

You should look at the hardware and the software of your existing system and make sure they will not only be compatible but also do the job that you need them to do.

Hardware   Almost certainly you will have to buy some hardware components. For instance, if you have never had a Web server before, you'll need to acquire one. However, if you discover that there is a server-class computer somewhere in your organization that can be drafted for the job, it can certainly be adapted to the task at a much lower cost than buying one.

You needn't scrap every bit of existing hardware in favor of a new system. For instance, if you decide that your client computers simply aren't capable of doing the job, you could probably just upgrade the computers, leaving the monitors in place. By not buying new monitors, you'll save a couple hundred dollars a shot.

However, you may have to make some hard fiscal choices. There may be equipment that simply must be upgraded, no matter how long you think it will hang in there. If your computer system is still programmed using punch cards, it's time to buy some new equipment. On the other hand, there are pieces of hardware that you can certainly keep and use with your new e-business network.

For instance, you can certainly keep networking hardware, assuming it is in good shape and will still meet your mission-critical needs. Let's take the example of using existing networking equipment. You're using a 10 Mbps Ethernet system, but your network traffic will increase considerably. Yes, you can still use the network, but when traffic levels get high, you'll experience a mess of bottlenecks and will have nothing but problems. On the other hand, if you have a 10 Mbps Ethernet system and your network traffic won't exceed those levels, then you can hang onto that equipment for a while.

Ultimately, however, you need to make sound decisions that will make your e-business successful. You can scrimp and save a couple bucks here and there, but in the end, if you've been too thrifty, you can expect trouble.

Software   If you are connecting into an existing EDI system, the software will be especially important. In the traditional model of EDI, the software was very rigid and expensive. However, with EDI's new life across the Internet, EDI translation software is reasonably affordable and easy to come by. Table 14-3 lists five vendors that offer EDI translation software.

The same caveats apply to software that apply to the general rules of upgrading. First and foremost, it's important to make sure that the software will be compatible with your existing system. Next, you have to make sure that the software will speak with your supply-chain partners' computers. This is where the X12 and EDIFACT standards come into play: remember, X12 and EDIFACT are the languages of EDI.

Another factor in selecting EDI software is deciding if it will work with your existing application software. The EDI software will be of little use to you if your back-office systems can't get the information from the software.

It wouldn't hurt to get software from the same vendor that you got the rest of your e-business applications from. For instance, Microsoft's BizTalk Server 2000 works seamlessly with its other Windows DNA products, such as SQL Server 2000 and Windows 2000 Server. Likewise, iPlanet's Commerce Xpert works with iPlanet's other applications for seamless data sharing.

Designing Web-Based EDI Applications

If you're ready to integrate your organization into an Internet-based EDI solution, there are two popular ways to do this using technology and processes we talked about earlier in this book. Both methods involve using a standard Web browser to take the EDI information from a customer, then transmitting it via the Internet to the purchaser.

Company	Web site
Sterling Commerce	www.sterlingcommerce.com
iPlanet	www.iplanet.com
Microsoft	www.microsoft.com
Perwill EDI	www.perwill.com
Peregrine	www.peregrine.com

Table 14-3.   EDI Translation Software Vendors

The two methods exemplified here—forms-based applications and intelligent Web clients—show different ends of the Web-enabled EDI spectrum. Your IT department's level of programming expertise and the degree to which you want to implement these solutions will tell you if you need a simple solution or something more complex.

Forms-Based Server Applications

With simple HTML programming, Web browser–viewable forms can be created. The browser acts as an interface to the sponsor's business applications. Once the forms are completed, the data is sent from the client to the server, and then the HTTP server sends the data through special interfaces or server application programming interfaces (APIs) to an external server program or to a dedicated Internet transaction server.

This EDI server translates the form data and forwards it to the sponsor's EDI business application. Finally, the script sends a transaction confirmation in the form of a dynamically created HTML page through the Web server, back to the browser.

A Web-based EDI program is a script, which provides predefined order forms for the client and then accepts the completed forms and converts the gathered information on the server side into the EDI standard format. This way, trading transactions are noted and data is passed on to the EDI business application. This process's structure is shown in Figure 14-7.

The communication between the Web client (your supply chain partner) and the Web server (your organization) is facilitated via HTTP and uses TCP/IP, which is the chief protocol used on the Internet.

The major advantage of this client/server architecture is the centralization of data and application management. Information can be selected on the server side and data— as well as functions—can be linked to unique user profiles. That means that specific data and functions can be applied to different supply chain partners.

Further, your server's components can be upgraded without affecting the client application. This means that your supply chain partner doesn't need a proprietary piece of software. Rather, they are able to use a standard Web browser. The downside of all this is that integration into internal business applications will be difficult, because they are accessed via a standard Web browser.

Intelligent Web Clients

The other type of Web client that you can use is a stand-alone application that utilizes an intelligent Web client. This requires more advanced technical skills: software engineering with experienced programming knowledge is necessary rather than crafting a Web site with an HTML editor, like FrontPage. Because more of the application's functionality is run on the client side, the server can be relieved of the processing tasks. With Java applets or ActiveX controls, portable, dynamic objects are employed on the client computer for specific functions, such as message translation.

This programming scheme reduces application development and deployment through prototyping, code reuse, and easier testing. Applications are adaptable to changing

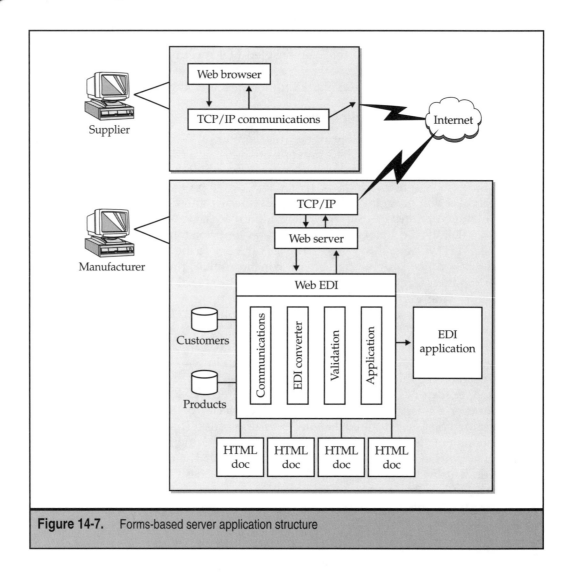

Figure 14-7.   Forms-based server application structure

business environments because users dynamically download program objects from individual organizations. Users with Java- or ActiveX-enabled Web browsers—like Microsoft Internet Explorer or Netscape Navigator—gain more flexibility and functionality. Additionally, easy-to-use graphical user interfaces make the process easier for the users. The overall functionality is even further improved when operating systems and these techniques are integrated together.

Figure 14-8 shows how a Java implementation of Web-based EDI works.

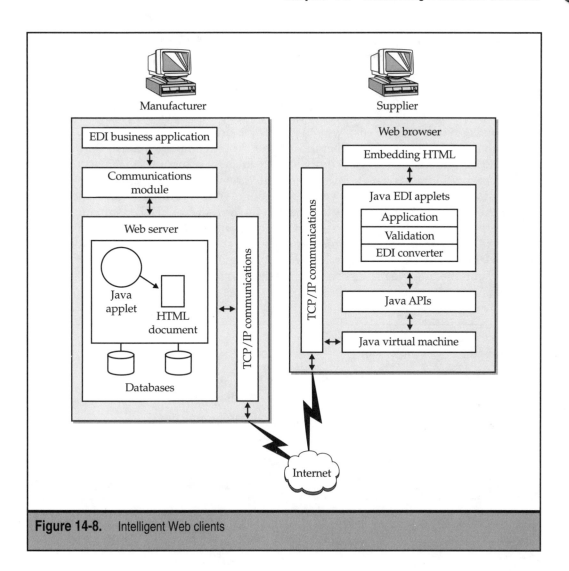

Figure 14-8.   Intelligent Web clients

As we mentioned in Chapter 5, Java is a software platform that delivers and runs dynamic applets or applications on internetworked computer systems. It resides on top of the common application platform. The Java code is machine independent and runs on a machine-specific Java virtual machine. Simply put, a program object written in Java and then compiled to a bytecode file can run on any operating system that runs a Java virtual machine. The two basic Java platform parts are the Java virtual machine and the Java application programming interface (Java API). Combined, these two components provide an end-user run-time environment for deploying Internet applications.

Outsourcing

It's simply not possible to integrate your existing system with an EDI solution overnight. If the task is beyond you, an easy way to get the job done is to hire an EDI service company to manage EDI transactions over the Internet. These companies consult to build and manage EDI solutions. EDI service companies are ideal for companies that just don't have the necessary resources to create and manage their own EDI solution.

Also, these companies can help you set up your own EDI solution. All you need do is write a check and click the Send button. Table 14-4 lists several EDI consultants.

Integrating your existing system with a new e-business solution is not a simple task. It requires planning from both a technical and a business standpoint. However, the payoff of EDI is fantastic. Whether you're ready to develop an EDI solution now or in the future, the Internet is making the process so much easier and so much less expensive.

Consultant	Contact
Research Triangle Commerce, Inc.	www.rtci.com
DLA Systems Consultants, Inc.	www.dlasys.com
Milgram Group	www.milgram.com
AT&T Global Network Services	www.att.com

Table 14-4. Some EDI Implementation Consultants

CHAPTER 15

E-Commerce Application
Service Providers

In previous chapters, we have looked in depth at issues such as configuring your own e-business server, WANs, LANs, and network security. In this chapter, we take a step back and ask, "Isn't there an easier way?"

The answer is a clear "maybe." Depending on your needs, an application service provider (ASP) could be the right solution for you. Or it may be better to build and maintain your own e-commerce site, or you can mix and match. An application service provider will deliver a standardized e-commerce software package from a remote data center for a rental fee. Your administrative staff is responsible for the content of the site. Thus you can avoid the costs of technical staff and expensive hardware. The ASP has to worry about software and hardware upgrades. You don't have to worry about the frustrating process of installing a new system. All of these services are provided for a fixed monthly fee, so you know what your costs are.

INTRODUCTION TO APPLICATION SERVICE PROVIDERS

The ASP option *could* save you lots of time, money, and headaches while you concentrate on running your business instead of managing a software development project and then operating a data center and an IT department. However, things are never quite as easy as they seem. As with any form of outsourcing, using an ASP means that you have less control over your data and less flexibility than you would with a system you build and maintain for yourself. Also, while you won't have to manage a technical staff, you will have to manage the relationship with the vendor.

What Is an ASP?

Before we go any further, let's make sure we know just what an ASP is. Since late in the last century, the computer trade press has been filled with stories about a whole New World emerging because of the booming ASP market. Worldwide ASP services revenue is projected to grow from $889 million in 1998 to $22.7 billion in 2003, according to Dataquest Inc. of San Jose, California. An analyst with Giga Information Group of Cambridge, Massachusetts, told the authors that by the year 2004 all software would be rented from application service providers.

Other observers challenge this glowing picture. Peter Slavid, a strategic analyst for ICL, a global IT services provider based in London, believes that the size of the ASP market is exaggerated. In ASPNews.com he wrote, "It is not easy to tell which types of business are included in the current market projections for ASP. I suspect that another large part comes from the 're-branding' of existing outsourcing contracts."

Before exploring this amazing New World any further, let's define what it is. A "pure" application service provider will deliver a standardized e-commerce software package from a remote data center for a rental fee. The client accesses these services through a wide area network (it may be the Internet or a private network). The client's data resides on the service provider's hardware, and the client pays a fee for use of the software.

The key features that distinguish the ASP from other forms of application software vendors are these:

▼ The application resides on a remote hardware platform operated by your vendor.

■ It is a standard application package with little or no customization.

▲ It is accessed through a wide area network.

For example, let's say your Seattle-based business sells hand-made guitars and accessories. You have decided to use an ASP for your e-commerce system. The e-commerce software and the database containing your product, sales, and order information sits on a server farm somewhere in Kansas. Customers in Tokyo, London, and Ottawa use the Internet to come to your Web site to place orders. Their orders are created and stored on the database in Kansas. When an order is made, a file with the information is sent to your office along with an e-mail notice to your order-processing department, which begins working on the order. Each month you pay a fee for the service. Promoting the Web site, fulfilling the order, and collecting on the invoice are all up to you.

As Figure 15-1 shows, using an ASP can be compared to shopping at a department store. In most towns and cities, if you want to get a new shirt, some jogging shoes, a set of earrings, and a new album by your favorite musician, you have two options. You can go to a clothing store, a shoe store, a jewelry store, and a music store, or you can go to a department store and get one-stop shopping. An ASP is really a package of hardware, software, communications, and data center services that you buy from a single vendor. This package can be taken apart and bought piece by piece. The vendors who provide the pieces include:

▼ Independent software vendors who produce applications software. In our case, we are talking about e-commerce applications. This includes electronic selling (e-tailing or e-stores), electronic procurement, and electronic collections and payments (also known as electronic data interchange or EDI).

■ System integrators and consulting companies who provide implementation and ongoing support that is necessary for all but the most standardized software packages.

■ Internet service providers (ISPs) who provide access to the Internet or network service providers who can set up your own private network.

▲ Data center operators who perform services such as Web hosting, database hosting and maintenance, back up and disaster recovery, virus protection, data security, and 24-hour operation of the hardware and operating systems, all of which you need to run your applications.

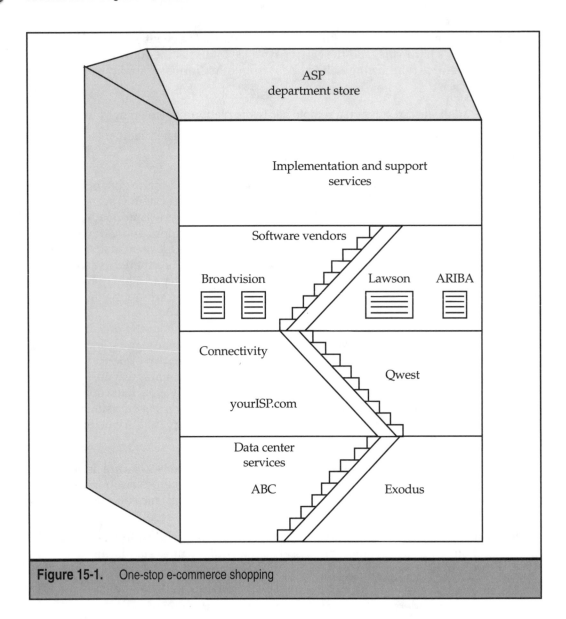

Figure 15-1. One-stop e-commerce shopping

Applications Software

Application service providers can theoretically provide software for any business task from highly specialized engineering design to general accounting systems to the latest versions of Word or Lotus Notes. However, our discussion will be limited to providers of e-commerce packages. This usually means retailing or selling through an e-store. What this actually involves is a number of processes. The first includes capturing the order, often through "shopping cart" software that allows a person to order multiple items. The order is then encrypted and sent to a secure server, which validates the customer's credit card and his or her address. Order notification is sent to your business either as e-mail or as a record to your order entry system. The funds are transferred to your bank account, usually within 24 hours. This all sounds wonderful and it is, but getting it set up takes a lot of work. Then you still have to do business the old-fashioned way and get the right order to the right customer.

Selling on the Net

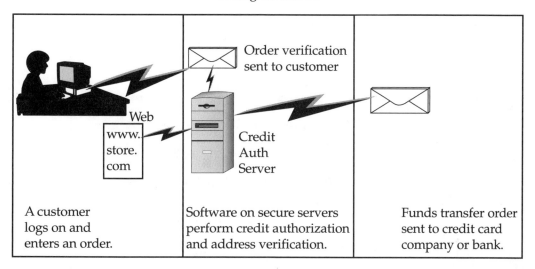

| A customer logs on and enters an order. | Software on secure servers perform credit authorization and address verification. | Funds transfer order sent to credit card company or bank. |

Selling over the Internet is getting so much attention that businesspeople often ignore e-procurement. Businesses always want to expand their customer base. The lure of hundreds of millions of customers on the Internet is a strong force pulling businesses into e-commerce. However, many businesses are being pushed into it for another reason. If your business supplies products or services to large corporations, you are or soon will be pressured to interface with their electronic procurement systems. Many corporations are telling their suppliers, "Become compatible with our systems or we will find someone else who is." Software is now available to translate your order and invoice data into formats that are compatible with the systems of your customers. As of the writing of this book, the price for sophisticated e-procurement software was in the $150,000 range, out of reach of most small and mid-sized businesses. However, an ASP could provide a solution for a fraction of this cost.

Some of the best-known independent software vendors (ISVs) who produce e-commerce applications are included in Table 15-1. However, a word of caution. There are many different systems and packages. These companies and their Web sites are listed as examples to give readers an idea of what is available. It is a long and confusing journey from browsing an ISV Web site to deciding what application to choose for your business. The rest of this chapter are designed to help dispel some of this confusion.

Name	Home Page	Description
BroadVision	www.broadvision.com	A leading supplier of personalized e-commerce products to businesses.
Commerce One	www.commerceone.com	Through its products, portals, and services, creates access to worldwide markets.
Ariba	www.ariba.com	Ariba business-to-business solutions are designed for ordering supplies and regulating operating resources.

Table 15-1. Some Large E-commerce Software Suppliers

Implementation and Ongoing Support Services

A well-designed software application can be easy to use and a great boon to your business. Unless you have experienced staff, however, implementation of that software package can be a major headache. Often software requires experts for maintenance and ongoing support, even if only to install new releases or provide training on new features. Keeping an expert on staff can be expensive. Finding a consultant at the right time can be problematic. So using an ASP for such support is often a good option. However, when choosing any consultant, remember three features of good consultants:

▼ They are good listeners and willing to learn about *your* business.

■ They are willing to transfer skills and teach you how to run the system without them.

▲ They are technically skilled, but even more important, they are quick learners.

Internet Service Providers

Another piece of the package is the communications software and hardware that connect you to the Internet. Other chapters in this book explore in detail how you can set up your own Internet communications and Web-hosting infrastructure. An ISP can also do this for you. Depending on your needs, they may be able to provide the service for you quicker and more economically than you can with a do-it-yourself connection. The trade-offs are control over the system and flexibility of fit. Even though a custom-tailored shirt is more expensive, it fits better than a one-size-fits-all model.

Data Center Services

People often speak of the World Wide Web as a virtual world existing somewhere out there and picture the Web as an enchanting if often frustrating land. However, even the most innovative and flashy Web site always gets down to physical bits and bytes residing in memory and on disks in a real data center housed in an ordinary bricks-and-mortar building. Someone has to keep the hardware humming and the power supply constant, maintain the air conditioning, upgrade the systems software, and do the ten thousand other tasks necessary to operate an up-to-date data center. Contracting out for this service relieves you of a lot of headaches and expenses. Very often application service providers themselves contract with other companies to build and maintain their data centers.

The preceding paragraphs have given you a nuts-and-bolts description of the application service provider concept, but the ASP industry is in a state of flux. There are mergers and new start-ups every day. Table 15-2 gives you some sources to get information on the latest developments in this sector. As always, the best information is that which you discover through your own experience; this table provides you with a starting point.

Name	Type	Address	Notes
Ambit	Seminars & expos	www.aspexpo.com	Ambit International advises computer industry clients on marketing and produces seminars and expos.
ASP Industry News	News & Analysis	www.ASPIndustryNews.com	Trade journal and Web site for the ASP Industry.
ASPIsland.com	News & Analysis	www.ASPIsland.com	Good explanations of the ASP model along with many press releases from ASP companies. Part of Internet.com.
ASPnews.com	News & analysis	www.ASPnews.com	Columns by analysts such as Peter Slavid and Laurie McCabe look at the industry with a critical eye. Part of Internet.com.
Web Harbor	ASP Industry Portal	www.WebHarbor.com	Look for their list of industry analysts who provide white papers on the ASP industry. Allied with ASP Industry News.

Table 15-2.   Some Sources of Background Information on Application Service Providers

NOTE: These sources are listed as examples. There are many other sources of information. In fact, there is much too much information from sources that are often connected to vendors. Remember to analyze every new and amazing claim carefully and ask how it can help your business.

Service Providers for Every Need

As we have seen, an application service provider offers one-stop shopping for many goods and services. However, there are still other options. These include total outsourcing to a business solutions provider and working with an industry portal.

Business Solutions Providers

Unlike an ASP, a business solutions provider (BSP) provides services in addition to the software. If you want to outsource the whole e-commerce piece of your business, a BSP will do it all for you. In the guitar maker example, an e-commerce provider would own and operate a Web site that would sell your guitars. Although detailed arrangements would vary, the BSP would take care of marketing, order processing, collections, and shipping. All you would have to do is make the guitars and have them ready for the shipper.

The advantage of the BSP is that everything is taken care of for you and you can concentrate on your core business. However, while you don't always get what you pay for, you always pay for what you get. Basically you are giving up the retail portion of your profits and becoming a wholesaler as far as the electronic marketplace is concerned. The key issues are how big is the provider's margin, how much more volume will come your way, and will that added volume increase your net profits.

Web Portals

A good option for marketing your wares on the Web is a vertical industry portal. A portal is a doorway to a community of interest. The Web is so huge and unstructured by nature that it is very difficult for the e-commerce site of a single manufacturer to get much attention. It is a bit like a craftsman who makes wonderful guitars setting up shop on a side street in a huge city like London, Calcutta, or San Francisco. The craftsman then stands outside her or his shop and shouts to passersby about how good the guitars are and wonders why so few people come in to shop. The problem is that most passersby are on their way to buy shoes or bread and couldn't care less about guitars. Before the advent of shopping malls, craftsmen and business people of one kind set up shop in the same district of the city. Customers then came down their street, but it was still up to the individual business owner to pull them into their store and distinguish their product or service from their competitors'.

Vertical industry portals work much the same way as a shopping district. For example, guitarsite.com pulls together information on guitar manufacturers, musicians from the Stones to Segovia, trends in the music industry, and almost anything that could be of interest to professional and amateur guitarists.

Some portals primarily offer businesses a marketing service. Others offer services such as Web hosting and design. Still others act like online commodity exchanges and meet all the needs of both buyers and sellers. For example, a seller of plastic resin can use the American Plastics Exchange (APEXQ) to make an offer and get a confirmed buy order within two hours. *APEXQ* will provide information on price, quantity, and quality to buyers. It will forecast shipping charges, confirm orders, and expedite payments all over the Web.

Table 15-3 refers to several application service providers that have produced results for their clients. These are just a few examples of the thousands of providers in the industry, but it will give you somewhere to start looking.

NOTE: The businesses listed here are merely examples of service providers. They are all relatively new start-ups in a fast-changing marketplace. At the time of publication, the authors see them as good examples of ASP vendors. The authors and publishers are not in any way endorsing these businesses or encouraging the reader to use their services.

Is Outsourcing a Part of the Solution or a New Set of Problems?

The answer, of course, is that it is both. The ASP vendor can help you manage your e-commerce problems, but you need to know how to manage the vendor. Vendor management is not a simple task. Before we examine the trees (what's involved in operating individual sites), let's take a look at this forest.

We are looking at the various service provider options as a means of outsourcing your e-commerce applications. The proponents for outsourcing always say that a specialized supplier can provide you with the goods quicker, easier, and cheaper. Every time someone tries to sell you something, you have to remember the unofficial motto of the state of Missouri and say to the sellers, "Show me."

Name	Address	Notes
Ejump-start.com	www.ejump-start.com	Means to jump-start small businesses into using the Internet.
Jamcracker	www.jamcracker.com	Has all sorts of software applications available for businesses.
Wizmo.com	www.wizmo.com	Includes a simple do-it-yourself package for very small businesses as well as sophisticated systems for all sizes of companies.

Table 15-3.   A Few Examples of E-Commerce Service Providers

There are many downsides to outsourcing your applications. These include:

▼ Loss of control

■ Security issues

▲ Lack of flexibility

Loss of control over your e-commerce applications has several implications. Renting software is like renting a home; you pay to use it for a specified amount of time and then you may be out on the street with no roof over your head. Building your own system can be expensive, but the software is yours. Also, if you have software problems, you have the ability to fix them. Neither option is cheap, so which option makes the most dollars-and-sense for you depends on the particular conditions of your business. If you have a capable IT department and you know their work, consider putting your trust in them; bringing in outside vendors can open you to potential problems in getting them to deliver what they have promised.

Another big issue is security. Look into the quality of the vendor's firewalls, their virtual private network, and their encryption techniques. However, technical issues are only part of the problem. Depending on the sensitivity of the applications information that you will be handing over to them, a bigger issue is, can you trust the vendor's security procedures? How will they protect you from careless or ill-intentioned employees?

And, again depending on your needs, loss of flexibility may be a red flag when going for the service provider option. Salespeople will always promise the moon, but if you need a truly custom-built application, then look for a provider that will put customization into your contract. Remember, customization is not the norm for an ASP.

In later sections, we will look in more detail at the issues involved in picking vendors. We will develop some guidelines on how to distinguish the bull from its own waste products. However, as in every buying decision, the first thing is to really know what you want.

WHO SHOULD CONSIDER USING AN ASP?

When the carpenters and bricklayers were building your storefront, they knew which tool to use for every job. Building your e-store is no different. The ASP solution is an excellent tool, but it is not for everyone. Instead of one tool, it is a bag of tools, and the tools in the bag are designed for a variety of needs. Some ASP e-commerce packages are ideal for small businesses that have a limited number of products and want to get them into the electronic marketplace as soon as possible. Many of these can be implemented in a half-day's work, and some are free of charge (see Wizmo.com in Table 15-2). Other ASP solutions require guidance in installing them and extensive training to use them. Still, they can be operated by a trained layperson and don't require a programming staff. And some packages are extremely sophisticated and require a team of experts to implement and support them. Many vendors offer a range of solutions. The free sites are loss leaders to attract small businesses and e-commerce beginners. The vendor hopes that they will remain customers as their business and e-commerce needs grow.

Definitely look into the ASP e-commerce packages if:

▼   You are a small business with a limited number of products

■   You are a mid-sized business just entering the electronic marketplace and lack the technical skills

▲   You have a limited budget for e-commerce (less than $50,000 in U.S. dollars)

Strongly question the service provider approach if:

▼   You plan to use your e-commerce site as a competitive edge

■   You have a need for large-scale customization of a package

▲   You are uncomfortable with managing vendors

There is a lot to consider before jumping on the ASP bandwagon. However, there is only so much you can look at on a theoretical level. In the following section, we will look at case studies of businesses that have used the ASP approach to their advantage.

EXAMPLES OF BUSINESSES THAT HAVE "ASP'ED"

These cases are based on a series of interviews, but the companies' names have been changed. Some examples are composites of several situations. However, all cases are based on real-life challenges. One supplier went beyond e-tailing and used an ASP to become a vertical portal for its customers, who could now get into the e-commerce game for themselves. Another company found that the preparation for selling online was very costly. The owners of the company did a lot of their own preparatory work and with the help of an ASP they were able to keep the costs down. Another business-person was at the height of a long climb to success when she suddenly faced a crisis. Her major corporate clients all told her she had to develop computer interfaces for their various e-procurement systems or lose their business.

Build Your Own Portal

SPI, a specialty office products supplier, sells over 8,000 office products to veterinarians across the country. For fifty years they have been taking mail and phone orders, sending sales people to offices, advertising in professional journals, and selling through direct mail. When they decided to go online, they knew that all of these sales efforts would continue. They would just have one more vehicle to communicate with their customers.

SPI analysts worked with consultants from a company that also provides application-hosting services. They formed a team to analyze their e-marketing strategy. Because they knew the market well, there was no need to do outside market research. The team analyzed SPI's customer base of over 80,000 vets. They analyzed the history in their sales database and surveyed their customers to find out their buying patterns and preferences. They had a very accurate picture of the degree of Internet connectivity in their market. The team analyzed the SPI product line and the additional services they offered their phone order customers. They developed a plan for phone support of the proposed Web site. Drawing on this work, they designed their Web site. The ASP vendor built it using a modular approach. The pages were designed using a template, and 90 percent of the site used packaged software. However, SPI wanted the Web site to match their catalog in appearance as closely as possible. They wanted the "shopping cart" software to resemble their current order forms. The vendor built a front end to the e-commerce package that met the needs of SPI. The site now allows veterinarians to easily shop for their office products, specialized forms, and informational flyers that they need to serve their clients.

However, SPI offered their customers an added bonus: a free Web site of their own. Using the service provider, SPI offers its customers the tools to set up their own Web sites and e-stores using template-driven software. Clinic staff can easily pick the look they want by choosing from a set of graphics or uploading their own photos or logo. They can create a store and offer up to 50 products for sale with no charge. SPI acts as a portal for the veterinary community and draws traffic to the sites of SPI customers. SPI gets additional Web exposure while providing a service for their customers, which builds their loyalty to SPI.

Build your own portal

A 20th century wolesaler

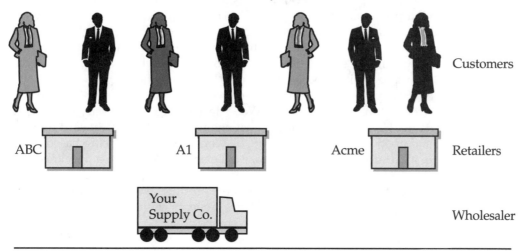

Customers

ABC   A1   Acme   Retailers

Your Supply Co.   Wholesaler

E-Reality: The view through the portal

Customers   Retailers

Your product portal

ABC

A1

Acme

Preparing to E-Tail

A landscape products company we'll call Land Sculpturing Inc. (LSI) sold to contractors who bought similar products time after time. The contractors were extremely busy during the day and wanted to place orders at night, sometimes after midnight. They also wanted to change their orders quickly. The supplier thought this was an ideal situation for putting up an e-commerce site. The contractors could order whenever they wanted to, and the orders would be available when they came by to pick them up.

The owner of LSI approached a local e-commerce consulting company and sketched out his ideas for the e-store he wanted. The Web pages had to look exactly like those in LSI's current catalog. He wanted standard functionality, including credit card billing, a shopping cart, and good security. In addition, he wanted variable pricing based on the customer's history. He also wanted a customer to be able to default to a previous order when entering a new one.

The consultant started asking questions about the products. Which products were ordered most often? How were the orders fulfilled? If clients could order any time of the day, would they expect to pick up at all hours? Were the products standardized? Did they have descriptions that adequately differentiated one model from another? How about digitized images? Were these available? Did they have plans for a call center to answer customer questions? What hours would it operate? How would the Web-generated orders fit into their current order entry and inventory control systems? What was LSI's strategy for marketing its Web site? How was this going to change their business model? What were competitors doing?

The owner's mind began swirling. He realized that a lot of preparatory analysis had to go on and asked for a bid for analysis, design, and development of the Web site that he had in mind. The proposal came a few days later with a price tag of $100,000. The owner of LSI said he'd have to think about it and did just that. During the following autumn and winter, the owner and LSI staff learned all they could about selling online. They talked with their customers about the idea and documented the existing methods that LSI used to fill its orders. The staff wrote detailed descriptions of each product and put these into a spreadsheet file. They photographed each product with a digital camera. By early spring they had a strategy, an operating plan for their site, and all of the preparatory work completed. They were ready to start developing the site.

By this time, the consulting company had become an ASP. With the preparatory work done by LSI and with rented software packages, the site was developed very quickly. The cost was under $20,000, and as the snows melted, landscapers were able to start placing their orders online.

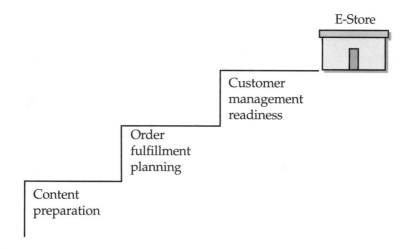

Meeting the E-Procurement Challenge

A small caterer in Atlanta had become a big success. The owner of a business that we shall call Alice's Restaurant In Your Office (RIYO) had started out providing box lunches to a friend who was conducting sales seminars at a local college. As the seminars grew, people came from all over the world and Alice was faced with a variety of requests from Indian vegetarian meals to Kobe beef. Her cooking skills were only exceeded by her resourcefulness in getting specialty foods from local marketplaces all around the globe. International businesspeople were thrilled to find favorite dishes from home delivered to their meetings. Atlanta grew as a center of international commerce, and Alice's business boomed. Alice first remodeled her garage into a deli kitchen, and then as her reputation and her customer list kept expanding, she moved into a new building with large storage coolers, a wine cellar, and a state-of-the-art kitchen.

Alice took orders by phone and by e-mail. She had each of her menu offerings broken down into their ingredients. Each order created a record, which she loaded into an Access database that she used to manage her inventory. She even had a custom-designed Web site that showed mouthwatering pictures of foods of the world taken by her husband, who was a gifted amateur photographer. The friend who had designed all of this had moved overseas. However, Alice and her manager had learned to tweak the system, and it served her well even as her business grew rapidly. Alice's RIYO became more and more involved with several multinational corporations with facilities in Atlanta. Alice was making money and having fun. Then within a few weeks, everything was threatened.

Three of her largest customers all launched e-procurement initiatives within a month of each other. They demanded that all of their suppliers conform to their electronically generated purchase orders, provide their catalogs in a standardized format, and invoice them electronically. Suppliers who failed to live up to the standards would have to give deep discounts or lose their business. What was worse, each of them had different formats that Alice's small business had to conform to. One company insisted she join Commerce One's MarketSite.net. Another used its own homegrown Web-based procurement system and wanted the catalog loaded in Excel format. The third company used the Ariba Commerce Services Network.

Alice's staff knew their business, but they did not know e-procurement. If she didn't meet this challenge, 60 percent of her sales were threatened. This was a real crisis.

Alice turned to a local systems integrator who worked with a large ASP with an e-procurement offering. They enabled Alice to use a robust e-procurement system that normally costs over $150,000 for the sales price alone. For just a fraction of that, Alice's RIYO rented access to software. What was better, the ASP did all of the electronic interfacing with her big corporate clients. For a few dollars per item, they were able to load Alice's large menu into their database. The ASP took Alice's enticing photographs of food, which were in GIF files, and stored them in their system. They received her client's purchase orders in whatever format the corporate client wanted to use. The ASP then translated it into a record that was easily loaded into Alice's Access system.

The solution wasn't cheap; it didn't bring Alice any new business, at least in the short term. However, it enabled a small business to keep playing in the big worldwide game known as e-procurement. What really helped Alice pull it off was that she knew exactly what she needed and what she could do for herself and where she needed help.

WEIGHING THE DECISION

Whether you build your own site from scratch or buy something off the shelf, your decision must be based on what your business needs. If you read the industry press to find out what you *should* be doing, you will be in for headaches and heart attacks. The gurus of the press always rave about the latest answer to all computing problems. In the Eighties, they said that the PC was going to make mainframes extinct within a few years. In the early nineties, client/server architecture was going to cure the industry's ills. As we noted earlier, the trend toward the ASP as an outsourcing solution has been greeted with similar grand prophecies. Already we are seeing that the fantastic predictions of growth in the ASP market were greatly exaggerated.

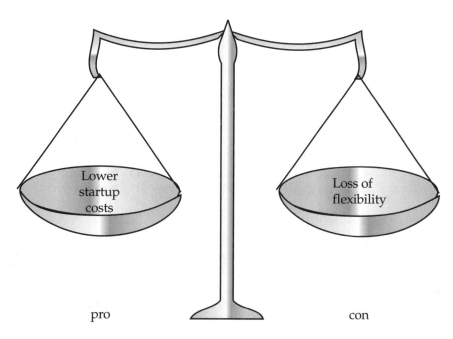

pro   con

As we mentioned, the ASP concept is nothing new. It's really just an improved version of the old time-sharing option where users all logged on to the same 1970s-style mainframe to share its processing power. It is a delivery mechanism for the same software that comes on a CD or a tape. However, this mechanism gives small and medium-sized business users a new tool. And just as you heard in shop class, "Choose the right tool for the job." You need to know what the particular service providers can do for you and, most of all, know your real needs. In the following sections, we try to provide you with some guidelines to use in deciding for yourself.

The Advantages of Using an ASP

In this section, we will outline what are normally the advantages of the ASP option. However, it is up to you to pull out your mechanical pencil and pad of paper or your hand-held supercomputer to see if these really are a plus for your business.

There are three main reasons to go with an ASP:

▼ Lower capital requirements for technology

■ Quicker start-up time

▲ Sharing the risks of a new e-commerce venture

We cover these issues in detail later in this chapter, but first let's take note of a few other points. One often mentioned is fixed maintenance costs. You won't have to ride the cost roller-coaster of paying for periodic software and hardware upgrades or new software development projects.

Another big advantage can be skill transfer, but this is not automatic. When the ASP consultants come to help you install the package, get them to teach you as much as possible about the application and about e-commerce in general. People talk about computer gurus as wizards, but "guru" is a Hindi word for teacher and guide. A good consultant teaches and guides his or her clients as well as being a skilled technician. If the consultants looks at their skills as trade secrets, you and your staff are going to be mystified and become dependent on them instead of learning how to get the most out of your new application.

Much Lower Capital Requirements

Setting up a full-scale e-commerce site requires significant start-up capital, and money is not going to pour in right away. Buying the necessary servers, routers, and hubs is expensive. So is the operating and applications software. Then consider the salaries of technicians with the expertise necessary to install and maintain the infrastructure. We haven't even started talking about development costs for the e-commerce application. An ASP with an operational data center and a functional software application that fits your needs is an attractive option. However, depending on your needs and your resources, the costs of developing your own systems may vary.

The real benefit, though, is that by using an ASP, a small or medium-sized business can gain access to sophisticated software that they could never afford to buy. As in the example of the catering business, robust products such as Ariba, BroadVision, or Commerce One can be out of reach of most small and even mid-sized businesses. Such products can cost hundreds of thousands in licensing fees and installation costs, whereas an ASP can offer them for a fraction of the cost.

Quicker Start-Up Time

In a marketplace dominated by lightning-quick innovations, a business requires speed to survive, but speed can also kill. If your e-business plan is not carefully thought out, it can bring you disaster instead of dollars. Even if you have done all the groundwork, a project to develop your own site can run into many unforeseen delays. It is hard to hire the necessary skills. Integrating software and hardware components will often cause delays. Designing your own application entails many unforeseen pitfalls as clients and developers try to sort out wish lists and assumptions. Then once the software is developed, the bugs need to be shaken out and fixed.

Instead, an ASP may offer you the ability to quickly take advantage of leading edge technologies without feeling the pain of a bleeding edge development effort. The ASP solution has felt all your pain for you and stands ready roll, *presumably*. However, that is precisely the gift horse that requires a close dental exam. Ask the vendor how widely this application is used. How many customers does this particular ASP have using this product? Ask to talk to several references. ISVs are notorious for selling systems that are actually in beta or even alpha testing. Even the largest software houses offer new releases that are filled with bugs to get a jump on the market. Just that a package is offered through an ASP is no guarantee that it lives up to its marketing claims.

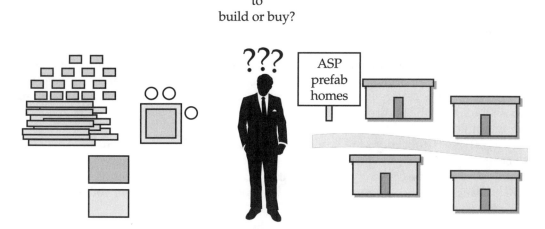

to
build or buy?

ASP
prefab
homes

Sharing the Risks of a New E-Commerce Venture

Even with the best market studies, you don't really know if an e-commerce venture will succeed until you implement it. A major development effort requires lots of capital and a great deal of time and energy in critical staff resources. An ASP gets you up and going with less up-front investment, so using an ASP means you share the risk. If you become the next amazon.com, you won't worry too much about paying monthly maintenance fees, and if you fail, then you haven't lost as much.

On the other hand, depending on whether your provider is a start-up company, you also share their risk. They may not be around to support you when your site really starts booming. The ASP market is facing rapid growth and a significant amount of shake-out. Some supposedly up-and-coming ASP start-ups that were interviewed in December 1999 weren't around the following summer—more on this in a following section.

The Problem Areas

There are good reasons that most people prefer to buy a home rather than rent it. Over the long term, renting can be expensive. It is true that you aren't forced to remodel your home every year or two, upgrading all of your plumbing, electrical, and telephone connections in the process. Still, there are some good reasons to think hard before jumping on the ASP bandwagon. The big questions revolve around three issues:

▼ Flexibility

■ Control

▲ Competitive advantage

Flexibility: How Does the Package Fit Your Needs?

If you use an ASP, be prepared to make your business process fit the flow of the software. By definition, an ASP provides minimal modifications of the package. If you demand software changes, they are often expensive and could create delays and software bugs. These are the problems you were trying to avoid by going to an ASP in the first place. Be highly skeptical of ASP salespeople who promise that they will modify the system to meet all of your requirements. There are often modules that can be added or options that can be tailored, but the reason it is being offered as a rented application is that it is a ready-to-use system. Remember that it is like going to an apartment and choosing between a handful of different model units. If you really need a bigger home and want to choose the size of the bathroom and design your own kitchen, you should hire an architect and build your own house.

All software applications are designed to reproduce and improve a business process. When you buy a package, you should know that the package was designed to reflect the workflow of another company. It won't fit your company exactly, and your staff may have to change how they perform their job. This could require retraining of your employees, and changing people's ways is never easy.

Control over Changes, Level of Service, and Data

You will have less influence over changes and improvements. If the ASP makes changes you don't like, you may have to live with them. Or even worse, what would happen if the changes don't work and they corrupt your data? Going back to the apartment analogy, what if the landlord decides to paint all walls military green and says you can move if you don't like it? Moving costs are high, and who pays if your furniture gets splattered while the painters are working? Find out how the ASP has handled changes to the application in the past. Investigate how it impacted other clients and ask to see a copy of the ASP vendor's change control procedures. Make sure they include data back-up and recovery plans.

Level of service is a key issue with ASP vendors. Many of these vendors are new in the field and have cobbled together offerings based on ad hoc alliances. Carefully look into their relationships with the data center and the ISV who developed the application. Remember that ISV stands for *independent* software vendor. Who's going to fix it when it is broken? You want solutions, not explanations. Make sure that you have one contact point regardless of the source of the problem. A selling point of the ASP model is that the provider is supposed to orchestrate all of the different vendors and give you a seamless application. As Figure 15-2 illustrates, the ASP can be seen as the conductor of an orchestra of service providers. However, if the violin section sounds flat or they just aren't playing the music you want to hear, make sure that you have the control you need to change the tune. Working with IT vendors is a difficult task. It is impossible if lines of accountability are not very clearly drawn.

Of course, the biggest level-of-service question is how the end game will be played. Whether you decide to transfer to another vendor or your vendor is bought by a competitor or simply goes belly-up, you must define their responsibilities to you during the

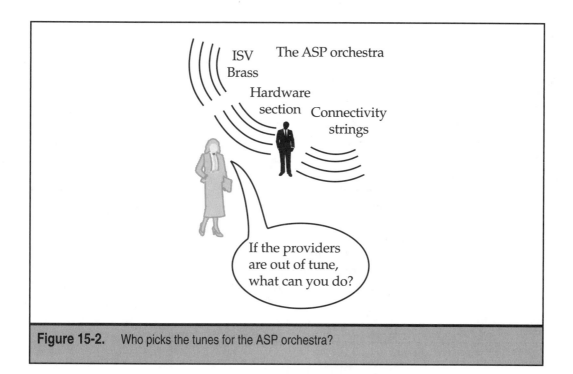

Figure 15-2.   Who picks the tunes for the ASP orchestra?

transition period. How do you get your data back—in what form, and with how much history? What will happen to transactions that come in during the transfer?

Data security is a big issue, as we mentioned before. You need to investigate their virus protection measures as well as their firewalls. Find out how they have dealt with security breaches in the past. Test their willingness to notify their customers of problems. Exposure of secure data gets worse if the problem is covered up. However, we need to look beyond the security of data and also ask about its availability to you. Will the data collected in your Web-based retail system be available to your marketing department? Can you use it to discover customer satisfaction with your products? Your customer data is one of your biggest assets, so look into how the ASP will let you access it.

An ASP Will Not Give You a Competitive Advantage

Don't use an ASP if you have a unique business approach and want to design your e-commerce site around your idea. By definition, an ASP provides the same package to any bidder. Maybe your competitors aren't selling online or offering e-procurement to your industrial customers. You see a chance to get the jump on them by getting online quickly using an ASP. It won't be long till they find out how you did it and copy you, and of course their Web sites will have a few more bells and whistles. The advent of the ASP model means that e-commerce capabilities have become a commodity, just like office space or telecommunications services. If you have a one-of-a-kind service to offer online, you may well need a one-of-a-kind Web site with custom software to support it.

KNOW YOURSELF

Business is often compared to a never-ending war. You constantly have to fight with your competitors and even with your vendors. Following this analogy, we offer you a quote from one of the world's first experts on the art of war, the ancient Chinese philosopher Sun Wu Tzu, who said, "Know the enemy and know yourself and you can fight a hundred battles with no danger of defeat." In the Web marketing battle, you will never know all of your competitors, so knowing yourself has to suffice. As Figure 15-3 illustrates, you have to ignore the wondrous claims of vendors and first understand what your business needs to succeed in e-commerce.

As we have stressed repeatedly, you must know what your needs are and carefully evaluate a package according to your own criteria. Forget how wonderful some expert says this new technology is; if it isn't good for your business, it is worthless. The other side of knowing yourself in this context is carefully evaluating your capabilities. Even if you don't have a whiz-bang e-commerce site, you probably have some pretty capable people working for you. By knowing your needs and your capabilities, you can find out what you can do in-house and where you must turn for outside help.

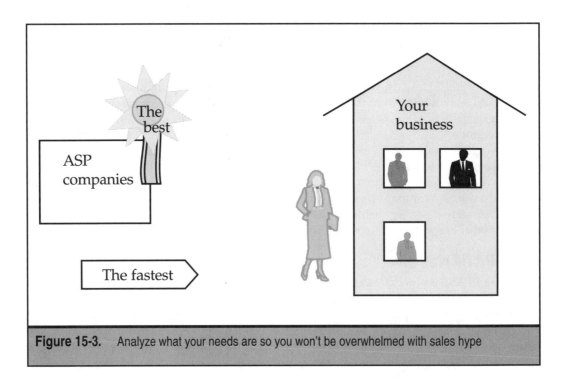

Figure 15-3. Analyze what your needs are so you won't be overwhelmed with sales hype

What Are Your E-commerce Needs?

There are four basic steps in analyzing your needs. These are:

1. Analyze your business process.
2. Set your goals. Define how you want e-commerce technology to improve it.
3. Specify the detailed requirements the technology must meet to fulfill your goals.
4. Prioritize these requirements.

For a few thousand dollars, a consultant would sit down and ask you questions based on this list, write up your answers, and present you with a document called a *requirements analysis*. You can do this work without any e-commerce experience or technical training. All the necessary skills already exist in your own organization. Once you complete this process, you are ready to move on to the next stage, evaluating how many of these requirements can be met by your own resources.

Analyze Your Business Process

First outline the general flow of your business, listing each discrete step. For example, going back to our guitar maker, his business essentially consists of five steps:

1. He takes an order for a custom guitar.
2. He orders the materials.
3. The shop craftspeople make the guitar.
4. The guitar is delivered.
5. The payment is collected.

Of course, each main step can be broken down into many smaller jobs. For example, ordering involves determining the materials list for the product, checking inventory, and ordering from many suppliers. When the main steps and the individual jobs are listed as a whole, you have an overview of your business process. It helps to put this into a flowchart to get a graphic image of how your work flows. The steps and jobs that you want to computerize must be broken down to very basic tasks and subtasks.

Set Your Goals

Once you understand your workflow and the specific jobs and tasks that make it happen, you can establish goals for your e-commerce site. In our custom guitar shop example, you would probably define order capture as the main function of your site. You might think that it would be great to automate the inventory ordering process as well. You should take a look at the specific jobs and tasks involved in ordering materials. If you have truly custom guitars, the materials list may vary greatly from one order to the next. You need to know which suppliers have the right type of wood in stock and check your own inventory as well. This requires either a lot of human interaction or a complicated series of interfaces between computer systems. Not every process is worth automating. Depending on the size of your shop, it might be more work to enter your entire inventory into a system and maintain a software system than have a person walk into the stockroom and take a look.

Specify the Detailed Requirements

Now that you know which jobs need to be automated on the Web site, you can define detailed requirements. At this point, you still do not need to know anything about Java code, Web-enabled data capture, or how even how to log onto the Internet. All you need to do is spell out in clear and simple English (or French or Japanese) what you want the e-commerce software to do. At this point, you also need to estimate the volume of your transactions and specify exactly what information you want captured.

Remember that online order capture is very different than taking an order over the counter or over the phone. The biggest difference is that the customer is driving the information gathering process rather than an experienced sales clerk asking for it. So the software has to do everything a clerk would, including checking for all required information. Everything has to be spelled out in great detail and communicated effectively. The online form must lead the customer through the process.

Prioritize These Requirements

Once you have defined everything you want your software to do, step back and take another look. Which of these really are necessary to process the order, and which are on a wish list? When you are shopping for a car, you know that leather seats, an automated sun-roof, and a robot that gives you a massage while you drive are on the "wouldn't it be nice" list while fuel economy, safety, and reliability are "must haves." Make the same distinction with your e-commerce requirements.

This is an easy thing to say, but we must also consider "political necessities" as well as business needs. In many organizations, there are numerous stakeholders who can block a purchasing decision. A "must have" for the marketing manager might seem like a frill to the order-entry department. So this means looking at everyone who will use the new Web site or be impacted by it. It means figuring out how to manage the messy political side of the decision. You have to look at who can cause trouble and how will you get them on board. The Web site has to work for everyone involved.

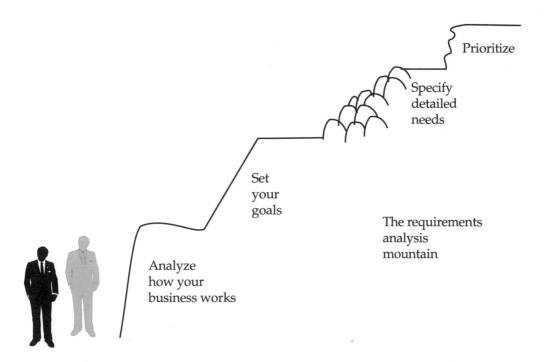

What Are Your Capabilities?

You have now completed a requirements analysis that you would previously have farmed out to a professional consultant. Perhaps by taking a close look at your organization, you will find that you have other capabilities you didn't know about. Do you have an existing IT staff that could maintain the infrastructure for an e-commerce site with a bit of training? What is their record with your current systems? Are there experienced staff members who could take on the responsibility to manage your Web site after a few classes? Who conducted the requirement analysis? If they did a good job, they have an excellent basis to take "ownership" of your Web site and manage the process of building it. They understand the business process, but they lack technical expertise, which is the perfect scenario for hiring a consultant. Now that you know your capabilities and your needs, you are at a point to begin making some decisions.

DECIDING IN THE REAL WORLD

Having just told you that you are ready, I'm going to throw out yet another word of caution. Don't make a decision on using an ASP while you are reading this book. Even after evaluating your needs and capabilities and reading everything you can, you don't really know what the pear tastes like until you bite into it. This means asking ASP vendors for detailed bids on a Web site that meets your requirements. If they don't have time to give you such a proposal, they won't have time to solve your problems later on.

NOTE: Artificial intelligence may be a great step for humankind, but artificial wisdom has led to false steps since ancient times. Choose your vendors wisely.

Vendor Selection

If selling on the Web is just an experiment, then choosing an ASP may not be a critical decision. However, if this is a strategic decision, remember that you are choosing a long-term partner. You are entrusting the ASP with some of your most important data and giving them a major influence over how you sell your products. Once this decision is made, it will be hard to reverse. Remember choosing a roommate in your college days? That person who seemed so friendly and interesting on their first visit turned out to be a slob who never picked up after himself. Think of this decision as choosing a housemate who will be using your heirloom china and be responsible for keeping your data clean.

Evaluating Each Bidder

Identify providers who offer software that claims to meet your requirements. Remember that you are from the "Show-me" state. Evaluate their claims carefully. Have an experienced person in your business that will actually use the system help you. Tell them to imagine using this software to do their job and ask them to evaluate it. Ask the salesperson to spend less time talking about the latest buzzwords and more time demonstrating how the software fits your business needs. Get multiple referrals and ask these clients about the provider's responsiveness to problems. If there are no problems, ask the same question in a different context or get the names of other clients. Ask existing clients how much time and money they had to spend to implement the system. Evaluate various pricing options carefully. Look into hidden costs such as upgrading your current hardware, software, and network infrastructure to interface with this vendor.

Start-Ups Versus Established Vendors

There are literally thousands of vendors who bill themselves as application service providers. Industry gurus classify them into all sorts of categories. Some are classified as a "pure play ASP," and others are called "best of breed." However, for you there are just two things you need to know about a prospective ASP vendor: What ways can they service your needs and how are they going to provide the service? However, the issue of locally based new start-ups versus nationally recognized ASP firms is important.

Name brands are supposed to give you reliability, and a company that has been around for a while does have a reputation to preserve. New start-ups are usually more responsive to customers' needs, although this depends on what you are looking for. If you are an established firm that is building a long-term e-commerce venture, then you want to be around after many of today's ASP vendors have disappeared. However, if you are a start-up yourself and are willing to take a risk, you may get better prices and service from the new ASP on the block. The other thing to look at is a firm's overall reputation and history, not just how long they have been waving the ASP banner. If a systems integration firm has managed complex projects in the past and has done a good job for their customers, they could very well be successful at playing the role of general contractor in building an e-commerce shopping center for your company.

A List of Hard Questions or How to Freeze the Smile on the Salesperson's Face

1. Could you please list *all* the start-up costs? Ask the salesperson, then ask the ASP technical staff. What installation prep does the ASP require of you? (This is rarely stated as a start-up cost, but in reality it is one.)

2. How widely used is this application? How many clients does this ASP have that actually use the specific application you are considering? What was the experience of some of these clients with installation? With ongoing support? Ask the same questions of several existing clients. (If they say that their clients are inundated with referral requests, then they don't have many clients and should be up-front about it.)

3. Which ASP staff members will be helping you implement the e-commerce solution? Interview them as well as the marketing and technical directors. What experience do these consultants have? What is their attitude toward transferring their skills to clients? (Are they green, eager-beaver MBAs with no real-world background, or are they crusty old curmudgeons who won't even tell you how to load data yourself?)

4. What are the ASP vendor's data security procedures? Investigate their virus protection measures as well as their firewalls. How have they dealt with security breaches in the past? How willing are they to notify their customers of problems?

5. How do they handle application or systems upgrades? What are their change control procedures? What is the average down time? Who bears the cost of converting data if that is required?

6. How will your costs change as you grow? What is their capacity to expand the database if your business booms? Can they add features such as customer relationship management?

7. What is their back-end architecture? How will they integrate new technologies coming down the pike? And how will this impact your application?

8. What is their relationship with their data center? With their software vendors? What are the service agreements between the various players? In order to know who you are going to call when things go bump in the night, make sure that you have *one* contact point regardless of the source of the problem.

9. Will the data collected in your Web-based retail system be available to your other departments? How can they access it?

10. What happens when the contract is terminated? How do you get your data back—in what form, and how much history? Make sure the contract specifies vendor responsibilities in turning over the data, whether they are transferring to another vendor or they go out of business. What will happen to transactions that come in during the transfer?

11. Ask to see their code of ethics—what protects you from their examining your accounts during contract negotiations? From using your data for unrelated purposes?

12. What service level are they committing to? Twenty-four hours, seven days a week with only a few hours down time is pretty standard these days, but get them to be specific, both about the service level and what they will offer if they fail to meet their commitments.

ASPSPEAK—A MINI-GLOSSARY TO HELP YOU CUT THROUGH THE HYPE

You have to talk the talk in order to know if salespeople can walk the walk. Language can be a means to communicate or a way to mystify. Experts in every field develop their own vocabulary so that they can discuss very precise conditions or processes. However, sales and marketing people often use the same language to mystify new customers. The goal is to make the customer feel ignorant so that the salesperson can appear to be a brilliant wizard who can solve all the customer's problems if you would just stop asking questions and sign on the dotted line.

Table 15-4 is a tool that can help the ASP newcomer feel a bit more at home in this brave new world. A step that the customer should take is to ask for a definition for every term they don't understand. If a salesperson acts like it is a stupid question, imagine how the support staff are going to respond to your staff or clients who use the system. The goal is for you to distinguish hype from help.

Acronym	Term	Definition
ASP	Application Service Provider	An application service provider will deliver a standardized e-commerce software package from a remote data center for a rental fee.
BSP	Business Solutions Provider	A business solutions provider is a vendor who provides business services, in our case an Internet retailer that would sell your products over the World Wide Web. Not to be confused with an IBSP.
CSP	Capacity Service Provider	Capacity service providers (CSPs) own and operate data-center infrastructures.
CLP	Co-Location Provider	Co-location providers are another form of capacity service provider. They can be brokers who lease network connections and data-center space to third-party ASPs and business services providers, BSPs.
ISV	Independent Software Vendor	In this context, an ISV is a producer of packaged software who sells through an ASP. It may be a corporation as large as BroadVision or a local software developer who specializes in esoteric systems like design-your-own-hat software.
IBSP	Internet Business Services Provider	In essence, an IBSP is an ASP that specializes in Internet services such as messaging, Web site hosting and Internet access.
ISP	Internet Service Provider	An ISP is a company that connects individual computers or LANs to the Internet. An ISP will often host Web sites as well.

Table 15-4.   Definitions for a Handful of E-Commerce Terms

Acronym	Term	Definition
MAP	Managed Application Provider	An MAP is an ASP that procures and manages the software and hardware components and needed services to install and run your application or package of applications.
NSP	Network Service Provider	An NSP is a company that can offer high-speed Internet backbone services. ISPs connect with network service providers for cross-country links.
	Portal or a vertical industry portal	Originally the term "portal" referred to a gateway site such as Yahoo or AOL that performed multiple services such as Web searching, news, and chat rooms. Now it usually refers to a vertical industry that provides an entry point to vendors of a particular industry. A corporate portal is generally the home page to the online services of a particular corporation.
RAI	Rentable Applications Integrator	An RAI is usually an ASP with consulting services that specializes in a specific set of applications (e.g., financial services) or in a particular industry (e.g., medical).
RAP	Rentable Applications Provider	An RAP is a specialized ASP that usually rents a specific solution.

Table 15-4. Definitions for a Handful of E-Commerce Terms *(continued)*

Acronym	Term	Definition
SLA	Service Level Agreement	An SLA is a contract between the software or service provider and the client that defines the level of service during a specified time period. SLAs can exist within an organization between the IT department and the business users as well as between vendors and their customers. They can be vague or very specific. The agreements can and should include such issues as system availability, help line response time, bandwidth availability, and response time for problem resolution (network down, machine failure, etc.), as well as pricing for additional services and detailed responsibilities for terminating the agreement.
SLM	Service Level Management	An SLM system is software that manages the network, reporting on events that threaten to interrupt service so that action can be taken to guarantee a specified level of system availability.
SME	Small and Medium Enterprises	A small enterprise is usually understood as one with less than 50 employees, whereas medium ones can have up to 500.
VSP	Vertical Solutions Provider	A VSP is an ASP that also provides content and portal services for a specific industry.

Table 15-4.   Definitions for a Handful of E-Commerce Terms *(continued)*

Index

B

C

D

 E

F

▼ O

▼ P

T

U

V

W

X